Designing and Implementing Microsoft DevOps Solutions AZ-400 Exam Guide

Prepare for the certification exam and successfully apply Azure DevOps strategies with practical labs

Subhajit Chatterjee
Swapneel Deshpande
Henry Been
Maik van der Gaag

BIRMINGHAM—MUMBAI

Designing and Implementing Microsoft DevOps Solutions AZ-400 Exam Guide

Group Product Manager: Rahul Nair
Publishing Product Manager: Niranjan Naikwadi
Content Development Editor: Nihar Kapadia
Technical Editor: Arjun Varma
Copy Editor: Safis Editing
Project Coordinator: Ashwin Kharwa
Proofreader: Safis Editing
Indexer: Tejal Daruwale Soni
Production Designer: Roshan Kawale
Marketing Coordinator: Nimisha Dua

First published: June 2020
Second edition: September 2022
Production reference: 3210922

Published by Packt Publishing Ltd.
Livery Place
35 Livery Street
Birmingham
B3 2PB, UK.

ISBN 978-1-80324-066-4
www.packt.com

Contributors

About the authors

Subhajit Chatterjee has a bachelor of engineering degree and a postgraduate diploma in information technology. He has also taken up many online certifications that have helped him learn and grow as a software engineering professional.

He has over two decades of experience in designing, implementing, and managing software development projects, using Microsoft and open source technologies. He is a seasoned engineering leader and has delivered many large and complex projects in Azure, IoT, enterprise integrations, web applications, and the mobility space.

He loves to solve problems and is passionate about sharing his learning with the community.

> *I want to thank the people who have been close to me and supported me all these years, especially my wife and my elder brother who have always been a source of motivation. I am also grateful to my work colleagues who are an inspiration themselves and have helped me learn and grow.*

Swapneel Deshpande is a solution architect, development consultant, and a trusted technology advisor, entrepreneur, start-up consultant, and more. He has been working in IT for nearly two decades, with expertise in .NET and web-related technologies. He has led the software architecture design, development, and delivery of large, complex solutions. He is passionate about embracing new technologies and teaching. His current role involves leading large and complex projects right from architecture to delivery.

> *To my family for their unwavering support, patience, and encouragement throughout the process of writing this book.*
> *I am also grateful for my elder sister who has always been a source of motivation for me.*

Henry Been has been working in IT for over ten years. He is an independent architect, developer, and trainer, who has worked with many different companies. With many of these companies, Henry has embarked on a journey implementing practices such as continuous integration and deployment, infrastructure as code, trunk-based development, and implementing feedback loops.

Alongside his work, Henry creates online training courses for Pluralsight and A Cloud Guru, and frequently speaks at meetups and conferences. He has held the Microsoft MVP award since 2019.

Maik van der Gaag is the CTO at 3fifty, an experienced consultancy company with a strong focus on the Microsoft cloud. He has over 15 years of experience providing architecture, development, training, and design expertise. During his career, Maik has worked on a variety of projects, ranging from cloud transformations to DevOps implementations.

Maik loves to share his knowledge, which was also one of the reasons why he founded the Dutch Cloud meetup. Maik is a Microsoft MVP, public speaker, talented blog writer, and an organizer of events.

About the reviewers

Shachaf Goldstein has 10 years of experience in the IT infrastructure and development fields alongside 3 years of experience in cloud infrastructure and solutions. He practices various DevOps methodologies and works with many platforms (GitHub, Azure DevOps, Atlassian Jira, GitLab). Shachaf is an experienced professional in automated cloud deployments, both for code and infrastructure elements, with a focus on Azure in recent years.

Jamel Achahbar has over 10 years of experience training people in several domains, is especially passionate about conveying technical knowledge to his audience in a practical way, and is an Azure geek. He has delivered Azure Immersion Workshops, created practical labs and blog content, and is a technical lead at his current company. He enjoys supporting his colleagues to achieve success for their customers. He has been instrumental in the move to the cloud of several customers. He has a degree in network and systems administration and is a Certified Azure Solutions Architect Expert and Microsoft Certified Trainer. He likes to get out of his comfort zone and take on challenges to keep learning and growing. Jamel has a never-ending learning attitude.

I'd like to thank my family and friends who understand the time and commitment it takes to keep abreast of everything that happens in the cloud. Working in this field would not be possible without the support system of a great Microsoft cloud community, passionate leaders, and great friends and family. Thank you to all of the giants who created these great tools, content, and services to make our work easier and help us achieve success!

Table of Contents

Part 2 – Getting to Continuous Delivery

4

Everything Starts with Source Control   55

5

Moving to Continuous Integration   81

6

Implementing Continuous Deployment and Release Management 121

Part 3 – Expanding Your DevOps Pipeline

7

Dependency Management   157

8

Implement Infrastructure and Configuration as Code   185

9

Dealing with Databases in DevOps Scenarios   223

10

Integrating Continuous Testing   237

11

Managing Security and Compliance   287

Part 4 – Closing the Loop

12

Application Monitoring   311

13

Gathering User Feedback   335

Part 5 – Advanced Topics

14

Adopting the Culture of Continuous Improvement   345

15

Accelerate Cloud Adoption through DevOps   353

16

Containers   363

17

Planning Your Azure DevOps Organization   401

18

AZ-400 Mock Exam   419

Preface

Every software engineering professional must be adept in their understanding of DevOps and the positive impact it brings to their teams. This book acquaints you with some of the most important DevOps practices, such as configuration management, release management, continuous integration, continuous deployment, infrastructure as code, continuous testing, and application monitoring and feedback. You will also learn to use tools such as Azure DevOps, GitHub, and other related tools for the implementation of the various practices.

With detailed case studies and hands-on labs, this book serves as a ready reckoner on *how* to implement the various practices. This book also covers additional topics that will help you develop deep expertise and a DevOps-oriented mindset, which will be impactful in your professional career.

Who this book is for

The target audience for this book is the following:

- Software developers or operations specialists who want to undertake the AZ-400 exam
- Software developers or operations specialists who want to learn how to use Azure DevOps to implement DevOps practices
- Technology enthusiasts who would like to enhance their DevOps skills

You should be familiar with software development and, more broadly, software development practices. You must be familiar with terms such as Waterfall, Scrum, Agile, and DevOps. Any serious practitioner with at least 2 years of team-based software development experience should be able to read this book. You should also have a basic understanding of Azure DevOps and GitHub.

What this book covers

Chapter 1, Introduction to DevOps, provides an overview of the DevOps movement and the culture it represents. This chapter introduces the practices and habits that will be the focus of this book.

Chapter 2, Site Reliability Engineering Fundamentals, introduces you to the principles and practices of **Site Reliability Engineering** (**SRE**), as well as the significance of adopting an SRE mindset to ensure the success of cloud applications.

Chapter 3, Getting the Best Out of DevOps Tools, provides a high-level overview of the various DevOps-related tools that can be used throughout an application development life cycle.

Chapter 4, Everything Starts with Source Control, discusses various approaches to source control and how proper source control is at the heart of continuous delivery.

Chapter 5, Moving to Continuous Integration, covers continuous integration, automated testing, quality control, metrics, code coverage, and the minimum standards necessary to produce a quality product.

Chapter 6, Implementing Continuous Deployment and Release Management, covers how to use the Azure DevOps release pipeline, as well as various deployment patterns and strategies to enable continuous deployment.

Chapter 7, Dependency Management, looks at how Azure Artifacts can help to manage shared components and how to use Azure pipelines to automate the build, release, and even use of these components.

Chapter 8, Implement Infrastructure and Configuration as Code, shows how to configure your application's infrastructure and how to fully automate the creation or updating of that infrastructure as part of your release.

Chapter 9, Dealing with Databases in DevOps Scenarios, discusses several strategies for treating your database like application code, an infrastructure, or a configuration.

Chapter 10, Integrating Continuous Testing, looks at different types of testing and how they relate to one another using the testing pyramid and how different types of tests can be embedded at different stages of our DevOps pipelines.

Chapter 11, Managing Security and Compliance, shows you how to collaborate with security experts to automate their concerns in a pipeline, rather than manually verifying them later using checklists.

Chapter 12, Application Monitoring, explores application monitoring, which is the process of instrumenting your application to understand application performance and usage patterns and extract key performance indicators.

Chapter 13, Gathering User Feedback, discusses how to use hypothesis-driven development to validate your ideas before putting them into action.

Chapter 14, Adopting the Culture of Continuous Improvement, concentrates on some aspects of organizational culture that have a direct influence on business outcomes.

Chapter 15, Accelerate Cloud Adoption through DevOps, provides an overview of using DevOps through scenarios and guidance while preparing an enterprise cloud adoption plan.

Chapter 16, Containers, provides an overview of containers, which allow you to package any application or tool (developed using any programming language) and deploy it on a basic host or cluster.

Chapter 17, Planning Your Azure DevOps Organization, discusses what works and what doesn't for your organization and team, as well as how to implement practices and approaches using Azure DevOps.

Chapter 18, AZ-400 Mock Exam, contains a mock test for you to assess your learning.

To get the most out of this book

Software/hardware covered in the book	Operating system requirements
Visual Studio 2019/Visual Studio 2022/VS Code	Windows, macOS, or Linux
An Azure subscription	-
An Azure DevOps subscription	-

If you are using the digital version of this book, we advise you to type the code yourself or access the code from the book's GitHub repository (a link is available in the next section). Doing so will help you avoid any potential errors related to the copying and pasting of code.

Download the example code files

You can download the example code files for this book from GitHub at `https://github.com/PacktPublishing/Designing-and-Implementing-Microsoft-DevOps-Solutions-AZ-400-Exam-Guide`. If there's an update to the code, it will be updated in the GitHub repository.

We also have other code bundles from our rich catalog of books and videos available at `https://github.com/PacktPublishing/`. Check them out!

Download the color images

We also provide a PDF file that has color images of the screenshots and diagrams used in this book. You can download it here: `https://packt.link/OADjU`.

Conventions used

There are a number of text conventions used throughout this book.

`Code in text`: Indicates code words in text, database table names, folder names, filenames, file extensions, pathnames, dummy URLs, user input, and Twitter handles. Here is an example: In GitHub Flow, there is one *master* branch that should always be in a deployable state. No unfinished changes are allowed to go onto the branch.

A block of code is set as follows:

```
{
"appServiceName": {
"type": "string",
"metadata": {
```

```
"description": "a free to choose text"
  }
}
```

When we wish to draw your attention to a particular part of a code block, the relevant lines or items are set in bold:

```
az aks update -n 'packtsbookaci' -g 'az400-dev'
--attach-acr 'packtbookacr'
```

Any command-line input or output is written as follows:

```
git add NewFile.txt

git push
```

Bold: Indicates a new term, an important word, or words that you see onscreen. For instance, words in menus or dialog boxes appear in **bold**. Here is an example: "Select **System info** from the **Administration** panel."

> **Tips or Important Notes**
> Appear like this.

Get in touch

Feedback from our readers is always welcome.

General feedback: If you have questions about any aspect of this book, email us at customercare@packtpub.com and mention the book title in the subject of your message.

Errata: Although we have taken every care to ensure the accuracy of our content, mistakes do happen. If you have found a mistake in this book, we would be grateful if you would report this to us. Please visit www.packtpub.com/support/errata and fill in the form.

Piracy: If you come across any illegal copies of our works in any form on the internet, we would be grateful if you would provide us with the location address or website name. Please contact us at copyright@packt.com with a link to the material.

If you are interested in becoming an author: If there is a topic that you have expertise in and you are interested in either writing or contributing to a book, please visit authors.packtpub.com.

Share Your Thoughts

Once you've read *Designing and Implementing Microsoft DevOps Solutions AZ-400 Exam Guide*, we'd love to hear your thoughts! Scan the QR code below to go straight to the Amazon review page for this book and share your feedback.

https://packt.link/r/1803240660

Your review is important to us and the tech community and will help us make sure we're delivering excellent quality content.

Part 1 – Digital Transformation through DevOps

In this part, you'll learn about the core principles and practices of DevOps that are foundational to achieving your software development goals in a faster and more efficient manner. We will explore how most organizations can build secure and reliable systems by incorporating **Site Reliability Engineering (SRE)** practices. You will also learn about the important DevOps tools that can improve the productivity of your teams.

This section establishes the necessary foundations for our work, after which the remaining chapters can be read (in any order) to get deeper insights into the respective topics.

This part of the book comprises the following chapters:

- *Chapter 1, Introduction to DevOps*
- *Chapter 2, Site Reliability Engineering Fundamentals*
- *Chapter 3, Getting the Best Out of DevOps Tools*

1

Introduction to DevOps

DevOps is not a product or tool that you can buy or install. DevOps is about culture and the way you write, release, and operate your software. DevOps is about shortening the time between a new idea and your first end user experiencing the value it delivers. In this book, you will learn about the tools and techniques you can use to apply that philosophy to your way of working. As the purpose of this book is to help you prepare for the AZ-400 certification exam, the core concepts and DevOps-related practices will be illustrated using Azure DevOps and its associated technologies.

DevOps has gained popularity in recent years, with almost all software engineering teams adapting themselves to a new world of doing things using a newer set of tools that activate productivity and better collaboration across development and operations. DevOps is often seen as an extension of Agile, but its scope is much wider, wherein it complements Agile.

In this first chapter, you will learn more about what DevOps is and how to recognize a successful DevOps team. By the end of this chapter, you will be familiar with the key terms and be equipped with a broader understanding of the high-level principles and practices of DevOps. You will also discover the benefits of DevOps as it applies to software engineering teams.

In this chapter, we will cover the following topics:

- What is DevOps?
- Creating your ideal DevOps organization
- Exploring DevOps practices and habits
- The five stages of the DevOps evolution

Technical requirements

There are no technical requirements for this chapter.

What is DevOps?

If you were to list all of the different definitions and descriptions of DevOps, there would be many. However, as different as these might be, they most likely share several concepts. These are collaboration, continuous delivery of business value, and breaking down silos.

With all the technical discussion in the rest of this book, it is important not to overlook the value proposition for adopting DevOps – namely, that it will help you improve the way that you continuously deliver value to your end users. To do this, you must decrease the time between starting work on a new feature and the first user using it in production. This means that you not only have to write the software but also deliver and operate it.

Over the last decade, the way we write software has fundamentally changed. More and more companies are now adopting an agile way of working to increase the efficiency of their software development. More and more teams are now working in short iterations or sprints to create new increments of a product in quick succession. However, creating potentially shippable increments faster and faster does not create any value by itself. Only when each new version of your software is also released to production and used by your end users does it start delivering value.

In traditional organizations, developers and operators are often located in different departments, and taking software into production includes a hand-off, often with a formal ceremony around it. In such an organization, it can be hard to accelerate that delivery to production, along with the speed at which development can create new versions.

Next to that, the development and operations departments often have conflicting goals. While a development department is rewarded for creating many changes as fast as possible, operations departments are rewarded for limiting downtime and preventing issues. The latter is often best achieved by making as few changes as possible. The conflict here is clear – both departments have optimizations for one subgoal, as shown in the following diagram:

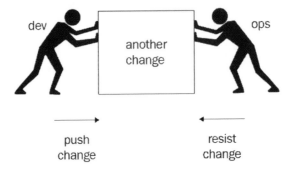

Figure 1.1 – Conflicting goals between development and operations

This defeats the purpose of these subgoals, which comes from the shared, overarching goal of quickly taking in new versions while maintaining stability. It's precisely this conflict between developmental and operational goals that is one of the things that should disappear in a DevOps culture. In such a culture, development and operations teams should work together on delivering new versions to production in a fast and reliable manner and share responsibility for both subgoals.

While it is good to know that DevOps is a cultural movement, tools and automation are an important part of that culture. In this book, we will focus on these tools and how to use them to implement many of the practices that come with a DevOps culture. In other words, this book will be mostly about the products and processes associated with DevOps. If you want to learn more about the cultural side of things and the people, there are many other books you can read. A very good read is *The Phoenix Project: A Novel About IT, DevOps, And Helping Your Business Win*, by Gene Kim.

The rest of this section will explore the relationship between DevOps and Agile to see how they complement each other. The focus will be on agile techniques and prices for work management. We will also discuss the goals and benefits of a DevOps culture.

The relationship between DevOps and Agile

If you take a look at Agile, you may notice that part of it focuses on business value and shortening the time of delivering a new business value. From that perspective, adopting DevOps is a logical next step after Agile. Agile advocates that the software development teams' responsibilities should extend forward by engaging with users and other stakeholders to deliver valuable and potentially shippable products quicker. DevOps is not just about something that might be shipped, but shipping it as well. With Agile and DevOps combined, you can create an end-to-end and continuous flow of value to your users.

You will need a common approach to managing the work to be done for everyone involved. In the next section, you will find some pointers on how to incorporate operational concerns in the way you manage your work.

Agile work management

When you are starting to increase the collaboration between development and operations, you will quickly notice that they have to cope with different types of work. In development, a large part of the work is planned: user stories and bugs that are picked up from a backlog. On the other hand, for operations, a large part of their work is unplanned. They respond to warnings and alerts from systems and requests or tickets from users or developers.

Integrating these two, especially if developers and operators are located on the same team, can be challenging. To learn how to deal with this, let's explore the following approach:

1. First, switch to a flow-based way of working for developers.

2. Next, allow for operations to also list their work in the same work management system as developers using synchronizations. You can also choose to implement *fastlaning*, a way to expedite urgent work.

3. Finally, you may choose to decommission existing ticketing tools for operations if possible.

Fastlaning is an approach to organizing work that allows for both planned and unplanned work by visualizing two separate lanes of work. To do this, the Scrum board is extended with a Kanban-like board on the top. This is the fast lane. On the Kanban board, urgent but unplanned work is added. Any work that's added to this lane is picked up by the team with the highest priority. Only when there is no work remaining in the fast lane is work from the Scrum board, along with planned work, picked up. Whenever new work is added to the fast lane, this takes priority again. Often, there is the agreement that any work in progress is finished before switching to work in the fast lane.

> **Important Note**
> Dependency management is also an important aspect of agile work planning. Hence, teams often make use of the prioritization attribute to qualify more important work for the short term.

Switching to a flow-based methodology

The first thing to consider when switching to a flow-based methodology is transitioning the way developers work from batch-wise to flow-based. An example of a batch-wise way of working is Scrum. If you are using the Scrum framework, you are used to picking up a batch of work every 2 to 4 weeks and focusing on completing all of that work within that time window. Only when that batch is done do you deliver a potentially shippable product.

When changing to a flow-based approach, you try to focus not on a batch, but just on one thing. You work on that one work item and drive it completely until it's done before you start on the next. This way, there is no longer a sprint backlog, only a product backlog. The advantage of this approach is that you no longer decide which work to perform upfront; whenever you are free to start on new work, you can pick up the next item from the backlog. In an environment where priorities shift quickly, this allows you to react to change quickly.

These changes to the way developers organize their work make it easier to include operations in work management, but there is also another benefit. When developers are focusing on getting a single work item done instead of a whole sprint at once, you can also increase the number of times you can deliver a small portion of value to your users.

Synchronizing work items to one system

Once the development team has changed the way it organizes its work, it should be easier for developers to also list their planned work on the shared backlog and pull work from that backlog when they have time to work on it. They now also have a place where they can list their unplanned work.

However, there may still be an existing ticketing system where requests for operations are dropped by users or automatically created by monitoring tools. While Azure DevOps has a great API to rework this integration to directly create work items in Azure DevOps, you may first choose to create a synchronization between your existing ticketing tool and Azure Boards. There are many integration options available and there is a lot of ongoing work in this area. This way, operators can slowly move from their old tool to the new one, since they are now in sync. Of course, the goal is for them to move over to the same tool, as the developers, completely.

Fastlaning

With the work of developers and operators in the same work management tool, you will notice that you have a mix of planned and unplanned, often urgent, work in the system. To ensure that urgent work gets the attention and precedence it deserves, you can introduce what is called a **fast lane** to your sprint board. The following screenshot shows an example of an Azure board that has been set up for fastlaning production issues:

Figure 1.2 – Azure Board setup depicting the fast lane

The horizontal split in this board is only used to work on tasks in the regular lane when there is no work to be picked up in the fast lane.

You can find instructions on how to configure swim lanes in your Azure (Kanban) boards for expediting work at https://docs.microsoft.com/en-us/azure/devops/boards/boards/expedite-work?view=azure-devops.

Decommissioning other work management tools

After creating a shared work management system between development and operations, there is an opportunity to increase the amount of collaboration between them. When this collaboration is taking off, old ticketing systems that were used by operations may now slowly be decommissioned over time. Integrations from monitoring tools can be shifted to the new shared tools, and the number of tickets between developers and operators should slowly decrease as they find new ways of working together.

> **Important Note**
>
> Azure DevOps allows you to customize work item templates, as well as define life cycle states. Using this feature, teams can easily model their work item template types based on any existing taxonomy they might be using in their existing tools. This significantly reduces the learning curve in the adoption of the new shared work management tool. For more information on this, go to `https://docs.microsoft.com/en-us/azure/devops/boards/backlogs/work-item-template?view=azure-devops&tabs=browser#manage-work-item-templates`.

Goals and benefits of a DevOps culture

At this point, you might be wondering about the point of it all. What are the benefits of DevOps and what's in it for you, your colleagues, and your organization? The most common goal of adopting DevOps is to achieve a reduction in **cycle time**. Cycle time is the time between starting work on a new feature and the moment that the first user can use it. The way this is achieved, by automation, also serves the goals of lower change failure rate, lower **mean time to repair** (**MTTR**), and lower planned downtime.

Next to all that, there may be other benefits, such as increased employee satisfaction, less burnout and stress, and better employee retention. This is attributed to removing opposing goals between developers and operators.

For a while, there was doubt about whether DevOps works, whether these goals can be met, and whether the extra benefits can be achieved since this was only shown using case studies. The downside of this is that case studies are often only available for successful cases, not for unsuccessful ones. This all changed in 2018 when the book *Accelerate* came out. This book shows, based on years of quantitative research, that modern development practices such as DevOps contribute to reaching IT goals and organizational goals.

Measuring results

To measure where you currently stand as a team or organization and the impact DevOps has on you, there are several metrics that you can start recording. As always, when working with metrics or **key performance indicators** (**KPIs**), make sure that you do not encourage people to game the system by looking only at the numbers. Several interesting metrics are detailed in the following sections and if you go over them, you will notice that they are all about encouraging flow.

Cycle time and lead time

Cycle time and **lead time** are metrics that come from Lean and Kanban and are used to measure the time needed to realize a change. Cycle time is the amount of time between starting work on a feature and users being able to use that feature in production. The lower the cycle time, the quicker you can react to changing requirements or insights. Lead time is the amount of time between requesting a feature and realizing that feature. It is the time between adding work to the backlog and when you start implementing it.

When you add cycle time and lead time together, you are calculating another metric, known as the **time to market**. This is often an important business metric when developing software. Hence, minimizing both cycle time and lead time will have a business impact.

The amount of work in progress

Another thing you can measure is the amount of work in progress at any point in time. DevOps focuses on the flow of value to the user. This implies that everyone should, if possible, be doing only one thing at a time and finish that before moving on to something else. This reduces the amount of time spent on task switching and the amount of time spent on not yet complete work. Measuring how many things a team works on in parallel and reporting on this can act as a source of encouragement.

You can even go as far as putting actual limits on the amount of work that can be in progress. The following is a small part of *Figure 1.2*, showing that these work-in-progress limits can even be shown in the tool:

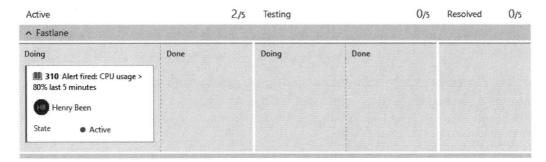

Figure 1.3 – Azure Boards depicting limits for each stage

The goal is to have as little work in progress at the same time as possible.

Mean time to recovery

The third metric is the **mean time to recovery**. How long does it take you to restore a service in case of a (partial) outage? In the past, companies focused on reducing the **mean time between failures**. This used to be the mean indicator of the stability of a product. However, this metric encourages limiting the number of changes going to production. The unwanted consequence is often that outages, though they might be rare, last long and are hard to fix.

Measuring the mean time to recovery shifts the attention to how quickly you can remediate an outage. If you can fix outages quickly, you can achieve the same – namely, you can minimize the amount of downtime without sacrificing the rate of change. The goal is to minimize the time to recovery.

Change rate and change failure rate

Finally, you can measure the number of changes that are delivered to production and the percentage of that which is not successful. Increasing the rate of change implies that you are delivering value to your users more often, hence realizing a flow of value. Also, by measuring not just the number of failures but also the percentage that fails, you are encouraging many small, successful changes instead of encouraging whether the number of changes is limited overall.

Your goal should be to increase the rate of change while lowering the change failure rate. Apart from the four major KPIs listed in this section, many other metrics may be useful in measuring your DevOps maturity. All these metrics must be linked back to the important business **objectives and key results (OKRs)** that are expected. You can find more information about OKRs here: `https://docs.microsoft.com/en-us/azure/cloud-adoption-framework/strategy/business-outcomes/okr`.

A representative sample, for illustration purposes, is depicted in the following table:

Objective	Key Results
Faster time to market	• Deployment Frequency: Every week • Deployment Time <= 4 hours • Lead Time (Major Releases): Once every quarter
Increase the business value that's been realized while maintaining or reducing costs	• CI/CD processes: 100% automated • Resource Utilization (95th percentile): 80% • Dashboards for monitoring both Health and Costs
Predictable and quality delivery and faster correction with fewer defects	• High Availability > 99.9% • RTO < 1 hour, RPO < 15 mins
Better processes across IT, automation, teamwork, and culture	• MTTR < 1 hour • Lead Time (Bugs) < 8 hour • Scaled Agile: Feature Teams > 5 • Technical Debt < 1 week
Improved customer engagement and ability to quickly respond to market demands	• CSAT: 4 or above • Product Planning: 50% of the backlog focuses on Customer Feedback

Table 1.1 – Using the OKR approach for your DevOps maturity

At this point, you might be wondering, how do I help my organization foster this culture and reap all of these benefits? The next section will answer this.

Creating your ideal DevOps organization

Well, maybe your organizational structure does not have to change at all. DevOps must start with a cultural change: openness, empathy, and collaboration are values that need to be encouraged. But still, changing your organizational structure may help accelerate this.

Traditionally, developers and operators are often organized into disparate teams or even different departments – organized in teams with people that have similar skill sets and responsibilities. A common change in organizations is changing this structure by pivoting and organizing teams behind a common goal, a single product, or a group of features, for example.

Now, you will need teams with different skill sets and responsibilities, teams most likely with developers and operators. It is important to realize that forcing such a change upon these people may not be the best way forward. Often, it works best to start with changing the culture and encouraging cooperation – then, this organizational change may come about naturally.

Finally, it is important to recognize one anti-pattern at this point. Some companies are trying to implement DevOps by hiring specialized DevOps engineers and positioning them between development and operations, interacting with both. While this, at first, may seem like a good idea, this goes against the DevOps values. If you do this, you are not breaking silos down, but you are adding a third one. You are not decreasing the number of hand-offs, you are most likely increasing them. Also, collaboration between developers and operations is often not enhanced by separating them using another organizational structure, and you may not see any increase in value to your end users at all.

Now that you know what DevOps is and you have a clear understanding of how you can form a DevOps team, it is time to explore how to start achieving your goals.

Exploring DevOps practices and habits

Since you are not the first team going on this journey, you can learn from the experiences of those before you. One example is the Microsoft team that built Azure DevOps. Being in the rare position that they can use their product for developing another product, they have learned a great deal about what makes DevOps successful. From this, they have identified seven key DevOps practices and seven DevOps habits that many successful DevOps teams share:

DevOps Practices	DevOps Habits
Configuration management	Team autonomy and enterprise alignment
Release management	Rigorous management of technical debt
Continuous integration	Focus on the flow of customer value
Continuous deployment	Hypothesis-driven development
Infrastructure as Code	Evidence gathered in production
Test automation	Live-site culture
Application performance monitoring	Myanage infrastructure as a flexible resource

Table 1.2 – DevOps practices and habits

Now, it is important to realize that just copying the motions described here will not guarantee success. Just as with Agile, you will have to spend time to understand these practices and habits, where they come from, and how they contribute to a continuous flow of value to your end users.

> **Important Note**
>
> Microsoft Services has introduced a more comprehensive **DevOps Dojo** model that aims to categorize the maturity of your DevOps practices. It gives you a good structure on how you should prioritize the DevOps-related investments within your teams. You can read more about it here: `https://docs.microsoft.com/en-us/learn/paths/devops-dojo-white-belt-foundation/`.

The following sections explore all of these practices and habits in more detail. Keep these in the back of your mind while reading the rest of this book. While the rest of this book will mostly focus on the *technical means* of *how* to do things, do not forget that these are only means. The real value comes from your mindset and creating a culture that focuses on creating a continuous flow of value for your customers.

DevOps practices

This section discusses all seven DevOps practices in turn. As you will quickly see, they are highly related, and it is quite hard to practice one without the other. For example, test automation is highly related to continuous integration and continuous deployment.

> **Important Note**
>
> If you plan on taking the AZ-400 exam, mastering all of these practices and performing them using Azure DevOps will help you significantly.

Configuration management

Configuration management is about versioning the configuration of your application and the components it relies on, along with your application itself. Configuration is kept in source control and takes the form of, for example, JSON or YAML files that describe the desired configuration of your application. These files are the input for tools such as Ansible, Terraform, Puppet, or PowerShell DSC, which configure your environment and application. These tools are often invoked from a continuous deployment pipeline.

The desired state can also be reapplied at an interval, even if no changes have been made to the intended configuration. This way, it is ensured that the actual configuration stays correct and that manual changes are automatically revoked. We call this the *prevention of configuration drift*. Configuration drift occurs over time due to servers being added or removed over time, or manual, ad hoc interventions by administrators. Of course, this implies that intended updates to the configuration are done in source control and only applied using tools.

Configuration management or **Configuration as Code (CaC)** is highly related to **Infrastructure as Code (IaC)**. The two are often intertwined and on some platforms, the difference between the two may even feel artificial. CaC will be discussed in detail in *Chapter 8, Implement Infrastructure and Configuration as Code*.

Release management

Release management is about being in control of which version of your software is deployed to which environment. Versions are often created using continuous integration and delivery pipelines. These versions, along with all of the configuration needed, are then stored as immutable artifacts in a repository. From here on, release management tools are used to plan and control how these versions are deployed to one or more environments. Examples of such controls include manual approvals and automated queries of open work and quality checks before allowing deployment to a new environment.

Release management is related to continuous deployment and focuses more on controlling the flow of versions through the continuous deployment pipeline. *Chapter 8, Implement Infrastructure and Configuration as Code*, will cover CaC as part of release management.

Continuous integration

Continuous integration is a practice where every developer integrates their work with that of the other developers in the team at least once a day and preferably more often. This means that every developer should push their work to the repository at least once a day. A continuous integration build verifies that their work compiles and that all the unit tests run. It is important to understand that this verification should not run only on the code that the developer is working on in isolation. The real value comes when the work is also integrated with the work of others.

When integrating changes often and fast, problems with merging changes are less frequent and if they occur, they are often less difficult to solve. In *Chapter 4, Everything Starts with Source Control*, you will learn more about how to set up your source control repositories to make this possible. In *Chapter 5, Moving to Continuous Integration*, you will learn about setting up a continuous integration build.

Continuous deployment

Continuous deployment is the practice of automatically deploying every new version of sufficient quality to production. When practicing continuous deployment, you have a fully automated pipeline that takes in every new version of your application (every commit), results in a new release, and starts deploying it to one or more environments. The first environment is often called **test** and the final environment is called **production**.

In this pipeline, multiple steps verify the quality of the software before letting it proceed to the next environment. If the quality is not sufficient, the release is aborted and will not propagate to the next environment. The premise behind this approach is that, in the pipeline, you try to prove that you cannot take the current version to the next environment. If you fail to prove so, you assume it is ready for further progression.

Only when a release has gone through all the environments in the pipeline is it deployed to production. Whenever a release cannot progress to the next environment, that release will be completely canceled. While you might be inclined to fix the reason for the failure and then restart deployment from the point where it failed, it is important not to do so. The changes you made at that point are not validated by all of the controls that the version has already passed through. The only way to validate the new version as a whole is by starting the pipeline from the start. You can see this clearly in the following diagram:

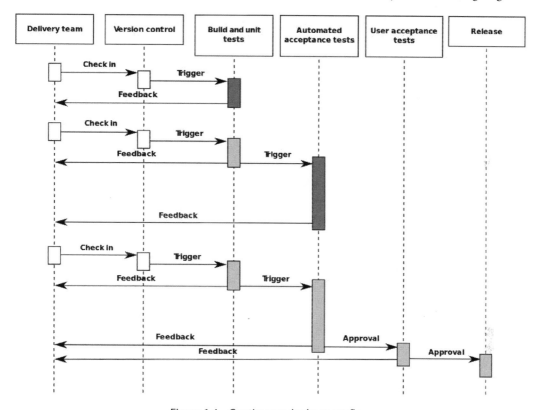

Figure 1.4 – Continuous deployment flow

In *Chapter 6, Implementing Continuous Deployment and Release Management*, you will learn about setting up continuous deployment using.

> **Important Note**
>
> The preceding diagram can be found at `https://en.wikipedia.org/wiki/Continuous_delivery#/media/File:Continuous_Delivery_process_diagram.svg`. The image is by Grégoire Détrez, original by Jez Humble, under CC BY-SA 4.0, at `https://creativecommons.org/licenses/by-sa/4.0/`.

Infrastructure as Code

When writing an application, the binaries that you are building must be running somewhere on some application host. An example of such an application host can be a web server such as IIS or Apache. Next to an application host, we may need a database and some messaging solution. This is called the infrastructure for our application. When practicing IaC, you are keeping a description of this infrastructure in your source code repository, alongside your application code.

When the time comes to release a new version of the application and you need to make one or more changes to the infrastructure, you are executing this description of your desired infrastructure using tools such as Chef, Puppet, Terraform, Azure Bicep, PowerShell DSC, or Azure ARM templates. The execution of such a description is idempotent, which means that it can be executed more than once, and the result is the same. This is because your description of the infrastructure describes the *desired state* you want the infrastructure to be in and not a series of steps to be executed. Those steps to be executed, if there are any, are automatically determined by your tool of choice. Applying the desired state can also be done automatically in a continuous deployment pipeline and is often executed before the application code is updated.

The big advantage of this is that you can easily create a new environment where the infrastructure is guaranteed to be the same as in your other environments. Also, the problem of configuration drift, where the infrastructure between your different environments slowly diverges, is no longer possible since every time you apply the desired state again to every environment, it's forced.

Chapter 8, Implement Infrastructure and Configuration as Code, will discuss IaC in more detail.

Test automation

To continuously deliver value to your end users, you must release fast and often. This has implications for the way you test your application. You can no longer execute manual tests when you release your application every few minutes. This means that you must automate as many of your tests as possible.

You will most likely want to create multiple test suites for the applications that you run at different stages of your delivery pipeline. Fast unit tests that run within a few minutes and that are executed whenever a new pull request is opened should give your team very quick feedback on the quality of their work, and it should catch most of the errors. Next, the team should run one or more slower test suites later in the pipeline to further increase your confidence in the quality of a version of your application.

All of this should limit the amount of manual testing to a bare minimum and allow you to automatically deploy new versions of your application with confidence.

Chapter 10, Integrating Continuous Testing, will cover test automation in detail.

Application performance monitoring

This last practice is all about learning how your application is doing in production. Gathering metrics such as response times and the number of requests will tell you about how the systems are performing. Capturing errors is also part of performance monitoring and allows you to start fixing problems without having to wait on your customers to contact you about them.

In addition to that, you can gather information about which parts of the application are more or less frequently used and whether new features are being picked up by users. Learning about usage patterns provides you with great insights into how customers use your applications and common scenarios they are going through.

Chapter 11, *Managing Security and Compliance*, and *Chapter 12*, *Application Monitoring*, will go into detail about both your application and your users' behavior in production.

DevOps habits

The seven habits of successful DevOps teams are more concerned with culture and your attitude while developing and delivering software, and less with technical means than DevOps practices are. Still, it is important to know and understand these habits since they will help make DevOps adoption easier.

You will notice that developing these habits will reinforce the use of the practices enumerated previously and the tools you use to implement them. And of course, this holds the other way around as well.

Team autonomy and enterprise alignment

An important part of working Agile is creating teams that are largely self-directed and can make decisions without (too many) dependencies outside the team. Such a team will often include multiple roles, including a product owner that owns one or more features and is empowered to decide on their way forward.

However, this autonomy also comes with the responsibility to align the work of the team with the direction the whole product is taking. It is important to develop ways of aligning the work of tens or hundreds of teams with each other, in such a way that everyone can sail their course but the fleet as a whole stays together as well.

The best-case scenario is that teams take it upon themselves to align to the larger vision, instead of taking directions now and then.

Rigorous management of technical debt

Another habit is that of rigorous management of technical debt. The term *debt* in itself suggests that there is a cost (interest) associated with the delay in addressing an issue. To keep moving at a constant pace and not slowly lose speed over time, it is crucial to keep the number of bugs or architectural issues to a minimum and only tolerate so much. Within some teams, this is even formalized in agreements.

For example, a team can agree that the number of unfixed bugs should never exceed the number of team members. This means that if a team has four members and a fifth bug is reported, no new work will be undertaken until at least one bug has been fixed.

Focusing on the flow of customer value

It is important to accept that users receive no value from code that has been written until they are using it. Focusing on the flow of value to a user means that code must be written, tested, and delivered and should be running in production before you are done. Focusing on this habit can drive cooperation between disciplines and teams.

Hypothesis-driven development

In many modern development methodologies, there is a product owner who is responsible for ordering all of the work in the backlog, based on the business value. This owner, as the expert, is responsible for maximizing the value that's delivered by the development team by ordering all the items based on the business value (divided by effort).

However, recent research has shown that even though the product owner is an expert, they cannot correctly predict which features will bring the most value to users. Roughly one-third of the work from a team adds value for users, while another third decreases the value. For this reason, you can switch your backlog from features or user stories to the hypothesis you want to prove or disprove. You only create a minimal implementation or even just a hint of a feature in the product and then measure whether it is picked up by users. Only when this happens can you expand the implementation of the feature.

Evidence gathered in production

Performance measurements should be taken in your production environment, not (just) in an artificial load test environment. There is nothing wrong with executing load tests before going to production if they deliver value to you. However, the real performance effort is done in the production environment. It should be measured there and compared with previous measurements.

This also holds for usage statistics, patterns, and many, many other performance indicators. They can all be automatically gathered using production metrics.

Live-site culture

A live-site culture promotes the idea that anything that happens in the production environment takes precedence over anything else. Next, anything that threatens production, is about to go to production, or hinders going to production at any time gets priority. Only when these are all in order is the attention shifted to future work.

Also, a part of a live-site culture is ensuring that anything that disturbed the operation of the service is thoroughly analyzed – not to find out who to blame or fire but to find out how to prevent this from happening again. Prevention is preferably done by shifting left; for example, by detecting an indicator of a repeat incident earlier in the pipeline.

Managing infrastructure as a flexible resource

Finally, a successful DevOps team treats its servers and infrastructure as mutable assets that can be continually changed, upgraded, tuned, or even decommissioned to meet the demands of the business. The ability to do this is fueled by configuration and IaC. This may even go so far as creating a new production environment for every new deployment and just deleting the old production environment after switching all traffic from the old environment to the new one.

Besides keeping these DevOps practices and habits in mind, there are certain stages that you will go through while trying to move to a DevOps culture in your organization. The next section will take you through them.

The five stages of the DevOps evolution

When you are trying to move to a DevOps culture in your organization, it is going to take time. There are motions you have to go through while everyone in your organization embraces the changes they have to make to their ways of working. Others that have gone before you have gone through the following five steps or stages, which may help you. Knowing about them can help you accelerate your journey. These steps were first published in the *2018 State of DevOps Report* and are discussed in the following sections.

Normalizing the technology stack

A common first step on the road to a DevOps culture is adopting. At a minimum, there are good tools for source control and often, a company standard and continuous integration and delivery are rolled out. Teams also work together to normalize the stack they develop software for. For example, one or two cloud vendors are chosen, and other deployment platforms are phased out. The same goes for tools for other purposes – they are standardized where possible. Homebrewed solutions are replaced with industry standards.

Standardizing and reducing variability

At this stage, teams work on further reducing the variation between and within applications and the development and operations teams that work on them, working together on aligning operating systems, libraries, and tools. Also, in this stage, deployment processes are changed to reduce the amount of variation between them, and configuration and infrastructure are often moved to source control.

Expanding DevOps practices

The remaining issues between development and operations are cleaned up, ensuring that the outputs of the development team are precisely what the operations team expects. Also, collaboration starts to grow between the two and they can work together without external dependencies on creating and delivering changes.

Automating infrastructure delivery

At this stage, the infrastructure that is used by developers and operations becomes fully aligned. Everything is deployed from source control and the same scripts or solutions are used by both teams.

Providing self-service capabilities

Before DevOps, virtual machines or hosting environments were often requested from operations, by developers manually, or through ticketing systems. Provisioning was done manually by operators, which could take days or sometimes even weeks.

Self-service capabilities mean that environments are no longer created manually, but through self-service APIs that operations teams make available to developers.

This way, developers can create and destroy environments on their own. They can create and test changes on their own and send them off or schedule them for automated deployment.

Summary

In this chapter, you learned what DevOps is (and what it is not) and its relationship with Agile. Moving to a DevOps culture helps you break down conflicting targets for developers on one side and operators on the other. This empowers them to work together on continuously delivering value to your end users, organizing their work in a single backlog, and working off a single board, while respecting the differences in their ways of working. Organizing developers and operators in product-oriented teams is the next important step in creating like-minded, goal-oriented teams.

Moving to DevOps can bring many benefits and you now know how these can be measured so that you can continuously keep improving. Next, you learned about the DevOps habits and practices that many successful DevOps teams exhibit. Mastering these yourself and with your team will enable you to go through a DevOps evaluation. All this helps continuously deliver value to your users.

In the next chapter, we will discuss **Site Reliability Engineering** (**SRE**) and how it complements DevOps for managing the reliability and scalability of your application.

Self-practice exercise

Make use of the concepts presented in this chapter to complete the following activities:

1. Identify 2-3 DevOps-related metrics that may be important for your team.
2. For each metric, identify the DevOps practices that apply.
3. Define the current baseline for these metrics and list the areas of improvement.

Questions

As we conclude, here is a list of questions for you to test your knowledge regarding this chapter's material. You can find the answers in the *Assessments* section:

1. True or false: Development and operations departments often have conflicting goals.
2. True or false: The seven DevOps practices discussed in this chapter are unrelated and one can be easily practiced without the other.
3. Which of the following is not a part of the five stages of DevOps evolution?

    A. Normalizing the technology stack

    B. Automating infrastructure delivery

    C. Standardizing and reducing variability

    D. Hiring dedicated automation teams

4. What is fastlaning?
5. Describe in your own words, in a few lines, what the essence of DevOps is.

Further reading

There are many other resources that you may find helpful to learn more about DevOps culture and the DevOps way of thinking. Some of them are as follows:

*   *The Phoenix Project*, by *Gene Kim*, *Kevin Behr*, and *George Spafford*.
*   *Effective DevOps*, by *Jennifer Davis* and *Katherine Daniels*.
*   *Accelerate*, by *Nicole Forsgren*, *Jez Humble*, and *Gene Kim*.
*   *Interview with Sam Guckenheimer*, available at `https://devops.com/11626/`.
*   *Microsoft Case Study on their DevOps Journey*, available at `http://stories.visualstudio.com/devops/`.
*   The *2018 State of DevOps Report*, available at `http://info.puppet.com/Eficode-Puppet-State-of-DevOps-Report.html`.

- More information on assessing existing development processes can be found at `https://docs.microsoft.com/en-us/learn/modules/assess-your-development-process/index`.

- More information about different Agile approaches and how to support them using Azure Boards can be found at `https://docs.microsoft.com/en-us/learn/modules/choose-an-agile-approach/index`.

2

Site Reliability Engineering Fundamentals

In the previous chapter, you learned about the DevOps culture, goals, and benefits. DevOps practices and habits enable collaboration between teams and shorten the loop within the delivery cycle from idea inception and design to deployment for the end user.

Site reliability engineering (**SRE**) and DevOps methods are complementary rather than competitive. SRE is not the next logical step after DevOps. Technically, teams that use SRE practices achieve better customer outcomes when measured with DevOps metrics.

Conventionally, organizations have maintained teams as different siloed units, such as **development** (**Dev**), **quality assurance** (**QA**), and **operations** (**Ops**) teams. The development team is primarily responsible for completing feature development, while the QA team is primarily responsible for performing and completing quality checks of developed functionalities. The operations team, on the other hand, is primarily responsible for the deployment and maintenance of applications in the production environment. Additionally, they also monitor and take necessary action to ensure the reliability and scalability of the deployed applications

Both SRE and DevOps have teams of engineers with development and operations expertise. As a result, the organization can prevent teams from working in silos.

The reputation and success of a business or product are dependent on the stability of cloud solutions in a production environment. To boost application stability and scalability, SRE will use automation to reduce repetitive and manual operational tasks. Adopting SRE practices into your software development life cycle is crucial for survival in this current era of building IT solutions.

In this chapter, we're going to cover the following main topics:

- Introduction to SRE
- Key principles and practices

Technical requirements

There are no technical requirements for this chapter.

Introduction to SRE

The term *SRE* was first coined by Ben Treynor Sloss at Google (`https://sre.google/sre-book/introduction/`). SRE has enabled Google to manage large-sized complex systems and massive infrastructure in the most efficient, reliable, scalable, and sustainable way.

> **Tip**
> SRE is primarily focused on the reliability of service.

Why is reliability so important?

Reliability is defined as the likelihood of services performing predictably under specified operational conditions. The most dependable systems will be more accessible, which will result in a better client experience. The reliability of your services is an important quality indicator.

Reliability and availability are interlinked; however, the difference is in the way they are measured. Although availability and reliability go hand in hand, the measures taken might produce different results. A system's availability may be modeled mathematically as a measure of its reliability. In other words, reliability can be considered as a subset of availability.

What is availability?

The availability of the systems can be measured as the percentage of time in which the system is available or fully operational. A software system is composed of several components, all of which must be evaluated to ensure availability. Let's assume we have a system that includes components such as database servers, storage servers, and application servers. Your system's availability will be defined by the combined availability of these components.

Refer to `https://uptime.is/` to learn more about the downtime allowed on your services based on availability guarantees, often known as **service-level agreements** (**SLAs**). The following table illustrates some availability percentages and downtime limits in seconds, minutes, and hours. The phrase *availability* or *uptime* is commonly given in nines (read as a count of nines) as shown in the table here (accordingly the allowed downtime is calculated):

Availability	Allowed Downtime				
Percentage	Daily	Weekly	Monthly	Quarterly	Yearly
99.999% (Five nines)	0 Seconds	6 Seconds	26 Seconds	1 Minute 18 Seconds	5 Minutes 15 Seconds
99.99% (Four nines)	8 Seconds	1 Minute 0 Seconds	4 Minutes 32 seconds	13 Minutes 8 Seconds	52 Minutes 35 Seconds
99.95% (Three nines)	43 Seconds	5 Minutes 2 Seconds	21 Minutes 54 Seconds	1 Hour 5 Minutes 44 Seconds	4 Hours 22 Minutes 58 Seconds

Table 2.1 – Availability percentage and downtime allowance

The formula to calculate the time-based availability percentage is as follows:

*Availability % = ((Service Uptime - Service Downtime) ÷ (Service Uptime)) * 100*

For example, to calculate the availability of production service in a single day, assuming the agreed service is expected to run *24*365, use the following*:

- The total number of seconds within a day that the agreed service is expected to be up and running = 86,400 seconds.
- The sum of downtime(s) on a specific day = 60 seconds for deployment + 60 seconds for rollback due to deployment error.
- Using the preceding formula for availability = ((86,400 -120) ÷ (86,400)) *100.
- The availability for your service on that day is 99.86%.

SRE advocates for monitoring and assessing the availability of important services that are essential to the business's success.

The goal of your IT department should not be to boost service availability across the board. Greater availability increases the cost of doing business because it necessitates more work and resources. However, because a lack of better availability can result in significant monetary losses (often, exceeding the cost of operations), the SRE team will take a pragmatic approach to define availability levels based on business demands.

Domain Name Services (DNS), for example, is the internet's directory. Domain names are matched with IP addresses using this service. DNS should be available 24 hours a day, 7 days a week. As a result, DNS availability is maintained at 100%.

In general, aiming for 100% dependability for any service or system is not a clever idea. It would be difficult for a user to identify the difference between a service that is 100% available and one that is 99.999% available.

According to *Table 2.1*, 99.999% availability allows for 26 seconds of downtime per month and 6 seconds per week, which is little in most circumstances.

However, some mission-critical systems, such as medical devices and aircraft, must be completely dependable and cannot afford any downtime.

Reliability challenges and SRE

Cloud architecture must be reliable, scalable, and performant. Cloud services will use auto-scaling to dynamically scale services to meet changing demand, and observability will be used for applications that provide support for monitoring system performance, availability, success, error and dependence error rate, request failure rate, latency, freshness, and throughput.

Service availability and reliability metrics will be used by organizations to determine the service levels required to keep business activities running smoothly. Your SRE strategy's key decision factors are reliability and availability, which have different meanings and are measured differently:

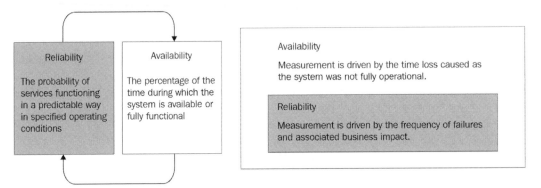

Figure 2.1 – Reliability and availability

As evident from the preceding figure, reliability can be considered as a subset of availability. Organizations have realized that maintaining system reliability is challenging while also maintaining development velocity, desired scalability, and operational stability.

The conventional team model includes a Dev, QA, and Ops team, with development, QA, and operations tasks separated. This type of separation has resulted in organizational silos or a *throw-it-over-the-wall* mentality, which influences the organizational team's ability to achieve long-term goals and foster a learning and blameless culture:

Figure 2.2 – Reliability challenges

The Dev team *throws* their code over the wall and expects the Ops team to run and manage it in production. The Dev team wants to release features at a fast pace to production and not be responsible for the stability of the applications. The Ops team, on the other hand, wants to minimize changes to the production service to avoid any disruptions to business to maintain the stability of services.

SRE helps the team in striking a balance between delivering new features and ensuring that the system operates appropriately and effectively. This collaborative method bridges the gap between development responsibilities and day-to-day system operation and customer service and support tasks. This daily customer support and operational activity create a feedback loop, which is essential for increasing system quality.

Although customers are increasingly anticipating shorter delivery times, just focusing on delivery speed or greater product velocity is insufficient. One of the most critical attributes for competing effectively in today's modern development is dependability. As a result, increasing product velocity while being dependable is a fundamental premise for any IT organization. The SRE team is responsible for the availability, latency, performance optimization, change management, monitoring, alerting, emergency response, and capacity planning of their service(s).

The fundamental goal of SRE is to improve system reliability and stability. The team understands that reliability metrics are driven by business needs, and not every business function might require the highest level of reliability, as there are cost tradeoffs associated with it.

Appropriate reliability

The level of reliability for a service must be appropriate to match its business needs. Online e-commerce businesses will have different requirements compared to traditional retail shops. For example, they will require a greater level of availability than traditional retail shops, which operate only throughout the day for a set number of hours.

Reliability is defined and measured using **service-level objectives** (**SLOs**). SRE practices can be tailored to achieve the appropriate level of reliability, and SLOs are usually defined as a percentage achievement over a period. SLOs are driven by key business objectives, whereas **service-level indicators** (**SLIs**) are driven by what's possible to measure while implementing the service.

Consistent reliability

Products are built on the foundation of reliable systems, services, and people. SRE considers it essential to build a culture and practices that will lead to consistent and predictable reliability. The connections and trust we build with our colleagues, sustainable operating procedures, and the learning culture that we nurture to provide a psychologically safe workplace for our team to achieve environmental sustainability are all part of reliability.

In the next section, the SRE team's key principles and practices are covered.

Key principles and practices

The SRE team's day-to-day activities include developing and maintaining large, distributed services. Operating a service successfully in good health requires a wide range of activities, such as building monitoring systems, planning capacity, responding to incidents, resolving the root causes of outages, and so on.

This section covers the key principles and practices that influence the SRE team's day-to-day activities. The following diagram depicts the elements necessary to make a service reliable, from the most basic to the most advanced:

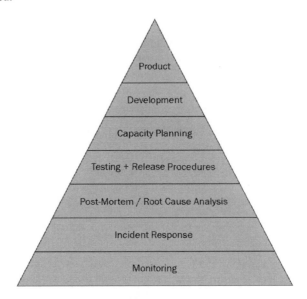

Figure 2.3 – Service reliability hierarchy according to Google's SRE book

From the most basic requirement to the capstone step of launching a product or service, Google has described the reliability hierarchy as necessary to boost the reliability of the system and maintain service health. Each level of this pyramid will be discussed briefly:

- **Monitoring**: Monitoring is the most essential strategy to maintain track of a system's availability, and is positioned at the bottom foundation layer of the service reliability hierarchy. Effective monitoring is simple and resilient, and it should provide alerts for critical failures in your service. Such alerts should be simple and clear to understand.

  There is no way to tell whether a service is operational, offline, or experiencing sporadic outages without monitoring. To establish a reliable system, you must be aware of problems and errors in your service before users notice them. After such problems are noticed, the SRE team should prioritize and manage incident response. To mitigate the impact or restore service to its previous state, the team should coordinate efforts in the most efficient way possible and maintain active communication.

  Microsoft Azure is a very robust cloud platform with a plethora of capabilities for dealing with every aspect of a solution. The services include tools for managing and deploying applications. When developing your solution on the Azure cloud, you must select the appropriate services to meet your SRE needs.

  To monitor your application, you can use the following services:

  - **Azure Monitor** provides a comprehensive solution for collecting, analyzing, and acting on telemetry from your cloud and on-premises environments, and supports operations at scale with *smart alerts* and *automated actions*.

  - **Azure Application Insights** is a feature of Azure Monitor that provides a powerful **application performance management** (**APM**) tool that easily integrates with your applications to send telemetry and analyze application-specific metrics. It also provides ready-to-use dashboards and a metrics explorer that you can use to analyze the data to explore business needs.

- **Incident response**: Once you have built effective monitoring around your service, you will need to configure notifications, such as SMS and **event management systems (EMS)** for unplanned, critical, and urgent incidents. Incidents and outages are unavoidable in a complex distributed system. Appropriate human intervention is required to identify the root cause and fix these outages.

  To minimize the business impact and run services smoothly, you would need to build up a process to mitigate and respond to these incidents in a structured way. Once the incident has been mitigated, the SRE team should follow the incident management response process to restore services as quickly as possible.

Incident response frameworks have three common objectives, widely known as the **three Cs** (**3Cs**) of incident management:

- Coordinate response effort.

- Communicate between incident responders, within the organization, and to the outside world.

- Maintain control over the incident response.

Although each organization's incident response process may change depending on organizational structure, skills, and previous experience, consider the following set of recommendations and best practices for responding to incidents:

- **Prioritize**: Fix frequently occurring problems, get the service back up and running, and keep the evidence for root-cause analysis.

- **Prepare**: In advance, develop and document your incident management procedures in consultation with incident participants.

- **Trust**: Provide all incident participants complete autonomy within their allocated roles and responsibilities.

During an incident, you must strike these critical balances:

- **Speed**:

  - Balance the need to move swiftly to satisfy stakeholders with the risk of making hasty decisions.

- **Sharing information**:

  - Inform investigators, stakeholders, and customers so that liability is minimized, and unrealistic expectations are avoided.

- **Post-mortem and root-cause analysis/blameless post-mortem**: Once an incident has been mitigated and handled, the SRE team implements post-mortem procedures. This post-mortem procedure offers an opportunity to cultivate a blameless post-mortem culture. A blameless post-mortem (or retrospective) is a post-incident document that helps teams figure out why an incident happened, what went well, what went wrong, and brainstorm how to prevent such issues from recurring.

Blameless post-mortems are a tenet of SRE culture. To build a sustainable culture, we would need to assume that everyone involved in an incident had good intentions and did the right thing with the information they had to minimize the business impact. Pointing the blame at people or at a team will discourage the team and will engender a fear of punishment, which will make it more difficult to bring concerns to light.

A blameless post-mortem is an opportunity for the team to learn from their failures or mistakes.

- **Testing and release procedures/testing for reliability**: The SRE team is responsible for building confidence in the reliability of the production systems they build and maintain. The SRE team will adopt a fully automated testing strategy along with classical software testing techniques to deploy in production and release it to users without any issues or downtime. The automated test suite(s) designed to support software reliability instills confidence that software will be deployed to production without major issues. As part of their QA activities, the SRE team must prioritize and make continuous investments in automated testing practices. Customers will be happier and platform adoption will increase, leading to a higher **return on investment (ROI)**.

- **Capacity planning**: As a member of the SRE team, you're in charge of determining the resource needs for your service, including the necessary hardware, software, and network resources, as well as ensuring that your service performs relatively well, even in the face of unanticipated demand. Capacity management is the process of ensuring that your service has enough resources to be scalable, fault-tolerant, efficient, and reliable. For example, SRE would estimate how much storage, service instances, or memory you will need over a specific interval of time. This data will help you create a scalable architecture for your service. You may be more flexible on required capacity in cloud-based models because you can dynamically increase or decrease required resources.

  Azure App Service, Azure SQL Database, Azure Kubernetes, and Azure Cache for Redis are examples of Azure cloud services that have built-in auto-scale features.

  For example, in **Azure App Service**, scale settings are applied in seconds and affect all apps in your App Service plan. You do not need to modify or redeploy your application. You can **scale up** and get more CPU, memory, disk space, and extra features, such as dedicated **virtual machines (VMs)**, custom domains and certificates, staging slots, autoscaling, and more. You can also leverage autoscaling, which automatically scales the number of instances depending on established criteria and schedules. Scaling rules are a more controlled approach to scale in or scale out.

  For example, every day at 21:00, you can scale down to two instances of Azure App Service, with a rule to scale up by one instance when CPU demand averages higher than 50%. A scale-out or scale-in action normally takes a few minutes to complete. Consider this when designing your scaling plan to match performance requirements and satisfy SLAs.

- **Development**: Although everyone expects services to run smoothly, there may be disruptions caused by events beyond anyone's control, such as natural disasters or hard drive failure, or even system process crashes that will impact your services adversely. Natural catastrophes can seriously damage many data centers in a region. To keep systems *functional*, the SRE team must design strategies to mitigate these failures. Such solutions would make use of deployment patterns/strategies such as **geo-replication and failover**, **geo-redundancy**, and **Active-Active, Active-Passive High Availability**:

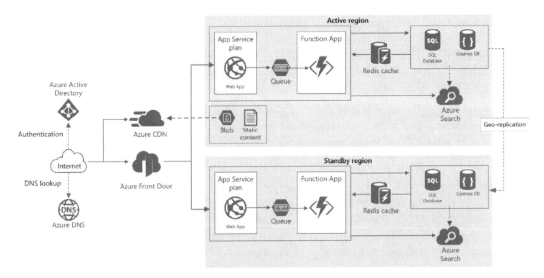

Figure 2.4 – Multi-region architecture

For example, as depicted in the preceding diagram, a multi-region architecture provides higher availability of service than when deploying to a single region. The architecture under consideration here includes the following components, to mention just a few:

- **Active and standby region**: Two regions to achieve higher availability. One is the primary region. The other region is for failover.

- **Azure Front Door**: A modern cloud **content delivery network** (**CDN**) service that delivers high performance, scalability, and secure user experiences for your content and applications. This service offers various layer 7 load-balancing capabilities and near-real-time failover for your applications.

- **Azure DNS**: A hosting service for DNS domains. It provides name resolution.

- **Azure App Service**: Azure's premier service for web applications and web-based APIs, which provides integrated security with **Azure AD** and **Azure Key Vault**. Supports auto-scaling.

- **Azure Functions**: A serverless compute option, it uses an event-driven model. In this architecture, the functions are invoked when a new message is pushed into the queue.

- **Azure Cache for Redis**: Applies a caching layer as a service to the solution, providing an in-memory managed cache to reduce latency and increase performance for the clients.

- **Azure Storage, Azure Cosmos DB, and Azure SQL**: Can store both structured and non-structured content.

- In the unlikely event of a disaster, a regional outage affects the active region, and Azure Front Door will fail over to the standby region. This architecture uses two regions, active and standby, to achieve higher availability. During normal operations, network traffic is routed to the primary region. If the active region becomes unavailable, traffic is routed to the standby region.

  - Active/passive with hot standby means resources in the secondary/standby region will be always running. These secondary region resources can be used for **A/B testing** for better value for money.

- **Product**: Companies launch new products at a slow pace. In the cloud and distributed modern world, the launch and release cycles need to be at a faster pace.

  Teams can create a checklist to document action items and roll back plans. A checklist plays an instrumental role in launching new services with reproducible reliability. A checklist needs to be tailored to the company's internal services, processes, and infrastructure.

The checklist needs to be created carefully or it will grow to an unmanageable size. This checklist can and should be documented and automated to minimize efforts. The checklist can cover the following themes:

- Architecture and dependencies

- Integration

- Capacity planning

- Failure modes

- Processes and automation

- Development process

- Rollout planning

- Gradual and staged rollouts

In the next section, we will cover patterns and principles that influence SRE operations.

Implementing SLOs and SLIs

SLOs define a goal level for your service's reliability. SLOs are at the heart of SRE practices because they are critical to making data-driven decisions regarding reliability. SLOs are a tool to help determine what engineering work to prioritize.

SLIs are a quantitative indicator of the level of service that you are providing. SLOs and SLIs always go hand in hand and are usually defined iteratively. SLOs are driven by key business objectives, whereas SLIs are driven by what is possible to be measured while implementing the service.

Your first attempt at an SLI and SLO doesn't have to be correct. The most important goal is to get something in place and measured, and to set up a feedback loop so you can improve. You can identify which metrics best match what your users care about in your service.

The SRE team recommends using a limited number of metrics based on critical services for greater user experience rather than developing an endless number of monitoring metrics. You could start with a broad target and then tweak it over time. This allows you to concentrate alerts on instances where you can reliably state that the services will be nonfunctional and will start to impact user experience.

Let's say that you are building a food delivery app from which users can do the following:

- Browse restaurants and menus.
- Select menu items and place an order.
- Pay for the order.

For this app, it is extremely important for a better user experience and overall business success that users can place an order for delivery and successfully make payments. Here, in the first attempt, the *Place order and pay* scenario will be the basis for defining SLOs, as this service would take precedence for business success over any other services.

The next step is to figure out which metrics to use as SLIs that will most accurately track the user experience. You can choose from a wide range of indicators, such as availability latency, throughput, correctness, and data freshness, as detailed next.

Most services focus on the following four key SLI metrics to monitor. These are the four golden signals of monitoring:

- **Request latency**: The time taken for your service to return a response to the request
- **Availability of service**: The fraction of time during which service is available to use
- **Success rate**: The number of requests successfully completed
- **Throughput**: The number of requests processed per second

The *measurement period* for defining an SLO is very important and can be defined over various time intervals. The SLO and SLIs need to be something that can be accurately measured and represented in your monitoring system. Over time, you will compare the SLO targets and SLIs with measured metrics. Now, for the *Place order and pay* service, which is a basis for the SLO, you will want to have an order confirmation received within an acceptable window.

In our example of the food delivery app, you can set a value of 700 ms for a response to be returned for a successful request for the *Place order and pay* service for a given specified time window of 1 month. These SLI goals and timeframes should be acceptable to businesses. So, if there are 10,000 HTTP requests in a calendar month and only 9,990 of them are successful, it corresponds to 9,990/10,000 or 99.9% availability for that month.

If your service is not meeting SLOs, then the SRE team will try to strike a balance between new feature development/deployment and increasing reliability of service to avoid SLO violations for a given measurement period.

An SLA is a legal agreement between the business and the customer that includes a reliability target and repercussions of not meeting it, whereas an SLO is an internal target that measures how customers use the service. SLOs are not shared with external stakeholders and have no legal bindings or consequences. If a service availability breaches the SLO, the SRE team must respond immediately to avoid the organization being penalized for failing to meet SLAs. SLOs should always be more stringent than corresponding SLAs. The SRE team does not typically get involved in constructing SLAs, because SLAs are closely tied to business and product decisions. However, the SRE team can help to define SLIs.

To find the right balance between reliability and innovation, it is better to create a rate against which SLO violations can be measured, and an *error budget* at which SLOs can be missed. In the next section, we will learn more about error budgets.

Establishing an error budget policy

An **error budget** is the maximum number of errors or the maximum amount of time your service is nonfunctional over a given period before it has a negative impact on the business and users become dissatisfied. The error budget is applied to several aspects of your service, such as availability, latency, and so on. The SRE team utilizes error budgets to strike a balance between service reliability and innovation speed.

An error budget will help you to know whether you are meeting expectations or not, and will help you to take appropriate actions to reduce the reliability failure of your service. If the service receives 1,000,000 requests in 4 weeks, a 99.9% SLO for successful requests allows us to budget for 1,000 errors throughout that period.

A service with 99.95% SLO has an error budget of 0.5% that translates to a overall downtime of 4 hours, 22 minutes, and 48 seconds within a year. The SRE team should take an appropriate course of action to restore stability to your service that is not meeting SLOs or has exhausted the error budget or comes close to exhausting it.

When your service is within budget, SRE practice encourages you to burn the error budget strategically, whether for a new feature or architectural modifications. Even though any new release inadvertently makes the service less reliable, for example, if the service goes down due to something such as a deployment configuration issue, the service is still within budget. Error budgets are often created for certain time periods, such as a month, quarter, or year.

Error budgets are frequently used strategically to apply automation for **toil** tasks such as manual deployment or environment setup, configuration changes, incident response, and many more. In the next section, we will learn more about reducing toil.

Reducing toil

Toil in an SRE context refers to operations that lack long-term monetary value and do not significantly advance the service. They are frequently repetitive and mostly manual (even though they could be automated). As the service or system grows, the number of manual requests for that system will likely grow proportionally, requiring even more human labor.

SRE engineers can only spend up to 50% of their time on *Ops* work such as tickets, on-call, and manual tasks, among other things.

SRE engineers should spend the other half of their time on activities such as the following (this is not a comprehensive list):

- Using automation to enable scalability
- Release deployment
- Test suite automation
- Applying database changes
- Automating response to incidents such as password reset and user creation
- Reviewing noncritical monitoring alerts
- Engineering work to develop new features to reduce toil and increase system reliability

To efficiently reduce the toil workload, the SRE team can start small and work their way up. Toil elimination requires automation, and the SRE team must work tirelessly to reduce or minimize toil. Automation engineering efforts, whether partial or complete, is necessary, but it should not endanger system reliability. **Azure Automation** can be used to automate human responses, as well as diagnosing and resolving issues. Team motivation will rise because of automation, and the team will be able to focus on engineering work.

Summary

In this chapter, we have learned about SRE principles and practices. We are now aware of how to calculate time-based availability and how to define availability based on business expectations and needs.

We also explored the typical reliability challenges associated with the traditional team model and how constituting an SRE team will help you find the right balance between system reliability and development. We underlined the role of proper and consistent reliability.

Then, we learned about all the necessary aspects, from conception to successfully launching the service on production. We also highlighted key techniques such as applying SLOs and SLIs, reducing toil, the post-mortem culture, and efficiently utilizing an error budget to improve system and cloud service dependability.

In the upcoming chapter, we'll look at DevOps tools and capabilities to see how they can help you manage your software development life cycle.

Self-practice exercises

1. Identify SLOs jointly with business stakeholders and development teams.

2. Perform blameless post-mortems for recent or hypothetical production incidents for your services in the production environment:

    - Refer to `https://sre.google/sre-book/example-postmortem/` for more guidance and an example post-mortem.

    - `https://docs.microsoft.com/en-us/azure/architecture/resiliency/failure-mode-analysis`.

    - `https://docs.microsoft.com/en-us/azure/architecture/framework/resiliency/overview`.

3. Identify tedious, repetitive tasks/toil associated with running your services in the production environment.

4. In the Azure portal, first, configure App Service logging with Application Insights to monitor your application, then configure email alerts.

Questions

As we conclude the SRE strategy, here is a list of questions for you to test your knowledge regarding this chapter's material. You will find answers in the *Assessments* section at the end of the book:

1. True or false? SRE is primarily focused on the reliability of service.

2. True or false? Availability is expressed in fives.

3. True or false? SRE adopts automation to enable application management.

4. What is the weekly, monthly, and yearly downtime allowance for a service with 95% availability?

5. What are the top three reliability challenges?

    A. Development velocity

    B. Quality

    C. Stability

    D. DevOps management

    E. Bug tracking

6. True or false? The appropriate level of reliability for services is identified by the key stakeholders.

7. What is toil in the SRE context?

Further reading

- Google's SRE book: `https://sre.google/sre-book/part-I-introduction/`

- Microsoft's SRE documentation: `https://docs.microsoft.com/en-us/learn/modules/intro-to-site-reliability-engineering/`

- *Azure Monitor*: `https://docs.microsoft.com/en-us/azure/azure-monitor/overview`

- *Azure Application Insights*: `https://docs.microsoft.com/en-us/azure/azure-monitor/app/app-insights-overview`

- *Azure Automation*: `https://docs.microsoft.com/en-us/azure/automation/overview`

3
Getting the Best Out of DevOps Tools

DevOps can be viewed as an approach aimed to improve the overall **Software Development Life Cycle** (**SDLC**) process, leading to greater collaboration between the teams involved. Hence, using the right set of tools for your DevOps processes and activities is critical to driving consistency and predictability across the various engineering teams. The goal is to establish a culture of innovation by automating the various processes, thereby synchronizing the efforts of the teams (or roles) while developing, testing, and deploying software faster with the highest quality possible.

Microsoft offers great products such as **Azure DevOps, GitHub, Azure Monitor,** and **Visual Studio Code** that help simplify the adoption of important practices spanning across the various life cycle phases of your DevOps implementation. These tools are feature-rich and offer a best-in-class experience to the developer community. The out-of-the-box experience can be further extended using marketplace extensions offered by other **Independent Software Vendors** (**ISVs**) and even the open source community.

By the end of this chapter, you will be familiar with some of these tool offerings, as well as the context in which they can be used within your respective software development programs.

In this chapter, we are going to cover the following main topics:

- SDLC and DevOps tools
- Azure DevOps and GitHub
- Azure DevTest Labs
- Azure Monitor
- Visual Studio Code

SDLC and DevOps tools

Be it a service or a product, the term SDLC refers to the set of processes and practices that are applied when building a software solution to ensure quality and meet other objectives, as outlined for the engineering team.

These processes are typically grouped as per the various phases in the development life cycle. The maturity of these processes has evolved over the years due to the evolution of technology. As engineering systems have become relatively complex with the use of distributed computing and cloud technologies, the development teams are expected to maintain strong rigor and discipline, as well as making use of automation to sustain their digital transformation journeys.

Depending on which software development methodology you may follow, be it **Waterfall**, **Agile**, **Scrum**, **Kanban**, or even a tailored version of your own, it is highly likely that you will make use of the DevOps-related practices in some form or the other. However, it is worth mentioning that Waterfall is not a recommended methodology to choose anymore if you wish to realize the true potential of your DevOps investments.

Let's look at some of the key activities that are executed in a DevOps life cycle.

Key activities in a DevOps life cycle

At a high level, the DevOps-related activities can be grouped into four different focus areas, as depicted in the following diagram:

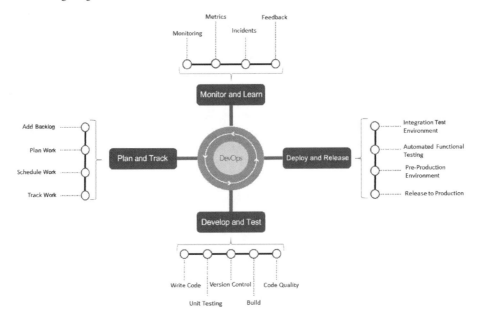

Figure 3.1 – Focus areas and key activities in a DevOps life cycle

The list of activities depicted here is meant to serve as a basic foundational list. Depending on your DevOps maturity level, you may implement many more practices to maximize your business outcomes. You must make use of the DevOps metrics discussed in *Chapter 1, Introduction to DevOps*, that are relevant to your context, and then identify the important practices that will help you achieve it.

In the next few sections, we will review these focus areas in detail to help you understand each of them better.

Plan and track

The development team identifies and organizes the product backlog and publishes work for the team. The work will be scheduled based on business priority and the available capacity. Backlog grooming and refinement is an ongoing activity throughout the life cycle of the product and shall span across multiple releases.

Develop and test

The development team starts producing the work outputs in the form of source code or scripts. All changes to the code base are checked for quality issues using static analyzers, unit tests, and even manual inspection. Once satisfied, the artifacts are compiled and built to produce a deployable package, also known as a solution.

Deploy and release

The solutions are initially deployed in a test environment, validated for correctness using automated tests, and then released to production environments. After this, the solution is then live and accessible to end users of the product or service.

Monitor and learn

Once the solution has gone live, this phase kicks in, and diagnostic and health monitoring information is captured from the live usage of the product or service. The data that's captured in the monitoring tools is periodically analyzed for faults and errors; any problems that have been identified are either mitigated using automation procedures or logged as bugs to be fixed by the team. Additionally, customer feedback can be channelized to suggest enhancements to the product or service. Now that you're aware of what goes on in the DevOps life cycle, let's review some of the commonly used tools for your DevOps practices.

Tools for your DevOps needs

Microsoft has a wide variety of tools to support your DevOps life cycle needs. Furthermore, it supports integration with other third-party tools to offer a cohesive experience to the developers of your team. So, whether you are building a new software system or maintaining one, you can easily adopt the Azure DevOps services and GitHub to innovate at scale.

Here we have listed the tools that you can plan to make use of for the various types of SDLC activities:

Practice/Activity	Choice of Tool
Manage your product backlog. Plan and track your work. Prepare dashboards and reports.	Azure Boards
Develop code locally, build, debug, and test.	Visual Studio Code/Visual Studio
Manage and track changes to your source code.	Azure Repos, Git
Define **continuous integration** (**CI**)/**continuous deployment** (**CD**) workflows to integrate changes and deploy the latest releases to different environments.	Azure Pipelines GitHub Actions Jenkins (third party)
Provision developer environments.	Azure DevTest Labs, Azure Virtual Desktop
Deploy and manage Azure cloud infrastructure and services (both IaaS and PaaS).	**Azure Resource Manager** (**ARM**) and the Azure **Command-Line Interface** (**CLI**)
	Ansible and Terraform (third party)
Manage the configuration of your resources.	Ansible, Terraform, Chef, Puppet, and Azure Automation
Advanced analytics and reporting.	Power BI
Capture and analyze logs (diagnostic, auditing, and health).	Azure Monitor and Azure Data Explorer
Prepare test plans and manage execution.	Azure Test Plans
Store reusable packages and artifacts.	Azure Artifacts
Improve productivity by using third-party extensions and plugins.	Azure DevOps Marketplace GitHub Marketplace

Table 3.1 – DevOps tools for your SDLC activities

Please go to https://azure.microsoft.com/en-in/solutions/devops/#practices for more details.

In the next few sections, we will look at the features and capabilities of a few of these tools. Detailed usage of these tools has also been explained in the subsequent chapters while providing illustrative examples of how the respective DevOps practices are being implemented.

Azure DevOps and GitHub

Azure DevOps and **GitHub** are two powerful **Software as a Service (SaaS)** offerings from Microsoft that serve as a complete DevOps toolset. From managing your backlog and team processes to a Git-based code repository to having the ability to execute CI/CD processes with automated testing, you will discover that GitHub and Azure DevOps is the perfect solution for you.

In the following subsections, we will explore the unique features of these two tools.

Azure DevOps

Originally, being part of the Visual Studio suite of products, the present-day Azure DevOps is perhaps the most used product by engineering teams to manage their source code and application life cycle processes. It was formerly known as **Visual Studio Team Services** and **Visual Studio Online** before that.

Azure DevOps is an Azure cloud-hosted version of the Azure DevOps server, previously known as **Team Foundation Server** (**TFS**) within the developer community. The main services that are available within this product are shown in the following diagram:

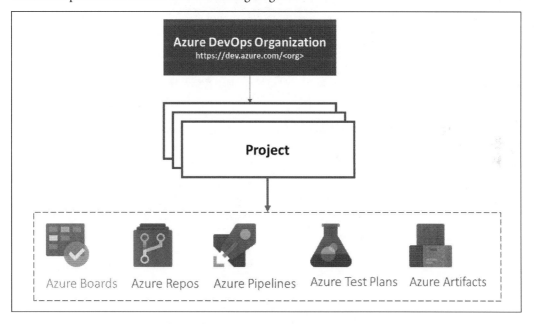

Figure 3.2 – Services available in Azure DevOps

Your access to these services will depend on the license type for your user account. For a complete list of the licensing options available for individuals and organizations, please go to https://azure. microsoft.com/en-in/pricing/details/devops/azure-devops-services/.

Let's take a brief look at each service.

Azure Boards

Managing your product backlog and tracking work has become a lot easier with Azure Boards. By making use of Kanban-style boards, you can create customized boards to track all your ideas to implementation:

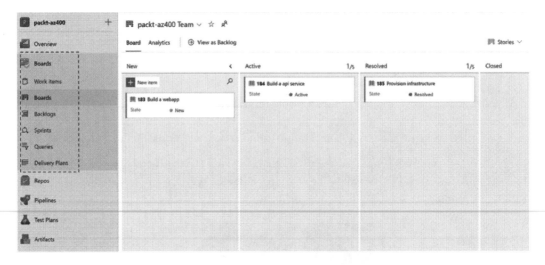

Figure 3.3 – Capabilities in Azure Boards

You can read more about Azure Boards here: https://docs.microsoft.com/en-in/azure/devops/boards/get-started/what-is-azure-boards?view=azure-devops.

Using Azure Boards, you can do the following:

- Manage and organize your backlog.

- Visualize stages and use them during daily standups and team meetings to track progress.

- Create customized dashboard reports for various stakeholders.

In the next section, we will look at Azure Repos, where you will store all your work products.

Azure Repos

Source Code Management (SCM) and **version control** are fundamental to engineering teams that are managing changes to the code base. Azure Repos offers a version control tool for managing a variety of software development projects.

Azure Repos offers two types of version control systems:

- **Team Foundation Version Control (TFVC):** This is a centralized version control system. Though not widely used in recent times, many project teams are continuing to use this approach for legacy purposes only.

- **Git:** This is the more popular distributed version control system. If you are just starting your DevOps journey, it is recommended to start with a Git-based version control system only:

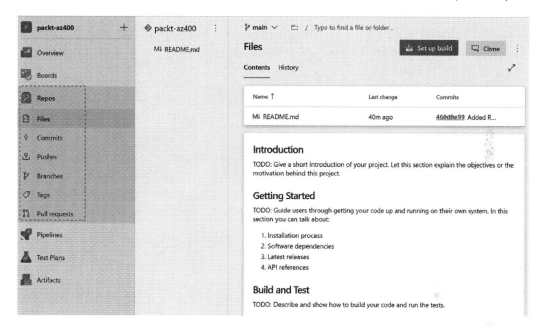

Figure 3.4 – Capabilities in Azure Repos

You can read more about Azure Repos here: https://docs.microsoft.com/en-us/azure/devops/repos/get-started/what-is-repos.

Using Azure Repos, you can do the following:

- Manage changes to your source code using the Git CLI or GUI-based tools.
- Configure branch policies and security to ensure compliance.
- Quickly find what you are looking for in your code base using semantic search.

Now, let's review Azure Pipelines, which you will use for your CI/CD processes.

Azure Pipelines

All code-based artifacts follow some sort of CI, CD, and **Continuous Testing** (**CT**) to certify their quality before they can be moved to a production environment. Azure Pipelines offers automation to execute the build, test, and release workflows. The sequence of tasks to be executed is configured using a YAML file. There are multiple source repositories (such as **Azure Repos**, **GitHub**, **Bitbucket**, and so on) you can choose from while building your pipelines. Also, separate pipelines are typically created for different workloads, along with gated approval checks as appropriate:

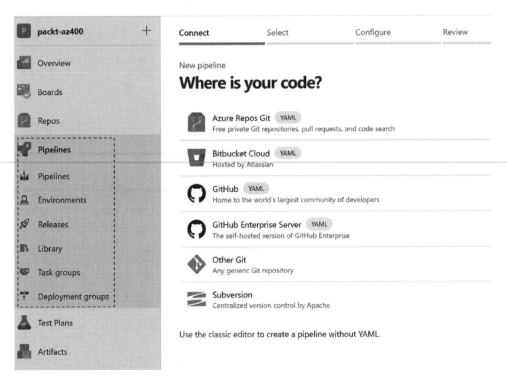

Figure 3.5 – Capabilities in Azure Pipelines

You can read more about Azure Repos here: https://docs.microsoft.com/en-us/azure/devops/pipelines/get-started/what-is-azure-pipelines?view=azure-devops.

Using Azure Pipelines, you can do the following:

- Create CI/CD pipelines (YAML-based) to execute various tasks, such as building the solution, running automated tests, and, subsequently, deploying the solution.

- Manage deployments to different environments. You can also implement gated checks and approvals.

Now, let's review how you can organize your test cases using Azure Test Plans.

Azure Test Plans

Testing is a very important step within an SDLC. There are different types of testing activities, such as functional testing (manual or automated), performance testing, user acceptance testing, and exploratory testing. Azure Test Plans allows you to create execution plans for any specific iteration or release, by including the applicable tests and tracking the results of the execution. Reports from executing a test plan can easily be created and inferred by the stakeholders to assess the quality of the software product or service under evaluation:

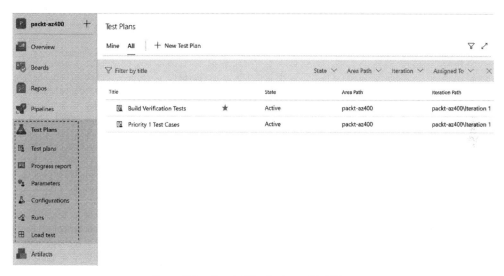

Figure 3.6 – Capabilities in Azure Test Plans

You can read more about Azure Test Plans here: `https://docs.microsoft.com/en-us/azure/devops/test/overview?view=azure-devops`.

Using Azure Test Plans, you can do the following:

- Create execution plans for various types of testing activities.
- Maintain traceability between test cases, defects, and product backlog items.
- Analyze the test reports using the charts and widgets that are available out of the box.

In the next section, we will review how your team can leverage Azure Artifacts as a store for all reusable code components.

Azure Artifacts

Azure Artifacts allows developers to manage different types of reusable packages for their solution development needs. These packages can be for internal use only or distributed externally. Essentially, it serves as a repository of packages, such as publicly available registries.

You can read more about Azure Artifacts here: `https://docs.microsoft.com/en-us/azure/devops/artifacts/start-using-azure-artifacts?view=azure-devops`.

Using Azure Artifacts, you can do the following:

- Publish packages to a central private repository. The supported package types are NuGet, npm, Maven, Python, and Universal Packages.

- Consume and share the packages for reuse and reference in other solution components.

Now, let's look at the GitHub offering from Microsoft.

GitHub

GitHub was acquired by Microsoft around June 2018. In its initial years, GitHub was a very popular code repository among the developer community as a code-sharing platform for open source projects. However, since its acquisition, it has added a variety of features to make it even more popular among developers to build and share code, as well as expanding on its enterprise usage footprint by offering a variety of other features.

GitHub is another very popular tool for implementing your DevOps practices. The main features that are available in the product are shown in the following diagram:

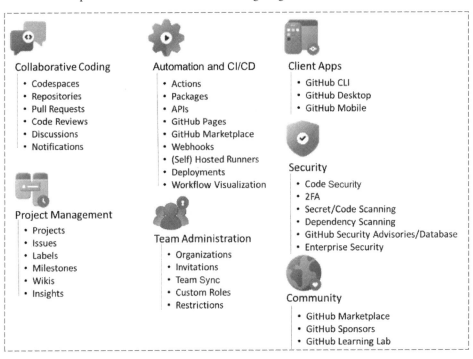

Figure 3.7 – Features available on GitHub

You can explore these features in more detail at `https://github.com/features`.

As the list of features is constantly evolving (you can refer to the public roadmap here: `https://github.com/github/roadmap`), please refer to the product documentation for more up-to-date information at any point in time.

In the next section, we will look at **Azure DevTest Labs**, which allows you to quickly provision non-production type environments to verify whether your solutions work.

Azure DevTest Labs

This is a service offering from Microsoft Azure that allows developers to quickly create development and test environments using reusable templates and artifacts that have been published. You can find more information at `https://azure.microsoft.com/en-in/services/devtest-lab/`.

While the service is available for free, it still requires developers to have access to a paid Azure subscription. However, the usage of the provisioned Azure resources will be charged at a highly discounted rate, as per their applicable pricing plans. You can refer to the pricing-related details here: `https://azure.microsoft.com/en-in/pricing/details/devtest-lab/`.

In the next section, we will take a look at the monitoring tools available in Azure.

Azure Monitor

Azure Monitor provides rich dashboarding capabilities to help you monitor application-specific metrics, resource health, and utilization to detect anomalies and provide timely intervention. It's a comprehensive service that allows you to collect, analyze, and act on the ingested monitoring data from a variety of sources, including applications, infrastructure, and other custom sources.

Some key features of Azure Monitor that you must plan to use are as follows:

- **Log Analytics** for digging into the monitoring data and deriving deep insights
- **Application Insights** for end-to-end transaction traceability, exceptions, and performance metrics
- **Container Insights** for microservices usage and health-related statistics
- **Custom dashboards** that are tailored to the use cases to track usage and reliability metrics
- **Alerts** to detect anomalies and notify teams about the appropriate action, as well as executing automated actions

To learn more about Azure Monitor, please go to `https://azure.microsoft.com/en-us/services/monitor/`.

The monitoring data from a variety of sources can be broken down into two parts, namely **logs** and **metrics**. They are separate big data stores within the Azure Monitor service.

Azure Monitor is comprised of a suite of products and services that offer the desired monitoring and dashboarding capabilities. In the following subsections, we will review three of the most commonly used services – that is, Azure Monitor Logs, Azure Monitor Metrics, and Application Insights.

Azure Monitor Logs

Generic log and performance data from a variety of sources can be collected and consolidated into a single workspace in Azure Monitor Logs.

Refer here for more information: `https://docs.microsoft.com/en-in/azure/azure-monitor/logs/data-platform-logs`.

Azure Monitor Metrics

This is a feature of Azure Monitor that captures numeric data from a variety of sources into a **time series database**. These values correspond to samples that have been collected at regular intervals for a list of metrics that have been captured from the system.

Refer here for more information: `https://docs.microsoft.com/en-in/azure/azure-monitor/essentials/data-platform-metrics`.

Application Insights

You can bake in support for rich telemetry capture in all your applications using Azure Application Insights. Use the logs to derive insights and detect performance issues, diagnose common errors, visualize an HTTP request using its end-to-end transaction flow, and collect metrics to derive various other metrics.

You can learn more about Azure Application Insights here: `https://docs.microsoft.com/en-us/azure/azure-monitor/app/app-insights-overview`.

In the next section, we will review Visual Studio Code, a popular tool among developers.

Visual Studio Code

Visual Studio Code is a free code editor from Microsoft that allows you to quickly develop, build, deploy, and test your modern cloud applications. It can be used on Windows, Linux, and macOS. It has built-in support for a wide range of programming languages. It also has a community of widgets and plugins that will immensely improve your productivity.

If you are a developer, you must try out Visual Studio Code. To find out more, please go to `https://code.visualstudio.com/`.

Summary

In this chapter, we reviewed a few of the important tools that can be used for your DevOps life cycle needs. We shall elaborate on the specific usage of these tools in the upcoming chapters via examples and hands-on labs. Whether you are a developer or an IT administrator (Ops), you will find usage of one or more of these tools in your day-to-day work.

With a continued focus on building automated workflows, a greater adoption of these tools will be beneficial for your organization to accomplish its DevOps objectives, as tracked through various metrics. Research indicates that enterprises that have transitioned into a DevOps-based delivery model have been more successful than their competitors in executing their various digital transformation initiatives.

Hence, it is imperative to understand that use of technology also plays a critical role in moving the needle on the DevOps maturity index. Adopting Azure DevOps and GitHub in your enterprise will not only activate greater productivity and potential of your teams, but also bolster your chances to become a top performer as a DevOps adopter.

In the next chapter, we shall explore the importance of having the right DevOps practices in place for your API platform life cycle processes.

Self-practice exercises

Make use of the concepts presented in this chapter to complete the following activities:

- Sign up for GitHub using your email at `https://github.com/`.
- Create a free Azure account by going to `https://azure.microsoft.com/en-us/free/`. The account creation step will require you to sign up using an existing Microsoft account (or a GitHub credential).
- Create a free Azure DevOps organization by going to `https://azure.microsoft.com/en-us/services/devops/?nav=min`. This will create an organization for you within the Azure DevOps directory.

Questions

As we conclude, here is a list of questions for you to test your knowledge regarding this chapter's material. You will find the answers in the *Assessments* section of the Appendix:

1. True or false: You need an enterprise user account to create an Azure DevOps project.
2. True or false: You can visualize and track your team's work using Azure Boards.
3. True or false: Azure Application Insights provides performance metrics such as response times for all the applications that are integrated with it.

4. True or false: You can use GitHub repositories within Azure Pipelines.

5. True or false: GitHub is only used as an open source code repository.

Further reading

To learn more about the topics that were covered in this chapter, take a look at the following resources:

- Enterprise DevOps report: `https://azure.microsoft.com/en-us/resources/enterprise-devops-report-20202021/`
- Agile: `https://docs.microsoft.com/en-us/devops/plan/what-is-agile`
- Scrum: `https://docs.microsoft.com/en-us/devops/plan/what-is-scrum`
- Kanban: `https://docs.microsoft.com/en-us/devops/plan/what-is-kanban`
- GitHub: `https://docs.github.com/en`
- Ansible: `https://docs.ansible.com/`
- Terraform: `https://www.terraform.io/docs`
- Chef and Puppet: `https://www.chef.io/puppet`

Part 2 – Getting to Continuous Delivery

In this part, you will learn about source control, continuous integration, and continuous deployment practices. Most organizations start with these DevOps practices first, as it allows you to produce quality solutions in the most effective and predictable way continuously.

This part of the book comprises the following chapters:

- *Chapter 4, Everything Starts with Source Control*
- *Chapter 5, Moving to Continuous Integration*
- *Chapter 6, Implementing Continuous Deployment and Release Management*

4
Everything Starts with Source Control

Source control is one of the most basic tools that is used in software development. Therefore, it is probably safe to assume that you have worked with source control before. For that reason, this chapter will contain only a brief introduction to source control and quickly move on to more advanced topics to help you to set up your source control to support DevOps practices.

Multiple DevOps practices rely on source control, so setting up your repositories to continuously deliver value to your users is a great way to get started and a prerequisite for many of the subjects in the following chapters.

The following topics will be covered in this chapter:

- The types of source control in Azure DevOps source control systems
- Selecting a branching and merging strategy
- Securing source control using branch policies
- Other tools that are available for source control

Technical requirements

To practice the subjects covered in this chapter, you may need an Azure DevOps organization. Also, ensure that Git tools are installed on your local machine. You can download Git tools from here: `https://git-scm.com/downloads`.

Types of source control in Azure DevOps

While there are many different source control systems in existence, they can be classified into two categories, centralized and decentralized, as follows:

- In a **centralized source control** system, only the server has the full history and the full set of branches that make up the repository.

- In a **decentralized source control** system, everyone working with the repository has a full copy of the repository, all of the branches, and its history.

Azure Repos, part of Azure DevOps services, offers both types of source control through **Team Foundation Version Control** (**TFVC**) and Git. The next two sections discuss both types of source control in more detail.

Centralized source control

In a centralized source control system, the server is the only location where the full repository, including all of the history, is stored. When you create a local version of the content, you only receive the latest version of the code. Receiving this latest version is called **checking out** the repository. In addition to this latest version, your own computer only has the changes you make locally.

Not checking out the full history obviously saves space on your local computer. However, disk space is hardly ever an issue nowadays. The downside of this is that you need to be continuously connected to the server to perform operations such as viewing the history of a file, recent commits of others, or which line in a file was last changed by who.

An advantage of centralized source control systems is that they often offer options for fine-grained control over who can access which branches, directories, and even files.

Decentralized source control

With a decentralized source control system, all files, history, and branches are also stored on a server. The difference with centralized source control comes when you **clone** the repository to have a local copy on your own computer.

Since you have a full clone of the repository, you can now view the history of a file and other branches without connecting to the server again. This obviously lessens the load on the server and allows you to continue working even when disconnected, which are two advantages of decentralized source control.

The downside is that decentralized source control can be harder to learn than centralized source control. Overall, the learning curve of decentralized source control systems is steeper. Also, access control on the level of individual directories and files is often more limited.

No matter which type of source control you are using, you must put a branching and merging strategy in place to allow developers to work on different features in parallel, while always keeping your `master` branch in a shippable state.

In a recent update to Azure DevOps, the default branch that gets created at the time of the repository creation is now named `main`. Azure DevOps also offers you the ability to rename your default branch to something else. Refer here for more information: `https://docs.microsoft.com/en-us/azure/devops/repos/git/change-default-branch`.

In the next section, we will look at the different source control systems that have been most commonly used within the developer community.

Source control systems

There are many source control systems in use, but in this chapter, we will only be looking at the three currently most used. They are the following:

- TFVC
- Git
- Subversion

Within Azure DevOps, only TVFC and Git are available. Subversion is a centralized source control system that is created by the Apache Foundation. In the upcoming subsections, we'll take a look at TFVC and Git in more detail and learn how to migrate sources between them. Subversion is discussed at the end of this chapter in the *Other tools for source control* section.

TFVC

TFVC is a centralized source control system that was introduced by Microsoft in 2013, as part of **Team Foundation Server** (**TFS**), the product that has evolved to become Azure DevOps. TFVC is still supported in Azure DevOps but is not recommended for new projects. If you are not already working with TFVC, there is no value in learning it as Microsoft will most likely not release new features for it, but it isn't necessary to move away from it without other drivers.

In Azure DevOps, there is a maximum of one TFVC repository per team project.

Git

Next to TFVC, Azure DevOps also supports hosting Git repositories. Git is a form of decentralized source control that is the standard now among the developer community. Git is not specific to Azure DevOps but is a general protocol that is used by many platforms that provide source control hosting as a service. Well-known examples next to Azure DevOps are GitHub and GitLab.

To work with a Git repository, you must first clone it:

1. Open *Command Prompt* and navigate to the directory where you want to store the repository.

2. Execute the following command and replace the example URL with the URL to your Git repository. The example URL shows how the location of a Git repository in Azure DevOps is built up:

```
git clone https://{organization}@dev.azure.com/
{organization}/{teamProjec t}/_git/{repository}
```

Now, you can start working on the changes you want to make. In this example, a new file, `NewFile.txt`, was added.

3. Next, this file must be staged for commit. Staging files is done to differentiate between files you want to commit and changes you want to keep for your own:

```
git add NewFile.txt
```

4. After staging all of the changes you want to group into a single commit, creating the actual `commit` is done by calling the `commit` command and specifying a description of the changes:

```
git commit -m "Added a new file that contains an
important text"
```

5. Finally, you can push your changes back to the central repository (also termed as the remote), by executing the following command:

```
git push
```

To make more changes, you can stage and commit changes as often as required. You can push the commits one at a time, or you can push multiple commits at once.

You can also work with Git through the **Visual Studio** (**VS**) or VS Code interfaces. Here, you execute precisely the same steps, but instead of your familiar command-line interface, you can use a visual interface.

Large File Storage

Git is designed and optimized for working with plain text files and tracking changes from version to version. However, you might want to store other things than just text files in source control. Examples are images or binary files that should be included with your application at runtime. While these are valid use cases, out of the box, they do not work very well with Git. To fix this, **Large File Storage** (**LFS**) was introduced.

Instead of storing the binary file itself, Git LFS allows you to store a small, text file that acts as a pointer to the binary file. The text file contains a hash of the binary file so that the client can download the file when cloning or fetching changes. Subsequently when you update the binary file, the hash within the text file is also updated.

To work with Git LFS, you must install the LFS client next to the Git client. This is a separate client that every user of the repository must download. Without this client, other users will only see the pointer files instead of the actual binary files. After installing the client, you must prepare the repository for the use of LFS. The following example commands enable the use of LFS for MP4 files:

```
git lfs install
git lfs track "*.mp4"
git add .gitattributes
```

From here onward, you can work with MP4 files just like any file, and behind the scenes, they will be stored separately from your text file changes.

Migrating between control systems

One of the steps on the DevOps journey is the consolidation of tools. This means that, at some point, you might be asked to migrate sources from one source control system to another, and companies might decide to move all of their sources from GitLab or Subversion to Azure Repos. There are multiple options available to you to do migrations like these.

The most likely event is that you will receive requests to move sources to one or more Azure Git repositories. Possible sources are other Git repositories, TFVC, or Subversion. There are tools and approaches available to do such a migration while retaining the history of changes in the original repository.

If there is no procedure available or you must import sources from another system, you can also fall back on creating a new, empty repository and initialize that with an existing code base. The disadvantage of this is that all history will be lost.

Migrating existing Git repositories

When it comes to migrating sources, moving to another location for hosting Git repositories is straightforward compared to other migrations. Let's learn how to do this:

1. First, clone the existing repository to your local computer:

   ```
   git clone https://{organization}@dev.azure.com/
   {organization}/{teamProjec t}/_git/{repository} .
   ```

2. Add another remote server that refers to the new, empty repository that you want to move the sources to:

   ```
   git remote add migrationTarget https://{organization}@
   ```

```
dev.azure.com/{organization}/{teamProjec t}/_git/
{newRepository}
```

3. Finally, push the changes to this new repository. You must do this separately for every branch you want to move next to the master:

```
git push migrationTarget master
```

Meanwhile, other developers might have continued to work with the existing repository.

4. To include those in the new repository as well, you must fetch them to your local computer from the original repository and then push them to the new repository. Again, repeat this for every branch:

```
git fetch origin master
git push migrationTarget master
```

5. Instruct all developers to start using the new remote repository. Subsequently, plan to decommission the original.

6. After a successful migration, it is often best to remove the old repository. This prevents anyone from continuing to work there accidentally.

The preceding steps will work for any Git-to-Git migration.

Now, if you specifically want to migrate to an Azure Git repository, you can also use the `Import` functionality that is included with Azure DevOps. To do this, follow these steps:

1. Navigate to **Repos** and, optionally, create a new Git repository.

2. Choose to import an existing repository.

3. Provide the requested information.

4. Click on **Import** to start importing the repository.

   The following screenshot illustrates these steps:

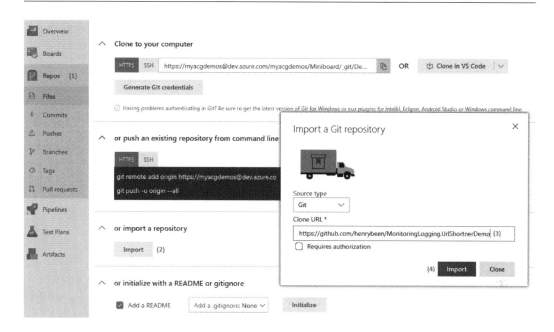

Figure 4.1 – Importing a repository

The disadvantage of this approach is that you cannot keep pushing changes from the source repository to the new repository. This means that all other developers on your team must make sure that they move their changes over on their own or do not have any pending work while you migrate the repository.

Migrating from TFVC to an Azure Git repository

To migrate from TFVC to Git, you can use the same import repository as for moving from any Git repository to an Azure repository. This wizard can move the history of changes for the last 180 days when doing the import. If this is not enough and you are required to move more than 180 days' worth of history to the new repository, there are other approaches you can use but they are more involved. Links to more detailed advice are included at the end of this chapter.

Migrating from Subversion to an Azure Git repository

A final type of request that you might receive is that of migrating from a Subversion repository to a Git repository. For this, there is no out-of-the-box solution from Microsoft available. However, Atlassian has created a tool that can be used to migrate a Subversion repository to a local Git repository while maintaining the changes history.

After running this tool, the only thing left to do is to add a remote repository to a new empty, hosted repository and push all of the branches. These are the same as the steps for migrating from Git to Git, starting at the step that adds a new remote repository.

Migrating without retaining history

If you are asked to do a migration without retaining history, you can just create a new, empty repository out of sources folder on your local computer and push existing changes there.

Execute the following commands from the directory that contains the files that should go into the master branch:

```
git init
git add
git commit -m "Initial import of existing sources"
git remote add https://{organization}@dev.azure.com/
{organization}/{teamProject}/_git/{repository}
git push
```

These commands initialize a new repository, create the first commit out of all of the files already in the directory, add a reference to the target server location, and push the newly created repository there.

If you want to retain multiple branches, you must repeat the following steps for every other branch:

1. First, go to the right directory for that branch:

    ```
    Git checkout {branchName}
    ```

2. Now, copy the files that need to go into this branch into your working directory. Then, continue with the following commands:

    ```
    git add .
    git commit
    git push
    ```

This completes the migration, and the latest version of the sources you had on your local computer is now available in Git. Other members of your team can now clone the repository and work with it. Next, we'll go on to learn about branching and merging.

Selecting a branching and merging strategy

Source control allows you to keep a history of all of the changes you have made to your files, and also allows working separately from your team members for a while if you so desire. We call this **branching**. When you are branching in source control, you **fork** the line of changes currently registered. We call such a fork a **branch**. A branch allows you to temporarily isolate some work from the rest. At any point, if you want to integrate the changes from a branch with the changes on the other fork, you can **merge** these changes back. Branches are often used for working on not-yet-complete features, proofs of concept, or hotfixes. Using branches allows you to later decide which changes to include in the next version and which not to.

Branching strategies

There are many branching strategies available, but the three most used nowadays are the following:

- GitHub Flow
- GitFlow
- Release Flow

The following subsections will discuss these in greater detail.

> Tip
>
> As an alternative to branching, trunk-based development is becoming more popular nowadays. To learn more about this, visit `https://trunkbaseddevelopment.com/`.

GitHub Flow

GitHub Flow is a simple, yet often sufficient, branching strategy. In GitHub Flow, there is one **master** branch that should always be in a deployable state. No unfinished changes are allowed to go onto the `master` branch.

If you want to start work on a new feature or bugfix, you need to create a new topic branch on the `master` branch where you commit your work. Only when you are completely done with that work should you merge this branch back to the `master` branch. An example commit flow might look like this:

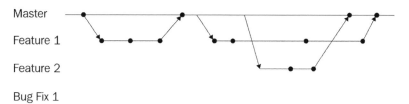

Figure 4.2 – GitHub Flow

As this is the branching scheme with the least branches involved, this is probably a good strategy to start with.

Refer here for more information: `https://www.geeksforgeeks.org/git-flow-vs-github-flow/`.

GitFlow

GitFlow is another well-known, elaborate branching scheme, and can deal with almost any situation that might arise when working with software. GitFlow describes creating a `develop` branch of the `master` branch whenever you start work on a new version. `develop` is the integration branch where you combine new features and do integration testing. It should only contain work that you believe is ready to be released.

From `develop`, you can create one or more `feature` branches where you start working on new features. Only when a feature is done should you merge that branch back to the `develop` branch.

When you want to release a new version of your application, you create a `release` branch of the `develop` branch. You can perform final testing on the code on this branch, and perform one or more bug fixes if needed. When you are satisfied with the quality of the code, you can merge this branch with `master` and tag the version. You can also merge these bug fixes back to `develop`, so they will also be incorporated in new developments. This flow is visible in the following diagram:

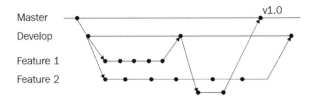

Figure 4.3 – GitFlow branching model

If there is ever a critical bug that you need to ship as fast as possible, or you want to do a hotfix, this is also possible using the GitFlow-based branching strategy. In that case, you can create a new branch of `master` on which you can fix the bug. After testing, you can merge this branch to both `master` and `develop`—just as you would with a `release` branch.

Release Flow

Release Flow is the branching system that is used by the Azure DevOps team to develop Azure DevOps. It is also based on working with short-lived topic branches that are made from and merged into the `master` branch.

The difference is that it is not the code that is on the `master` branch that is deployed to production. Instead, whenever a new version of the product needs to be released, a new branch is created of `master` with the name `release-{version}`. The code from this branch is then deployed to production. Once a new `release` branch is deployed, the previous one can be disregarded. This results in the following flow:

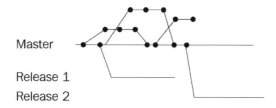

Figure 4.4 – Release flow branching model

The advantage of this model is that it allows for taking a snapshot of the current state of the master branch and taking that to production. If there is ever a bug in production that needs to be fixed ahead of a new complete release, then the necessary commits can be merged from the master branch to the current release branch.

Trunk-based development

In many companies, branching and merging are done to retain flexibility when releasing a new version of the software, and being able to cherry pick changes for a particular version only at the last moment. This flexibility comes at the cost of having to merge or integrate your changes at some point.

This cost is not only the time it takes but also the risks that a merge operation introduces. Merging the changes from two different branches that contain perfectly working software might still produce non-working code.

For this reason, you might consider switching to **trunk-based development**. In trunk-based development, you are no longer using branching for picking the changes that go into a version. Instead, every developer on the team continuously works from the same branch (often the master branch) and only creates a short-lived branch for preparing one single change, which is then merged into the master branch.

Benefits of Trunk-Based Development

Trunk-based development facilitates increased agility for the development teams when releasing features to production. The features teams will develop features using temporary and short-lived features branches. The changes will be unit tested and verified in the development environment, and then subsequently pushed to the master branch using the Git PULL request feature. This is explained in the subsequent sections.

You can read more about trunk-based development here: https://trunkbaseddevelopment.com/.

When you adopt this, you will need another way to determine which changes will and won't yet be available to your users when releasing a new version of your software. You can do this by using **branching by abstraction**.

Branching by abstraction

When branching by abstraction, you do not keep two versions of your code side by side using branches, but you keep them side by side in your code base instead. For example, when you want to change the implementation of a class called `FoodClassifier`, which implements the `IFoodClassifier` interface, you go through the following steps:

1. Refactor the name of the `FoodClassifier` class to `FoodClassifierToBeRemoved`.

2. Create a copy of the complete `FoodClassifierToBeRemoved` class.

3. Change the name of this copy back to `FoodClassifier`.

    At this point, your changes should look like this:

    ```
    public class FoodClassifier : IFoodClassifier
    {
    public FoodClassification Classify(Food food)
    {
    // Unchanged classification algorithm
    }
    }
    public class FoodClassifierToBeRemoved : IFoodClassifer
    {
    public FoodClassification Classify(Food food)
    {
    // Unchanged classification algorithm
    }
    }
    ```

Please note that at runtime, your application will behave just as it did before. You have just added a new, yet unused, class with a behavior change. It is safe to commit these changes and even ship the new binaries to a user. Now you can start changing the implementation of the new `FoodClassifier` class, test it, and establish trust in its implementation.

Meanwhile, you can keep committing and pushing your changes, even to customers. Switching to the new implementation can be done using your dependency injection configuration, a Boolean flag, or environment variables. Just choose what makes sense in your scenario.

Only when you are fully satisfied that the new implementation is working do you remove the `FoodClassifierToBeRemoved` class and update any references back to `FoodClassifier`.

We will expand on branching by abstraction in *Chapter 6, Implementing Continuous Deployment and Release Management*, when discussing feature toggles. While being a recommended way forward to further accelerate your delivery, branching by abstraction is a double-edged sword. If you do not have a process to keep the number of side-by-side implementations under control and clean them up after switching implementations, the quality of your code base might decline.

Merging strategies

Depending on the source control system you are working with, there might be multiple ways you can merge your changes from one branch to another.

TFVC

When you are working with TFVC, you can prepare a merge locally by choosing both a source and target branch and then picking the list of changes you want to merge. TFVC will then execute the merge and will show you the changes that are the consequence of this merge as *local* changes. You can review, correct, or change these changes, and resolve any conflicts. After this, you can commit the changes just as you would any regular change.

Git

A merge using Git can be performed by switching to the target branch and then merging all of the changes from the source branch. If there are conflicting changes between the branches, you must resolve those just as you would when fetching new changes from the server. After merging the changes from the source branch and resolving any changes, you can commit the changes. This will result in a merge commit, which you push to the remote just as any other change.

The merge commit can be done using the visual interface of Visual Studio or VS Code, or by using the following sequence of commands:

```
git checkout targetBranch
git merge sourceBranch
```

During the merge process, if there are any conflicts, you have to resolve these at this point. Otherwise, you cannot continue:

```
git commit -m "Merged changes from sourceBranch"
git push
```

As you will read in the *Securing repositories* section, it is possible to protect some branches by disallowing merging this way. When it comes to merging changes to master, you might want to use another mechanism, namely, pull requests. Using a pull request, you can open a request for someone else to pull changes from your local branch to the target branch. This way, another team member can first review your changes and then merge them when they meet all agreed standards. Others can comment on your changes or request updates before they perform the merge. This is the most common way of enforcing the *four-eyes principle* for source code when working with Git. The *four-eyes principle* says that every change or action should be viewed by at least two people.

When you are approving a pull request, there are different strategies you can use for generating the merge commit. The most commonly used are a merge commit, squash commit, or rebase.

Merge commit

A regular **merge commit** is a type of commit that maintains visibility of all previous commits. It has a reference to two parents, showing both origins of the change, namely the source and target branch. This is the same type of merge as you can perform manually using a Git merge. The advantage of this type of commit is that it clearly shows where the new state of the target branch comes from.

Squash commit

When performing a so-called **squash commit**, you are combining all of the individual commits from the source branch in one new commit. This is useful when all of the commits on the source branch relate to one feature and you want to keep a clear, concise change history on the target branch. This approach makes most sense when there are commits with bug fixes or clean-up operations on the source branch. The disadvantage is that you might lose the rationale for some incremental changes that were made on the source branch.

Rebase

Rebasing a branch means that all of the new commits or changes in your local branch that is not yet merged with the `master` branch are put aside for a bit. Meanwhile, all of the commits for which the `master` branch is ahead of your local branch are now merged into your local branch. Finally, all of your own commits that were set aside are now reapplied. The following diagram shows a branch before and after a rebase commit:

Figure 4.5 – Rebasing

After rebasing the source branch, it is now merged into `master`. The advantage of this kind of merge is that you retain all individual changes in one single commit history.

Managing repositories

When working in Azure Repos, every team project can have a maximum of one TFVC repository. However, when working with Git, you can have multiple repositories in the same team project. A discussion that is gaining more attention lately is that of having a single repository for all applications or a repository per application. Other topics that are important when managing repositories are creating and removing repositories, securing them, and setting policies on them.

Monorepo or multi-repo

You use a **monolithic repository (monorepo)** when you store all of the code from all of your projects and applications in one single source control repository. Contrary to this, you might use multiple repositories where every application, library, or project is stored in its own repository. Both approaches have their own pros and cons, and both approaches are used by companies from small to large.

Possible advantages of a monorepo can include the following:

- Easier reuse of existing code: If all of the code is in a single repository, it is accessible and visible to everyone. This means that the chances of reuse are increased.

- Having all applications in one repository also means that any change affecting more than one application can be made in a single commit in a single repository. A typical example is an API change.

- With all of the code being accessible to and maintained by everyone, there is less chance that a developer or team claims a specific repository as its own. This encourages learning from each other.

Disadvantages of mono repositories include the following:

- A monorepo can become very, very large, even up to the point that developers checkout or clone only part of the monorepo. This effectively defeats most of the advantages of a monorepo.

- Having one repository with all of the code encourages tight coupling between components or applications. If you have multiple repositories, you could update an API and release it under a new version and upgrade clients one by one. In a monorepo, you might be tempted to upgrade the API and change all of the consumers in one commit, with all of the risks attached.

Which approach works best for you is influenced not only by the advantages and disadvantages discussed but also by the background and makeup of your team and organization. If you have a single team doing all the development for internal applications, a monorepo might make more sense. If you have multiple teams working on different applications for different clients, multiple repositories make more sense.

Creating and removing repositories

In Azure DevOps, you can have multiple Git repositories per team project. Try doing the following:

1. First, visit the **Manage repositories** interface. The following screenshot shows how to access this interface:

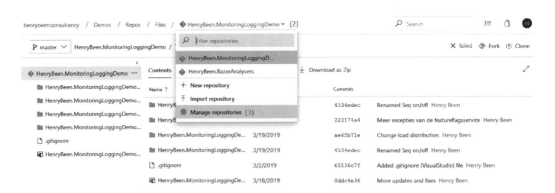

Figure 4.6 – Managing repositories

2.   After opening this interface, a new interface (as shown in the following screenshot) opens up. Here, you can add new repositories by clicking on the **Add...** button with a plus sign (refer to the vertical section next to the left navigation menu) and filling out a repository name.

3.   Repositories can also be removed by clicking on their name and then **Delete repository** (marked with **2**; refer to the context menu shown for the repository name):

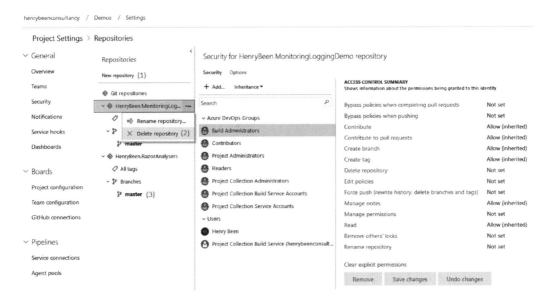

Figure 4.7 – Deleting a repository

Removing repositories is not something that is often done. It might make more sense to make a no-longer-used repository read-only or remove all authorizations on it.

Now, let's learn how to secure the repositories that we create.

Securing repositories

While the security options with distributed source control are often not as broad as with centralized source control, Azure Repos offers some means to set authorizations on a repository or a server-side branch. In the last figure of the previous section, you can also see how you can select a group or user in the middle column and then update the authorizations on the repository. By default, all authorizations are inherited from project defaults.

> **Tip**
>
> It is recommended to only change authorizations as little as possible and if you do, it is often best to work via groups and allow authorizations.

You can also change the authorizations for a specific branch by opening the repository branches in the drop-down menu on the left and clicking on the branch you want to override the authorizations for. In the preceding screenshot, this is marked with **3**; refer to the expansion of the `HenryBreen.RazorAnalysers` repository.

Branch policies

Finally, it is possible to enforce one or more policies on pull requests to a specific branch. The interface for branch policies is shown in the following screenshot and can be accessed by choosing the **Branch policies** option while managing the authorizations on a repository branch:

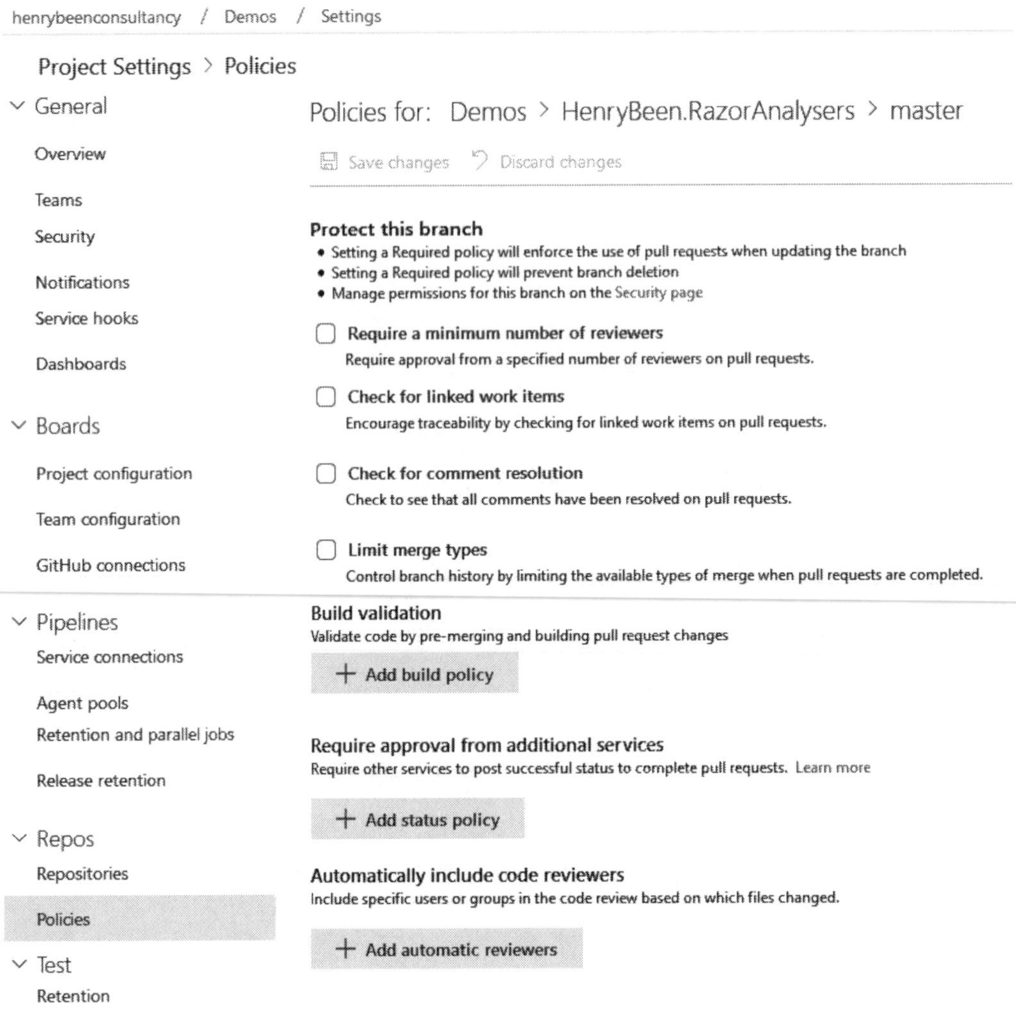

Figure 4.8 – Branch policies

The first four checkboxes are related to default policies that can be enabled (or not) on your preference. By default, they are all disabled.

Build validation can be used to disallow the merge of any pull request if one or more of the select builds have not been completed successfully. How to set up such a build is something you will learn in the next chapter.

Next to builds, you can also call external services to inspect the pull request and to allow or disallow it. An often used integration here is with a code quality tool. You might also call your own APIs here to enforce team agreements on things such as pull request titles, relation to work items, or more complex constraints.

Finally, you can enforce that a specific user or group has to be included in the review of a pull request. This might be needed to enforce a specific level of quality, but it can also be a limiting factor in your development speed and flow.

Other tools for source control

Next to the source control systems available in Azure Repos, there are also some other well-known systems that you should know about:

- GitHub
- GitLab
- Subversion

We'll go over each of these in the upcoming subsections.

GitHub

GitHub is a hosted source control provider that delivers hosted Git repositories. GitHub allows anyone to create as many publicly visible repositories as they want. When you create private repositories that require three or more contributors, you must switch to a paid subscription.

This model allows unlimited free usage of the platform if developing in public, which has made GitHub by far the largest host of open source software in the world.

GitHub was acquired by Microsoft in 2018 and since then, Microsoft and GitHub have worked together to create a great integration experience between GitHub repositories and Azure DevOps, specifically with Azure Boards and Azure Pipelines. In addition to this, Microsoft has stated that GitHub and Azure Repos will continue to exist next to each other and that there are currently no plans to terminate one of the products in favor of the other.

There is also an enterprise offering by GitHub called GitHub Enterprise, which comes with two deployment options, namely cloud-hosted and self-hosted (or on-premises).

You can read more about the various GitHub products and pricing plans here: `https://docs.github.com/en/get-started/learning-about-github/githubs-products`.

The public roadmap for GitHub can be viewed here: `https://github.com/orgs/github/projects/4247/views/1`.

GitLab

GitLab is another platform that delivers hosted Git repositories. Just like Azure DevOps, source control hosting is one of the services it provides.

Subversion

An older source control system is Subversion. Subversion was developed and first used in 2004 and is maintained by the Apache Software Foundation. Subversion is a centralized source control system that supports all the features that you would expect of such a system.

There are many false arguments as to why Subversion would be inferior to Git; however, most of them are not true for more recent versions of Subversion. The reality is that Subversion is a widely used type of source control system that performs well, especially for very large repositories, or repositories that have very specific authorization needs.

While Azure DevOps cannot host Subversion repositories, it can connect to and work with sources that are stored in Subversion.

Summary

In this chapter, you have learned about source control. You saw that there are two types of source control: centralized and decentralized, both supported by Azure DevOps. TFVC is no longer recommended for new projects. You should use Git whenever starting a new project.

When using Git, you can have more than one repository in your team project. For each repository, you can assign policies to lock down specific branches and enforce the four-eyes principle. You have also learned about access control, and how to provide users access to one or more repositories. Finally, you have learned about alternative tools, and how to migrate sources from one tool to the other.

You can use what you have learned to make decisions on which type of source control system to use in your products. You can now professionally organize the repository or repositories you work in. You are now able to work with different branching strategies and use policies for enforcing security or quality requirements.

The next chapter will take what you have learned about source control and use that to set up continuous integration.

Questions

As we conclude, here is a list of questions for you to test your knowledge regarding this chapter's material. You will find the answers in the *Assessments* section of the *Appendix*:

1. What are the differences between centralized and decentralized source control, and which works best in what situation?

2. True or false? Git is an example of decentralized source control.

3. Which of the following is not a common branching strategy?

    A. Release Flow

    B. Rebasing

    C. GitFlow

    D. GitHub Flow

4. Many companies want a code review to be performed before code is merged into the `master` branch. What construct is used to do so when working with Git, and how can this be enforced in Azure DevOps?

5. Which of the following are not valid merge strategies?

    A. Rebasing

    B. Trunk-based development

    C. Merge commit

    D. Squash commit

Exercises

- Prerequisite reading: `https://docs.microsoft.com/en-us/azure/devops/boards/best-practices-agile-project-management`.

- Create your first team project, and name it `PacktBookLibrary`. Apply other settings as per the following screenshot:

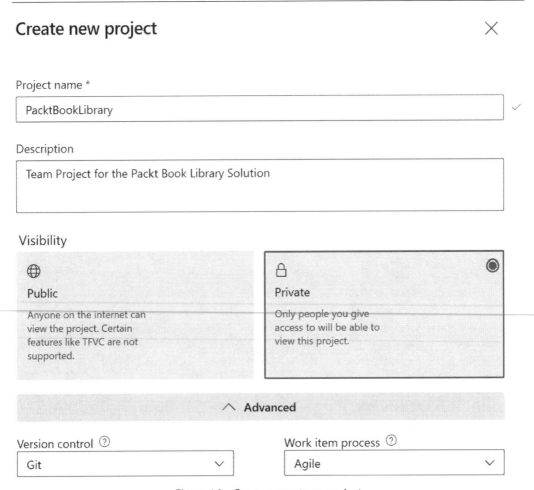

Create new project   ✕

Project name *

PacktBookLibrary   ✓

Description

Team Project for the Packt Book Library Solution

Visibility

⊕	🔒 ⊚
Public	Private
Anyone on the internet can view the project. Certain features like TFVC are not supported.	Only people you give access to will be able to view this project.

∧ **Advanced**

Version control ⑦   Work item process ⑦

Git   ∨   Agile   ∨

Figure 4.9 – Create a new team project

- Once the PacktBookLibrary team project has been created, using the left navigation, go to **Boards | Queries**. Create a new query with filter options as defined in the following screenshot, and save it as Product-Backlog within **My Queries**. Note that it should show you a tree of work items starting with **Epic** items as the parent work item entry in the listview. The objective here is to visualize the breakdown of the entire Product-Backlog query in a hierarchical manner:

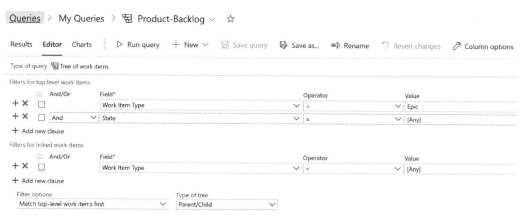

Figure 4.10 – Query editor

- Using the **Column options** section within the **Editor** view, choose columns (Stack Rank, ..) and **Sorting** on **Stack Rank**:

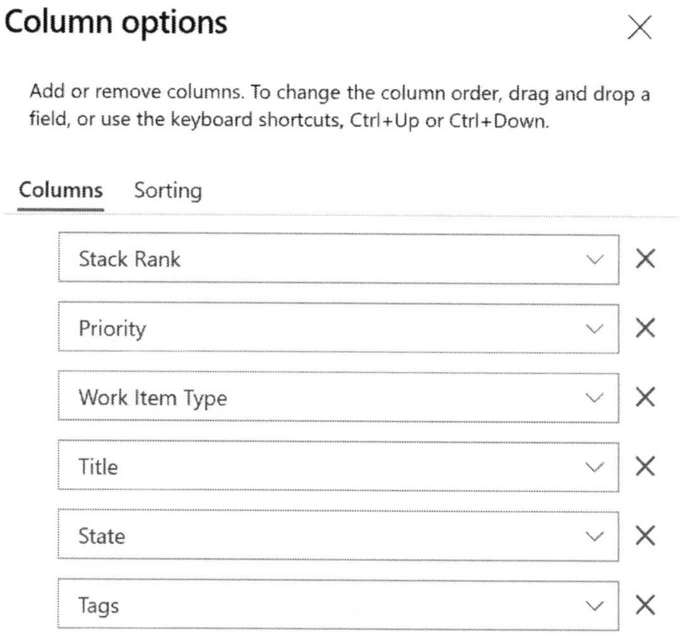

Column options   ×

Add or remove columns. To change the column order, drag and drop a field, or use the keyboard shortcuts, Ctrl+Up or Ctrl+Down.

Columns   Sorting

Stack Rank   ∨   ×

Priority   ∨   ×

Work Item Type   ∨   ×

Title   ∨   ×

State   ∨   ×

Tags   ∨   ×

Figure 4.11 – Add columns and apply sorting

- Add an initial Product Backlog (Epics and Features) as shown in the following screenshot:

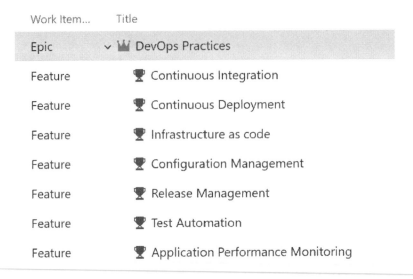

Work Item...	Title
Epic	👑 DevOps Practices
Feature	🏆 Continuous Integration
Feature	🏆 Continuous Deployment
Feature	🏆 Infrastructure as code
Feature	🏆 Configuration Management
Feature	🏆 Release Management
Feature	🏆 Test Automation
Feature	🏆 Application Performance Monitoring

Figure 4.12 – DevOps feature list

The goal here is to track the implementation of the important DevOps practices through the same product backlog so that those are included during the work planning and prioritization process. Eventually, it is the same set of team members who will work on implementing these practices as well.

- You can either configure a new Git repository to start adding your code or import code from an existing Git repository. The starter code for the PacktBookLibrary solution is available here: https://github.com/PacktPublishing/Exam-Guide-AZ-400-Designing-and-Implementing-Microsoft-DevOps-Solutions.

The dialog in the following screenshot is shown when you import an existing repository:

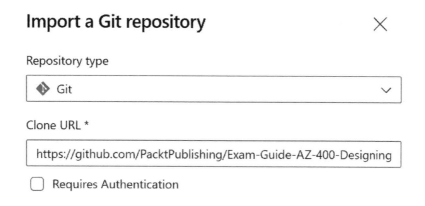

Figure 4.13 – Import a Git repository

- Once the code has been imported, you should be able to view the code files within the repository.

- Configure branch policies for the `main` branch in the repository within the following settings:

  - Turn on (use the toggle button) **Require minimum number of reviewers**. Set the minimum reviewer count as **1**.

  - Turn on (use the toggle button) **Check for linked work items** to **Required**.

- Turn on **Limit merge types**. Select **Squash merge** as the only option from the allowed merge types list.

- Clone the `PacktBookLibrary` repository (the `main` branch) to a local folder within your workstation.

- Check out the source code by creating a branch off `main`, and then start using it for making commits. Periodically plan to raise a `PULL` request to merge your changes with the `main` branch.

After completing the steps mentioned in the exercise list, your source control repository will be set up. We will build upon this foundation in the next chapters through exercises.

Further reading

- More information about working with Git can be found at `https://docs.microsoft.com/en-us/learn/paths/intro-to-vc-git/`.

- The original Microsoft advice on TFVC versus Git can be found at `https://docs.microsoft.com/en-us/azure/devops/repos/tfvc/comparison-git-tfvc?view=azure-devopsviewFallbackFrom=vsts`.

- More information about Git LFS can be found at `https://docs.microsoft.com/en-us/azure/devops/repos/git/manage-large-files?view=azure-devops`.

- Instructions for downloading Git LFS can be found at `https://git-lfs.github.com/`.

- More information about migrating to Git can be found at `https://docs.microsoft.com/en-us/azure/devops/repos/git/import-from-TFVC?view=azure-devops`.

- An Atlassian tool for converting an SVN repository to a local Git repository can be found at `https://www.atlassian.com/git/tutorials/migrating-convert`.

- More information about GitFlow can be found at `https://datasift.github.io/gitflow/IntroducingGitFlow.html`.

- More information about GitHub Flow can be found at `https://guides.github.com/introduction/flow/`.

- Release Flow is described in more detail at `https://docs.microsoft.com/en-us/azure/devops/learn/devops-at-microsoft/release-flow`.

- Trunk-based development is discussed at `https://trunkbaseddevelopment.com/`.

- More information about GitLab can be found at `https://about.gitlab.com/`.

- More information about Subversion can be found at `https://subversion.apache.org/docs/`.

5

Moving to Continuous Integration

After setting up source control for your organization and deciding on a branching and merging strategy that supports parallel work, you are ready to move on to continuous integration. Continuous integration is a method where every developer takes their work and integrates it with the work of others, and then verifies the quality of the combined work. The value of this is an increase in quality early on in the pipeline. This reduces the risk of error later on when merging code changes and reduces the number of bugs that are found in production, thereby reducing costs and protecting your reputation.

Continuous integration is only possible when you have the proper setup with the necessary tools. In this chapter, you will learn how to use Azure DevOps pipelines to set up continuous integration.

The following topics will be covered in this chapter:

- Introducing continuous integration
- Creating a build definition
- Running a build
- Working with YAML pipelines
- Agents and agent queues
- Automate **Continuous Integration** (**CI**) builds using GitHub Actions
- Other tools

Technical requirements

To go through the examples that are covered in this chapter, you will need the following:

- An Azure DevOps organization
- Git command-line tools
- A code editor such as Visual Studio Code

Introducing continuous integration

Continuous integration is a methodology where you integrate your own changes with those of all of the other developers in your project and test whether the combined code still works as expected. This way, you create a fast loop that provides you with feedback on your work.

When working with extensive branching strategies for isolating code changes, it is not uncommon for one or more developers to work for days, weeks, or even months on an isolated branch. While this is great for making sure that their changes do not disrupt others, continuous integration is a great way to make sure that there won't be merge issues later. If you have ever had to merge weeks or months of work back into the main branch, you will know how much work is involved and how often this results in bugs or other issues.

To prevent this, developers should make it a habit to integrate their changes with those of all the other developers at least once a day. Here, integrating means at least merging, compiling, and running unit tests. This way, there is a constant stream of feedback on the quality of the developer's changes, and since this feedback is combined, it is a great way to prevent merge issues later.

Continuous integration also enables you to embed other concerns in your pipeline to automatically preserve the quality of your code. Static code analysis, unit testing, and security scanning are three prime examples of this. These topics are discussed in later chapters, but a good continuous integration pipeline is the basis for these practices.

In the rest of this chapter, you will learn about the technical means to set up continuous integration using Azure Pipelines. But first, let's look at a common misconception and the four pillars of continuous integration.

> **Important Note**
> While an automated continuous integration build is an important ingredient for performing continuous integration, continuous integration entails more than just having a build pipeline. The important thing to remember is that continuous integration is a process where every developer integrates their work with that of their colleagues at least daily. Then, the integrated sources are compiled and tested. The value comes from compiling and testing the integrated work, not the isolated work.

The four pillars of continuous integration

There are four pillars that underpin the successful adoption of continuous integration:

- **A version control system**: Used for storing all of the changes made to a system since its inception. Version control systems were discussed in the previous chapter.

- **A package management system**: Used to store the binary packages that you use in your own application and the packages that you create. This will be discussed in detail in *Chapter 7, Dependency Management*.

- **A continuous integration system**: A system that can pull the changes of all developers together – several times a day – and create one integrated source version. This can be done using Azure DevOps pipelines.

- **An automated build process**: Used to compile and test the combined sources. We will look at how to implement this process using Azure DevOps pipelines.

Continuous integration and automated builds can be set up in Azure DevOps. The next section explains how to set both up in Azure DevOps.

Creating a build definition in Azure DevOps

The main way to perform continuous integration is by using a continuous integration build. In Azure DevOps, builds can be configured as part of the Azure Pipelines offering. There are currently two approaches available for creating a build definition:

- Via the visual designer (also called **classic builds and releases**)
- Through **Yet Another Markup Language** (**YAML**) files (also called YAML pipelines or multistage pipelines)

The rest of this section will focus on the visual designer. The following section, *YAML build definitions*, will go into more detail about YAML pipelines. Both approaches support roughly the same capabilities, although there are some differences. Some features that are available in classic builds and releases are not (yet) available in YAML build definitions. Also, some new features are only provided to YAML pipelines.

If you have no experience with pipelines, the classic editor is a good way to get familiar with the workings of continuous integration/continuous development pipelines before moving on to YAML pipelines. Almost all of the concepts in classic builds translate to YAML builds as well.

In the following sections, we will start by building a classic build pipeline.

Connecting to source control

To get started with a build definition, follow these simple steps:

1. Open the **Pipelines** menu.

2. From this menu, click on **Builds**. Here, you will be presented with a button to create a new build. After clicking on this button, a new view for creating a build will open, as shown in the following screenshot:

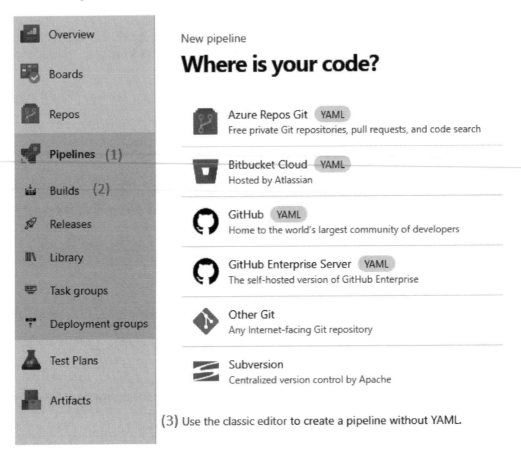

Figure 5.1 – Source code repository options for pipelines

3. You will then be guided to the new YAML experience, but you can still opt to go back by choosing the classic editor.

After choosing the classic editor, you can configure how to connect to the source control. The classical editor is the editor that is visible in all of the screenshots in the following sections.

Many source control systems are supported. If you are working with a hosted Git repository, pick your specific product, if available, and only choose **Other Git** if your product is not available; currently, **GitHub**, **GitHub Enterprise Server**, and **Bitbucket Cloud** are supported. The reason for this is that continuous integration using **Other Git** works by using a polling model, where all the specific products use their known integration Webhooks. The following example works with a Git repository that is in the same Azure DevOps organization.

When you select the **Pipeline** header, you can set the name of the build definition and select an agent pool that the phases will run on by default. Agents take care of the actual execution of your tasks and will be looked at in more detail in the *Agents and agent queues* section of this chapter.

Below the **Pipeline** header, you can see the chronological layout of your build definition. First up is downloading sources. Here, you can once again choose to connect to a source control system. You can also specify more advanced settings that relate to the way sources are fetched, such as whether to clean the build directory first, select a branch, or add tags.

Configuring a job

Below the source's node, you can add one or more jobs that will perform the bulk of the work that you want to perform. Jobs can be added using the ellipsis on the **Pipeline** header. There are two types of jobs available:

- **Agentless jobs**: Agentless jobs can be used to run tasks that do not require an agent. They are run on Azure DevOps Server.

- **Agent jobs**: Agent jobs are used to run tasks that require an agent to run on, which is the case for the bulk of the tasks.

Some examples of agentless tasks are as follows:

- Waiting for manual approval before continuing

- Inserting a delay before proceeding

- Calling a REST API

- Calling an Azure function

The main benefit of an agentless job is that it does not keep an agent occupied while running. This frees the agent up to do other work, meaning that you need fewer agents, which can save costs. Also, the number of agents that you can use concurrently is governed by the number of parallel pipelines that you have bought in Azure DevOps. Limiting the number of agent jobs will save money here as well.

Let's go over the process of configuring a job:

1. Select any job. You will see the view shown in the following screenshot. In this view, you can change the name of the job and, for agent jobs, override the agent pool to execute this job on:

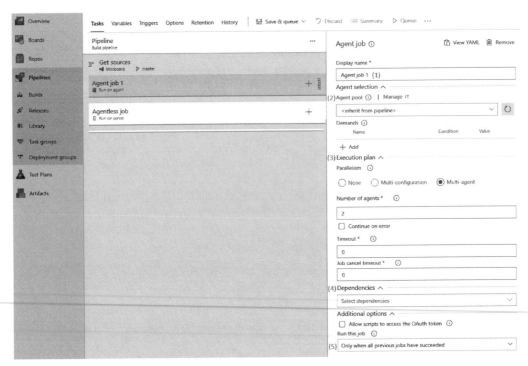

Figure 5.2 – Add/update jobs for the pipeline

2. Next, specify which agent pool to use for running the job. Here, it also specifies the demands that you have of the agent that will execute this job. Demands will be discussed in the *Agents and agent queues* section of this chapter.

3. As part of the execution plan for an agent, you can specify **Parallelism** and choose one of three options:

    - **None**: This will just execute all the tasks you add to the agent job one after another on the same agent.

    - **Multi-configuration**: Here, you can specify a series of variables that determine the number of variations of the build to run. This is useful if you want to create, for example, x86 and x64 builds from the same code.

    - **Multi-agent**: Here, you can specify the number of agents that will run the same tasks in parallel.

4. Next, you can specify one or more dependencies. These are the other jobs that need to be completed before the selected job runs.

5. Also, for any job, you can specify how to cope with errors in previous jobs by telling it to continue or stop.

As an alternative to *step 3* and *step 4*, you can also specify a custom expression to specify whether a job should run. This expression should evaluate to a Boolean and support rudimentary operations, such as `or()`, `and()`, or `eq()`. The following is an example condition:

```
and(succeeded(), ne(variables['Build.SourceBranch'], 'refs/
heads/main'))
```

This condition specifies that the job will only run when all previous jobs have succeeded and the build is not started from the main branch. A link to a detailed description of the conditions syntax is included at the end of this chapter.

Agentless jobs have fewer options available than agent jobs. For example, it is not possible to execute the same build for multiple variable values in parallel.

Adding tasks to your job

After adding one or more jobs, you can add tasks to a job. Tasks define the actual work that is to be done during the execution of your build. The following screenshot shows you how to add a task and then configure it:

1. Click on the plus sign next to the job you want to add tasks to:

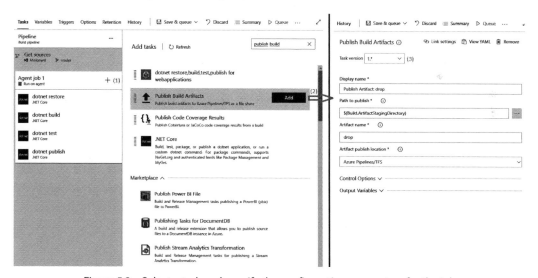

Figure 5.3 – Select a task and specify the configuration parameters for the job

2. You will then be presented with a task picker, where you can find any task that matches your search input and add one or more tasks by clicking the **Add** button. A new screen will then open, where you can configure the individual task. The options provided here differ for each task.

3. There can be multiple versions of a task, and you can switch between the major versions of it. This means that the maintainer can push non-breaking updates and you will receive them automatically. Major or breaking updates can be pushed with a new major version number, and you can upgrade them at your own discretion.

It is possible to add as many tasks as needed to a pipeline job.

Publishing build artifacts

An important part of a build definition is its outcomes. Builds are often used to produce one or more artifacts that are later used for the deployment of an application. Examples of artifacts can be executables or installer files. These files need to be made available for use after the execution of the build pipeline has beencompleted.

The **Publish Build Artifacts** task that is shown in the preceding screenshot is a task that is specifically designed to do this. It allows you to select a file or directory and publish it under an **artifact name**. The result of this is that the file(s) in the selected path are retained with every execution of the pipeline for manual download or use in a release definition later. Release definitions will be discussed in *Chapter 6, Implementing Continuous Deployment and Release Management*.

Next, we'll learn how to integrate our pipeline with other tools and configure our service connection.

Calling other tools

When building pipelines, we will often need to integrate them with other tools. For source control systems, this is part of the flow when creating a pipeline and you are limited to the built-in options. For tasks, you can create references to any tool or location you want using service connections. An example of a task that uses a service connection to an Azure app service is shown in the following section.

A service connection is a pointer to an external system, with a name and series of properties that differ for each type of service connection. Often, you will need to put in a URL to locate the other service and a mechanism for authentication. The following steps will help you configure your service connection:

1. After defining one or more service connections, you can select the one to use from a drop-down menu:

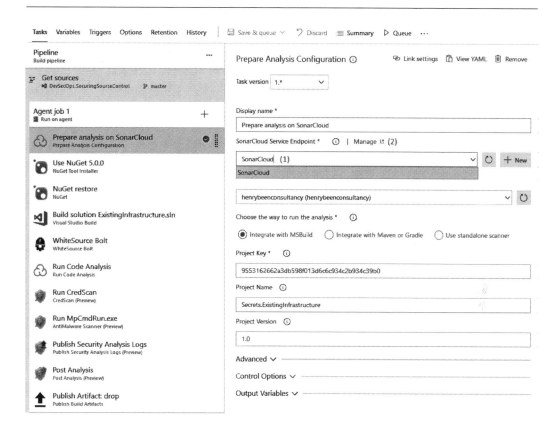

Figure 5.4 – Use the service connection in the task

2. Service connections are managed in a central location as project settings. You can access them by going to the management view directly from the task you are currently configuring, as shown in the preceding screenshot. You can also do this by navigating to **Project Settings** and then to **Service connections**, as in the following screenshot (see **2**):

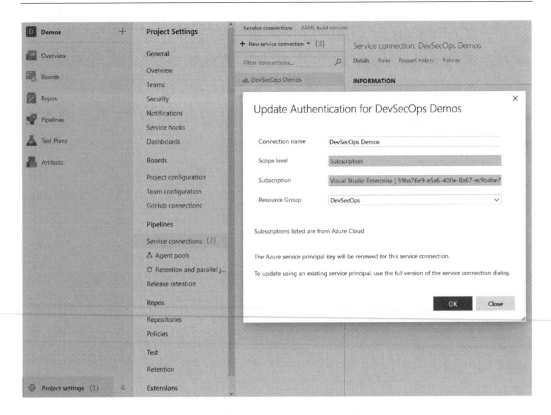

Figure 5.5 – Service connection dialog

3.   In this view, you can then either add a new service connection or update an existing service connection (see **2** and **3** in the preceding screenshot).

By default, service connections are scoped to the project level, meaning they are not available for everyone in the Azure DevOps organization. To encourage the reuse of service connections, Azure has made it possible to share them between projects since mid-2019.

Task Marketplace

A set of frequently used tasks is built into Azure Pipelines; however, there are even more available using the Visual Studio Marketplace for Azure DevOps. If you are an administrator of the DevOps organization, you can find and install extensions that add tasks here. If you are a regular user, you can find tasks here as well; however, you cannot install them, only request them. Your Azure DevOps administrator will then be notified and can install the extension on your behalf if they approve.

Of course, you can write and distribute extensions with tasks of your own as well.

Creating variables and variable groups

When you are configuring your build, there might be values that you need to use more than once. It is often wise to extract these values into variables, rather than just repeating them throughout your tasks.

Variables can be used to note down values that you do not want to have stored in source control. Values such as passwords and license keys can be safely stored as non-retrievable values when locked down using the lock symbol (see **1** in the following screenshot). After saving the build definition, these values are encrypted and can only be used by the build that they belong to.

To learn how to work with variables in Azure Pipelines, go through the following steps:

1. In Azure Pipelines, you can add variables to your build definition by going to the **Variables | Pipeline variables** tab (see **3** in the following screenshot). Here, you can enter them as name values, as can be seen in the following screenshot:

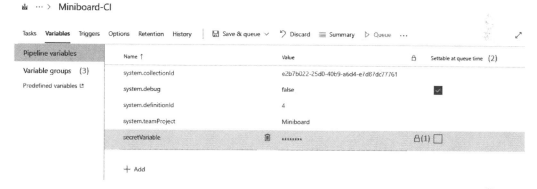

Figure 5.6 – Pipeline variables

2. Once defined, you can use the variables in the configuration of all tasks in all jobs of the same build. For this, you can use the following notation:

```
$(variableName)
```

3. Finally, you can mark variables as **Settable at queue time** (see **2** in the preceding screenshot), which means that their value can be changed whenever someone queues a new build. An example of a variable for which this is used is the system.debug built-in variable. When this variable is set to true, there is a verbose debug logging included in the build.

Next to your own variables, system variables are also defined. These are variables that contain information about the build that is currently running, including version numbers, agent names, build definition details, and the source version. A link to the full list of system-defined variables is included at the end of this chapter.

Variable groups

As well as creating the variables that go with a specific build, you can create variable groups. These variable groups can, in turn, be linked to one or more builds. This is an effective way of sharing variables between builds; some examples of these might be the name of your company, trademark texts, and product names. Let's see how we can work with variable groups:

1. Access variable groups through the menu by clicking on **Library** in the **Pipelines** menu (see **1** in the following screenshot). This displays a list of the existing variable groups that you can edit, and you can add a new group here as well, as shown in the following screenshot:

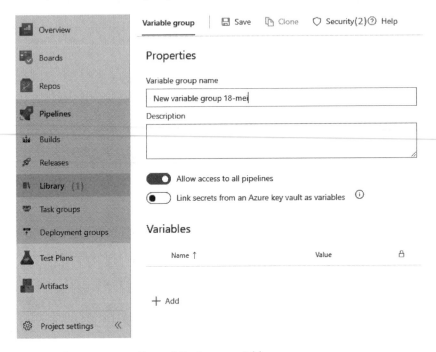

Figure 5.7 – A new variable group

2. Here, you can work with variables in the same way that you would with the variables that come with a build. The only differences are highlighted in the following list:

   - You cannot mark variables in a group as settable at queue time.

   - You can allow or deny the use of this group in all pipelines. If you deny their use in all pipelines, then only you can use the variable group. You can authorize other users or groups through the **Security** option (see **2** in the preceding screenshot).

- You can reference an Azure key vault for which this variable group will act as a placeholder. After logging into Azure, you can select a key vault and which values that are stored in the key vault you want to be accessible through the variable group.

Azure Key Vault is an Azure offering that can be used for the secure storage of secrets. Secrets in a key vault are automatically versioned, so older values are not overwritten but replaced by a newer version. In addition to this, you can specify segregated access policies that specify, per user, whether they can read, write, update, or delete values. All these actions are audited in a key vault, so you can also find who has made which change. If you are linking Azure DevOps to a key vault, then a new service principal will be created in your active directory that has access to that key vault. Now, whenever Azure DevOps needs a variable from the variable group, the actual values will be pulled from the key vault.

Variable groups can be linked to the variables of a build under the **Variable group** tab (refer to the screenshot in *Figure 5.7*).

As well as working with variable groups, you can also work with files in the library. You can upload files that are not accessible by other users but that can be used within a build. This is useful for files with private keys, license keys, and other secrets. Refer to this link for more information: `https://docs.microsoft.com/en-us/azure/devops/pipelines/library/secure-files?view=azure-devops`.

Just as you can with variable groups, you can specify whether each secure file can be used by any build or authorize specific users only.

Triggering the build

The next tab in a build definition governs what should start or trigger the build. To implement continuous integration, go through the following steps:

1. Click on the **Triggers** tab and select the first header on the left:

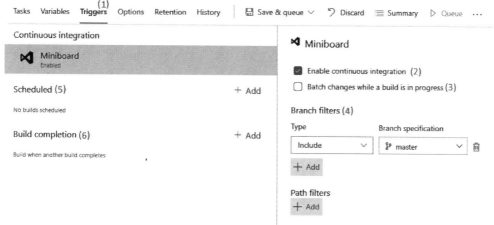

Figure 5.8 – Defining triggers for the pipeline

2. Check the **Enable continuous integration** box. This means that Azure DevOps will track for changes in your repository and queue a new build as soon as a new chance is available.

3. Next, you can choose whether you want to build every incoming change individually or batch multiple changes when more than one new change comes in while building a change. It is recommended that you build every single change separately if this is feasible.

4. Along with the continuous integration trigger, specify one or more branch and path filters. Here, you can specify which branches and files to queue a new build for. You can specify either inclusions or exclusions, depending on your needs. A common example is to limit your build to the main branch. If you have folders named `doc` and `src` in your repository and all your sources are in the latter folder, then it might make sense to limit the trigger to this path.

5. As well as choosing to have a continuous integration trigger, you can also opt to execute a build on a recurring schedule where you select one or more weekdays and a time.

6. You can also schedule a build to run whenever another build completes. This is called **chaining** builds.

Next, let's learn how to change the configurations of our build definition.

Build options

You can change the advanced configuration options for your build definition. These options include a description, the format of the build number, and the automated creation of work items on failures and times. To set this up, go through the following steps:

1. Click on the **Options** tab. You should arrive at the following screen:

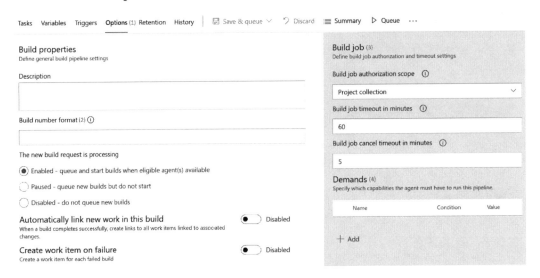

Figure 5.9 – Build options

2. Now, create your build number format. If this field is left empty, then the build number for your application will be set to an ever-increasing number that will increase by one with every build. This number is unique within a team project and counts over all the build definitions. You can also specify a format of your own using the variables available to you. A common approach is to specify a major and minor version number manually and then add an increasing number using a variable. The following example specifies a version of 4.1.xx, where the last part is replaced by a two-digit increasing number:

```
4.1($Rev:.rr)
```

3. On the right, there are advanced (but rarely used) options for specifying the authorization scope for the **Build job** timeouts for each job in the build definition.

4. It is also possible to specify the agent demands that every agent, for every job in the build definition, should fulfill. Again, we will look further at demands in the *Agents and agent queues* section of this chapter.

Other options on the left enable you to suspend the pipeline temporarily.

Build history

The final tab, called **History**, shows you a list of every change that has been made to the build definition. Build definitions are stored in JSON format, and you can pull up side-by-side comparisons for every change. The comment that you put in when saving a build is also stored here and can be used to provide the rationale for a change. You can revert to an older version of the pipeline as well.

Since builds are an important means of preserving quality, it is important to keep track of who has changed them to ensure that automated quality metrics are not removed.

With this, you are now ready to run your first build. You can directly run it using the **Save & queue** button that is visible in most of the screenshots in this section. The *Running a build* section of this chapter will teach you how to work with the results that you obtain.

Task groups

When working in a team or organization that has more than one pipeline, it often doesn't take long before multiple pipelines that have the same shape emerge. For example, in some companies, all pipelines contain tasks for security scanning, running tests, and calculating the test coverage.

Instead of repeating these tasks everywhere, they can be extracted from an existing pipeline into a task group. Task groups, in turn, can be used within multiple pipelines as if they are tasks themselves. Doing this reduces the effort needed to create a new pipeline or update all the pipelines with a new requirement. Doing this also ensures that all the pipelines using the task group have the same task configuration.

To create a new task group, open any existing build definition and go through the following steps:

1. Select one or more tasks by clicking on them while holding down *Ctrl*, or by using the selectors that appear when hovering the mouse over a task:

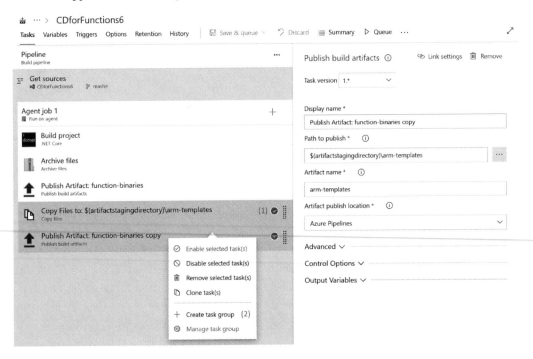

Figure 5.10 – Creating a task group

2. Right-click on the selection and select **Create task group**.

3. In the popup that now appears (not shown in the screenshot), choose a name, description, and category for the task group. If any of the selected tasks have a variable value specified, you can now provide a default value and description for these parameters. These parameters will be available within the task group and need to be configured when the task group is used.

4. After clicking **Create** (not shown in the screenshot), the existing build definition is updated by removing the selected tasks and replacing them with the new task group.

Adding an already existing task group to a build or release definition is done in precisely the same way as adding regular tasks. Task groups show up in the same list of tasks to choose from.

A list of all the existing task groups can be found by navigating to the **Pipelines** menu and then **Task groups**. To edit an existing task group, select it in the list that is shown, and then select the **Edit** option. Editing task groups works in precisely the same way as editing a build definition.

This section was all about creating a build definition and describing how an application should be built. The next section is about executing the build.

Running a build

In this section, you will learn how to work with the build results and use them to report and generate builds. You will also learn how to run a build with every pull request and report the quality of the changes back to that pull request to assist the reviewer.

Viewing the build results

While a build is running, an agent will perform all the configured steps. Azure Pipelines will capture detailed information and logs from all these steps. As you can see in the following screenshot, a build will display a list of all the steps it has executed on the left. Clicking on any of these steps will open a detailed view that displays the logs per step:

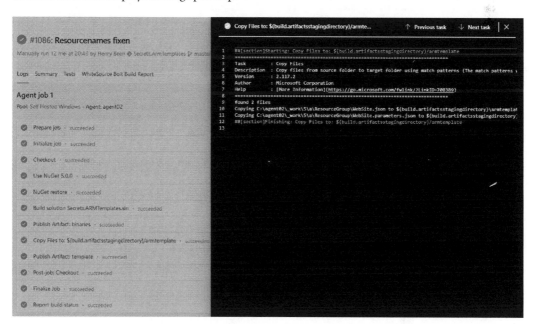

Figure 5.11 – Build results

Whenever there are warnings or errors during the build, they show up in orange or red, respectively.

Building a pull request

After setting up your build definition and running your first builds, you might also see the first failures coming in – for example, when someone accidentally commits and pushes changes that do not compile or contain unit tests that do not run successfully. You can prevent this by having a build definition run automatically whenever a pull request comes in. To configure this, go through the following steps:

1. Click on **Policies** under **Project Settings**. The following screen will open. Click on **Add build policy**:

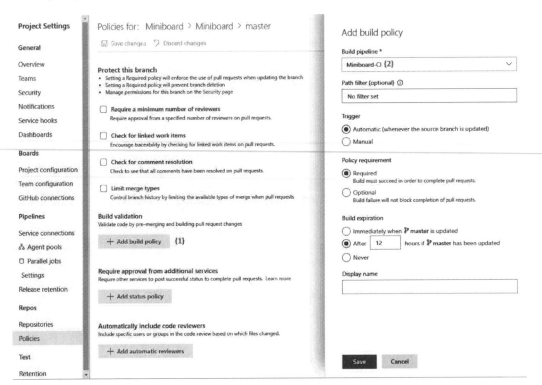

Figure 5.12 – Adding a build policy

2. Select a build definition that you want to use to validate the pull request.

3. Next, there will be three more things that you can configure:

    -   **Trigger**: When the build definition should start, either automatically or manually. Of course, the real value comes from running a verification build automatically.

    -   **Policy requirement**: This determines whether a pull request can be completed if the build fails. In other words, this determines whether you can ignore a failing build. It is recommended that you avoid setting this to **Optional**, if possible.

- **Build expiration**: This determines how long a positive build result is valid for. The default value is **12** hours, but you should consider changing this to **Immediately when main is updated**. The advantage of this is that you cannot merge changes without first running the build against a combination of the current state of the branch that you will merge to and the proposed changes.

You can add more than one build policy. If you have a lot of things that you can automatically validate and want to keep automated validation times to a minimum, then this is a good approach.

Accessing build artifacts

As well as compiling, testing, and validating your source code, builds can also be used to generate what are called **artifacts**. Artifacts are outputs from a build and can be anything that you want to save and publish from a build, such as test results and application packages.

An application package is intended to be an immutable build of a version of your application. This package can later be picked up in a release and deployed to one or more environments:

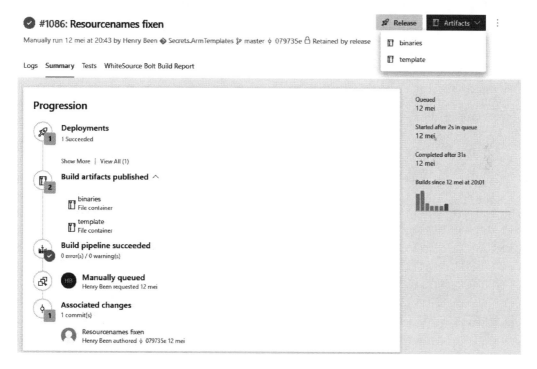

Figure 5.13 – Viewing application packages

In the preceding screenshot, you can see that, as part of the summary of an executed build, there were two artifacts published. Artifacts can be accessed from either the **Artifacts** drop-down menu in the top-right corner of the screen or from the **Summary** tab. You can download and explore artifacts from this page, and in the next chapter, you will see how to work with them to set up continuous delivery.

Great! With this, you have learned how to create a definition using the visual designer. But wait – as we mentioned earlier, there is another way of doing this, which is by using YAML files. Let's see how this works in the next section.

Working with YAML pipelines

You have seen how to create a build definition using the visual designer. A new, alternative approach, which has been available since early 2019, is the use of YAML pipelines. When working with YAML pipelines, you specify your complete build definition in a YAML file and store it in source control, often next to the source code that the build is for.

While both pipeline systems coexist, using YAML pipelines is now the preferred approach for defining pipelines. This means that it is very likely that new features will only surface in YAML pipelines.

The reason for using build definitions as code

When you first start working with YAML build definitions, you might find that the learning curve is steeper than it is when working with a visual designer. This might raise the question as to why you would use YAML-defined builds. There are two main advantages that YAML build definitions have over visually designed definitions.

When you are writing your definition in YAML, it can be hosted in source control next to your code. The consequence of this is that all the policies that you have in place for changing source control now automatically apply to your build definition. This means that any change must go through a pull request, be reviewed by a peer, and can be built and verified ahead of time. Enforcing the **four-eyes principle** on your build definition, as well as your code, increases the stability of your build process. Of course, it also benefits security and compliance, topics that will be discussed in later chapters.

As well as this increase in security, having the build definition in source control also means that it is available in every branch. This means that it can be changed in every branch to build that specific branch before merging it with the main branch. When working with a visually designed build definition, this single definition is responsible for building not only your main branch but also all the branches that you want to merge through a pull request.

This means that you must do one of the following:

- Update the build definition for the change that you will merge. However, this will terminate the building of the current state of the main branch.

- Merge the change, which will also result in a broken build, since the build definition has not yet been updated.

Either option has the risk of allowing faulty changes to flow through the target branch, defeating the purpose of a continuous integration build. With a build definition per branch, we eradicate this problem.

Writing a basic YAML pipeline

To get started with YAML builds, there are two things you need to do:

1. First, you need to write your YAML file.
2. Then, you need to create a build definition out of it.

So, let's get started.

Writing the YAML file

The following code sample contains an example YAML definition for building a .NET Core application and running unit tests. Save a file with any name – for example, `pipeline.yaml` – in any Git repository in Azure DevOps. Then, it can be used to create a pipeline out of it later on:

```yaml
trigger:
- main

pool:
  name: Azure Pipelines
  vmImage: windows-2019

steps:
-   task: DotNetCoreCLI@2
    displayName: 'dotnet build'
    inputs:
        projects: '**/*.csproj'
-   task: DotNetCoreCLI@2
    displayName: 'dotnet test'
    inputs:
        command: test
        projects: '**/*.csproj'
```

This YAML example defines a basic pipeline. Every pipeline needs to be triggered in some way. Just as with classic builds, this can be done by connecting the pipeline to a change in a source code repository. The default repository for this is the repository that also contains the YAML definition. The **trigger** keyword is used to specify a push to which branches should trigger the pipeline. A good starting point is the main branch. As the trigger keyword accepts a list, multiple branches can be specified, and wildcards can be used.

A trigger is not mandatory, as a pipeline can also be started manually.

> **Tip**
> There are also alternative options to using the trigger keyword, such as including or excluding one or more branches, tags, or paths in the repository. These options are described in detail at `https://docs.microsoft.com/en-us/azure/devops/pipelines/yaml-schema#triggers`.

As well as a trigger, every pipeline contains one or more tasks, just as in classic build definitions. All these tasks need to execute on an agent pool – again, just as in classic build definitions. The `pool` keyword is used to specify a set of key/value pairs that determine which pool the tasks will run on by specifying the name of the pool. When working with the default agents that Microsoft provides, the default name of `Azure Pipelines` can be used. When using this specific pool, a **Virtual Machine** (**VM**) image has to be specified. This determines which operating system and what software is available on the agent that will execute the task.

> **Tip**
> An up-to-date list of all the VM images that are available can be found at `https://docs.microsoft.com/en-us/azure/devops/pipelines/agents/hosted#use-a-microsoft-hosted-agent`.

Finally, the definition contains a list of the steps that make up the pipeline itself. These steps correspond one to one with the tasks that you can drag into a classic build pipeline. A task is added by specifying the name and version – separated by the @ sign – of the task that you want to run. Next, you can optionally specify a display name for the task. This display name will later be visible in the views that show the results of an executed pipeline. Finally, specify one or more inputs for the task. These inputs relate to the task-specific configuration that you have already seen for the visual designer.

Creating a YAML pipeline

After saving your YAML file in a repository, you can create a build definition from it. When creating a new build definition (see the *Creating a build definition* section of this chapter), you should go through the following steps:

1. Choose the **Azure Repos Git YAML** option when the wizard starts.
2. From here, go through the wizard to select and review the YAML you want to build, as shown in the following screenshot:

Figure 5.14 – A YAML pipeline for a repository

3. Then, locate the repository that contains the YAML file that you want to use as your pipeline.

4. Next, configure the pipeline by choosing an example YAML file to start from or by referring to an already existing file.

5. Finally, you can review the YAML file that you have selected and start a build from it.

Your pipeline is saved automatically. Once the pipeline is saved, it can be started, and you can interact with it in the same way as you would with classic build pipelines.

Multi-job pipelines

The pipeline you saw in the previous section does not specify any jobs, as you may recall from the section on classic builds. Instead, it contains a list of tasks under the `steps` keyword. This means that it implicitly contains only a single job. With YAML pipelines, it is also possible to create a definition that contains more than one job. To do this, the following structure can be used:

```
trigger:
- main

pool:
    name: Azure Pipelines
    vmImage: windows-2019
```

```
jobs:
- job: job1
  displayName: A pretty name for job1
  steps:
  - task: DotNetCoreCLI@2

    ...
- job: job2
  displayName: My second job
  pool:
      name: Azure Pipelines
      vmImage: ubuntu-18.04

  ...
```

Instead of adding the `steps` keyword directly to the pipeline, a list of jobs is created first. Within that list, one or more `job` keywords are added, followed by the name for that job. Next to this technical name, a display name (`displayName`) can be specified for each job.

As the second job in the preceding example shows, it is also possible to specify which agent pool to use per job. When no pool is specified for a job, the default pool specified at the top of the file is used.

> **Tip**
> The jobs that are discussed in this section are called agent jobs. Besides agent jobs, there are also server jobs, container jobs, and deployment jobs available. More information about these types of jobs can be found at `https://docs.microsoft.com/en-us/azure/devops/pipelines/process/phases#types-of-jobs`.

By default, all the jobs in a pipeline run in parallel, but there are control options available to change this.

Control options

To control the order of jobs, the `dependsOn` keyword can be used in the definition of a job. This signals that the job can only be started after one or more jobs are completed. Besides this, the `condition` keyword can be used to specify a condition that a job should run under. These two keywords can be combined to realize more complex scenarios, such as the one shown here:

```
jobs:
- job: compile
  steps:

    ...
- job: test
```

```
      dependsOn: compile
      steps:
      ...
   - job: build_schema
      dependsOn: compile
      steps:
      ..
   - job: report
      dependsOn:
      - test
      - build_schema
      condition: or(succeeded('test'), succeeded('build_schema'))
      steps:
      ..
```

This pipeline will start by running the job named `compile`. Once this job completes, the next two jobs, `test` and `build_schema`, will run in parallel, as they both depend on the `compile` task. After both of these tasks complete, the `report` task runs, as it declares a dependency on both the `test` and `build_schema` jobs. Before this job actually starts, the condition is evaluated to determine whether the job should actually run or be skipped.

Conditions can be built using a syntax that is similar to many programming languages. It checks the successful completion of a job using the `succeeded()` and `failed()` functions. There is also support for Boolean operators such as `or()`, `and()`, and `ne()`.

You can combine the `dependsOn` and `condition` keywords in any way you see fit. The only requirement is that there should be at least one job that does not depend on any other job.

Variables

Just like classic build pipelines, YAML pipelines support the use of variables. Variables can be defined at every level of a YAML pipeline (except for within a task) using the following syntax:

```
variables:
  name: value
  anotherName: otherValue
```

Variables can later be retrieved using the syntax that you already know from classic build pipelines – `$(name)` and `$(anotherName)`.

It is also possible to reference existing variable groups from within a YAML pipeline. This is done by using the `group` keyword, instead of specifying the name of a variable. To also retrieve all the variables from a variable group called `myVariableGroup`, you would extend the preceding YAML, as follows:

```
variables:
  name: value
  anotherName: otherValue
  group: myVariableGroup
```

Variables can be set at every level in a YAML pipeline, but only variables set at the root level can be overridden when queuing a new execution manually. You can learn more here: `https://docs.microsoft.com/en-us/azure/devops/pipelines/process/variables`.

Pipeline artifacts

Just like classic builds, YAML pipelines can be used to build and publish artifacts. As the task used to do this is a task like any other, it can be added directly to the list of steps in a job.

However, with the introduction of YAML pipelines, a new type of artifact has become available – the so-called pipeline artifact. This comes with the benefit of improving the speed at which large artifacts can be uploaded and downloaded. When working with classic releases, pipeline artifacts are not automatically downloaded, whereas build artifacts are.

To publish a pipeline artifact, the following YAML can be used in the `steps` keyword of a job:

```
steps:
- publish: folder/to/publish
  artifact: artifactName
```

Pipeline artifacts are mainly intended to be downloaded in multi-stage YAML pipelines, which are also covered in the next chapter.

Tips for writing YAML pipelines

Writing YAML pipelines from scratch can be complicated when you are just getting started. There are two tools available that can help you.

First, there is the option to export YAML from the visual designer. For every task, there is a link with the **View YAML** title. This opens a small pop-up box that shows you the YAML corresponding to the task and configuration that you currently have open. The same can be done for jobs and, under specific conditions, complete build definitions.

The other tool available for writing YAML is the built-in YAML editor:

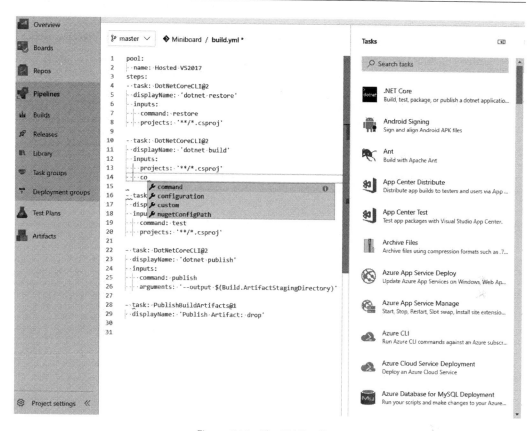

Figure 5.15 – The YAML editor

Whenever you open a YAML build definition, there are two tools available to help you. First, there is autocompletion for every location in your YAML file. This shows you the options available at that point in the file. As well as this, there are snippets available in the task picker on the right. When selecting any of the tasks on the right, you configure them visually and then click the **Add** button to add the generated YAML to your definition.

These two tools aim to bring the ease of the visual designer to the YAML build experience as well, combining the best of both worlds.

Refer to these docs for a complete YAML schema reference: `https://docs.microsoft.com/en-us/azure/devops/pipelines/yaml-schema/?view=azure-pipelines`.

Agents and agent queues

The build definitions that you have created so far can contain agent jobs, which in turn contain tasks. These tasks are not executed within your Azure DevOps organization directly but are instead executed by agents that run on VMs or in containers. In turn, agents are grouped in agent pools. There are two types of agent pools that you can work with:

- Built-in agent pools
- Self-hosted agent pools

Let's go through them one by one.

Built-in agent pools

Built-in agent pools are managed by Microsoft and are made available to you as part of the Azure DevOps product itself. There are different agent pools available, depending on your needs. Pools run different versions of Windows and Visual Studio, and there are also pools available that run Linux (Ubuntu) and macOS.

The disadvantage of these managed pools is that you cannot install extra software on the machines or containers that host the agents if you need to. This means that, in these cases, you have to create your own private agent pools.

Creating a private agent pool

Private pools are defined in your Azure DevOps organization and are provisioned from there to one or more of your team projects. However, you can also create your private pools at the team project level if they are created and provisioned in one go. To do so, go to **Project Settings | Agent pools**. You should see the following **Add agent pool** option:

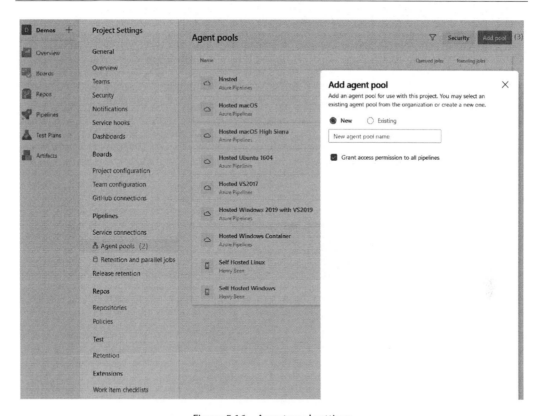

Figure 5.16 – Agent pool settings

After giving the pool a name and determining whether you want to automatically provide access to all pipelines, you can save the pool. After creating the pool, you can add or remove agents.

Adding and removing agents

Adding an agent is done in two steps:

1. Download and extract the agent runtime. You can find the agent runtime by going to the section with the overview of the agent pools and opening the details of any private agent pool. After the details of the pool are opened, click on **New agent** in the top-right corner:

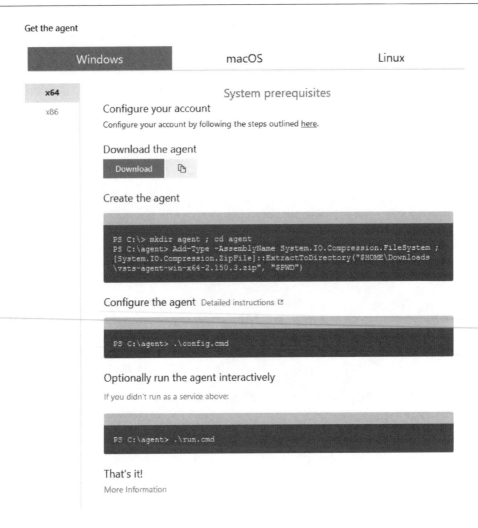

Get the agent

Windows	macOS	Linux

x64
x86

System prerequisites

Configure your account

Configure your account by following the steps outlined here.

Download the agent

[Download]

Create the agent

```
PS C:\> mkdir agent ; cd agent
PS C:\agent> Add-Type -AssemblyName System.IO.Compression.FileSystem ;
[System.IO.Compression.ZipFile]::ExtractToDirectory("$HOME\Downloads
\vsts-agent-win-x64-2.150.3.zip", "$PWD")
```

Configure the agent   Detailed instructions ↗

```
PS C:\agent> .\config.cmd
```

Optionally run the agent interactively

If you didn't run as a service above:

```
PS C:\agent> .\run.cmd
```

That's it!

More Information

Figure 5.17 – Adding a new agent

2. In the dialog that opens, you can download a ZIP file with the agent and instructions for extracting and installing the agent.

Important Note

During the configuration phase, you will be prompted to authenticate with your Azure DevOps organization and provide the name of the agent pool you want to install the agent in. While there are x86 and x64 agents available, it is recommended that you work with the x64 agent unless you have a specific reason not to.

To remove agents from the pool, you can use one of two methods:

- You can return to the PowerShell command line, just as you did for the installation, and use the following command:

```
.\remove.cmd
```

- Alternatively, you can also remove agents from the agent pool overview using the **Agents** tab. Go to **Project Settings** | **Agent pools** (see **1** in the following screenshot) | **Agents** (see **2** in the following screenshot), and then select the options button (see **3** in the following screenshot) on the agent you want to remove. Then, click **Delete** (see **4** in the following screenshot):

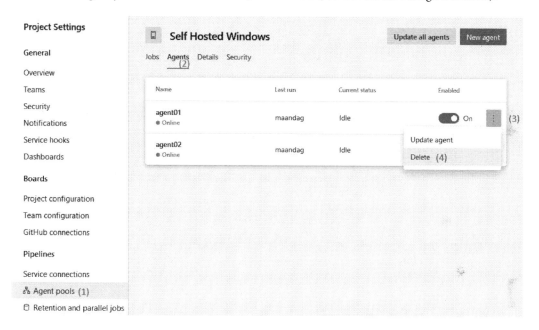

Figure 5.18 – Deleting an agent

In the preceding screenshot, you can see the steps to remove an agent using the interface. Be aware that this does not clean up the binaries and any files on the host machine; however, if a machine that is hosting an agent breaks down or a VM is removed, this is the only way to remove the agent.

Agent selection

Whenever a build job starts running, an agent is selected from the pool that will perform the tasks that you have defined in the pipeline. The selection of an agent is done in two steps:

1. Only agents that are part of the selected pool are eligible for running the tasks. This means that when working with private agent pools, it is wise to have multiple agents in a pool. If you then take one agent offline for maintenance, the agent jobs that rely on the agent pool can continue running.

2. Before an agent job can run, the demands from each job and the tasks it contains are gathered. As you learned in the *Variable groups* section, an agent job can specify the demands it has of the agent that it uses. The same goes for tasks – they can also specify demands. To run a job, only agents that meet all of these demands are used. Demands and capabilities are key/value pairs, where the value is an integer. Refer to these docs for examples of demands: `https://docs.microsoft.com/en-us/azure/devops/pipelines/process/demands`.

When there is no eligible agent for a build definition, the build eventually fails after a timeout.

Finding agent capabilities

To find the capabilities that are available on the individual agents, go through the following steps:

1. Navigate to **Organization Settings | Agent pools**:

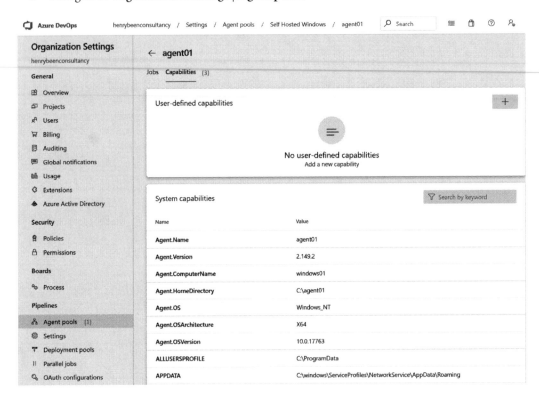

Figure 5.19 – Viewing agent settings

2. Navigate to the correct agent pool (either hosted or private), then **Agents**, and then open the agent details (not shown in the preceding screenshot).

3. Open the **Capabilities** tab.

Here, you can specify one or more custom capabilities for the agent using the top block, called **User-defined capabilities**. For self-hosted (private) agents, all the capabilities that were discovered on the machine when you installed the agent are also shown.

The benefits of self-hosted agent pools

Use of Microsoft (cloud)-hosted agents is a fairly common practice and saves you a lot of time in managing and configuring your build infrastructure. Self-hosted agents have proven to be beneficial on many occasions. Due to the availability of a lot of good documentation, it has become an easy task for administrators to provision and configure a self-hosted agent for use in their pipelines.

The main benefits of using a self-hosted agent are as follows:

- Optimizing the cost of your build agents.

- Installing additional software as required for your specific build tasks.

- Improving the performance of your builds, making them run faster by caching resources, and enabling incremental builds.

- The debugging and troubleshooting of build issues are easier.

- Allows for **Virtual Network** (**Vnet**) integration, and you can securely run your builds behind the firewall.

- Accessing other corporate resources securely using whitelisted IP addresses.

In the next section, we will explore the option to automate CI builds for repositories hosted on GitHub.

Automating CI builds using GitHub Actions

If you are using a GitHub repository, you can also automate your CI builds using GitHub Actions (available as a tab within the repository's top navigation menu). You can either choose from an existing template workflow (with more than 50 workflows available) or set up a custom workflow of your own:

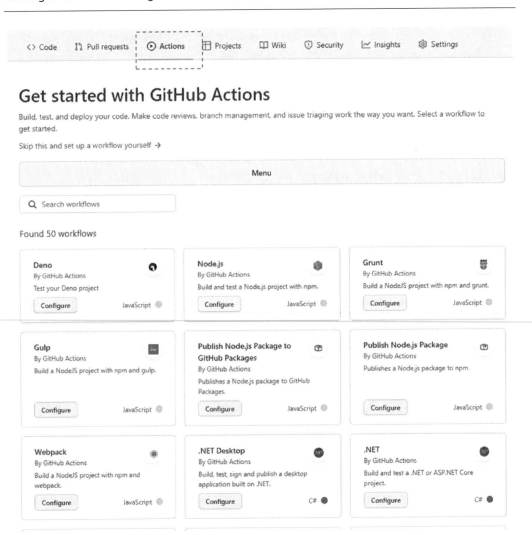

Figure 5.20 – The available options in GitHub Actions

The experience of authoring a workflow is similar to creating a YAML file and saving it within your GitHub repository:

Figure 5.21 – Editing a YAML file in the GitHub repository

In the next sections, we will introduce alternative tools that can be used for managing the CI processes.

Other tools

There are many tools available besides Azure DevOps. Two other well-known tools are GitLab CI and Jenkins. Some very basic knowledge of these tools will help you to understand how to integrate with them if that is ever necessary. Also, a limited understanding of other tools will help you to quickly understand the concepts and generalize your knowledge of how to work with these other tools.

To highlight how these tools work with the same concepts, both examples in this section are equivalent to the Azure DevOps YAML pipeline in the *Writing a YAML build definition* section.

GitLab CI

GitLab offers build pipelines using the GitLab CI capabilities. GitLab CI is configured by putting a file with the `.gitlab-ci.yml` name in the root of a repository. In this file, you can define one or more stages and jobs, along with the tasks that they should perform. An example YAML file for GitLab CI can appear, as shown in the following example:

```
stages:
    - build
    - test

build:
        stage: build
        script: dotnet build **/*.csproj

test:
        stage: test
        script: dotnet test **/*.csproj
```

Just as Azure DevOps uses agent pools with agents, GitLab CI relies on **runners** to perform the actual work. In GitLab CI, there is currently no support for visually creating or editing your pipelines.

Jenkins

Jenkins is another tool used to run build pipelines. Complex builds can be run using Jenkins pipelines, which get their work from a Jenkinsfile. A **Jenkinsfile** is written in a Jenkins-specific notation, as shown in the following code:

```
pipeline {
        agent any
        stages {
                stage('build') {
                agent any
                    steps {
                            dotnet build **/*.csproj
                    }
                }
```

```
        stage('test') {
                agent any
                steps {
                        dotnet test **/*.csproj
                }
        }
    }
}
```

Jenkins has limited support for visually creating and editing a pipeline. This is referred to as a freestyle project.

Summary

In this chapter, we looked at continuous integration and learned how it is a combination of your mindset, the processes, and tools used by the development teams. You learned how to create build definitions using Azure Pipelines, using both the graphical designer and YAML, as well as how to run builds. You learned that you can use build pipelines to compile and test your code, as well as report the outcome back to pull requests.

You learned that builds can produce outputs, termed as Artifacts. Artifacts are stored and retained within Azure pipelines and can be used to store reports, but they are also the starting point of deployment pipelines, which you will learn about in the next chapter. You also learned about the infrastructure that you need to run builds – namely, agents and agent pools. Finally, you saw two brief examples of how to run a continuous integration build using GitLab CI and Jenkins, which are two other tools that you can use for build pipelines.

With this knowledge, you are now able to create build pipelines for your projects. You can hook up to source control and produce the builds that you will use in the next chapter to deploy your applications. With this deep knowledge of the underlying structure of tasks, jobs, stages, and pipelines, you can solve complex application-building problems.

In the next chapter, you will continue learning about pipelines but this time, for releases. You will learn how to pick up builds and release them to one or more environments.

Questions

As we conclude, here is a list of questions for you to test your knowledge regarding this chapter's material. You will find the answers in the *Assessments* section of the appendix:

1. True or false? You achieve continuous integration if you compile all the branches of your project at least daily.

2. True or false? A classic build definition is always connected to a source code repository.

3. True or false? A YAML pipeline definition is always connected to a source code repository.

4. Which of the following is needed to call an external tool from an Azure pipeline?

    A. An external service definition

    B. An Azure service connection

    C. A service connection

    D. A service locator

5. What are some common reasons for using self-hosted agents? Choose all of the correct answers from the following:

    A. Access to closed networks is needed.

    B. Specific extension tasks need to be available to the agent.

    C. The number of parallel pipeline executions needs to be larger than 10.

    D. Specific software needs to be installed in order for the agent to use it.

Exercises

- Add a folder named `pipelines` under the root directory of the `PacktBookLibrary` repository.

- Create a subfolder named `build` under the `pipelines` directory.

- Add a build file named `main-ci-build.yml`.

- Insert the following code block in the file:

```
trigger:
- main

pool:
  vmImage: ubuntu-latest
```

```
variables:
  buildConfiguration: 'Release'

steps:
- script: dotnet build --configuration
$(buildConfiguration)
  displayName: 'dotnet build $(buildConfiguration)'
```

- Save the file and commit your changes to the branch. Push and then raise a pull request to merge your changes with the main branch.

- Create a new pipeline in your team project. In the **Configure your pipeline** step, select the **Existing Azure Pipelines YAML file** option:

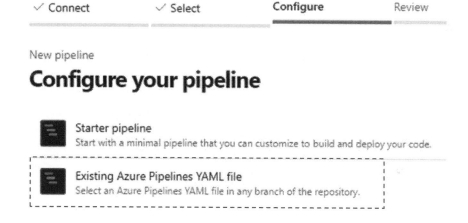

Figure 5.22 – Using an existing pipeline option

- When prompted to select the build pipeline, specify the main-ci-build.yml file. Click **Continue** to finish creating your build pipeline.

- Run the pipeline job to verify that the build pipeline works. On the pipeline status page, review for any errors and the successful execution of the pipeline job.

> **Important Note**
>
> The pipeline is composed of tasks to build a .NET Core project. To build other types of code components, make use of the appropriate task library.

The source code repository for the starter kit can be found here: `https://github.com/PacktPublishing/Designing-and-Implementing-Microsoft-DevOps-Solutions-AZ-400-Exam-Guide`

Further reading

- An in-depth definition of continuous integration by Martin Fowler is available at `https://martinfowler.com/articles/continuousIntegration.html`.

- A detailed description of the conditions syntax is available at `https://docs.microsoft.com/en-us/azure/devops/pipelines/process/conditions?view=azure-devopstabs=classic`.

- Exercises for practicing with Azure DevOps builds can be found at `https://docs.microsoft.com/en-us/learn/modules/create-a-build-pipeline/index`.

- You can find the Visual Studio Marketplace for Azure DevOps at `https://marketplace.visualstudio.com/azuredevops`.

- You can find a detailed description of the Azure Pipelines YAML syntax at `https://docs.microsoft.com/en-us/azure/devops/pipelines/yaml-schema?view=azure-devopstabs=schema`.

- Details of the pricing of the Azure Pipelines' hosted and self-hosted agent pools are available at `https://azure.microsoft.com/en-us/pricing/details/devops/azure-pipelines/`.

- More information about GitLab CI can be found at `https://about.gitlab.com/product/continuous-integration/`.

- More information about Jenkins can be found at `https://jenkins.io/`.

- Build tasks for .NET Core projects: `https://docs.microsoft.com/en-us/azure/devops/pipelines/ecosystems/dotnet-core?view=azure-devops&tabs=dotnetfive`.

- *Develop a web extension*: `https://docs.microsoft.com/en-us/azure/devops/extend/get-started/node?view=azure-devops`.

6
Implementing Continuous Deployment and Release Management

In the previous chapter, you learned how to use Azure DevOps pipelines for continuous integration. Due to this, you now know how to pick up a version of your sources and create artifacts that you can deploy. In this chapter, you will learn how to extend this with continuous delivery and continuous deployment practices so that you automatically deploy these artifacts to the servers or platforms that your code is running on.

To do this, we will start by introducing Azure DevOps release definitions so that you can define and run the releases of your application. Next, a series of strategies will be introduced that you can use to perform deployments in a low-risk manner. Doing this makes it possible for you to automate the process of deploying new versions unattended, with a limited risk of incidents occurring. From here, we will shift our attention to automating the creation of release notes. After this, we will introduce Visual Studio App Center, which is used for building, testing, and releasing mobile and desktop applications. Finally, other tools for continuous deployment will be introduced.

The following topics will be covered in this chapter:

- Continuous delivery and continuous deployment
- Working with Azure DevOps releases
- Writing multi-stage **Yet Another Markup Language** (**YAML**) pipelines
- Implementing continuous deployment strategies
- Deploying mobile applications
- Automating release notes
- Other tools

Technical requirements

To experiment with the techniques described in this chapter, you might need one or more of the following:

- An Azure DevOps account for building release definitions and multi-stage YAML pipelines
- An App Center account for deploying mobile applications

Free trial options are available for both of these.

Continuous delivery and continuous deployment

The difference between continuous delivery and continuous deployment is a common source of confusion. Some people think these terms are interchangeable and see them as two synonyms for the same concept, but they have, in fact, two different meanings.

Continuous delivery is a practice where teams ensure that the artifacts they build are continuously validated and ready to be deployed to a production environment. Often, this is done by deploying the artifacts to a production-like environment, such as acceptance or even a staging environment, and applying a series of tests, such as verification tests, to ensure that an application is working correctly.

Continuous deployment is a practice where every version that is deployed to a production-like environment and passes all tests and verifications is also deployed to production automatically.

It is a recommended practice to plan for continuous delivery irrespective of whether your team decides to deploy more frequently or not. Deployment and upgrades are dependent on multiple factors, which may change over time. Hence, continuous delivery will be a prerequisite for faster release cycles.

When working with Azure DevOps, Azure Pipelines is the tool of choice for implementing continuous delivery and deployment. This can be done using either the visual classic editor or with multi-stage YAML pipelines, both of which will be discussed in the following section.

Working with Azure DevOps releases

Continuous delivery and deployment can both be implemented in Azure DevOps by using releases. When creating a new release definition, an outline of the release process is created. This process will often start with an artifact that triggers the creation of a new release. Next, it is possible to define one or more stages that the release can be deployed to. Often, these stages correspond to the different application environments – for example, test and production – but this is not mandatory.

Let's learn how to create a new release definition and explore the various options we have. First, navigate to **Pipelines** and choose **Releases** from the menu. From here, it is possible to start creating a new release pipeline, which will take us to a screen that looks similar to the one shown in the following screenshot:

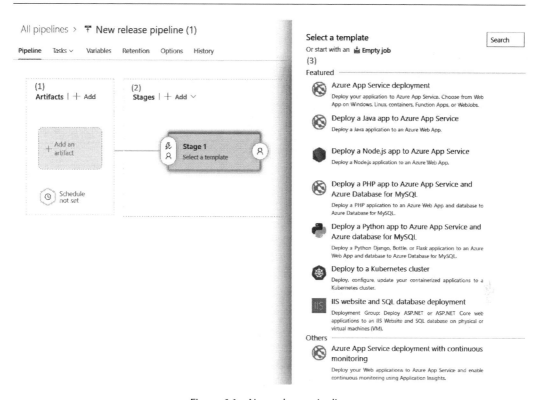

Figure 6.1 – New release pipeline

On the preceding screen, we can perform the following actions (which are numbered in the preceding screenshot):

1. First, note that, on the left, it is possible to see the outline of the release pipeline with a box. Here, you can select one or more artifacts that can be used in the release pipeline.

2. To the right of this, there is a box where the different stages of the release can be seen. By default, one stage is created already.

3. It is possible to pick a template as a starting point for the deployment pipeline for this pre-created stage. Choosing to start with an empty job in this view allows you to craft a custom deployment pipeline from scratch.

After choosing a job template or an empty job to start with, the pane on the right will close, and it will be possible to start editing the release pipeline from left to right, starting with the artifacts.

Once a skeleton release pipeline is visible, the first things you will need to configure are the artifacts that the release should work with. This is the subject of the next section.

Creating artifacts and release triggers

The previous chapter described build definitions and YAML pipelines, which create artifacts. These artifacts are picked up in releases and form the basis for deploying an application.

To start editing a release pipeline, follow these steps:

1. Click on the **Add an artifact** button to start building the starting point of the release definition. This will open the right-hand pane shown in the following screenshot:

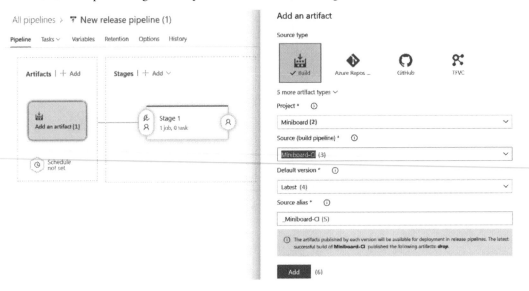

Figure 6.2 – Add an artifact

2. In the picker for the project, the current project will be selected by default.

3. Now, specify the artifacts that the release pipeline should pick up.

4. After this, the default version to use and the source alias will be automatically selected. The default version can always be overridden when manually starting a release, so **Latest** is a sensible default.

5. The source alias is the name of the folder where the artifacts can be located when we add jobs to the release stages at a later date. The default is often fine.

6. Finish adding the artifact by clicking **Add**.

Now that we've specified the artifacts to work with, it is time to specify when a new release should be created. Let's learn how to do this:

1. To configure the availability of a new artifact to trigger the release, click on the lightning bolt next to the artifact to open the configuration pane. This can be seen in the following screenshot:

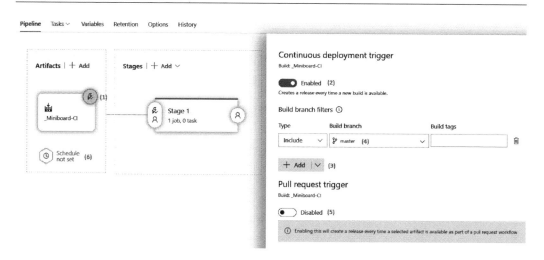

Figure 6.3 – Specifying a deployment trigger

2. In this pane, it is possible to create a new release, when one is available, using the top slider. This will expand a new section where you can define one or more filters so that you can specify conditions under which a new artifact should trigger a release.

3. Click the **Add** button to start adding a condition.

4. A common example is to only include artifacts that come from the master branch, as shown in *Figure 6.3*.

5. In addition to artifacts that come from regular builds, it is possible to also allow artifacts that come from pull request builds to start a new release.

6. Finally, it is possible to create a new release on a fixed schedule.

If no schedule and no trigger are specified, a new release will only be created when someone does so manually.

Specifying the stages to deploy the release

After specifying the artifacts to release, it is time to specify one or more stages to deploy the release to. Often, every environment (test, acceptance, and production) will correspond to a stage, but it is also possible to have other stages if the situation calls for it.

Let's learn how to add a new stage and explore various options. First, click on **Pipelines** to arrive at the following screen:

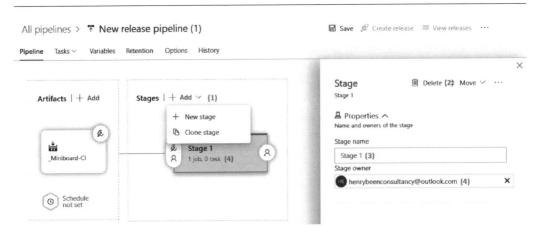

Figure 6.4 – Configuring a stage within a new pipeline

Now, complete the following steps:

1. Click the **Add** button to create a new stage. A stage can be either new or a clone of an existing one.

2. After selecting an already existing stage, it can be removed using the **Delete** button on the top right.

3. Other actions that can be performed on this screen include renaming the stage and designating a stage owner. The owner will be notified when a release is deployed to the environment.

4. After creating and naming a stage, it is possible to add jobs and tasks to a stage, just like it was possible for a build pipeline. To do this, click on the link in the box that denotes the stage.

From here on, this works exactly the same as building pipelines. There is only one addition: besides agent jobs and agentless jobs, it is also possible to use deployment group jobs.

These will be discussed in the *Working with deployment groups* section later on. But first, let's understand which stages we need.

Which stages do I need?

One of the questions that frequently arise when working with releases is, *which stages do I need in my release pipeline?* According to the documentation, stages should denote the major divisions of a release pipeline. When starting out with releases, this often boils down to having one stage per environment in a release pipeline. Appropriate stages include **test**, **acceptance**, and **production**.

When working with releases for a long time, we might incorporate more automation in the pipelines and want to add extra checking stages to them. An example might be a stage called **load test**, which is executed in parallel to the **test** stage. Another example might be the introduction of a stage for **automated UI tests**.

No matter which stages are added, the approach to propagating a release to production should always stay the same. When a release propagates from stage to stage and gets closer to production, this should show that there is confidence in this release, that it is working correctly, and that it can be promoted to production.

Stage triggers, approvals, and gates

After defining the required stages and adding jobs and tasks to them, it is time to configure when the release to a specific stage should be triggered. The steps for this can be seen in the following screenshot:

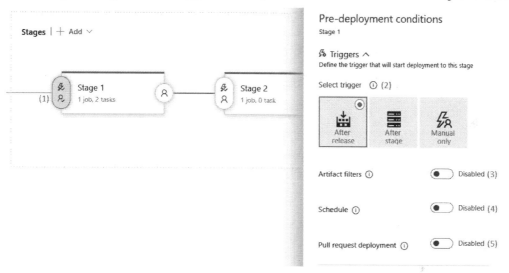

Figure 6.5 – Post-deployment configuration

Note that the following steps need to be carried out for every stage individually:

1. To trigger a release to a specific stage, click on the button with a lightning bolt and a person icon, to the left of the square that denotes the stage.

2. The first thing to configure here is when a release should propagate to this stage. This can be either upon the availability of the release, after completing another stage, or only upon manual request. The choice you make here will also be reflected in the visual representation of the pipeline.

3. Separate from the trigger, it is possible to define one or more filters that limit which artifacts will trigger a deployment to the stage. There can be one or more include or exclude branch filters for every artifact.

4. It is also possible to redeploy on a fixed schedule.

5. Finally, if the creation of a new release is specified for builds that were started from a pull request, the release can also be allowed to propagate to the current stage using the **Pull request deployment** slider.

Next to these triggers, approvers and gates can be added so that you can configure how to handle deployment queue settings. These settings can be accessed from the tabs below the section for **Triggers**, as shown in the following screenshot:

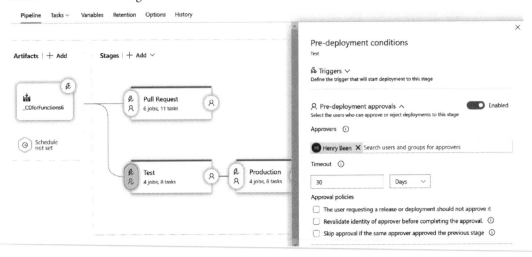

Figure 6.6 – Pre-deployment conditions

Once the trigger condition has been configured, the next section is about approvers. Here, groups or users are specified. They must give their approval before release to this stage can begin. Multiple people can be added, and if so, an order can be defined that they have to approve, or it can be specified that a single approval is enough. By scrolling down, you will find the following options:

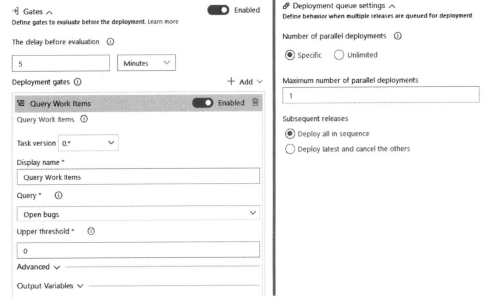

Figure 6.7 – Deployment gates

The second tab (on the left) allows you to add one or more gates. Gates are automated checks that have to succeed before the release can continue. Currently, this shows the configuration details for configuring a work item query and a threshold on the number of results – for example, to ensure that there are no open bugs before a release proceeds. There are also gates available that can call in Azure Monitor, Azure Functions, or a RESTful API. This set of gates can be extended using the Azure DevOps extension mechanisms. Some of these extensions also integrate with common change management systems.

The final section (on the right) allows you to configure how to handle a situation where different versions of the release are ready for deployment to the same stage. Here, it is possible to specify how many releases can run in parallel. If there are even more releases coming in, you can queue them up and deploy them one after the other, or only deploy the latest.

Working with deployment groups

Another topic that you might run into at some point is deploying an application to on-premises servers or servers that are behind a firewall. You may also come across situations where it is necessary to run scripts on all of the machines hosting the application or situations where the target environment does not supply a mechanism for deploying applications.

The approach to performing releases, which was shown in the *Working with Azure DevOps releases* section of this chapter, relies on being able to connect to the target machines or services that will host the application. We call these **push-based deployments**, and this is not always possible.

When deploying to target machines that cannot be connected to, another approach needs to be taken. This approach is called **agent-based deployment**. In an agent-based deployment, an Azure DevOps agent is installed on every machine that the application will be installed on. Next, these agents must be grouped into deployment groups. Once this is done, a **deployment group job** can be added to the release.

This is very similar to an agent's job, except for one thing. In an agent job, the tasks in the job will run on **one of the agents** against the target machine. In a deployment group job, all of the tasks will run on all of the agents in the release group on the target machines. This difference between both approaches can be seen in the following diagram:

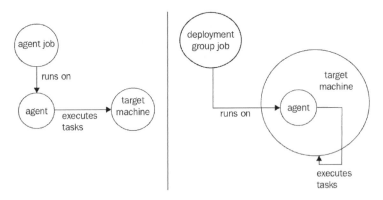

Figure 6.8 – Jobs are run on an agent

When using this approach, it is necessary to have agents on the machines that the application needs to be deployed to. These agents listen to Azure DevOps, and whenever a new release is requested, they retrieve the work and execute it on the local machine.

Managing deployment groups

Before you can add a deployment group job to a release pipeline, you need to create a deployment group. To do so, perform the following steps:

1. Navigate to the **Pipelines** menu.

2. Open the **Deployment groups** menu.

3. Click on **New** to add a new deployment group.

4. Enter a deployment group name and description and click **Create**.

Once the new deployment group has been created, a script will appear on the right, as shown in the following screenshot:

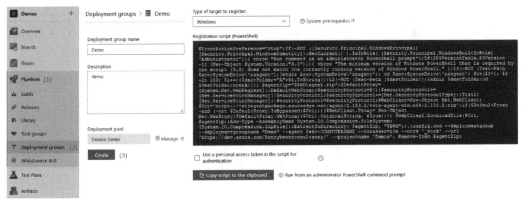

Figure 6.9 – Creating a new deployment group

Executing this script on the target machine will install the agent and automatically register that machine as part of the newly created deployment group.

If an application must be deployed to three stages (test, acceptance, and production) using deployment groups, there will need to be three separate deployment groups, one for each environment.

Creating a release pipeline with a deployment group

After creating the necessary deployment group(s), those can be used in releases from the **Tasks** view, as shown in the following screenshot:

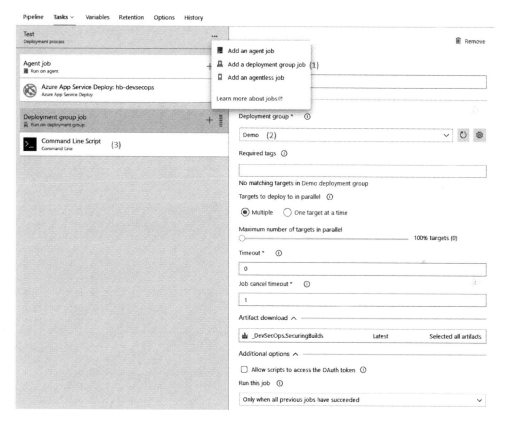

Figure 6.10 – Specifying the deployment group in the pipeline

To do this, perform the following steps:

1. Add a new deployment group to the pipeline.

2. Specify which deployment group the job should run on by picking it from the drop-down menu.

3. Add one or more tasks to execute the job. The functionality of the user interface is the same as that for regular agent jobs.

Besides the different approaches to executing on all agents in a group instead of one, deployment group jobs behave the same as regular agent jobs.

Writing multi-stage YAML pipelines

In addition to the visual designer for release definitions, it is also possible to implement continuous deployment using YAML pipelines. When doing so, it is still recommended to differentiate between the build (**Continuous Integration (CI)**) and release (**Continuous Deployment (CD)**) phases of a pipeline. The concept of stages is used to make this possible. A YAML pipeline can be divided into one or more stages. A stage can represent an environment such as test, acceptance, or production, but this isn't always true. If, in an application scenario, it makes sense to add extra stages such as pre-production or staging, you can include additional stages as applicable. It is good practice to publish **pipeline artifacts** in earlier stages and to consume or **download artifacts** in later stages.

Multi-stage YAML pipelines are the new default for creating pipelines in Azure DevOps. Since working with YAML pipelines can have a steeper learning curve than working with classic releases, you may find it easier to work with classic releases first and switch to YAML pipelines later. Just like with builds, many of the concepts of classic releases translate to multi-stage YAML pipelines as well.

Adding stages to YAML pipelines

If no stages are defined in a YAML pipeline, there is always one implicit stage that holds all the jobs. To convert a pipeline into a multi-stage pipeline, you need to add the `stages` keyword and a list of stages, as shown in the following code:

```
stages:
  - stage: stage1
    displayName: My first stage
    jobs:
    - job: job1
      steps:
      - task: DotNetCoreCLI@2
        displayName: 'dotnet build'
        inputs:
        projects: '**/*.csproj'

  - stage: stage2
    jobs:
  ...
```

The preceding syntax shows that a list of stages is defined at the top of the YAML file. Each stage starts by defining a name. This name can be used later so that you can refer to this stage.

While jobs (unless otherwise specified) run in parallel by default, stages always run sequentially by default. But just like jobs, stages accept the `dependsOn` and `condition` keywords to change the ordering and parallelism, and (potentially) to skip stages.

Downloading artifacts

A common use of multi-stage pipelines is to separate the build stage and the deployment stage. To make this possible, the build stage often publishes one or more pipeline artifacts. This was discussed in *Chapter 5, Moving to Continuous Integration*.

All the artifacts that were published in a previous stage of the current pipeline can be downloaded using a `download` task:

```
steps:
  - download: current
    artifact: artifactName
```

It is also possible to download artifacts from another pipeline. To do this, the `current` constant has to be replaced with the name of that pipeline. Pipeline artifacts are downloaded to the `$(Pipeline.Workspace)` directory.

> **Tip**
>
> If you want more fine-grained control over downloading pipeline artifacts – for example, over the version of the artifact to use or the location to download the artifact to – you can also use the **Download Pipeline Artifacts** tasks, which are documented at `https://docs.microsoft.com/bs-cyrl-ba/azure/devops/pipelines/tasks/utility/download-pipeline-artifact?view=azure-devops`.

Publishing and downloading artifacts within a pipeline ensures that code that is built in the first stage is also the code that is deployed in the second stage – even if the stages run days apart. In essence, each pipeline run builds a local stage of all the artifacts associated with that specific run.

Approvals

In a multi-stage YAML pipeline, it is not possible to define approvers as compared to what was possible when creating a classic release pipeline. The reason for this is that the pipeline – *the build and deployment process* – is viewed as code. Code is worked on by developers and operators only. Approvals are worked on by, for example, product owners. However, this does not mean that it is impossible to implement approval flows for the progression of a pipeline to the next stage.

To control whether a pipeline is allowed to proceed to a certain stage, the concept of environments needs to be introduced. An environment is defined when we give it a name and a description. One or more approvers can be attached to these environments. Once this is done, jobs can be configured to target such an environment. If there is at least one job in a stage that targets an environment, then that environment is said to be used by the stage. If an approval has been configured on that environment, the deployment to that stage will not continue until the approver has given permission.

To start working with environments, you'll need to access the list of environments. This list can be found in the **Pipelines** menu, as shown in the following screenshot:

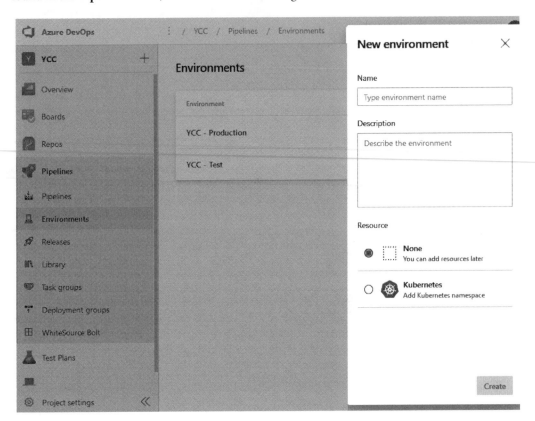

Figure 6.11 – Adding a new environment

To add a new environment, perform the following steps:

1.   Open the **Pipelines** menu and choose **Environments**.

2.   Select **New environment** from the top right.

3.   Specify a name and description.

4.   Click **Create**.

It is possible to associate resources with an environment. Resources that are coupled with an environment can be used in a pipeline if, and only if, that pipeline is also targeting that environment. To protect the resources of an environment, the owner of that environment can add one or more approvers. An example of a configured approver can be seen in the following screenshot:

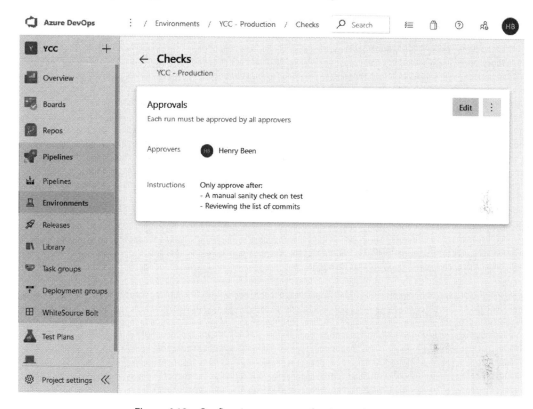

Figure 6.12 – Configuring approvers for the environment

Approvers can be added to an environment as follows:

1. Navigate to the **Environments** overview pane.
2. Open an environment by clicking on it.
3. Click the top-right menu marked with the three dots and choose **Approvals and Checks**.
4. Click the **Create** button.
5. Pick a user or group from the list and add extra instructions if needed.
6. Click the **Create** button again.

Approvals make it possible for you to control the progression of a pipeline to the next stage if that pipeline targets the correct environment. Targeting an environment is done by specifying a specific type of job – the deployment job. The following YAML shows how to do this:

```
jobs:
 - deployment: deploymentJobName
   displayName: Friendly name
   strategy:
   runOnce:
     deploy:
       steps:
         ...
```

Deployment jobs do not directly contain the steps to execute as an agent job does. Instead, they first must specify an execution strategy for the tasks outlined under the `steps` keyword. At the time of writing, the only strategy supported is `runOnce`. Other strategies are expected to be announced in the future.

At the time of writing, only Kubernetes clusters are supported as environment resources, but more types of resources have been announced for the future.

Now that we know about the technical means for creating release definitions and writing multi-stage YAML pipelines, it is time to look at the different strategies we can use to apply this in practice. These CD strategies are designed to minimize the risk of deploying new versions of an application automatically.

Implementing CD strategies

Before we deploy an application continuously, it is important to think about the strategy we should use. Just doing deployment after deployment may have more risks associated with it than a business is willing to accept. It is important to think about how to deal with issues that might occur during or after deploying a new version of your application.

There are a few deployment strategies that can be applied to reduce the risks that might come with deployments, all of which will be covered in this section. Please note that it is possible to combine one or more of the following patterns. For example, it is perfectly possible to use a blue-green strategy for every ring in a ring-based deployment. Also, all deployment strategies can be combined with the use of feature flags.

Blue-green deployments

Blue-green deployments is a technique where a new version of an application never gets deployed to the production servers directly. Instead, it gets deployed to another set of servers first. Once this has been done successfully, users are directed to the new deployment.

Let's assume that an application runs on a total of three hosts by default. A typical setup for blue-green deployment would be two sets of three hosts – the blue group and the green group. In front of these two sets, there is a reverse proxy that functions as a load balancer and redirects the incoming requests to the blue group. The following diagram shows how this works:

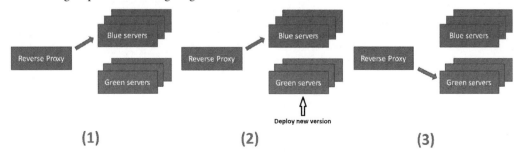

Figure 6.13 – Blue-green deployments

To deploy a new version of the application in this situation, it needs to be deployed to the green group of servers. Since these servers are not receiving any traffic from end users, this way of upgrading the servers has no impact on them at all.

After the deployment, the new deployment can be verified to ensure that it was successful and that the application is running correctly. After this verification, the load balancer is reconfigured to redirect traffic to the green group. Now, the new version of the application is served.

Should there suddenly be any unexpected issues, it is very easy to switch back to the previous deployment by reconfiguring the load balancer back to the blue group. If the deployment is successful and there are no issues, it is possible to start the deployment of the next version by going through the same procedure, but now with the roles of the green and the blue groups switched.

Immutable servers

A variation of the blue-green deployment pattern is immutable servers. With immutable servers, there is no going back and forth between two groups of servers. Instead, the group of servers that is serving the old version of the application is completely disregarded or removed. Often, this is done after a grace period.

The result of this is that there will still be means to roll back to a previous version – almost instantaneously if the old servers are kept around for a while. The other benefit is that there is now a guarantee that no remains from a previous deployment are being carried over into the newer deployments. Using immutable servers, the change of active servers over time might look as follows:

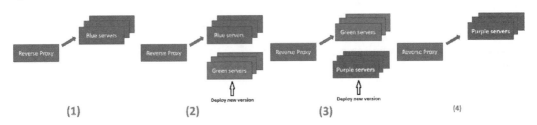

Figure 6.14 – Immutable server deployments

Of course, an approach like this is only feasible when using technologies such as containers or virtual machines. Nobody would expect anyone to disregard physical servers after every redeployment.

Progressive exposure

Progressive exposure is a deployment strategy in which the number of users that have access to a new deployment or a new feature is slowly increased over time. The goal of this strategy is to limit the number of users that are experiencing issues when a faulty release of a feature is made available.

We can also look at this more positively and in line with the CD way of thinking: exposing a new feature to only a few users at first and increasing that number over time allows us to increase the amount of trust in a new version or feature of an application before exposing it to all users.

Canary deployments

The first strategy for progressive exposure is to use canary deployments. In a canary deployment, not all users are routed to the new version immediately – only a limited percentage of the users get access to that version. These users are the canaries and they are monitored very closely. If they experience any issues or if degradation in performance of a service is observed, the new deployment is quickly rolled back.

A typical approach to realizing canary deployments is to use them in combination with blue-green deployments. The difference is that instead of switching all users over at the same time, only a small percentage is moved over to the new version at the start, and then the number of users that are moved over is gradually increased over time. This might look something similar to the following:

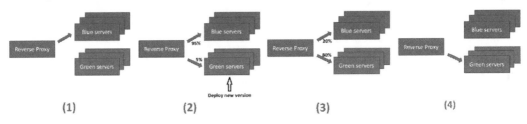

Figure 6.15 – Canary deployments

If a deployment is rolled back because errors have been observed, this is not a fun experience for users. To prevent the same small group of users from running into issues repeatedly, it might be beneficial to select a different group of canary users afterward.

Ring-based deployments

In a ring-based environment, there is not just one production environment – there are multiple. Each production environment serves only a portion of the users. It differs from a canary deployment in that, instead of just two environments, there can be as many as needed. Also, every new version goes to all the rings, one after the other.

So, instead of redirecting the users, in a ring-based environment, the new version propagates to the servers used by those users. The new version just keeps propagating from one ring to the next, until they are all done:

Figure 6.16 – Ring-based deployments

Ring-based deployment architectures are especially suitable for products that are accessed by customers from all around the world. The different rings can be positioned around the world, thus combining the deployment benefits with the added benefit of reduced latency for users.

Blue-green versus canary deployments

While both approaches are useful in minimizing the impact on your production workloads, there are some subtle variations that must be remembered when choosing one over the other:

- You can opt for blue-green deployment only when your production environment has an identical yet redundant secondary instance. Basically, you can upgrade the secondary instance first, and then route the traffic to it. Once satisfied with its working, you can continue with the deployment on your primary instance. This type of setup is similar to what is used during a disaster recovery situation.

- If you do not have an extra second instance but are able to partition your primary instance in a way that a subset of the user traffic can be routed to separate physical compute units, you can benefit from using the canary deployment strategy. Canary provides a relatively easier way to activate or deactivate features based on certain criteria to a subset of users of the application. Canary deployment is preferred for right-shift testing strategies, wherein the performance and usability of a new feature can be initially verified with a limited load, before rolling it out with the entire user base of the application.

In general, both methods require some initial planning and investment to straighten out the processes of deployment.

Feature flags

The third form of progressive deployment can be achieved using feature flags, also called feature toggles. Whereas canary deployments and ring-based deployments rely on slowly exposing new binaries to an increasing number of users, feature flags are used to slowly expose new features to an increasing number of users. This can be achieved even if they are all sending requests to the same server. Feature flags are generally used to mitigate the risk of releasing new features when upgrading to a new version of the application binaries that contain them. These flags act like a toggle switch whereby providing the ability to system administrators to enable or disable specific features at runtime.

The best example of a feature flag is showing or hiding a button that gives users access to a new feature. Application settings, a database, or an external service are used to keep track of which feature has been enabled for which user. Depending on that setting, the feature is shown or hidden. Examples of such external services include LaunchDarkly, split.io, and Prefab.Cloud.

Microsoft Azure also offers a resource named Azure App Configuration that can be used for centrally managing your feature flags and other application settings. You can read more about it here: `https://docs.microsoft.com/en-us/azure/azure-app-configuration/overview`.

Other feature flags might toggle bug fixes or performance improvements on or off. This can help to gradually expose these enhancements or fixes to ensure there are no issues. There should be a process in place when introducing feature toggles within the code base. It adds complexity, as the feature must support on-off toggles without having any impact to end users. This process should not only describe adding feature toggles but also how to remove them as soon as possible. An example of such a process can be as follows.

A new feature flag is introduced by a developer as soon as the business needs to release the feature independently of the deployments that were made by the development team, or for a change that the development team qualifies as high-risk and wants to be able to pull back at any time without redeploying it. Introducing a feature flag means a new database entry or a declaration of a new setting is applied in the application settings.

After introducing the feature toggle, the new feature or change is developed and tested. This means that there are one or more `if` statements in the code base that execute different code paths, depending on the state of the feature flag. At this point, the application must maintain two code execution paths until they remove the feature flag again. It is a good practice to separate these two code paths as much as possible using existing engineering practices, such as dependency injection.

While the code is continuously being shipped to users, the feature is not enabled for anyone. Only when the development team is fully satisfied with the change or the product owner feels the time is right for releasing a new feature is the feature flag turned on.

It is important not to stop here. After turning the feature flag on, it should actively be determined whether the feature or change is working properly, and if it is, the feature flag should be removed as soon as possible. This way, the time the two code paths need to be maintained for is as short as possible.

Also, note that besides maintaining an increased number of execution paths, there is now a larger number of paths to test. The impact of this consequence quickly grows if dependencies or exclusions between feature flags are introduced. Feature flags that can only be turned on or off, depending on the state of another feature flag, can be costly, and it is recommended to avoid this.

If implemented properly and removed as soon as possible, the added cost of feature flags is often worth it. As with every engineering practice, start small and evaluate what works in the given context, before adapting the practice at scale.

Roll back or fail forward

No matter which strategy is being used, it is necessary to think about the ability to roll back one or more versions and how long that will take. For example, blue-green deployments give us the ability to go back one version almost instantaneously, if a new version has not been deployed to the non-active servers yet. On the other hand, performing a rollback in a ring-based deployment will require a full redeployment of the previous version, which will probably take longer and comes with all the risks of deployment. This may even need to be done on multiple rings, making it more challenging.

Another approach that can be adopted is that of failing forward. When adopting this approach, it is stated that there will never be a rollback to a previous version. Instead, when any issue is encountered, this will be addressed by redeploying a new version with the fix of that issue in it. This strategy is gaining traction lately since it saves time, as we don't have to prepare, test, and practice rollbacks. However, there can be risks involved with this process:

- There is no guarantee that the fix will be correct. The issue might not be resolved by the newly deployed version or, even worse, the new version might result in transitioning from one issue to another.
- Working out a detailed root cause of any issue takes time, just like writing a fix does. The consequence of this might be that the fix might take longer than a rollback would have taken.

No matter which approach is taken, consider the consequences and prepare for them.

So far, we have mainly focused on web-based applications. In the next section, we will shift our attention to mobile applications.

Deploying mobile applications

One type of application that needs a special approach to deployment is a mobile application. These applications are often not downloaded and installed by end users directly and are mostly consumed via an app store on their mobile device.

Visual Studio App Center is a Microsoft offering that can be used for distributing (deploying) mobile applications to end users via app stores, but also via private distribution lists.

You can discover more about App Center here: `https://visualstudio.microsoft.com/app-center/`.

After logging into App Center, you will be taken to the following screen:

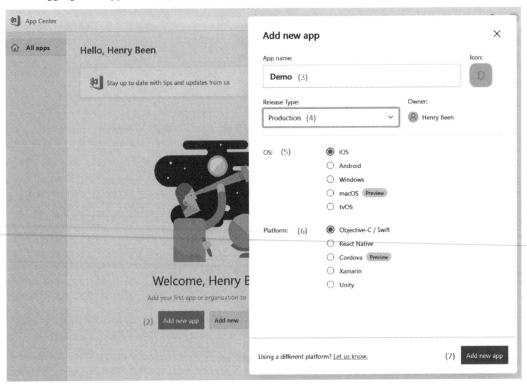

Figure 6.17 – Adding a new app

Here, you can create a new app definition. An app definition should be created for every target operating system of an application. If the same application is going to be deployed to both Android and iOS, at least two apps have to be created.

Creating an app is done by performing the following steps:

1. Log in to App Center.

2. Click the blue **Add new app** button. If there are no existing apps, this button will be in the center of the screen; otherwise, it will be at the top right (hidden under the popup shown in the preceding screenshot).

3. Enter the name of the app.

4. Select the type of release.

5. Select the operating system.

6. Select the platform to use.

7. Click **Add new app** to create the app.

Once an app has been created, it can be connected to the correct app store and distribution groups can be created.

Connecting to the app store

The app store is the main mechanism for distributing an application for all mobile platforms. Once a build is delivered to an app store, users can install and use the application. The current list of connections to app stores can be opened using the **Stores** tab on the left-hand side of **App Center**. From this list, an individual store connection can be opened, which will take us to a screen similar to the one shown in the following screenshot:

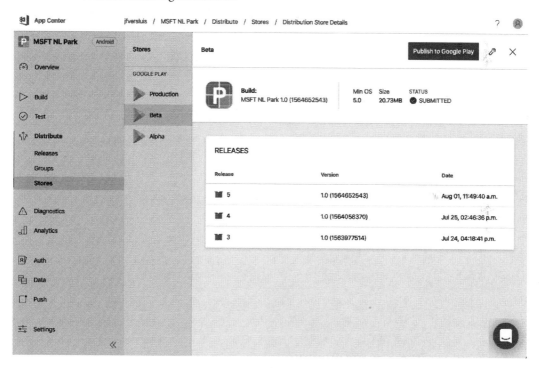

Figure 6.18 – An app store within Visual Studio App Center

This view shows a list of all the versions of the application that have been published to the connected store account. This is also where a new version of the application can be selected for publication to the store. This is done using the blue **Publish to Google Play** button at the top. This will open a popup where you can select the correct release. You only have to confirm this once to publish this version.

New connections to the store can be created by navigating back to the list of all store connections and clicking the **Add** button. This will open a wizard where two pieces of information have to be entered:

- **The type of store connection**: This list is limited to the stores that are available to apps of the type that was chosen when creating the app definition. For example, for iOS, this is limited to the Apple App Store and the Intune Company Portal.

- **Connection details**: Often, they include the means of authentication between App Center and the app store.

Once the new connection has been created, it can be found on the list shown previously and can be used to distribute the app.

Another means of distribution is using distribution groups, which we'll introduce in the next section.

Using distribution groups

Distribution groups are used to create named lists of one or more users, often testers or alpha users, that install an application through an invitation, rather than via the app store. Distribution groups can be found in the left-hand menu, under **Groups**:

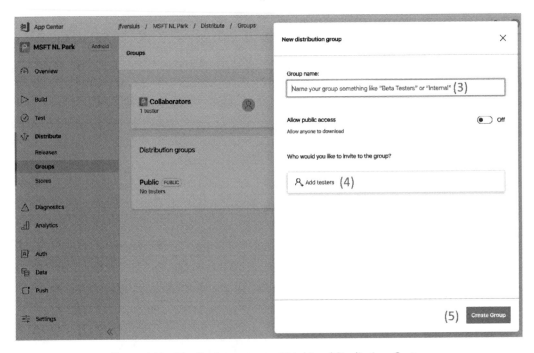

Figure 6.19 – Distribution groups within Visual Studio App Center

Here, a new group can be added, as follows:

1. Navigate to **Distribution groups** using the menu on the left.

2. Click the blue button labeled with a plus (+) sign (hidden under the popup in the preceding screenshot).

3. Choose a name for the group.

4. Add one or more members.

5. Save the new group.

Once a distribution group has been created, it can be used for publishing releases, which we will discuss in the next section.

Publishing an app

To publish the first or a new version of an app, it has to be shared with App Center. This can be done using the **Releases** tab on the left-hand side. When opening up the releases, the following view, detailing all the current releases, will appear. From here, any release can be selected so that you can view the details of it:

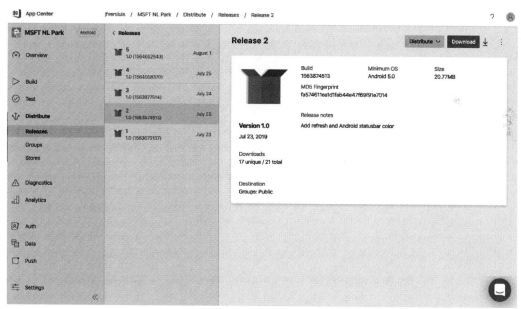

Figure 6.20 – Viewing the releases of an app'

In this view, a list of the most recent releases is shown in the middle column. After selecting an individual release, the details of that version will be shown. This includes its formal version, the store(s) and/or distribution group(s) it has been shared with, and other details.

From here, it is possible to distribute this specific version to a store connection or distribution group directly using the **Distribute** bottom at the top right.

From here, a new release can also be created by uploading a new build of the app. To do this, follow these steps:

1. Click on the **New release** button, which is available from the list of all releases (it might be necessary to close the details of a specific release first). This will open the following view:

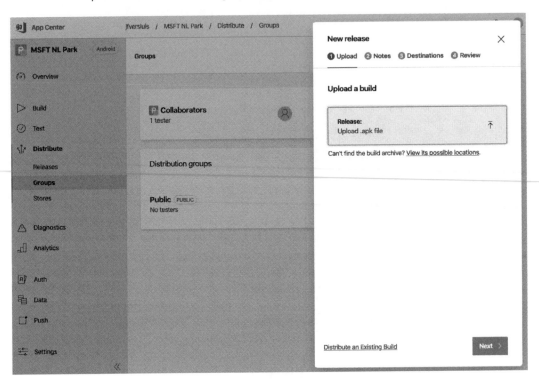

Figure 6.21 – Uploading a new build

2. A new wizard will open, where a build needs to be uploaded. Depending on the type of app, the correct type of file will be requested. After uploading the binaries, click **Next**.

3. Now, the release notes have to be filled in. After detailing the changes in this release, click **Next** again.

4. Now, it is time to specify where this new build should be distributed. At least one destination – either a distribution group or a store – has to be selected. After selecting one or more destinations, click **Next** again.

5. The final wizard tab will show the selections you've made so far. Check the details and click **Distribute** to complete the creation of a new version and its initial distribution.

Often, the same version or release needs to be distributed to other groups or stores over time as well. It is not necessary (nor useful) to create a new release every time. Instead, going to the **Detail** pages of the new destination store connection or distribution group allows you to publish an existing release to that destination as well.

As an alternative to using App Center to perform release management this way, it is also possible to use Azure Pipelines for release management.

App Center via Azure Pipelines

App Center can also be integrated with Azure Pipelines. If teams are familiar with the release process in Azure Pipelines, it can be sensible to build the app in Azure Pipelines and only use App Center for deployment to stores and distribution groups.

To make this possible, there are tasks available in Azure Pipelines that allow you to upload a release and trigger the deployment of a release to a store or distribution group. That way, release management can be done in Azure Pipelines while the App Center-specific capabilities are still leveraged where applicable.

This section is focused on mobile applications specifically, while the next section will apply to all types of releases. When creating releases is automated and new versions follow each other quickly, it is useful to start automating the creation and publication of release notes as well. This will be discussed in the next section.

Automating release notes

After automating the build, releasing an application, and working on increasing the flow of value to end users, many developers find that it becomes harder and harder to keep documentation and release notes up to date. As the amount of releases increases, this becomes more and more work, and eventually, the team will fall behind or even give up completely.

To combat this, it is possible to automate the creation and publication of release notes. One way to do this is by using the *Azure DevOps Release Notes Generator*. Refer this for more details: `https://docs.microsoft.com/en-us/samples/azure-samples/azure-devops-release-notes/azure-devops-release-notes-generator/`.

The generator is an Azure Functions application that is available on GitHub. To use the Release Notes Generator, the following needs to be done:

1. Download or clone the function code from GitHub at this link: `https://github.com/Azure-Samples/azure-devops-release-notes`.
2. Create an Azure App Service Plan, function app, and storage account in Azure.
3. Create a new Blob Container in the storage account called `releases`.

4.   Compile the function code and deploy it to an Azure App Service.

5.   Create a new Azure DevOps WebHook to call the deployed function whenever a new release is created. (Please refer to the Wiki documentation on GitHub for more detailed instructions.)

After setting this up, the generator will run whenever a new release is created. It will then do the following:

1.   Query the created release for its name, all associated work items, and all the commits that are new since the previous release

2.   Generate a Markdown file containing all of this information

3.   Upload that file to the blob container – that is, `releases`

Of course, the Azure DevOps Release Notes Generator is just one example of automating tasks around releases, and there are other alternatives available as well. Also, many companies create tailored, in-house automation scripts for updating and publishing documentation and other tasks.

Other tools

In addition to Azure DevOps and App Center, there are other tools that can be used for deploying and releasing software. GitLab CI/CD and Jenkins, which were discussed in the previous chapter for executing builds, can also be used for releases. Besides those, Octopus Deploy is also a commonly used tool that integrates well with Azure DevOps.

Octopus Deploy

Octopus Deploy is a deployment automation tool that is based on the concept of running a series of tasks on one or more target machines.

Octopus reaches these machines through a tentacle (an agent) that is installed on these machines. In Octopus Deploy, it is possible to define applications and environments and assign one or more machines to each of those. To do deployments, execution steps can be defined in a graphical editor, comparable to the visual release editor of Azure DevOps.

One of the main differences is that these steps are not defined per environment, only once per pipeline. Next, it is possible to specify which environments each task should run on. This way, it is easier to see where the deployment to different environments varies.

There is an integration between Azure DevOps and Octopus Deploy available, in the form of a build and release task. Using this integration, you can start a deployment using Octopus Deploy from an Azure DevOps build or release pipeline.

Summary

In this chapter, you learned about continuous deployment and how you can implement them using Azure DevOps. In addition to the visual release editor, you also learned about multi-stage YAML pipelines, which you can use for releasing your software to multiple stages, all of the way to production. Next, we discussed a series of strategies that you can use for releasing. You now know about blue-green deployments, using immutable servers, and different strategies for progressive exposure. You also learned how to choose between making sure you have rollback capabilities and accepting a fail-forward strategy.

Then, you learned about automating release notes and documentation and how you can generate those automatically as part of your pipeline. After that, you learned about continuous deployment for mobile applications and how that differs from the delivery of web applications. Finally, you learned about the existence of Octopus Deploy, how it operates, and how it integrates with Azure DevOps.

In the next chapter, you will learn about topic dependency management using Azure Artifacts. This can be used to host your own NuGet packages or to host build artifacts when you are using other products for building or releasing your application, in combination with Azure Pipelines.

Questions

As we conclude this chapter, here is a list of questions for you to test your knowledge of this chapter's material. You will find the answers in the *Assessments* section of the *Appendix*:

1. True or false: an Azure DevOps Classic release is always triggered by the availability of a new version of an artifact.

2. Which of the following platforms can App Center publish apps to? (You can choose more than one.)

   A. Google Play Store

   B. Apple App Store

   C. Microsoft Intune

3. Which of the following techniques use progressive exposure for minimizing the risks of deploying a new version? (You can choose more than one.)

   A. Feature toggles

   B. Ring-based deployments

   C. Canary deployments

4. True or false: deployment groups can be used for deploying software to on-premises servers when an Azure Pipelines agent is installed on the machine that will be running the software.

5. What is the advantage of integrating App Center with Azure Pipelines if you have an Azure Pipelines release definition triggering actions in App Center?

Exercises

- **Prerequisites**: The exercises in this chapter have a dependency on *Chapter 8, Implement Infrastructure and Configuration as Code*. Please complete the exercises mentioned in that chapter so that you have provisioned the necessary resources in Azure to continue with the build deployment-related pipeline creation.

- **Dependency**: Please ensure that a **Service connections** record has been created for the PacktBookLibrary project. This will be used as a service account for deploying resources and builds to Azure:

  - Navigate to **Project Settings | Service connections** (under **Pipelines**) and then click on the **New Service Connection** button.

  - Within the **New service connection** dialog, ensure that the **Azure Resource Manager** option is selected and then, in the next step, that **Service Principal (automatic)** is selected.

  - Keep scope as **Subscription** and specify the Service connection name as **Azure Service Connection**.

  - Under **Security**, check the option to grant access to all pipelines.

- Create **Environments** and define approvals:

  - Navigate to **Pipelines | Environments**, and create three environment records as DEV, TST, and PRD. Don't add any resources for now:

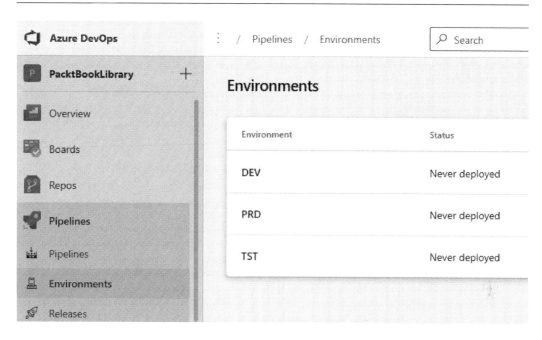

Figure 6.22 – Environments for deployment

- For each environment entry, configure the approvers for it. The list of approvers should be the members who can approve any activity in their respective owned environment:

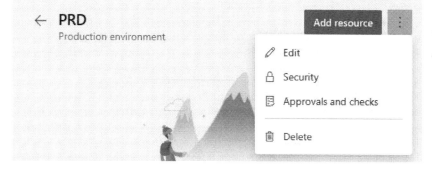

Figure 6.23 – Configuring environment settings

- Create **Variable groups** and specify values for the variables:

  - Navigate to **Pipelines | Library | Add Variable group**. Add the following set of variables for three different variable groups (one per environment):

    - `Environment`: Refers to the name of the environment

    - `azureSubscription`: Refers to the service connection name to be used

- Webappname: Refers to the Azure App Service resource name

- Resorucegroup: Refers to the resource group in which the App Service resource has been provisioned

- Slotname: Refers to the slot of the App Service that the build has to be deployed to

- You should now see three different variable groups:

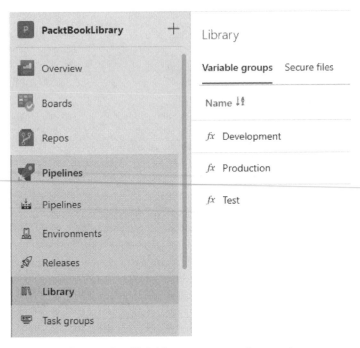

Figure 6.24 – Variable groups per environment

- Open your code repository for the PacktBookLibrary repository and create a subfolder named deploy in the pipelines directory:

  - Create a file named template.yaml. Insert code as per the file present in this directory: https://github.com/PacktPublishing/Designing-and-Implementing-Microsoft-DevOps-Solutions-AZ-400-Exam-Guide

- Place another file named template.yaml in the build subdirectory:

  - Insert code as per the file present in this directory: https://github.com/PacktPublishing/Designing-and-Implementing-Microsoft-DevOps-Solutions-AZ-400-Exam-Guide

- In the pipelines directory, create a file named main-cd-pipeline.yaml. Insert code as per the file present in this directory: https://github.com/PacktPublishing/Designing-and-Implementing-Microsoft-DevOps-Solutions-AZ-400-Exam-Guide

- Create a CD pipeline to provision the latest build to three different environments:

  - Click on **Pipelines | New Pipeline**, and then select the repository, set the branch as main, set the path as the relative path to main-cd-pipeline.yaml, and then save the pipeline under the name main-cd-pipeline.

- Grant permissions to the pipelines to all the variable groups. You should see the following two pipelines now:

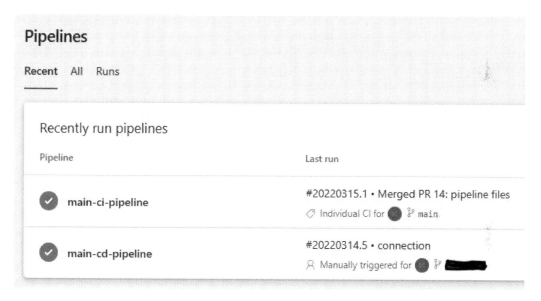

Figure 6.25 – Viewing the pipeline run statuses

- Run main-cd-pipeline and verify whether the build deployment is succeeding or not.

Further reading

- More information on using stages in YAML pipelines can be found at https://docs.microsoft.com/en-us/azure/devops/pipelines/process/stages.

- More information on the idea of immutable servers can be found at https://martinfowler.com/bliki/ImmutableServer.html.

- More information about LaunchDarkly can be found at `https://launchdarkly.com/`.

- More details about the build and release extension for integration with Octopus Deploy can be found at `https://marketplace.visualstudio.com/items?itemName=octopusdeploy.octopus-deploy-build-release-tasks`.

- The Azure DevOps Release Notes Generator can be found at `https://docs.microsoft.com/en-us/samples/azure-samples/azure-devops-release-notes/azure-devops-release-notes-generator/`.

- Some Microsoft hands-on labs for practicing the topics we covered in this chapter can be found at the following links:

  - `https://docs.microsoft.com/en-us/learn/modules/create-multi-stage-pipeline/index`

  - `https://docs.microsoft.com/en-us/learn/modules/create-release-pipeline/index` and `https://docs.microsoft.com/en-us/learn/modules/manage-release-cadence/index`

Part 3 – Expanding Your DevOps Pipeline

In this part, you will learn about other DevOps practices that build upon the strong foundation of **Continuous Integration (CI)/Continuous Delivery (CD)** discussed earlier in *Part 2 , Getting to Continuous Delivery*. You will learn about how to establish a robust **Application Lifecycle Management (ALM)** process to manage your infrastructure in the cloud, as well as streamlined upgrades and migration of your backend databases without incurring any loss of information.

We will also look at continuous testing practices to understand more about the concept of "shift-left quality." This involves embedding quality concerns in our pipelines from the start and continuously verifying them, resulting in the faster delivery of a secure and high-quality product.

This part of the book comprises the following chapters:

- *Chapter 7, Dependency Management*
- *Chapter 8, Implement Infrastructure and Configuration as Code*
- *Chapter 9, Dealing with Databases in DevOps Scenarios*
- *Chapter 10, Integrating Continuous Testing*
- *Chapter 11, Managing Security and Compliance*

7

Dependency Management

In part one of this book, you learned how to continuously deploy your application. In modern enterprise software development, applications are developed by cross-functional teams and involve complex solutions and projects. Complex solutions with hundreds of modules and functions have a greater probability of code duplication – that is, identical implementation for the same functionality within projects. Duplicated code is one of the cardinal sins of programming. You can solve problems by copying and pasting, but it usually creates maintenance nightmares later. **Don't Repeat Yourself (DRY)** is a basic principle of software development aimed at reducing the repetition of information.

For a small or a single project, you may be able to handle dependencies on your own, but for complex solutions, a team will descend into **dependency hell**. One approach to solve this is by introducing package management. Developers need to identify the components to reuse within internal projects or from open source. Reusing libraries will increase the development velocity and the quality of the solution. Instead of copying and pasting code from one project to another, you can create a shared library using it. In this chapter, you will learn how to identify shared components and how to make them reusable using Azure Artifacts. In addition to this, you will learn how you can use Azure Artifacts for storing pipeline artifacts when working in a heterogeneous architecture. Here, you will also work with other **Continuous Integration (CI)/Continuous Deployment (CD)** tools than just Azure DevOps. To do so, you will learn how to use Azure Artifacts for Universal Packages.

The following topics will be covered in this chapter:

- Identifying shared components
- Creating a feed for publishing packages
- Consuming packages
- Working with Universal Packages
- Exploring other tools

Technical requirements

To experiment with the topics mentioned in this chapter, an Azure DevOps organization is required.

Identifying shared components

Adopting DevOps practices, such as CI/CD, can greatly reduce the amount of time you have to spend on building and testing your applications. Besides building your applications, there are also many other concerns that you can address in your pipelines.

When you start adding more and more tasks to your pipelines, you might run into a situation in which a single execution of your pipeline starts taking too long. In order to combat this, you might be interested in splitting your solution up into smaller builds and maybe even repositories. Splitting solutions into smaller builds is not viable with monolithic applications, since it would break the build process. Microservice applications or solutions, which have components decoupled into separate projects, could adopt this approach to split the build process. To do this, you could build parts of that application in isolation and then use the results of these builds in your main application as ready-built components.

Componentization is a process to structure your projects into reusable components that application developers independently write and deploy.

With source componentization, you split your solution into parts to use as shared projects. Imagine that you have two solutions that work closely together: one is a REST API and the other is a client package that you ship to your customers to work with that API. It is likely that in their source code, these two solutions share at least one project comprising common reusable objects, such as data models, that will serve as data contracts to exchange data between the two solutions. Here, you can also leverage package componentization and make a third solution with only the shared project, which you could then use as a package in your other solutions. Packages are rarely functional as a standalone unit.

Alternatively, what if you work in a team that is responsible for maintaining a whole series of solutions, and you find that you have complete namespaces that are copied and pasted between these solutions? It is not a desirable situation and one that probably comes with a lot of issues. What if you could write all of this code just once, build it, package it, and then reuse it in all these solutions? To summarize, three reasons for starting to work with packages and artifact feeds are as follows:

- Extracting shared components into packages
- Building packages that are used by other teams
- Reducing build and CI times by splitting a larger solution into parts

> **Tip**
> The three main aspects of dependency management are standardization, package formats and sources, and versioning.

In the remainder of this chapter, you will learn techniques for doing this by building packages out of (parts of) your application code, hosting them in a centralized location, and reusing them in one or more solutions.

In all three scenarios, you might be looking to increase the reusability of the code, but also to reduce the time taken between checking for a change and receiving feedback for that change in the form of automated test results. Before you start breaking up your application, remember that moving a part of your solution to a separate component does not always achieve this.

If you break your application up into three components and one remaining main part, make sure that you can build and test these three components completely in isolation, or at least close to 100% isolation. If you cannot test a component of your application in isolation, creating a separate repository and build for that component will actually increase the time between checking for a change and receiving feedback to you as a developer. Both separate builds might run quicker, but now you need to wait for two builds before you receive any feedback.

> **Tip**
>
> If you break your application up into separate components, make sure that each component can be built and tested in a high degree of isolation.

As well as this, you have to make sure that making a reusable component out of part of your application makes sense from a conceptual point of view. For example, components that are addressing a cross-cutting concern such as logging libraries or database abstraction layers are great candidates for factoring out to shared libraries. (On a side note, after you have done so, you might also want to consider replacing your own general-purpose libraries with off-the-shelf alternatives – for example, for database abstraction, use Entity Framework, and for logging providers, use Serilog, NLog, and so on wherever possible.)

However, if splitting your solution into components makes sense, it can bring great benefits.

Types of feeds

Once the solution has been separated into different components. some components will be reused by multiple teams and projects. A feed will be required to store, share, and manage these reusable components/packages.

There are many types of package feeds that can be hosted in Azure Artifacts. How you will use an artifact feed depends on the language and ecosystem used by the application.

The following ecosystems are supported in Azure Artifacts:

- **NuGet**: When working with Microsoft .NET languages, the package management used is NuGet. Technically, a NuGet package is just a ZIP file that's been renamed with the .nupkg extension and whose contents match certain conventions.

- **npm**: The npm protocol is used when building applications with JavaScript or TypeScript.

- **Maven or Gradle**: Maven and Gradle are used for the Java ecosystem.

- **pip and Twine**: When working with Python packages, they can be obtained using these pip and Twine utilities.

- **Universal Packages**: Universal Packages are not associated with a specific ecosystem but are a generic means for uploading and retrieving packages.

Whenever a new feed is created, no type needs to be specified. In fact, every feed can be accessed using any protocol, even with different protocols over time. However, in general, this does not make sense.

Creating a feed

Once you have identified one or more packages that you want to publish, you will need a place to store them. For this, you can use Azure Artifacts. The following diagram shows the structural makeup of Azure Artifacts:

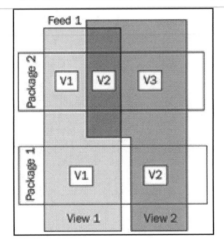

Figure 7.1 – Azure Artifacts views

Within Azure Artifacts, you can create one or more feeds where you can store your packages. For each package, you can have multiple versions in a feed. The feed is the level at which you can set up authorizations for publishing packages. Within a feed, you can create one or more views that you can use for setting up authorizations for consuming packages. A specific version of any given package can be in more than one view at the same time. The following sections discuss all these concepts in more detail.

Setting up a feed

Within Azure Artifacts, the feed is the location where your packages are stored. Each feed is a separate and fully isolated repository. To create a new feed, follow these steps:

1. First, navigate to Azure Artifacts in the menu on the left and then click on the **Create feed** button (partially visible in the following screenshot behind the pane for creating a new feed):

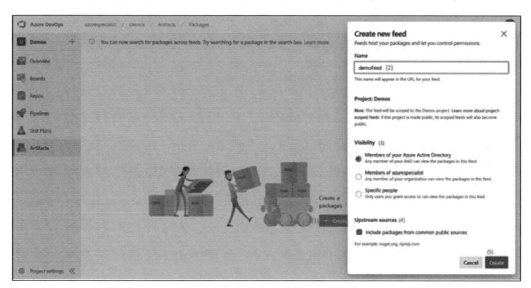

Figure 7.2 – Creating a new feed

2. Specify a name for the feed. It should not contain any spaces and should preferably contain only letters and numbers, since it will become part of a URL.

3. Next, it is possible to specify the initial settings for visibility. This determines which users can view the feed. This will be discussed in more detail in a later subsection, *Managing views on a feed*.

4. Configure the use of upstream sources. This will also be covered in more detail in a later subsection, *Configuring upstream sources*.

5. A few seconds after selecting **Create**, your feed will be available.

Once the feed is created, you can configure various settings, such as hiding deleted packages, enabling package batches, and configuring retention policies. To learn how to do this, follow these steps:

1. After the feed is created, access the settings for the feed by clicking on the gearbox in the top-right corner.

2. Choose **Feed settings** in the view shown in the following screenshot. In this view, you can configure a few more things:

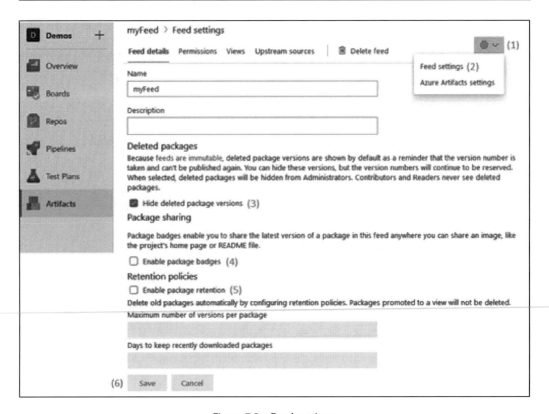

Figure 7.3 – Feed settings

3. Besides changing the name and adding a description, you can choose to hide deleted packages. When you do this, versions of a package that have been removed are no longer visible to administrators of the feed. Regular users are never able to view or use deleted packages, but this setting enables the same view logic as administrators.

4. Another setting you can enable is that of package badges. A package badge is a visual element with the name of a package and the latest available version. If you enable this option, Azure DevOps Feed management will provide a direct URL link to the package badge. Using this link, you can always reference the latest version of the package. This is useful for people who want to keep tabs on the latest version of a package.

5. Finally, you can configure a retention policy. Here, you can configure the automated removal when the number of versions of a package exceeds a certain threshold. While this helps you to save disk space and therefore costs, this can have the unintended effect of breaking the code references to these specific versions for downstream users of the feed. To safeguard against this, you can prevent removing a package for **x** number of days after it has been downloaded for the last time. Furthermore, keep in mind that any package version that is currently a member of a feed will not be removed.

6. Once done, click on the **Save** button.

After you have created and configured your feed, it is time to specify which users have access to the feed and what permissions they have. Let's learn how to do that next.

Securing access

There are four roles you can assign to a user or group, where the rights of each successive role include the rights of the previous roles as well:

- **Readers** are able to list all packages in a feed and can download them.

- **Collaborators** are also able to use packages from upstream sources.

- **Contributors** can also publish their own packages and unlist and deprecate packages.

- Finally, **owners** have full control over a feed and can also change permissions, rename the feed, or delete it.

To change the permission of a user, follow these steps:

1. Navigate to the **Permissions** view that you can see in the following screenshot. In this view, you can see a list of every user or group that has permissions assigned:

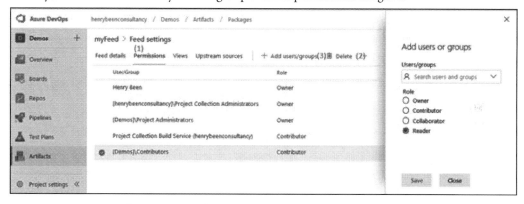

Figure 7.4 – Feed settings – adding/removing permissions

2. To remove permissions, select the row and click on **Delete**.

3. To add a new row, click on the **Add users/groups** button. This will open the view you see on the right.

As an alternative to adding users or groups as a reader on the whole feed, it is also possible to create one or more views on the feed and set access rights per view.

Managing views on a feed

A feed is a repository of packages that you can publish and download packages to and from. However, there are many cases where you do not want every uploaded package to be available for download. Often, you might find that you want to control who can use which versions of a package – for example, when you are implementing the CD of a shared library but want to share only stable versions with the rest of your organization.

To do this, you can create views. A view is a subset of the package versions within a feed. As a consumer, when working with a view, it behaves just as if it were a feed.

Views can be managed as follows:

1. Navigate and click on **Views**; you should see something similar to the following screenshot:

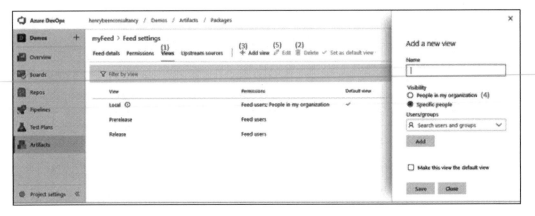

Figure 7.5 – Feed settings – managing views

2. Here, you can see a list of all the current views and remove any views by selecting the row and clicking on **Delete**.

3. Adding new views can be done using the **Add view** button, which opens the view you see on the right.

4. You can set permissions for reading from a view here as well. You can allow read access to your whole Azure DevOps organization, or specify specific users. Any user or group you add here will get reader permissions on this view only.

5. Editing permissions can be done by selecting any row and choosing **Edit**.

Once one or more views are available, packages can be promoted to a view for consumption through it.

Configuring upstream sources

The final thing that you can configure on your feed is the upstream sources. Azure Artifacts feeds give you a repository where you can publish your own packages for reuse from one or more locations.

However, you will probably also use packages that are publicly available on repositories such as NuGet.org or npmjs.org. In this case, you could use a combination of an Artifacts feed and NuGet.org, but you can also configure your feed to serve packages from NuGet.org as well. If you do this, NuGet.org is called an upstream source.

Along with simplicity, this gives you the added benefit of having one central location where you can see all the packages you are using in your solution(s). This enables you to quickly check which packages and versions you are using, which can be useful for compliance or security checks. Using the different permissions between the reader and collaborator roles, you can also configure which users are authorized to pull packages from NuGet.org to your feed and which users are not.

Of course, you can do this for any repository that is accessible over the internet and implements one of the protocols that Azure Artifacts supports. To configure upstream sources, follow these steps:

1. Upstream sources can be configured after navigating to the following screen:

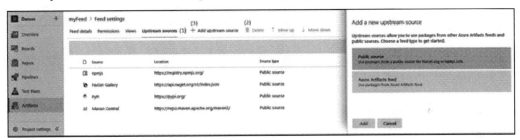

Figure 7.6 – Configuring upstream sources

2. Upstream sources are configured in the same way as permissions and views. You can delete upstream sources using the **Delete** button in the menu bar.

3. Adding upstream sources is done by clicking on the **Add upstream source** button, which opens the view on the right.

> **Important Note**
>
> A final thing to note about the use of upstream sources is that it is not possible to have the same version of a package published to your own feed if it is already available on an upstream source.
>
> For instance, when you enable the NuGet.org upstream, you cannot publish the Newtonsoft.Json 10.0.3 package because that same package version is already present on NuGet.org.

This section discussed how to create and connect feeds. Now that these are in place, we will learn how to publish packages to those feeds in the next section.

Publishing packages

Now that you know how to create and manage feeds, it is time to learn how to publish packages to them. If you have experience of publishing packages to public feeds, you will see that publishing to Azure Artifacts works in precisely the same way. There are two ways in which you can publish packages to a feed:

- Manually from your own computer
- By using Azure Pipelines

Both options are explored in the following sections.

Publishing packages manually

To upload packages manually, the following steps need to be performed:

1. First, you will have to retrieve the URL to your feed. To do this, click on **Connect to feed** for any of your feeds, as shown in the following screenshot:

Figure 7.7 – Connect to feed

2. In the list on the left, select the protocol to use for accessing the feed.

3. Select the correct view to use. Remember that for publishing packages, the full feed URL needs to be used, since views are read-only.

4. After making the correct selections, copy the correct URL to the clipboard using the **Copy** button.

5. Execute the following command to create a NuGet package from a regular `.csproj` file. If you do not have the `NuGet.exe` tool already available, you can download it using the link provided at the end of this chapter:

```
nuget.exe pack DemoSolution\MyPackage.csproj -Version
1.1.0
```

6. Execute the final command for uploading the package to NuGet:

```
nuget.exe push
    - Source "{feedUrl}" "MyPackage.1.1.0.nupkg"
```

After executing the final command, the package will be published and becomes available in your feed.

Publishing packages from a pipeline

Uploading a package manually is not a convenient solution if you need to do it more than once. In cases where you want to frequently generate and publish a new version of a library, you can use an Azure pipeline. As well as the automation that this gives you, it is also a great way to introduce repeatability and reliability, since you can now use all of the benefits that pipelines offer you.

You can find a possible build definition for creating and publishing an npm package, as shown in the following example. The sources for this build are from an open source Microsoft GitHub repository called `tfs-cli`.

In this pipeline, there are three usages of the built-in npm task:

*   The first occurrence is an `npm install` command. This command is used for installing the dependencies for this package:

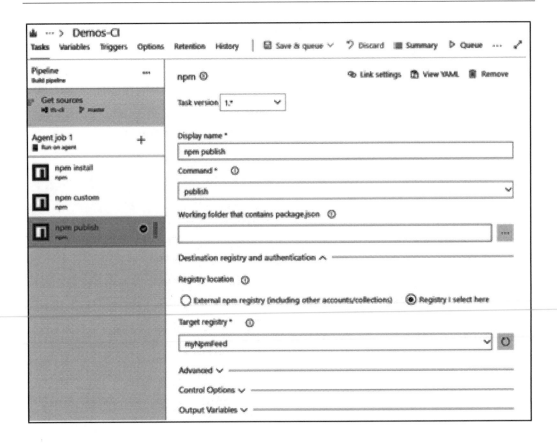

Figure 7.8 – Publishing an npm package through an Azure pipeline

- The second occurrence is running a custom command, build. This command is defined in the source code itself using package.json and is used for transpiling the source files from TypeScript to JavaScript:

Figure 7.9 – Building the npm package command in an Azure pipeline

- The final and third task is running the npm publish command to publish the generated package to an npm feed. In this instance, there is no external feed selected but a built-in target registry, the Azure Artifacts feed:

Figure 7.10 – Publishing an npm package in an Azure pipeline

After running this build, your package is available in your feed.

Versioning packages

One thing that is not done automatically when using the tasks to upload an npm package, or most types of packages for that matter, is managing the version number. Of course, there are many ways in which you can make sure your packages have proper versions, but a common approach is setting (part of) the version number during the build of a package.

> **Tip**
>
> Semantic versioning, also known as SemVer, is the most common practice to use within a versioning system.

Version basics

Applications adopting **Semantic Versioning (SemVer)** will have a version number naming standard in the Major.Minor.Patch[-Suffix] form. The SemVer standard constructs a version in four parts and has the following meanings:

- **Major**: This indicates that this release includes breaking changes or incompatible changes with previous versions.

- **Minor**: This indicates that this release includes new features but is compatible with a previous version – that is, backward-compatible.

- **Patch**: This indicates that this release is backward-compatible but only for minor bug fixes.

- **Suffix (optional)**: This is a hyphen followed by a string, denoting a pre-release version.

A recommended approach is to publish a new version of the package with an updated version number in the package.json file.

Expanding on the npm package build that we demonstrated before, three changes can be made to the build definition:

1. First, the build number format for the build definition is updated to the following: 1.0$(Rev:.rrr). This guarantees that a unique number is automatically generated for every build. The Ref:.rrr variable will generate a number with three positions, leading with zeros if needed. The first time, this number will be 000, and it will increase by one every time the rest of the build number is not changed.

2. Second, a task is added to replace the version number that is currently specified in the source control, using the {#Build.BuildNumber#} token. This is a reference to the build variable with the name Build.BuildNumber, which contains the build number that was specified in *step 1*.

3. Finally, a **Replace Tokens** task is added to the build before all other tasks. A possible configuration to replace the fixed-version number with the automatic version number for this task is shown as follows:

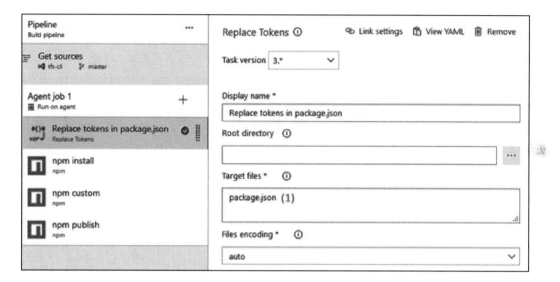

Figure 7.11 – Replace Tokens tasks

This task can be configured to replace the tokens in one or more target files (**1** in the preceding screenshot). It will look for any series of characters starting with {# and ending in #}, take the text between these two markers, and then replace the whole text with the value of the corresponding variable.

For example, if we send the following json file as input, it will replace the variable1 pipeline variable values within the tag:

```
{
    "property1": "{#Variable1#}"
}
```

If the value is configured as `Variable1: "validToken"`, then the output `json` file will be as follows:

```json
{
    "property1": "validToken"
}
```

With this in place, every package that is built using the definition will have a unique and ever-increasing patch version number. Whenever the major or minor version number needs to be updated, this can be done by updating the build number format.

As an alternative to this approach, there are many tasks available from the extensions marketplace that can help with versioning, including more complex scenarios.

This section discussed how to publish packages to a feed. With packages published to a feed, the next section will detail how these can be used with either Visual Studio or an Azure pipeline.

Restoring packages

Uploading packages to an Azure Artifacts feed or repository makes them available for use in many different scenarios. Two common scenarios are using your own packages with Visual Studio or from Azure Pipelines. Both scenarios will be detailed in the following sections.

Restoring packages from Visual Studio

Once you have your shared libraries available as NuGet packages in an Azure Artifacts feed, you can start using them from Visual Studio. Before you can do this, you will have to register your feed in your Visual Studio instance.

To do this, you first have to grab the URL of your feed. In order to do this, refer to the *Publishing packages manually* section. Once you have your URL ready, go to manage NuGet files for your solution, as you would do normally. If you are not familiar with working with NuGet packages in Visual Studio, you can find this option in the Solution Explorer on the solution and project headers:

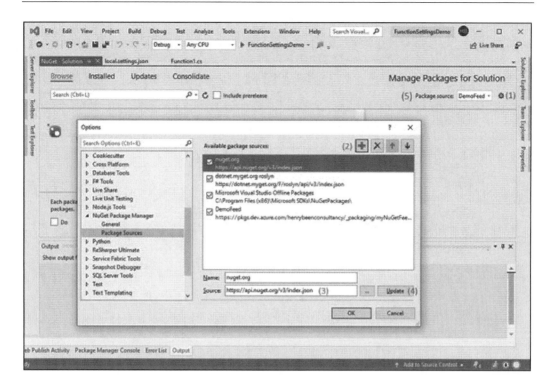

Figure 7.12 – Configuring the NuGet package sources

Once you are here, follow the following steps:

1. Click on the small gearbox in the top-right corner to open the dialog where you can configure which NuGet feeds to use.

2. Add a new feed.

3. Fill in both the name and the source of your own feed.

4. After doing so, do not forget to click on **Update**; otherwise, your changes to the **Name** and **Source** fields will not be saved, and there will be no warning prompting you that you have unsaved changes.

5. After you have made these changes, you can now select your feed as the package source at the top right of the screen.

From here onward, it is possible to work with these packages from your own feed, just as you do with packages from NuGet.org.

Restoring packages from a pipeline

Once you start using your packages in Visual Studio, it is very likely you will need them in Azure Pipelines as well. This is in order to perform CI/CD on the dependent application that uses your packages.

Fortunately, this can be achieved with a small configuration change on your NuGet restore task, as shown in the following screenshot. The following screenshot relates to the NuGet restore task that can be used with both the Visual Studio build tasks and the .NET Core build tasks. Both contain the same interface and can be used in the same way:

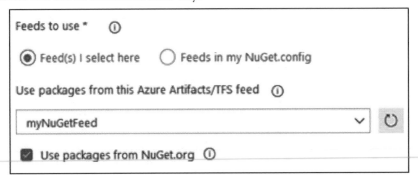

Figure 7.13 – Restoring the NuGet package feed configuration

By default, only the radio button for using packages from NuGet is checked; therefore, to include packages from your own feeds as well, you need to select the correct feed in the drop-down list.

If you ever find the need to include packages from more than one feed, you will be forced to create one aggregator feed and use the other feeds as upstream sources for it.

This section covered how to consume component packages from Visual Studio. The next section will dive into working with Universal Packages to share general binary packages.

Working with Universal Packages

The previous sections have all focused on using Azure Artifacts as a means for redistributing application packages, such as libraries or other shared components. However, there is also another important use for Azure Artifacts – to maintain Universal Packages.

A Universal Packages feed can be used to store different types of packages other than those widely used, such as **NuGet** for .NET, **npm** for Node.js, **pypi** for Python, and **Maven** for Java application development.

You can use Universal Packages for storing and serving your build artifacts in sizes up to 4 TB. Packaging build artifacts into a Universal Package enables quick rollback to the desired version. Packages can be published and retrieved to and from Artifacts feeds using the Azure CLI or Azure Pipelines.

> **Tip**
> Universal Packages are only available in Azure DevOps services.

To use Universal Packages for staging your build artifacts in a heterogeneous architecture, there are four basic operations you should understand: uploading and downloading Universal Packages from an Azure pipeline and uploading and downloading Universal Packages using the Azure CLI. The latter one you can invoke from other tools.

Universal Packages are a lightweight, easy-to-use, and efficient way to transfer files with dependency management. Universal Packages provide client- and server-side deduplication, which can substantially reduce the network traffic you're using to move files around. These Universal Packages are managed as part of feeds in package management, so you can easily control access to them.

Uploading and downloading Universal Packages from Azure Pipelines

Uploading build artifacts to a Universal Packages feed works in a similar way as uploading a regular build artifact. There are two changes you need to consider.

Firstly, you have to use another task for performing the upload. Instead of using the *publish build artifact* or *publish pipeline artifact* tasks, you have to use the task named **Universal Packages**. When using this task, you can still give a name to the artifact and specify a location on the filesystem of the build agent to upload it from. Next, you can specify a target feed and a version to use. This version can be either automatically incremented whenever a new package is uploaded or specified using a build variable.

Secondly, you have to consider the fact that the uploaded package is not associated directly with the build that produced it – as is standard with regular build or pipeline artifacts. This means that no matter where you are using the package that has been uploaded, you have to find another way to find the correct version to download.

To perform the actual download, you can use the **Universal Packages** task again, as shown in the following screenshot:

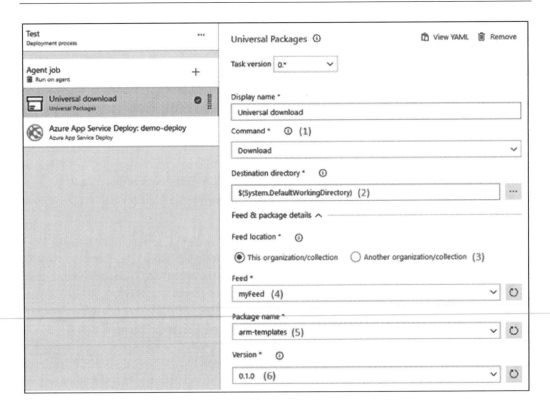

Figure 7.14 – The Universal Packages download

Refer to the screenshot and follow these steps:

1. After adding the task, you can toggle it between **Upload** and **Download**.

2. You can also specify a directory that is uploaded as the artifact for the **Upload** command. Alternatively, for the **Download** command, you can specify where the artifacts should be downloaded.

3. Furthermore, the name of the feed needs to be specified.

4. Also, specify the name of the package.

5. Specify the version to be either an upload or a download.

> **Important Note**
>
> Note that you can also use feeds that are not part of your own organization by choosing to use another feed at *step 5*. If you do so, you will need to create a service endpoint to reach that feed.

Uploading and downloading Universal Packages using the Azure CLI

When you want to work with Universal packages from a product other than Azure Pipelines, you will have to use the Azure CLI. To do this, perform the following steps:

1. The first thing you have to do to work with Universal Packages using the Azure CLI is to install the CLI itself. The link to the CLI can be found at the end of this chapter.

2. Next, it is time to install the extension for Azure DevOps. This can be done using the following command:

```
az extension add -name azure-devops
```

3. After making the extension for Azure DevOps available, you have to log in using the account that you also use to work within the Azure DevOps UI. You can log in by giving the following command:

```
az login
```

4. Once logged in, you can upload a file as an artifact using the following command:

```
az artifacts universal publish
  --feed {yourFeedName}
  --name {yourPackageName}
  --version {yourVersion}
  --organization https://dev.azure.com/
{yourOrganizationName}
  --path {sourceFileName}
```

5. To download a particular version of an artifact again, you can use the following:

```
az artifacts universal download
  --feed {yourFeedName}
  --name {yourPackageName}
  --version {yourVersion}
  --organization https://dev.azure.com/
{yourOrganizationName}
  --path {targetFileName}
```

Using the CLI and these commands, you can use Azure Artifacts as a means to share build artifacts between multiple tools. When working with a number of tools on the same project, Universal Packages are a great tool for moving binaries around.

In the next section, other tools available for package management will be explored.

Exploring other tools

There are many other tools available to do binary management. Four commonly used products are MyGet, Artifactory, GitHub Packages, and **Azure Container Registry** (**ACR**). The features they deliver do overlap, but they also have unique attributes at which they excel.

MyGet

MyGet is an alternative location for hosting your NuGet packages and allows you to create both public and private feeds that are managed by you. It also supports defining upstream sources and delivers built-in dependency scanning to give you continuous feedback on the level of security of your dependencies.

Since MyGet is an implementation of the NuGet protocol, you can publish and use packages using the default NuGet tasks from Azure Pipelines.

Artifactory

Artifactory, a product by JFrog, is another tool that you can use to host your package feeds. Artifactory was originally an on-premises product, but it is now also available as a **Software as a Service** (**SaaS**) offering. Just like Azure Artifacts, it supports multiple protocols to interact with package feeds. At the time of writing, Artifactory supports more repository protocols than Azure Artifacts. Examples of this include PHP Composer and **Red Hat Package Manager** (**RPM**).

JFrog has published an Azure Pipelines extension to download and upload packages.

Azure Container Registry

Another type of storage for reusable packages is ACR. This was designed specifically for container images and was developed with the layering of containers in mind. This allows it to receive only partial uploads when a new version of an image becomes available if not all of the layers have changed. This makes ACR a very good location for storing container images. Uploads are faster and ACR storage is cheaper than Azure Artifacts storage. This is a big benefit, since container images can be large.

You can integrate with ACR from Azure Pipelines using the Docker integration extensions.

Summary

In this chapter, you learned how to identify shared components in your solutions – pieces of code that appear not only in multiple locations but that are also logical units for reuse. You learned how to use Azure Artifacts feeds for hosting packages that contain these libraries. Furthermore, you learned how to use these hosted packages to build dependent solutions using both Visual Studio and Azure Pipelines. You also learned about using Universal Packages to share build artifacts between Azure Pipelines and other tools that you might use for CI/CD.

With this knowledge, you will now be able to identify shared components in your solutions. Once you have identified such a component, you will also be able to isolate it in source control, build it, and publish it to an artifact feed. From here, you can distribute it to one or more consuming solutions. Finally, you are now also capable of using Artifacts feeds to share build artifacts between different CI/CD products.

In the next chapter, you will learn about infrastructure and configuration as code. This is one of the fundamental DevOps practices that allows you to have your infrastructure definition in source control and use that as part of your release pipeline.

Questions

As we conclude, here is a list of questions for you to test your knowledge regarding this chapter's material. You will find the answers in the *Assessments* section of the *Appendix*:

1.   True or false: Any version of a package can be deployed to only one view within a feed.

2.   True or false: Pipeline artifacts can be used for sharing build outcomes (packages) from Azure DevOps to other products.

3.   True or false: Azure Artifacts feeds with Universal Packages can be used to share build outcomes (packages) from Azure DevOps to other products.

4.   True or false: **Standardization**, **package formats and sources**, and **versioning** are valid aspects of a dependency management strategy.

5.   Which of the following is needed to enable building a solution that uses packages from an Azure Artifacts feed in Visual Studio? (You can select more than one option.)

    A.   Adding the full package URL to your project dependencies, instead of only the package name

    B.   Having at least *reader* access to the feed or one of the views in the feed

    C.   Having at least *consumer* access to the feed

    D.   Configuring the location of the feed as a package source for Visual Studio

6.   What are some reasons for splitting a solution into multiple parts that are separated by Azure Artifacts feeds?

Exercises

- Let's create a shared component to maintain model classes and extract it as a package. This package, as it has model classes, can be used with multiple projects, such as mobile, API, or website projects.

- Add a **New Class Library** project template in the same solution folder created in *Chapter 5, Moving to Continuous Integration*, and name it `packtbookslibrary.Shared.Models`.

- Add a new class for the `Book` model as follows:

```
namespace packtbookslibrary.Models
{
    public class Book
    {
        public string? Id { get; set; }
        public string? ISBNNumber { get; set; }
        public string? Title { get; set; }
        public string? Description { get; set; }
        public string? Author { get; set; }
        public string? AuthorName { get; set; }
    }
}
```

- In Azure Artifacts, create a `PacktBooksLibraryFeed` feed.

- Under **Feed Permission,** provide a contributor to the `[PacktBookLibrary]` group named **Build Administrators**.

- Alternatively, set the **Project Collection Build Service** identity to be a contributor on your feed:

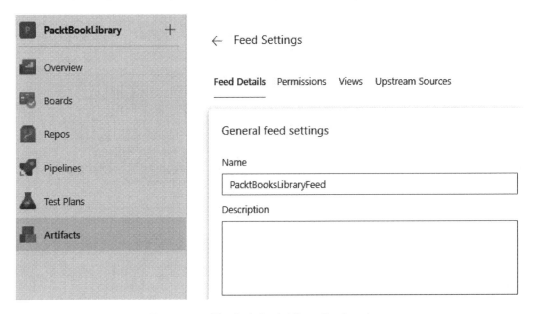

Figure 7.15 – The PacktBooksLibraryFeed settings

- Now, create a `packtbookslibrary-Shared-Models-ci-pipeline.yaml` pipeline to create a NuGet package for our `packtbookslibrary.Shared.Models` class library project.

- Add the YAML code from the file present in the following directory in `packtbookslibrary-Shared-Models-ci-pipeline.yaml`: `https://github.com/PacktPublishing/Designing-and-Implementing-Microsoft-DevOps-Solutions-AZ-400-Exam-Guide`

To push a package, run `packtbookslibrary-Shared-Models-ci-pipeline.yaml`.

- Once the package is successfully executed, you will see a new entry in the list for `packtbookslibrary.Shared.Models`:

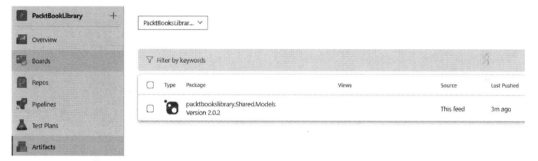

Figure 7.16 – The shared model package published in Azure Artifacts

- Now, add this NuGet feed to your project by navigating to **Manage NuGet packages** and **Settings**:

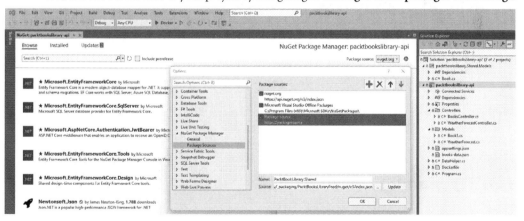

Figure 7.17 – Managing the NuGet package sources for packtbooklibrary-api

- Select the package and install it in your project:

Figure 7.18 – Installing the package in the packtbooklibrary-api project

- You can use this package in `BookController.cs` as follows:

Figure 7.19 – The shared model package in packtbooklibrary-api

Further reading

- Exercises for practicing with Azure Artifacts can be found at `https://docs.microsoft.com/en-us/learn/modules/manage-build-dependencies/`.

- You can find and download `NuGet.exe` from `https://www.nuget.org/downloads.`

- More information on creating a package can be found at `https://docs.microsoft.com/en-us/nuget/create-packages/creating-a-package`.

- Information on downloading and installing the Azure CLI can be found at `https://docs.microsoft.com/en-us/cli/azure/install-azure-cli?view=azure-cli-latest`.

- More information about JFrog Artifactory is available at `https://jfrog.com/artifactory/`.

- The extension for Azure Pipelines can be found at `https://marketplace.visualstudio.com/items?itemName=JFrog.jfrog-artifactory-vsts-extension`.

- More information about ACR is available at `https://azure.microsoft.com/en-in/services/container-registry/`.

- You can find the Docker extensions for Azure Pipelines at `https://marketplace.visualstudio.com/items?itemName=ms-vscs-rm.docker`.

- More information on semantic versioning can be found at `https://semver.org/`.

- More information on `tfs-cli` is available at `https://github.com/microsoft/tfs-cli`.

- More information on Universal Packages can be found at `https://docs.microsoft.com/en-us/azure/devops/pipelines/artifacts/universal-packages?toc=%2Fazure%2Fdevops%2Fartifacts%2Ftoc.json&bc=%2Fazure%2Fdevops%2Fartifacts%2Fbreadcrumb%2Ftoc.json&view=azure-devops&tabs=yaml`.

8
Implement Infrastructure and Configuration as Code

In the previous chapter, the focus was on storing and building application code and releasing the created binaries. You learned how to create a pipeline, from source control to a target environment, for the automated, repeatable deployment of your applications.

In this chapter, you will learn how to apply the same principles to the infrastructure that your application runs on and the runtime configuration of your application. Doing so will help you to further increase the speed at which changes can be delivered to production, increasing the flow of value to your end users.

This chapter will start off by explaining the value of having everything, infrastructure and configuration included, as code. After that, it continues by explaining **Azure Resource Manager** (**ARM**) templates. The syntax will be explained, as well as how to deploy ARM templates. Then, it proceeds to explain the Azure Automation offering, available in the Azure cloud. Azure Automation can be used to run scripts on a schedule or load and apply PowerShell DSC modules. Next up is managing application settings for PaaS offerings, such as Azure App Service. Finally, it concludes by discussing several other tools that have similar capabilities.

The following topics will be covered in this chapter:

- Having everything as code
- Working with ARM templates
- Deploying ARM templates
- Reverse engineering a template
- Using Azure Automation
- Managing application settings
- Other tools

Technical requirements

To experiment with one or more of the technologies described in this chapter, one or more of the following may be required:

- An Azure subscription, for executing ARM templates and running Azure Automation

- PowerShell with the Azure PowerShell modules, for executing ARM templates, available from `https://docs.microsoft.com/en-us/powershell/azure/install-az-ps?view=azps-7.3.0`

- The Azure CLI, for executing ARM templates, available from `https://docs.microsoft.com/en-us/cli/azure/`

Having everything as code

If you have been responsible for creating and maintaining application infrastructure and configuration in the past, you have most likely experienced what is called **configuration drift**. Configuration drift is the name for the phenomenon where the configuration between servers in acceptance and the production environment differs. Or, even worse, when having multiple servers in the production environment, it might be the case that the configuration of these is not always the same.

The most common cause of configuration drift is manual change. When making changes manually, maybe under the pressure of a production issue, there is always the risk that you apply different settings to different servers or hosts. If you ever need to scale out and add another server to your production environment, the chance of that server taking on the same configuration as all already-existing servers is very slim.

> **Tip**
> Declarative (functional) and imperative (procedural) are two of the main approaches adopted to implement **Infrastructure as Code (IaC)** and **Configuration as Code (CaC)**.

With IaC and CaC, you no longer make changes to application configuration and infrastructure manually, but through automation. The first step to do this is specifying the desired state of configuration and infrastructure. The desired state is then fed into configuration management tooling that enforces this configuration on your infrastructure. Specifying only the desired state is called a *declarative* approach, which differs from an *imperative* approach, where you specify all of the steps that need to be taken.

Some of these tools are often also capable of checking the current state of your infrastructure and configuration at regular intervals and reapplying your desired state if any deviation is detected. This is possible due to the declarative approach. This makes applying configuration an idempotent operation.

> **Tip**
> An operation is idempotent if it can be repeated one or more times, while the outcome remains the same.

When adopting IaC and CaC, you can even go so far as to recreate the complete infrastructure before deploying an application, deploy the application on that new infrastructure, and then disregard the old infrastructure after switching to the new deployment. This is an extreme form of immutable servers. The added benefit of this approach is that you are now guaranteed that there will be no traces from any configuration or binaries from the previous deployment.

In the following sections, you will learn about different IaC technologies and how to use them. It is important to understand that they are complementary and are often used together. For example, ARM templates can be used to create virtual machines in Azure and, once that is done, PowerShell DSC or Ansible can be used to configure those virtual machines.

Working with ARM templates

When working on the Azure platform, infrastructure is described using ARM templates. ARM templates are written in JSON, and a skeleton template looks as follows:

```
{
    "$schema":
"https://schema.management.azure.com/schemas/2019-04-01/
deploymentTemplate. json#",
    "contentVersion": "1.0.0.0",
    "parameters": {
    },
    "variables": {
    },
    "resources": [
    ],
    "outputs": {
    }
}
```

The template itself is, at the highest level, a JSON object. There is a mandatory property, $schema.

$schema is a required element and the value version number depends on the scope of the deployment and the JSON editor. The contentVersion property is also required and can be specified to version the contents. This version can be used by the author to version the template if necessary.

The rest of this chapter will discuss the different parts that make up ARM templates in more detail. You will find a link to the online documentation at the end of this chapter. A link to a formal, detailed breakdown of the structure and syntax of ARM templates is also provided at the end of this chapter.

Parameters

The parameters section is usually near the top of the template. Before beginning deployment activities, ARM will resolve the parameter values. The resolved value is referenced whenever the parameter is found in the template by ARM.

This section takes the form of a JSON object, which can be empty but cannot be left out. The use of this section is to declare one or more parameters that can be specified by the caller of the ARM template before deploying it. A common reason for using the parameters section is to use the same template for both the test and production environments but vary the names of resources between the two. An example parameters section might look like this:

```
{
  "appServiceName": {
    "type": "string",
    "metadata": {
      "description": "a free to choose text"
    }
  }
}
```

For every parameter, a new key is specified with the parameter's name. The value is an object. This object has one mandatory key, type. The allowed values for type are string, int, bool, object, array, secureString, and secureObject. The secureString and secureObject variations can be used to make sure that the runtime values of these parameters are scrubbed from any log and output. They are intended to hold passwords, keys, or other secrets.

The metadata object, with the description key, is optional and can be used to add a description to the parameter for future reference.

Other properties that can be specified on a parameter object are the following:

- minValue and maxValue for specifying bounds on an integer value
- minLength and maxLength for specifying bounds on the length of a string value

- defaultValue for specifying a default value that will be used if no value is specified when applying the template
- allowedValues for specifying an array of allowed values, limiting valid inputs

Next, let's understand what parameter files are.

Parameter files

You can make use of a JSON file that contains the parameter values instead of specifying them as inline values in your script. In this section, we will discuss how to use parameter files to use with the templates. Often, a single template is accompanied by more than one parameter file, for example, one for test and one for production. The JSON for a parameter file appears as follows:

```
{
  "$schema":
"https://schema.management.azure.com/schemas/2019-04-01/
deploymentParameter s.json#",
  "contentVersion": "1.0.0.0",
  "parameters": {
    "exampleParameter": {
      "value": "exampleValue"
    }
  }
}
```

Just like an ARM template, every parameter file is a JSON object with mandatory $schema and contentVersion properties. The third property parameter is used to specify one or more parameter values. For each parameter, specify its name as the key and an object as the value. This object can hold the value key for providing the actual value of the parameter.

While very valuable for specifying names for resources, scaling options, and other things that have to vary between environments, this solution is not useful for secrets.

The following diagram shows how the parameter file references the secret and passes that value to the template:

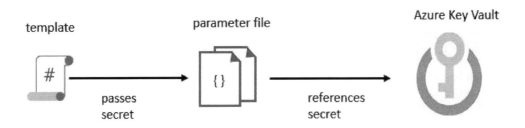

Figure 8.1 – Using secrets in an Azure template

Keys, passwords, and other secrets should not be stored as plaintext in source control in a parameter file. For secrets, another notation is available:

```
{
  "$schema":
"https://schema.management.azure.com/schemas/2019-04-01/
deploymentParameter s.json#",
  "contentVersion": "1.0.0.0",

  "parameters": {
    "exampleSecretParameter": {
      "reference": {
        "keyvault": {
          "id": "/subscriptions/…/Microsoft.KeyVault/
vaults/<vaultname>"
        },
        "secretName": "myKeyVaultSecretName"
      }
    }
  }
}
```

With this notation, instead of specifying the value directly, there is a pointer to a location in an Azure key vault where the correct value is stored. When deploying the template, this secret is (within Azure!) taken from the key vault and used in deployment. This is allowed only if the user or service starting the deployment has either an owner or contributor role in relation to the key vault, and the key vault is enabled for template deployment.

> **Important Note**
>
> Strictly speaking, any role that includes the `Microsoft.KeyVault/vaults/deploy/`
> `action` permission will work. By default, these are the owner and contributor roles, but you
> can create custom roles that include this action as well.

Variables

The variables section is used to specify one or more values that will be used throughout the template. A common approach is building the names of all resources in the variables section, based on a single parameter called `environmentName`. This ensures that resources will have the same name between environments. Variables are also used to specify values that cannot be specified from outside the template but should be recognized as configurable. An example might look like this:

```
"Variables": {
  "appServicePlanType": "B1",
  "appServiceName": "[concat('myAppService-',
parameters('environmentName'))]"
}
```

Please note that the example for `appServiceName` contains functions, which are discussed in the next section.

Functions

Functions are used to allow the dynamic evaluation of properties in ARM templates. Calling functions uses a notation very similar to that of many programming languages: `functionName(arg1,` `arg2, ...)`. Functions can return either a value, such as `string` or `int`, or an object or array.

When an object is returned, any property can be accessed using the `.propertyName` notation. Accessing elements in an array can be done using `[index]`. To indicate which parts of a string should be evaluated as a function, they must be enclosed in brackets:

```
"myVariable": "[concat('myAppService-',
parameters('environmentName'))]"
```

The preceding section shows two examples of functions. In the first, the `concat` function is called to concatenate two string values. One is hardcoded and the other one is the result of a second function call to retrieve the value of a template parameter.

There are a fair number of functions available. They can be used for string manipulation, retrieving details about the current subscription, resource group, or **Azure Active Directory** (**AAD**) tenant, or getting resource details.

Functions can also be used to retrieve account keys or other secrets. This is often done to automatically insert keys directly from the service that exposes the key to the application settings or a key vault. This eliminates the need for the manual transfer of secrets. Variables and functions can help make your templates easier to maintain.

You can also add your own functions to your template. These functions can be used in your template. User-defined functions exist independently of regular template functions. In most cases, you define complex expressions that you don't want to repeat throughout your template.

Comments and metadata

An ARM template can contain sections that aren't related to the JSON language itself. You have a few options to add comments and metadata.

Comments

To comment the rest of a line, `//` is used, or to comment a block, the `/*  */` notation is used. This makes the following snippets both valid as part of an ARM template:

```
{
    "appServiceName": {
        // this is a single line comment
        "type": "string",
        /*
            This is a multi-line comment
        */
        "metadata": {
            "description": " The name of the web app that you
wish to create.",
            "author": "author Name"
        },
    "location": "[
        parameters('location')
        ]", //defaults to resource group location
}
```

Another deviation from JSON is that ARM templates allow for a multiline string. You can break a string into multiple lines. See the `location` property in the preceding example.

In the preceding example, you will notice the use of comments and metadata in your templates.

> **Important Note**
> To deploy templates with multiline strings and comments, use Azure PowerShell or the Azure CLI. For the CLI, use version 2.3.0 or later, and specify the `--handle-extended-json-format` switch.

metadata

Text you add to a metadata description is automatically used as a tip for that parameter. ARM will ignore the `metadata` object, and this can be added anywhere in the template.

Resources

Resources are the main part of the template, where all of the resources to be created are specified. This section is the only one that is not an object, but an array. Within that array, one or more objects of the following form are specified:

```
{
    "type": "Microsoft.Sql/servers",
    "apiVersion": "2021-02-01-preview",
    "name": "mySqlServer",
    "location": "West Europe",
    "properties": {
        "administratorLogin": "myUsername",
        "administratorLoginPassword": "myPassword",
        "version": "12.0"
    }
}
```

Each resource is specified in the form of an object. The first four properties are mandatory for every type of resource:

- The type of the resource to be created or updated needs to be specified. This takes the form of the name of `resourceprovider` followed by a slash and the name of a resource type that belongs to that `resourceprovider`.

- The version of the REST API to use for this resource: A list of supported API versions can be retrieved from `https://docs.microsoft.com/en-us/azure/templates/microsoft.resources/allversions`.

- The name for the resource: Every resource type has its own rules for determining what a valid name is. These can also available in the reference link shared in preceding point.

- Many resources will need to have a location. If the resources require a location, you must specify one for each resource. The location does not have to be the same as the location of the resource group. The location must be a valid Azure region.

All other properties on the object vary from resource type to resource type and are all specified in the resource.

Dependent resources

A special type of resource is the dependent resource. For example, SQL databases are hosted on SQL Server and Service Bus topics are located within a Service Bus namespace.

For a nested resource type, the type and name reflect this nesting. The following example shows the explicit dependency of Service Bus topics on a Service Bus namespace:

```
{
    "apiVersion": "2021-11-01",


    "name": "myNamespaceName/myTopicName",
    "type": "Microsoft.ServiceBus/namespaces/topics",
    "dependsOn": [
        "Microsoft.ServiceBus/namespaces/myNamespaceName"
    ]
}
```

Next to nesting the type and the name, the extra property, dependsOn, is also mandatory to specify that this nested resource can only be created after the containing resource exists. A location property is not necessary since this will be inherited from the containing resource.

The following sample depicts a logical dependency between Azure SQL Server and Azure SQL Database. When the dependson property is utilized, an explicit deployment dependency between a child resource and the parent resource is established automatically. The child resource will be deployed after the parent resource. Here, you will notice the use of the built-in important resourceID function. The resourceID function returns the unique identifier of a resource:

```
{
    "type": "Microsoft.Sql/servers",
    "apiVersion": "2020-02-02-preview",
    "name": "[parameters('serverName')]",
    "location": "[parameters('location')]",
    "resources": [
```

```
    {
        "type": "databases",
        "name": "[parameters('sqlDBName')]",
        "location": "[parameters('location')]",
        "dependsOn": [
            "[resourceId('Microsoft.Sql/servers',
concat(parameters('serverName')))]"
        ]
    }
    ]
}
```

> **Important Note**
>
> A **circular dependency** is a problem with dependency order, resulting in the deployment running in a loop, unable to continue and complete the deployment. ARM identifies circular dependencies during template validation.

Nested templates

A second special type of resource is template deployment. This way, one template can trigger the deployment of another. An example of defining a template deployment as a resource in a template looks as follows:

```
{
    "type": "Microsoft.Resources/deployments",
    "apiVersion": "2021-04-01",
    "name": "linkedTemplate",
    "properties": {
        "mode": "Incremental",
        "templateLink": {
            "uri":"https://.../myLinkedTemplate.json"
        },
        "parametersLink": {
            "uri":"https://.../myParameters.json"
        }
    }
}
```

The locations of the template and parameter file can be specified using both HTTP and HTTPS, that is, with a valid **Uniform Resource Identifier** (**URI**), but have to be publicly accessible locations. Although the template URI needs to be accessed externally, we would like to enable security and restrict access for these templates. To gain access during deployment, append an SAS token to the template file URI As an alternative, a single property template can be specified. This should then contain a whole template as a JSON object. However, you can't use both inline parameters and a link to a parameter file.

Outputs

The next section of a template is the outputs section. Here are the keys returned to the caller of the template. The caller can use these values to start another task or script and use one or more of the values created or used by the template.

The main use for this is to prevent hardcoding names and other dynamic values, especially IPs, in downstream automation. The outputs section is a JSON object of the following format:

```json
{
    "outputName":
    {
        "type": "string",
        "value": "myValue"
    }
}
```

When specifying outputs, the same types can be used as for parameters. Of course, it does not make much sense hardcoding the values, so functions are used to retrieve values from parameters, variables, or even created resources.

To continue with the previous example in the *Dependent resources* section for creating a SQL server, a sample of the output would be as follows:

```json
"outputs": {
    "SqlServerURL": {
        "type": "string",
        "value": "[reference(parameters('serverName')).
fullyQualifiedDomainName]"
    }
}
```

The output would be as follows:

```
sqlServerURL String serverName.database.windows.net
```

Well, so far, we have learned about the different parts that make up an ARM template, which you should be able to write on your own. Now it's time to learn how we can deploy them with the help of various tools.

Deploying ARM templates

Once an ARM template and its accompanying parameter files are written, they can be applied to an Azure environment. There are PowerShell cmdlet and Azure CLI commands available for applying an ARM template from a scripting environment. When ARM templates are used for the infrastructure of an application, Azure Pipelines can be used for deploying not only code but also ARM templates. Other alternatives for deploying templates in Azure include the Azure portal, Azure CLI, REST API, and Azure Cloud Shell or ARM template specs.

Whatever deployment method is used (REST API, Azure CLI, or ARM templates), it will all have a *deployment mode*. This can be either *Incremental* or *Complete*. In Incremental mode, all resources specified in the template will be created in Azure or their properties will be updated if the resource already exists. In Complete deployment mode, any resources that are not defined in the ARM template will be deleted. This mode does not redeploy all resources; instead, it verifies that the resources stated in the template have been created and removes those that have not been defined and already exist in Azure.

The default deployment mode is Incremental.

In the next sections, several tools for executing deployments are discussed, starting with PowerShell.

PowerShell

For the local development and testing of ARM templates on a local machine, PowerShell has a quick command to apply an ARM template to a resource group:

```
New-AzResourceGroupDeployment -ResourceGroupName
myResourceGroup - TemplateFile "c:\my\template.json" `
-TemplateParameterFile "c:\my\parameters.json"
```

The preceding command will pick up the specified template and parameter file and apply it to the specified resource group. This command assumes that the current session has already been logged in to Azure.

There are a few variations of the command available:

- A parameter called -Mode with a Complete or Incremental value is available. This can be used to specify deploymentmode.

- If no parameter file is specified and the template requires parameters, the cmdlet will prompt for these values on the command line.

- As an alternative, the -TemplateUri and -TemplateParametersUri options can be used to specify the location of the template and parameters to be retrieved from another location.

The next tool that we'll look into is the Azure CLI.

The Azure CLI

The Azure CLI is another way of deploying ARM templates from the command line. The benefit of the CLI is that it is completely cross-platform and runs on Windows, macOS, and Linux. The Azure CLI command for deploying an ARM template is as follows:

```
az group deployment create -resource-group myResourceGroup
-template-file "c:\my\template.json" -parameters "c:\my\
parameters.json"
```

All other options that are available in PowerShell are also available in the CLI.

Azure Pipelines

A third mechanism for deploying ARM templates is from an Azure pipeline. This is particularly useful for deploying the infrastructure and configuration of an application, together with the binaries. To deploy an ARM template deployment from a pipeline, at least one service connection of the ARM template needs to be configured. After doing this, a pipeline can be configured, as shown in the following screenshot:

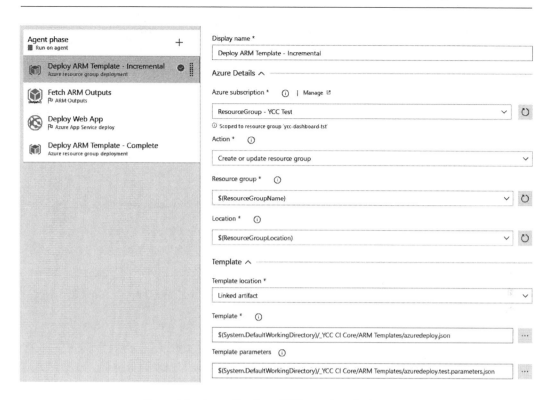

Figure 8.2 – Azure Pipelines ARM template deployment

In this example, there are two deployments of an ARM template, surrounding the deployment of the application code. The first deployment is of the Incremental mode, while the second deployment is of the Complete mode.

> **Tip**
>
> The ARM template test toolkit is available at `https://github.com/Azure/arm-ttk` for you to make ARM templates compliant with standard practices.

Using this approach, the first deployment will create all new infrastructure needed by the new version of the application. This deployment is done in Incremental mode, so infrastructure that is no longer present in the template but still in use by the currently deployed version of the application will not yet be removed. The second deployment will take care of removing these elements after the new version of the code is deployed.

ARM REST API

ARM provides REST API operational groups to deploy and manage infrastructure to Azure. In order to get a list of resources in a subscription, run the following command:

```
GET https://management.azure.com/subscriptions/
{subscriptionId}/resources?api-version=2021-04-01
```

You can use ARMClient, a simple command-line tool, to send HTTP requests to the new ARM REST API:

```
armclient GET /subscriptions/{subscriptionId}/resources?api-
version=2021-04-01
```

The preceding command gets a list of resources in the subscription. Please note that ARM client is not an official Microsoft tool. It is an OSS project that is maintained on GitHub.

Also, you can use the `az rest` command to run these commands. Take the following example:

```
az rest --method get --uri /subscriptions/{subscriptionId}/
resources?api-version=2021-04-01
```

Azure Cloud Shell

Azure Cloud Shell provides a Bash and PowerShell experience to manage and deploy Azure resources from within the browser itself. Azure Cloud Shell is hosted in Azure.

Figure 8.3 – Azure Cloud Shell

The Azure Cloud Shell command for deploying an ARM template in a resource group is as follows:

```
az deployment group create --resource-group testrg --name
rollout01 --template-uri https://myresource/azuredeploy.json
--parameters @myparameters.json
```

All other options that are available in the Azure CLI are also available in Azure Cloud Shell.

Reverse engineering a template

Writing an ARM template from scratch can be a tedious and time-consuming task. Luckily, there are two approaches available to generate an ARM template from existing infrastructure:

- Using **Export template**
- Using **Resource Explorer**

Let's discuss both of these in the upcoming subsections.

Using Export template

The first approach is using the **Export template** option, which can be found on every resource and resource group in the Azure portal. This will generate an ARM template of the current state of the resource (group), as shown in the following screenshot:

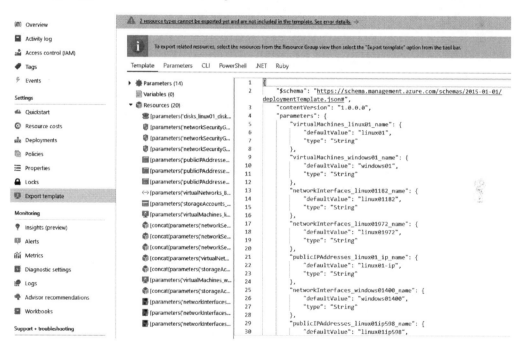

Figure 8.4 – Exporting an ARM template

Please note that not every service currently supports reverse engineering an ARM template using this approach. For any service not supported, there will be a warning at the top of the screen. To work around this limitation for retrieving the JSON template for an individual resource, there is another approach, which is our next topic of discussion. The `Export template` process will create a reusable ARM template. However, most exported templates require some modifications before they can be used to deploy Azure resources.

Using Resource Explorer

To retrieve the JSON template for an individual resource, we can use **Resource Explorer**. Resource Explorer is shown here and can be found in the Azure portal by using the menu (**1**):

Figure 8.5 – Azure Resource Explorer

After opening Resource Explorer, two new panes open up. The left pane can be used to navigate through subscriptions and drill down into the resource groups, down to the individual resources. For every element that is selected, the corresponding JSON will be displayed on the right. In the preceding example, the JSON for a hard disk is shown. This JSON is the same as the JSON that can be used in the resources array of an ARM template, except the ID element. Note that due to the different API versions used, the JSON output and the relevant template resource may vary.

Subscription-level templates

The discussion of ARM templates up to this point has all been about ARM templates for a resource group deployment. A template describes one or more resources that are deployed to a resource group. Additionally, there are also subscription-level templates. An example ARM template for a resource group is as follows:

```
{
    "$schema": "https://schema.management.azure.com/
schemas/2018-05-01
/subscriptionDeploymentTemplate.json#",
    "contentVersion": "1.0.0.1",
    "parameters": { },
    "variables": { },
    "resources": [
        {
            "type": "Microsoft.Resources/resourceGroups",
            "apiVersion": "2021-04-01",
            "location": "West Europe",
            "name": "myResourceGroup",
            "properties": {}
        }
    ],
    "outputs": {}
}
```

The format for a subscription template is completely the same as that for a resource group. The differences are $schema, which points to another schema location, and the types of resources that are supported. Subscription templates do not support the creation of resources directly and support only the creation of resource groups, the initiation of template deployments, creating and assigning Azure policies, and the creation of role assignments.

Azure Blueprints

Next to subscription-level templates, there is also another offering available: Azure Blueprints. Blueprints can be used to describe the desired state of an Azure subscription and apply that to an existing subscription.

All of the things that can be done using a blueprint can nowadays also be done using an ARM template. However, the other way around is not true. Azure Blueprints only supports the following constructs, which are called artifacts:

- Policy assignments
- Role (RBAC) assignments
- Resource group creation
- Nested ARM templates at the subscription or resource group level

These are all of the elements that are needed to build the default layout, or a blueprint, for Azure subscriptions.

There are a number of key differences between blueprints and ARM templates:

- A blueprint is a resource you can create and navigate to in the portal. The authoring experience is also in the portal, not in text files on a local computer.
- The relationship between a subscription and the blueprint that was used to create it remains, also after the deployment completes.
- With the assignment of a blueprint to a subscription, it is possible to mark the assignment as locked. If this is done, all of the resources deployed through the blueprint cannot be deleted or edited as long as the blueprint is applied—not even by the owners of the subscription that it is assigned to.
- There are many built-in blueprints available that can be used to implement controls from well-known standards such as ISO, NIST, or HIPAA.

Azure Blueprints is still in preview at the time of writing. While using Blueprints, you can install RBAC roles, ARM templates, and Azure policies all at once and assign them to a certain scope. Removing the assignment does not delete or remove the resources, thus this soon becomes tedious, and Azure DevOps has no tasks or automation to manage blueprints at scale.

Bicep

Bicep is a **Domain-Specific Language** (**DSL**) that allows the declarative deployment of Azure resources. Everything you can do with an ARM template can be accomplished with Bicep as well.

Bicep provides all resource types and API versions. Bicep provides a better authoring experience as it supports type safety and a simple declarative syntax. Bicep files are idempotent, and one file will represent the desired state. You can then use that file to repeatedly deploy your infrastructure in a consistent manner.

Bicep is a transparent abstraction over ARM template JSON and supports JSON template capabilities. The Bicep CLI converts a Bicep file into ARM template JSON. You can use the Bicep Playground (`https://aka.ms/bicepdemo`) to view Bicep and equivalent JSON side by side.

To decompile ARM template JSON to Bicep in the Azure CLI, use the following:

```
az bicep decompile --file deployment.json
```

The command creates a file named `deployment.bicep`. Decompiling an ARM template helps you get started with Bicep development.

Using Azure Automation

Azure Automation is a service in Azure that is designed to help users to create, manage, deploy, and maintain their Azure resources. Azure Automation contains several concepts that remove some of the complexities and low-level details from these actions. Azure Automation allows for the formulation of workflows in the form of runbooks. These runbooks can be executed against Azure resources on behalf of the user.

Automation account resources

Within an Azure Automation account, there are several resources that make this more than just a scripting engine. These resources are shared on the level of the Automation account and can hence be reused within multiple runbooks.

Run As account

The first of these constructs is the *Run As* account. This account is a service principal that will be created in the AAD that the Azure subscription containing the Automation account is linked to. The credentials to authenticate as this service principal are securely stored within the Automation account. These credentials are non-retrievable directly from an Automation account. The service principal is also added as a contributor to the Azure subscription. As a result, runbooks can now be set up to execute using this account. Run As accounts can be automatically created when creating the Automation account.

Run As account functionality is still available for current and new Automation accounts. However, the Run As account has been replaced with managed identities. Managed identities are the recommended way to authenticate in your runbooks and the default authentication method for your Automation account. Because no credentials are saved, a managed identity is more secure and easier to use. If you use Run As in your runbook code, you should change it to use managed identities instead.

Schedules

A common way of automating workflows is scheduling them to run on a specific date and time or at a fixed interval. Instead of specifying a schedule for every workflow, shared schedules can be created and reused in runbooks. To create a new schedule, first, open the list of all schedules. After that, a new schedule can be added, as shown in the following screenshot:

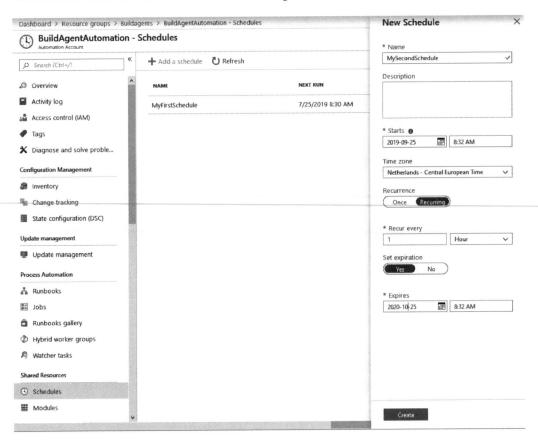

Figure 8.6 – Azure Automation workflow schedules

A schedule has a name and a description. These values are for the users interacting with the schedule only. Next, a starting date and time can be configured, along with an optional recurrence interval, and, if a recurrence interval is specified, an expiration date and time.

Once the schedule is created, it can be used for a runbook.

Modules

The runbooks that are used in Azure Automation are written in PowerShell or Python. PowerShell has a very rich ecosystem of modules with predefined functionalities that can be used. To use PowerShell modules from an Automation account, only modules that have been uploaded to the modules section can be used. One major benefit of this is that it is possible to fix the version of a module to use. This guarantees that scripts will keep working and not break in case of updates to dependencies.

The PowerShell modules for interacting with Azure are by default installed into every Automation account. Furthermore, more modules can be added, and existing modules can be upgraded or removed by administrators.

Variables

Within runbooks, a lot of variables might come into play: the names of resource groups, virtual machines, startup or shutdown times, and so on. Hardcoding these values inside a script is not good practice but storing them together with a runbook also has downsides. For example, in the case that there are three runbooks for the same virtual machine, this would mean that a number of variable values (for example, resource group name and virtual machine name) would be repeated at least three times. To prevent this, it is possible to store variable values at the Automation account level, from where they can be reused throughout every runbook that is executed in that account.

Once a variable is set, it can be accessed from a runbook using the following command:

```
$exampleVar = Get-AutomationVariable -Name 'ExampleVar'
```

In addition to reading and using variables inside a runbook, they can also be updated from within a runbook:

```
Set-AutomationVariable -name 'ExampleVar' -value 'ExampleValue'
```

While a very powerful feature, updating variables from within runbooks can have unexpected consequences. If a variable value that is used in multiple runbooks gets updated by one of them, this might break the other runbooks. Keeping track of which variables are read-only and which are written to as well is important.

Credentials

A special type of variable is the credential. Credentials contain not one but two values: a username and a password. Credentials are treated as secrets everywhere they are used. This means that they will not appear in logs and that they have to be retrieved using a specific PowerShell syntax:

```
$myCredential = Get-AutomationPSCredential -Name 'MyCredential'
```

After executing this command, the `myCredential` object can be used to retrieve both the username and password.

Connections

It is a very common scenario to have to connect to one or more external services from within a runbook. A common example is the ARM template that is used to manage all resources within Azure. To avoid having to store a series of variables and build the corresponding connection in a runbook, Automation accounts allow for the creation beforehand of one or more connections.

> **Tip**
> In most scenarios, it is not necessary to create connections manually as they are provided along with a Run As account.

Once all of the shared resources are in place, it is time to start writing one or more runbooks, which is our next topic of discussion.

Runbooks

Azure Automation supports a number of types of runbooks: PowerShell, Python 2, and graphical. The first two allow for writing scripts in the specified language. Graphical runbooks allow for composing a runbook from all uploaded PowerShell modules, assets, and existing runbooks using drag and drop.

In addition to these three basic types of runbooks, there are PowerShell workflow and graphical workflow types available. The difference between a regular runbook and a workflow runbook is that workflow runbooks also support parallelism. Another benefit of PowerShell workflow is that it supports the use of checkpoints, which allow a script to be resumed if it encounters an exception mid-execution.

Runbook execution

Once the runbook is written, there are a number of ways to execute it:

- **Manually**: Any runbook can be run at any time by opening it in the Azure portal and pressing **Start**. Of course, these operations are also available using PowerShell or the Azure CLI.

- **By attaching a webhook**: Once a runbook is published, one or more webhooks can be generated for executing the runbook. Each webhook can be enabled or disabled or given an expiration date. These tools allow a new webhook to be generated for every user of the runbook and fine-grained control to be initiated if ever, in the future, access should not be accorded to a particular user.

- **On a schedule**: Published runbooks can be attached to one or more of the shared schedules. Being able to attach to multiple schedules means that it is easy to precreate a series of schedules for typical reoccurrences, such as hourly, daily, or every Monday, and reuse and combine these for the appropriate runbooks.

When executing the runbook from a webhook or on a schedule, the option to run it manually will stay available.

Jobs

Every time a runbook is executed, a new entry is created in the **Jobs** log. This log will show an entry for every time the runbook has run, no matter how the execution was initiated. Every entry will contain the date and time the run was started, whether there were errors, and a full execution log.

Runbooks gallery

Runbooks are a great way of automating common tasks. Of course, there are tasks that are only for specific customers, but there are also many tasks that are applicable to all Azure customers. Examples include the automated startup of a virtual machine every Monday at 8 A.M. or scaling up a database every morning and back down every evening.

For these common scenarios, there is the runbooks gallery, which is enabled within every Automation account. In this gallery, hundreds of premade runbooks can be browsed and searched. Once an appropriate runbook has been found, it can be imported directly into the account as a runbook.

Besides executing scripts at set intervals or upon the invocation of a webhook, Azure Automation can also be used as a PowerShell DSC pull server. Let's discuss this next.

Before you run a new runbook that you've created or imported, you must first publish it. Each Azure Automation runbook has a Draft and a Published edition. Only the Published version can be run, and the Draft version can be modified. Any modifications to the Draft version have no effect on the Published version. When the Draft version is ready, you publish it, replacing the existing Published version with the Draft version.

PowerShell DSC

PowerShell DSC is a notion for specifying the configuration of servers. This configuration is stored on a pull server, where it can be accessed by one or more virtual machines. These virtual machines are configured to check this server at a specified interval for the latest DSC configuration and update themselves to comply with this configuration.

PowerShell DSC is an extension to the PowerShell language specification that is used for writing desired state configurations. A configuration enables the desired state of one or more nodes to be specified. A node specifies which server, or set of servers, is to be configured. The configuration for a node is written in the form of one or more resources. An example configuration is as follows:

```
configuration ServerFarmConfig
{
    Node FrontEndServer
```

```
{
    WindowsFeature IIS
    {
        Ensure = 'Present'
        Name = 'Web-Server'
        IncludeAllSubFeature = $true
    }

    File LogDirectory
    {
        Type = 'Directory'
        DestinationPath = 'C:\logs'
        Ensure = "Present"



    }
}
}
```

In this example, the configuration for a server farm with a single type of server is described. This server contains two resources. The first one, of the `WindowsFeature` type, with the name **Internet Information Services** (**IIS**), ensures that `IIS` is installed together with all of its subfeatures. The second resource, of the `File` type, ensures that a directory, `c:\logs`, exists. The resource types of `IIS` and `File` and many more are built into the PowerShell DSC specification. A full reference of all resources is available online and a link is included at the end of this chapter.

Compiling and applying PowerShell DSC

PowerShell DSC files are saved in plaintext, often in a `.ps1` file. These files can be compiled into **Managed Object Format** (**MOF**) files. These MOF files can then be pushed to one or more servers to update the state of the server to the state described in the MOF file. This is called **push mode**.

Besides push mode, there is another mode for deploying MOF files. This is called **pull mode**. In pull mode, MOF files are not directly pushed to individual servers but stored on a central server, which is called the **pull server**. This way, the pull server has a complete record of all configurations and node definitions within those configurations.

Once the pull server is up and running, individual servers are configured to fetch their DSC configuration at a fixed interval and apply that configuration. Applying a configuration means that, for every defined resource, the described state will be enacted. This can be done by doing nothing if the actual state already matches the desired state, or by running commands to achieve the desired state. In this process, all previous changes—even by administrators—will be reverted if necessary.

Using PowerShell DSC with Azure Automation

Azure Automation has built-in capabilities for PowerShell DSC and can fulfill the role of pull server for one or more virtual machines.

To start using the built-in pull server capabilities, upload one or more configuration files to the Automation account. This is done from the **State configuration** view that is shown in the following screenshot. Now, complete the following steps:

1. Open by clicking the menu option on the left.
2. Select **Configurations** in the tab bar at the top.

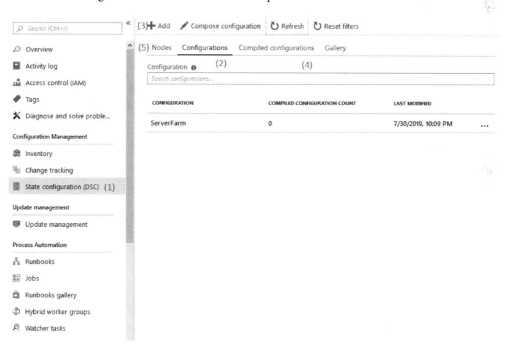

Figure 8.7 – Azure Automation state configuration

3. Once the overview of all configurations is opened, new configurations can be added using the **Add** button. In `topHere`, a local `ps1` file can be selected, and that will be added to the list. Any valid configuration in the list can be clicked on and compiled in place.

4. Now, the configuration will also be shown in the tab with compiled configurations and can be applied to one or more virtual machines.

5. Once a compiled configuration is available, the **Nodes** tab can be used for adding one or more virtual machines from the subscription to a configuration node.

6. Clicking the **Add** button while this tab is shown opens the view shown here:

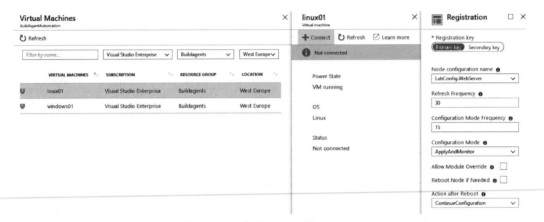

Figure 8.8 – Azure Automation – adding a new virtual machine

7. In this view, a virtual machine can be selected to which the selected configuration should be applied.

8. The local configuration manager on that machine will be configured to refresh the configuration at fixed intervals.

9. Whenever the configuration is refreshed, it will be reapplied to the server.

Azure Automation enables users to manage virtual machines, for example, to apply application configuration. When working with PaaS offerings, this cannot be done using techniques such as PowerShell DSC; other techniques have to be used to manage application settings. These will be discussed in the next section.

Managing application settings

Another part of the infrastructure of an application is the application configuration. In this section, a number of approaches for storing and loading the application configuration for an Azure App Service are discussed. They include the following:

- Storing the configuration in the app settings

- Using a combination of a managed identity and key vault

- Using the Azure App Configuration service

The disadvantage of the first approach is that the app settings can be read by any user who has administrative (read) access to the app service that is configured. The next two approaches do not have this disadvantage.

Azure App Service settings from an ARM template

The first way to configure application settings as code is by specifying app settings as a resource in an ARM template. This should be specified as a nested resource. This can be done as shown in the following screenshot:

```
{
    "name": "[concat(variables('websiteName'), '/
appsettings')]",
    "type": "config",
    "apiVersion": "2021-03-01",
    "dependsOn": [
        "[concat('Microsoft.Web/sites/',
variables('webSiteName'))]"
    ],
    "properties": {
        "key1": " [listKeys(parameters('storagename'), 2021-03-
01').keys[0].value]",
        "key2": "value2"
    }
}
```

The use of the listKeys function is especially useful in these scenarios. It allows for the direct copying of secrets from supported services to the application settings without ever storing them in an intermediate solution. For secrets that do not come from Azure sources, template parameters should be used.

The configuration specified in the ARM template corresponds to the configuration of an app service that can be found in the portal. These settings are used to override corresponding entries in the appsettings.json or appsettings.config files. Updating this configuration automatically reloads the application as well.

The downside of this approach is that secrets that are stored this way are readable through the Azure portal. Any user with read access to the app service can retrieve all secrets stored this way.

Loading settings at runtime from a key vault

The next possible location for storing app service settings is in an Azure key vault, where the application loads them at runtime. To make this possible, the following has to be in place.

To be able to authorize an application with access to a key vault, the application first has to be able to authenticate itself against AAD. Of course, this can be done by registering a service principal manually, but this would return a username and password that have to be stored somewhere. Usernames and passwords are secrets but cannot be stored in the key vault since they are needed for accessing it. This problem of how to keep the key to the vault safe can be solved by using an Azure capability called a **managed identity**.

> **Important Note**
> The problem of securely storing secrets but getting another secret in return for accessing them is often referred to as the problem of *turtles all the way down*. This refers to an old anecdote to which a link is included at the end of this chapter.

With an Azure managed identity enabled on an app service, Azure automatically generates a service principal with a non-retrievable username and password. Only at runtime, using specific code, can an application authenticate itself as this principal. Azure will ensure that this will only work for code that is running with the app service that the managed identity belongs to.

Now that an application can have its own identity, that identity has to be granted access to the key vault. This can be done in the key vault description in an ARM template, using the following syntax for reference:

```
{
    "type": "Microsoft.KeyVault/vaults",
    "name": "[parameters('keyVaultName')]",
    "apiVersion": " 2021-11-01-preview",
    "location": "[resourceGroup().location]",
    "dependsOn": [
        "[resourceId('Microsoft.Web/sites/',
parameters('appServiceName'))]"
    ],
    "properties": {
        "enabledForTemplateDeployment": false,
        "tenantId": "[subscription().tenantId]",
        "accessPolicies": [
            {
```

```
                    "tenantId": "[subscription().tenantId]",
"objectId":
                    [reference(concat(resourceId('Microsoft.Web/
sites',parameters('appServiceNa me')),  '/providers/Microsoft.
ManagedIdentity/Idntities/default'), ' 2021-11-01-preview').
principalId]", "permissions": {     "secrets": [ "get", "list" ]
                    }
                }
            ],
            "sku": {
                "name": "standard",
                "family": "A"
            }
        }
    }
}
```

In this example, the reference() function is used to retrieve the information of the managed identity and uses this to create an access policy on the key vault.

Finally, with the key vault and access to it set up, the application has to retrieve the contents at startup time. To do this, config builders can be used. They are introduced with .NET Core 2.0 (and .NET Framework 4.7.1) and are used in the StartUp class, as shown in the following code snippet:

```
var tokenProvider = new AzureServiceTokenProvider();
var kvClient = new KeyVaultClient((authority, resource, scope)
=> tokenProvider.KeyVaultTokenCallback(authority, resource,
scope));


var configurationBuilder = new ConfigurationBuilder().
AddAzureKeyVault(
    $"https://{ Configuration["keyVaultName"]}.vault.azure.
net/", kvClient,
    new DefaultKeyVaultSecretManager());
Configuration = configurationBuilder.Build();
```

All types in this code example are available in the NuGet Microsoft.Configuration. ConfigurationBuilders.Azure package.

Azure App Configuration

Another location for storing the configuration of applications is Azure App Configuration. This is a new service, and at the time of writing, it is still in preview. App Configuration allows for the creation of a central register of key-value pairs that can be used as configuration by such a register, but also multiple applications.

App Configuration is another type of resource that can be created from the portal. The main component is a **Configuration explorer,** as shown in the following screenshot:

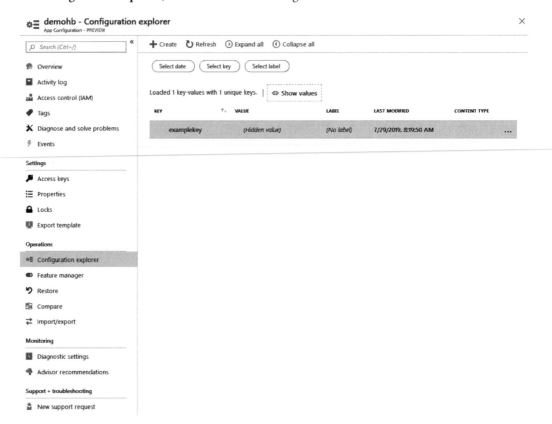

Figure 8.9 – Azure App Configuration

In addition to the Configuration explorer, there is a keys section for retrieving access keys that applications can use to read the configuration. There are also options to view recent changes to the configuration and restore earlier versions and for importing or exporting all configuration settings.

After the App Configuration resource has been created and configuration keys added, they can be retrieved from within an application by using an extension method of the **IConfiguration** framework type:

```
config.AddAzureAppConfiguration(settings["ConnectionStrings:
AppConfig"]);
```

The loader for settings from an app configuration is part of the NuGet `Microsoft.Azure.AppConfiguration.AspNetCore` package.

Compared to storing settings in Azure Key Vault, App Configuration has two downsides:

- First, the application needs to be configured with a connection string to the Azure App Configuration, storing at least one new secret in the app settings.

- Second App Configuration does not have access control options that are as rigid as Key Vault. For this reason, it might make sense to distribute configuration over both App Configuration and Key Vault, depending on the type of configuration value.

This concludes our discussion of Azure and Azure DevOps capabilities for IaC. The next section will discuss a series of other tools available that offer similar capabilities.

Other tools

There are many other tools available for managing infrastructure and configuration through code. Next to the native Azure and Windows options discussed in the previous sections, there are many alternatives widely in use and some of them are listed in this section. It is important to know which tool can be used for which scenarios and how to integrate with them.

CloudFormation

CloudFormation is the IaC language for the AWS cloud. CloudFormation templates can be written in either JSON or YAML format. One example of creating an AWS S3 storage bucket that is publicly readable would look like this:

```
Resources:
  HelloBucket:
  Type: AWS::S3::Bucket
  Properties:
  AccessControl: PublicRead
```

There is an extension available that allows the execution of CloudFormation templates on AWS from Azure DevOps. This extension provides tasks for creating, updating, or deleting AWS stacks. A stack has a function that is comparable to a resource group in Azure and the tasks are comparable to the tasks for applying an ARM template.

Chef

Chef is a tool for CaC, with support for describing and enforcing the configuration of servers. Chef uses a centralized server, the **Chef server**, where all configuration for all servers is saved. Here, the correct desired state for every server is determined, which is then pulled by the **Chef client**, an agent that runs on the *node* that is being managed.

Defining the desired state for a server is done using a number of constructs. The lowest level is the recipe. A recipe contains one or more resources, which are built-in capabilities that can be used. An example resource is `execute`, which runs a Bash command. Another example resource is `apt_update`, which provides the means to interact with the `apt` package manager. One or more recipes are combined in cookbooks, which describe a capability that can be assigned to a node. The assignment of one or more cookbooks to a node is done using the run list. The run list contains all cookbooks that have to be applied to a node.

Interaction with the Chef server is done using a command-line tool called `knife`.

While the terminology is completely different, there are many conceptual parallels between PowerShell DSC and Chef.

Puppet

Puppet is a deployment and configuration management tool that operates using a server-client model. There is a centralized server called the **Puppet master** that is responsible for taking in all of the desired state descriptions and compiling them to an internal catalog that holds the desired state for every managed server. All servers that are managed by Puppet need to have the Puppet agent installed on the local server. The agent connects to the server to pull the state for the server it manages, and applies that locally. A managed server is called a **node**.

The base building block used by Puppet is called a **resource**. A resource is defined by specifying a resource type and a series of attributes. There are many resource types available, for example, for managing users and installed applications. Resources are grouped into one or more *classes*. These classes are, in turn, assigned to one or more nodes.

Puppet can be installed on any Linux or Windows virtual machine in Azure. There is also a prebuilt image with Puppet Enterprise available in the Azure Marketplace.

Puppet is comparable to Chef and PowerShell DSC. All three have a comparable model for describing the desired state and they all serve the same purpose.

Ansible

Ansible is yet another configuration management tool that is mostly used on Linux but also has support for Windows. One aspect that differentiates Ansible from other tools is that it does not have a centralized server that hosts all of the desired states, nor does it work with agents. All commands executed by Ansible are executed using SSH or other relevant protocols—HTTP(S), WinRM, and so on.

Any server can initiate the deployment of a *playbook* against one or more *items* in an *inventory*. An Ansible inventory contains all of the servers that can be managed by Ansible. They can be grouped into one or more groups, which can be nested into other groups as well. Each individual server and every group is an inventory item. In Ansible, the desired state is written in playbooks. A playbook is a series of tasks or roles that need to be run on the target server. A role is a group of tasks. Roles are intended to be reused in more than one playbook and should, therefore, be general enough to be usable in multiple situations. Roles should also be idempotent. This means that the tasks in the role should ensure that the outcome of running the playbook is the same, no matter the number of times it is run.

Ansible scripts can be executed using command-line tools or an Azure DevOps extension that wraps this tool. There are also other management systems available, such as Ansible Tower, which provides a graphical user interface on top of the capabilities of the Ansible command-line tools.

Terraform

Terraform is a multicloud infrastructure management solution. It is comparable to ARM templates or Bicep, the difference being that it also supports Amazon Web Services, Google Cloud Platform, and other supported cloud services. Terraform uses a custom file format for specifying one or more resources to be created using one or more providers. The resources correspond to the cloud resources, and the providers are responsible for knowing how to interact with the APIs of the different vendors.

Optionally, you can use a JSON format instead of the Terraform proprietary format called **HashiCorp Configuration Language** (**HCL**). Terraform also supports the use of modules for creating packages that are reusable components.

Terraform configuration files are executed using CLIs.

You can refer to the Terraform fundamentals (`https://learn.hashicorp.com/collections/terraform/cli`) to learn about these core components.

Summary

In this chapter, you learned about the concepts of IaC and CaC, their value, and how to use them in practice. To implement these, you learned about ARM templates, the IaC mechanism for Azure. You also learned about PowerShell DSC to manage the configuration of virtual machines and about different techniques for managing the configuration of your applications. Finally, you learned about several other tools available on the market. You learned which tool can be used in which situation and whether these tools can integrate with Azure DevOps.

With this knowledge, you are now able to start describing the infrastructure and configuration of your application(s) in source control using one or more of the tools you have read about. You are also capable of setting up the means to deliver the infrastructure using automation, either from a release pipeline or using dedicated infrastructure management tools. But no matter which solution you choose, you now have the capabilities to incorporate infrastructure into your DevOps processes.

In the next chapter, you will learn about another challenge you might encounter when implementing DevOps practices, related to databases. When increasing the speed at which features flow to production, you may also have to change the way you manage your database schema and how you apply changes. The next chapter will discuss this subject.

Activity

- Create And Deploy Empty ARM template using Azure CLI
- Add a resource to create Storage account in your ARM template

Questions

As we conclude, here is a list of questions for you to test your knowledge regarding this chapter's material. You will find the answers in the *Assessments* section of the Appendix:

1. True or False: ARM templates in Incremental deployment mode can be used for creating, updating, and deleting Azure resources.

2. Which of the following is not an Azure Automation account resource?

   A. Modules

   B. Containers

   C. Managed identities

   D. Variables

3. True or False: One disadvantage of IaC is that you have to put sensitive information in source control as ARM template parameter files.

4. True or False: Azure Automation accounts allow for the execution of PowerShell runbooks at a predefined schedule.

5. What are some of the benefits of using IaC?

Further reading

- A formal breakdown of the ARM template structure and syntax can be found at https://docs.microsoft.com/en-us/azure/azure-resource-manager/templates/template-expressions.

- The complete ARM template documentation can be found at `https://docs.microsoft.com/en-us/azure/templates/`.

- An overview of all functions that can be used in ARM templates can be found at `https://docs.microsoft.com/en-us/azure/azure-resource-manager/templates/template-functions`.

- More information about Azure Blueprints can be found at `https://docs.microsoft.com/en-us/azure/governance/blueprints/overview`.

- Details about the `WhatIf` command for ARM templates can be found at `https://docs.microsoft.com/en-us/azure/azure-resource-manager/templates/deploy-what-if`.

- Documentation for all PowerShell DSC built-in resources, can be found at `https://docs.microsoft.com/en-us/powershell/dsc/overview/decisionmaker?view=dsc-1.1`.

- More information about CloudFormation can be found at `https://aws.amazon.com/cloudformation/`.

- More information about Chef can be found at `https://www.chef.io/`.

- More information about Puppet can be found at `https://puppet.com/`.

- More information about Ansible can be found at `https://www.ansible.com/`.

- More information about Terraform can be found at `https://www.terraform.io/`.

- More information about Azure resource manager commands `https://docs.microsoft.com/en-us/cli/azure/deployment/group?view=azure-cli-latest#az-deployment-group-create`

- Bicep overview:

  - `https://github.com/Azure/bicep`

  - `https://docs.microsoft.com/en-us/azure/azure-resource-manager/bicep/learn-bicep`

- Learning path to explore the *Infrastructure as Code*: `https://docs.microsoft.com/en-us/learn/paths/az-400-manage-infrastructure-as-code-using-azure/`.

- There are many online references to the story of *turtles all the way down*, but an early reference can be found digitized at `https://dspace.mit.edu/handle/1721.1/15166`.

9

Dealing with Databases in DevOps Scenarios

In the previous chapters, you learned about the continuous integration and continuous deployment of your software. You also learned how the same principles can be applied to the delivery of configuration in infrastructure. Once you have adopted these principles and started increasing the flow of value delivery, you might run into another challenge: managing your database schema changes.

Applying DevOps to databases can feel like trying to change the tires on a running car. You must find some way of coordinating changes between the database schema and application code without taking the system down for maintenance.

In this chapter, you will learn about different approaches for doing just that: managing these schema changes while avoiding downtime. With proper planning and a disciplined approach, this can be achieved in a way that manages risks well. You will see how you can treat your database schema as code, and you will learn about the different approaches that are available to do so. You will also see another approach that avoids database schemas altogether, namely, going schema-less.

The following topics will be covered in this chapter:

- Managing a database schema as code
- Applying database schema changes
- Going schema-less
- Other approaches and concerns

Technical requirements

In order to practice the ideas that are laid out in this chapter, you will need to have the following tools installed:

- An application with the Entity Framework Core NuGet package installed
- Visual Studio with SQL Server Data Tools
- Access to Azure Pipelines
- An Azure subscription, for accessing Cosmos DB

Managing a database schema as code

For those of you who are familiar with working with relational databases from application code, it is very likely you have been working with an **object-relational mapper** (**ORM**).

ORMs were introduced to fill the impedance mismatch between object-oriented programming languages and the relational database schema, which works with tables. Well-known examples are Entity Framework and NHibernate.

ORMs provide a layer of abstraction that allows for the storage and retrieval of objects from a database, without worrying about the underlying table structure when doing so. To perform automated mapping of objects to tables, or the other way around, ORMs often have built-in capabilities for describing a database schema, the corresponding object model, and the mappings between them in a markup language. Most of the time, neither of these have to be written by hand. Often, they can be generated from an object model or an existing database, and the mappings between them are often, by convention, generated or drawn in a visual editor.

While all this allows for the current database schema to be defined as code, this alone does not help with coping with schema changes, yet. For handling schema changes as code, two common approaches are available. The first one describes every change in code; the other one describes only the latest version of the schema in code. These approaches are known as migration-based and state-based approaches, respectively. Both can rely on third-party tooling for applying the changes to the database.

Migrations

The first approach is based on keeping an ordered set of changes that have to be applied to the database. These changes are often called **migrations**, and they can be generated by tools such as Microsoft Entity Framework or Redgate SQL Change Automation, or they can be written by hand.

Tools can automatically generate the migration scripts based on a comparison of the current schema of the database and the new schema definition in source control. This is called **scaffolding**. The scripts generated by tools are not always perfect, and they can be improved by applying the domain knowledge that the programmer has. Once one or more new migrations are scaffolded or written, they can be applied to a database using the chosen tool. The following is a diagram showing how that works:

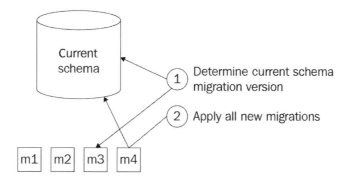

Figure 9.1 – Migration approach

Here, we see how an ever-growing series of migrations, labeled **m1** to **m4**, are generated to describe incremental changes to the database. To update the database to the latest version, the latest applied migration is determined and all migrations after that are added one after the other.

When editing migration scripts by hand, the following have to be kept in mind:

- The migration scripts should be ordered. Migrations describe the SQL statements that need to be executed in order to move the database from version x to version $x+1$. The next migration can be started only when this step is completed.

- A migration script should migrate not only the schema but also the data. This can mean that a few steps are needed in between migrations. For example, moving two columns to another table often implies that the new columns are first created, then filled with the data from the old columns, and only then are the old columns removed.

- It is advisable to include all database objects in the migration scripts. Extra indexes and constraints should be applied not only to the production database but also to test environments. With migrations, there is already a mechanism for delivering those from source control. Having these in the same migration scripts also ensures that indexes and constraints are applied in the same order and cannot unexpectedly block migrations by existing only in production.

- If possible, migration scripts should be made idempotent. If there is ever an issue or the suspicion of an issue, being able to just rerun the last migration is a great way to ensure that it is fully applied.

One disadvantage of this approach is the strict ordering requirement that is imposed on generating and applying the generated migrations. This makes it hard to integrate this approach into a development workflow that relies heavily on the use of branches.

Migrations created in different branches that are merged together only later might break the ordering of migrations or, even worse, merge a split in the migration path. For example, imagine the case where two migrations, b and c, in two different branches have been created after an existing migration, a. How are these going to be merged? Neither order—a, b, c or a, c, b—is correct, since both b and c are created to be executed directly after a. The only way such an error can be fixed is by performing the following steps:

1. Remove all migrations apart from the first new one, which is c in this case.

2. Apply all other migrations to a database that has none of the new migrations applied, in this case, only b if a was already applied, or both a and b.

3. Generate a new migration for the other migrations, in this case, a replacement for c.

An advantage of this approach is that every individual schema change will be deployed against the database in the same fashion. Irrespective of whether one—or more than one—migration is applied to the production database at the same time, they will still run one by one in a predictable order and in the same way in which they ran against the test environment, even if they were applied there one by one.

End state

A different approach to managing schema changes is to not keep track of the individual changes (or migrations), but only store the latest version of the schema in source control. External tools such as Microsoft Visual Studio and Redgate's SQL Data Compare tool are then used to compare the current schema in source control with the actual schema of the database, generate migration scripts, and apply these when running. The migration scripts are not stored and are single-use only.

Unlike writing migrations, it is not feasible to execute a task like this by hand. While tracking the newest version of the schema by hand in source control can be managed, the same is not feasible for an end-state approach. Generating a migration script while comparing the existing schema and the new schema and applying this migration script can only be done using a tool. Examples of suitable tools are Redgate SQL Source Control and SQL Server Data Tools. How these tools work is shown in the following diagram:

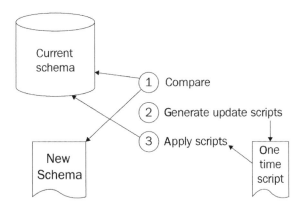

Figure 9.2 – Managing schema changes

Here, we see how the current, actual database schema and the description of the desired database schema are compared to generate an upgrade and directly apply a script for making the changes needed to make the actual schema the same as the desired schema.

One advantage of this approach is that there is no series of scripts generated that have to be executed in a specific order. Therefore, this approach combines easily with extensive branching schemas, where changes are integrated more slowly over time. It also removes the need to write migrations by hand for simple scenarios, such as adding or deleting a column, table, or index.

The disadvantage of this approach is that it makes it harder to handle changes that need data operations as well. Again, imagine a scenario of moving two columns to another table. Since the tooling only enforces the new schema, this will lead to data loss if there is no further intervention.

One possible form of intervention to circumvent this is the addition of pre- and post-deployment scripts to the schema package. In the pre-deployment script, the current data is staged in a temporary table. Then, after applying the new schema, the data is copied from the temporary table to the new location in the post-deployment script.

This section was about managing database schema changes in a format that can be stored in source control. The next section discusses how these changes can be picked up at deploy time and then applied to a database.

Applying database schema changes

With the database schema and, optionally, a series of migrations defined in source control, it is time to start thinking about when to apply changes to the database schema. There are two methods to do so. Database schema changes can be applied prior to deployment of the new application version, or by the application code itself.

Upgrading as part of the release

The first approach to applying database changes is as part of the release pipeline. When this is the case, the tool that is responsible for reading and executing the migration scripts is invoked using a step in the pipeline.

This invocation can be done using a custom script in PowerShell or another scripting language. However, this is error-prone, and with every change of tool, there is a risk that the scripts need to be updated. Luckily, for most migration-based tools, there are Azure Pipelines tasks that are readily available for starting the migration from the release.

For example, there is an Azure Pipelines extension available for applying Entity Framework Core migrations to a database directly from the dll file where they are defined. This task can be added to the release pipeline for updating the database before the new application code is deployed. A link to the **Build & Release Tools** extension is provided in the *Further reading* section at the end of this chapter.

Another variation is a split between the build and release phases of an application. In this case, the migration scripts are exported as a separate build artifact, either directly from the source code—if written in SQL—or after executing a tool that generates the necessary SQL scripts as output. This artifact is then downloaded again in the release phase, where it is applied to the database using an Azure Pipelines task for executing SQL.

Upgrading with the application code

Instead of applying schema changes from the release pipeline, they can also be applied by the application itself. Some of the ORMs, with migration support built in, have the capability to automatically detect whether the database schema matches the latest migration. If not, they can automatically migrate the schema to that latest version on the spot.

An example of an ORM that supports this is Entity Framework. The core version of Entity Framework does not have support for automatic migrations built in. In Entity Framework Core, a single line of application code can be used to initiate an upgrade at a time that is convenient from the perspective of the application. The code for doing so is shown in the following code snippet:

```
using (var context = new MyContext(...))
{
    context.Database.Migrate();
}
```

The advantage of this approach is that it is very simple to enable. Just a Boolean switch in the configuration of, for example, Entity Framework can enable this workflow. However, the disadvantage is that most ORMs that support this will enforce a global lock on the database—stopping all database transactions while the migrations are running. For any migration or set of migrations that take more than a few seconds, this approach might be impractical.

This approach is normally only used for migration-based approaches. Approaches that use an end-state approach require an external third-party tool that is used to generate the necessary migration scripts and apply them. This is normally done from the release pipeline and is not wrapped in the application itself.

Adding a process

As the previous section illustrated, it is important to think about how and when changes to the database schema or the application (or applications!) that use that schema are applied. But, no matter how the deployment of schema changes and code deployments are scheduled, there will always be a period where one of the following is true:

- The new application code is already running while the schema changes are not applied yet or are in the process of being applied.

- The old application code is still running while the schema changes are already applied or are in the process of being applied.

- The application code is not running while the schema changes are being applied.

The third situation is highly undesirable. This is true in general, but especially when practicing DevOps. If changes are shipped often and during working hours, it is unacceptable to take the application down for every schema change.

To prevent having to take the application down while schema changes are being applied, one of the following conditions has to be met:

- The schema changes are backward-compatible in such a way that the old version of the application code can run without errors against a database where the schema changes have already been applied or are being applied.

- The new application code is backward-compatible in such a way that it can run against both the old and new versions of the schema.

Meeting the first of these conditions ensures that the old application code can continue to run while the schema changes are being applied. Meeting the second of these conditions ensures that the new version of the application code can be deployed first, and once that is completed, the database can be upgraded while this code is running. While either will work, it is often desirable to aim for the first condition. The reason is that schema changes often support application code changes.

This means that the following is a safe process for deploying schema changes without downtime:

1. Create a new database.
2. Apply the database changes.
3. Verify that the changes have been applied properly or abort the deployment pipeline.
4. Deploy the new application code.

It is important to realize that this process assumes failing forward. This means that if there ever is an issue with the deployment of schema changes, they should be resolved before going forward with the code changes.

Finally, meeting the condition of backward compatibility for schema changes can sometimes be impossible to fulfill for a schema change. If this is the case, the change can often be split into two partial changes that together have the same end result, while they both meet the condition of backward compatibility. For example, renaming a property, or changing the unit in which it stores a distance from feet to meters, can be executed as follows:

1. Generate a migration that adds a new column to a database table, storing the distance in meters.

2. Add application code that reads from the old column but writes to both columns.

3. Deploy these changes to production.

4. Add a new migration that migrates data from the old column to the new column for all cases where the new column is not yet filled, but the old column is.

5. Update the application code to read and write only the new column.

6. Deploy these changes to production.

7. Add a new migration that removes the old column.

Using the correct tools and a proper process, it is possible to execute effective and safe deployments of schema changes. In the next section, another approach, using schema-less databases, is introduced.

Going schema-less

In the previous sections, the focus was on relational databases, where strict schemas are applied to every table. A completely different approach to database schema management is to let go of having a database schema altogether. This can be done by using schema-less or document databases. A well-known example of a schema-less database is **Azure Cosmos DB**. These databases can store documents of different forms in the same "table." Table is in quote marks here since these types of databases often do not use the term "table," but call this a database, a container, or a collection.

Since these databases can store documents with a different schema in the same collection, schema changes no longer exist from a database's point of view. But of course, there will be changes to the structure of the corresponding objects in the application code over time. To see how to handle this, it is best to differentiate between storing objects in the database and reading them back.

Writing objects to the database

The documents that are stored in a schema-less database are often serializations of objects in application code. When working with a relational database, these objects are often stored using an ORM, such as Entity Framework, Dapper, or NHibernate. When working with a document database, these objects are often serialized and stored in the database. Serialization is the process of converting an object into a stream of bytes so that it can be saved or transmitted easily across process boundaries. Deserialization is the reverse process of constructing a data structure or object from a stream of bytes. This means that a change in the definition of that code object will also result in a different document structure when saving the object. Due to the nature of document databases, this will work fine.

As an example, take the following C# class and its JSON representation.

This code is using the `JsonConstructor` attribute to indicate that the constructor of the class should be used to create an instance of the class during deserialization:

```
public class Person
{
    [JsonConstructor] private Person() {}
    public Person(string name) {
        Name = name ?? throw new ArgumentNullException();
    }
}
```

The following code shows a JSON representation of the instance of a `Person` class after serializing it to a document database:

```
{
    "Name": "Mark Anderson"
}
```

After this code has been running in a production environment for a while, and thousands of people have been saved, a new requirement comes in. Next to the name of the person, the city where they live must also be recorded. For this reason, the `Person` class is extended to include another property. After performing this change and deploying the new code, whenever a person is saved, the following code is used:

```
public class Person
{
    [JsonConstructor] private Person() {}
    public Person(string name, string city) {
    Name = name ?? throw new ArgumentNullException();
    City = city ?? throw new ArgumentNullException();
    }
    [JsonProperty]
    public string Name { get; private set; } [JsonProperty]
    public string City { get; private set; }
}
```

The definition of the `Person` class has changed; the corresponding JSON representation of a new instance is shown in the following snippet. Both document variations can be saved into the same collection:

```
{
    "Name": "Mark Anderson",
    "City": "Amsterdam"
}
```

This shows that from the viewpoint of writing information to the database, the schema-less approach is very convenient since developers do not have to think about schema change management at all.

Reading objects from the database

While schema-less databases make it extremely easy to write documents of different forms to the same collection, this can pose problems when reading documents back from that same collection and deserializing them. In reality, the problem of schema management is not removed but deferred to a later point in time.

Continuing the example from the previous section, deserializing the first person that was saved on the new C# `Person` class definition will result in a null value for the city property. This can be unexpected since the C# code guarantees that a person without a city can never be constructed. This is a clear example of the challenges that schema-less databases pose.

In this example, the issue can be circumvented by updating the `Person` class to the following:

```csharp
public class Person
{
    [JsonConstructor]
    private Person() {}

    public Person(string name, string city) {
        Name = name ?? throw new ArgumentNullException();
        City = city ?? throw new ArgumentNullException();
    }

    [JsonProperty]
    public string Name { get; private set; }

    [JsonIgnore]
    private string _city;
```

```
[JsonProperty]
public string City {
   get { return _city; }
   private set { _city = value ?? _city = string.Empty}
}
}
```

Aside from this scenario, where a property was added, there are many other scenarios that require the C# class to be adapted in order to handle deserialization scenarios. Some examples are as follows:

- Adding a property of a primitive type

- Adding a complex property, another object, or an array

- Renaming a property

- Replacing a property of a primitive type with a complex property

- Making nullable properties non-nullable

Adding code to objects to handle these situations increases the size and complexity of the code base and pollutes the primary code base with the capabilities for coping with past situations. Especially when this happens often, this can lead to unwanted complications in a code base. To prevent this, a possible solution is to go through the following process whenever the schema of an object changes:

1. Change the schema of the object, ensuring that there are only properties added. Even when the goal is to remove a property, at this stage, only a property with the new name is added.

2. Implement logic on the object to cope with the deserialization of old versions of the object.

3. Deploy the new version of the object.

4. Start a background process that loads all objects of the type from the database one by one and saves them back to the database.

5. Once the background process has processed all existing entities, remove the code that is responsible for coping with the schema change during deserialization from the code base, along with any properties that are no longer used.

Using this approach, all changes are propagated to all stored versions of the object over a period of time. The downside to this approach is that the change to the object's structure is spread over two changes that must be deployed separately. Also, deployment of the second change must wait until all objects in the database have been converted.

Other approaches and concerns

Besides the more common approaches that were discussed previously, the following tips and approaches might help with reducing the amount of work in dealing with databases or help reduce the risk associated with making database changes.

Minimizing the influence of databases

A first step in dealing with databases can be to reduce the chance that a database change has to be made. In many databases, it is possible to write stored procedures—or some other code or script—that executes within the database engine. While stored procedures come with some benefits, changing them can also count as a database schema change, or at the least, result in changes that can be difficult to test.

One simple approach for this is to just replace stored procedures with application code that allows for easier side-by-side changes using feature toggles.

Full side-by-side deployment

When working in a high-risk environment, or with a fragile database, there is also another approach to database schema changes that can be taken. This approach is based on applying feature toggles and the blue-green deployment pattern and goes as follows:

1. Change the application code in such a way that it writes any update to not just one but two databases.

2. In the production environment, create a complete, full copy of the existing database and configure the application code to write all changes to both databases. These databases will be called *old* and *new*, from now on.

3. Introduce the required changes to the new database schema and the application code *only* in the path that writes to the new database.

4. Introduce the necessary changes in all code paths that read data in such a way that all queries run against both databases.

5. Update the application code to detect differences in the query results between the new and old databases and log an error when it finds any discrepancy.

6. If the changes run without any issues, remove the old database, and the old read and write access paths, from the application code.

7. If the changes run with errors, fix the issues. Then, restart by restoring the backup of the intended new database, and resume at *step 5*.

The advantage of this approach is that it is very lightweight. The downside is that it is very involved, takes a lot of work, and is more expensive. Also, the extra database costs and duration of backup and restore operations should be taken into account.

Testing database changes

Just as with application code, insights into the quality of database schema changes can be gathered through testing. Links to performing tests on database schemas can be found at the end of this chapter.

In most cases, in order to fully cover the risks introduced by database changes, system tests are needed that execute against a fully deployed stack of the application. This type of test can cover most of the risks that come from faulty schemas, invalid stored procedures, and database and application code mismatches.

Summary

In this chapter, you have learned how to manage your database schema and schema changes using source control. You know about both the migration-based approach and state-based approach for storing changes, and how to apply them to your production database in a safe manner.

Additionally, you have learned how schema-less databases can remove the burden of traditional schema management. However, this comes at the price of having to cope with schema differences when reading older versions of an object back from the database.

In the next chapter, you will learn about continuous testing. You will not only learn about testing techniques, but also about which to apply at what point, and how testing is a crucial part of DevOps and a critical enabler of a continuous flow of value to end users.

Questions

As we conclude, here is a list of questions for you to test your knowledge regarding this chapter's material. You will find the answers in the *Assessments* section of the Appendix:

1. True or false: When working with Entity Framework, schema management is built in using migrations-based support.

2. True or false: When working with a migrations-based approach for schema management, you do not need extra tracking tables in your database schema.

3. True or false: When working with an end-state-based approach for schema management, you do not need extra tracking tables in your database schema.

4. What are the benefits of a full side-by-side approach to database schema changes? (Choose multiple answers):

    A. The risks are reduced to almost zero.

    B. You can measure the actual performance impact of changes in a production-like environment.

    C. Side-by-side migrations reduce cycle time.

5. True or false: Schema-less databases remove the need for thinking about schema changes completely.

6. What is a possible technology choice that you can make to limit the impact of changes on your database schema?

Further reading

- More information about Entity Framework and Entity Framework migrations can be found at https://docs.microsoft.com/nl-nl/ef/and https://docs.microsoft.com/en-us/ef/ef6/modeling/code-first/migrations/.

- More information about Redgate and its database tooling can be found at https://www.red-gate.com/.

- More information on SQL Server Data Tools can be found at https://docs.microsoft.com/en-us/sql/ssdt/download-sql-server-data-tools-ssdt?view=sql-server-ver15.

- Build & Release Tools Azure DevOps extension: https://marketplace.visualstudio.com/items?itemName=bendayconsulting.build-task&ssr=false#overview.

- Database changes deployment with Redgate SQL Change Automation and Azure DevOps: https://azuredevopslabs.com/labs/vstsextend/redgate/.

10
Integrating Continuous Testing

In previous chapters, you learned about the different types of techniques that are used to help increase the rate at which you deliver changes to your production environment. If you are already using these techniques in your daily work, you will quickly notice that this is only possible if your work is of sufficient quality. If the quality of your work is not high enough, you will face many outages or issues and your end users will not be happy. To be successful, increasing the rate of change and increasing the quality of your work must go hand in hand. To assess the quality of your work and increase it, you first need to know what is meant by quality. This is where testing comes in. Testing is the discipline of reporting on the quality of software.

To introduce the topic of testing, this chapter will start by looking at how the quality of software development can be measured. After that, the topic of functional testing will be explored. As we progress through this chapter, we will explore the different testing strategies to determine what types of tests are needed and how many of each should be used. After this, the different types of tests will be discussed one by one. You will learn about how they work, what they test, and the benefits and downsides of each one. Finally, the last section will focus on how all metrics and test results, once generated and collected by your pipelines, can continuously report on the quality of the work of your team and even prevent changes of insufficient quality propagating to your users. All of this will help you maintain the high quality of your software and enable you to confidently deliver that software quickly and frequently.

The following topics will be covered in this chapter:

- Defining quality
- Understanding test types
- Executing tests in a pipeline
- Maintaining quality

Technical requirements

To experiment with the techniques described in this chapter, you might need one or more of the following:

- An Azure DevOps project with access to build and release pipelines and dashboards
- Visual Studio Code, Visual Studio 2019, or Visual Studio 2022
- A Basic + Test Plans license for Azure DevOps
- A SonarCloud subscription

All of these are available for free or can be obtained for free for a limited trial period.

Defining quality

One of the primary goals of the DevOps mindset discussed in *Chapter 1, Introduction to DevOps*, is increasing the flow of value to end users. To do this, software must be deployed frequently, maybe even multiple times per day. To make frequent deployments possible, two things are important: automation and quality. Automation has been discussed extensively in the previous chapters, so now it is time to move on to the topic of quality.

Once an automated build and release pipeline is in place and changes are starting to flow to production at an increasing speed, it is time to start measuring the quality of these changes. Even more importantly, this allows us to abort changes that are not of sufficient quality.

What actually makes quality *sufficient* can differ from project to project. When creating games, a few bugs might be annoying for the user but nothing more. When creating software for airplanes or medical use, a single bug may cost lives. In software, higher quality is more expensive and/or takes more time. So, there is a trade-off between the number of features we can deliver and the quality that can be guaranteed. For every project, there is a different optimal trade-off between these.

Before quality can be measured, it is important that you first establish how to measure the quality of software. A common approach to monitoring the quality of software is to gather one or more metrics. For example, it could be decided to collect a set of five measurements every week. Graphing these metrics over time provides insight into how the quality of the software is evolving. An example of this might look something like the graph shown here:

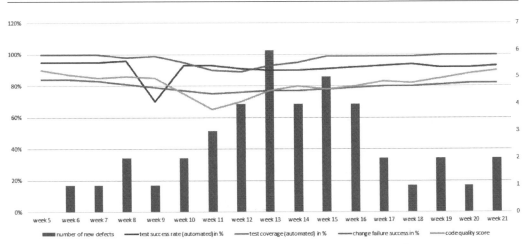

Figure 10.1 – Software quality metrics measurement example

The next sections discuss several examples of metrics.

Metrics for quality

Metrics are a means of capturing something that is measured as a number. In software development, metrics are often used to represent a particular quality aspect that can be hard to quantify in itself. For example, the quality of a piece of software can be very hard to describe by itself. This holds even more for how quality changes. For this reason, we often capture numbers that, taken together, say something about the quality of software.

It is important to realize that metrics are a great tool but should always be used with caution. For one thing, there might be more factors influencing the (perceived) quality of software than the metrics that are being measured. Also, once people know that a specific metric is recorded, they can optimize their work to increase or decrease the metric. While this might show the desired numbers in reports, it might not necessarily mean software quality is really improving. To combat this, often, more than one metric is recorded.

A well-known example is that of story point velocity in Agile work environments. Recording the sprint velocity for a team to see whether it is becoming more efficient over time sounds effective; however, if the team size varies from sprint to sprint, then the metric might be useless since attendance is influencing velocity as well. Also, the metric can be easily falsified by a team agreeing on multiplying all estimations by a random number every sprint. While this would increase the numbers every sprint, it would not relate to an increase in team throughput anymore.

Moving on to metrics for measuring the quality of software, it can be difficult to objectively measure the quality of written code. Developers often have many opinions as to what constitutes *good code*, and the more the topic is discussed, the harder it can be to find consensus in a team; however, when shifting attention to the results that come from using that code, it becomes easier to identify metrics that can help provide insights into the quality of the code.

Some examples of this are as follows:

- **The percentage of integration builds that fail**: If code does not compile or pass automated tests, then this is an indication that it is of insufficient quality. Since tests can be executed automatically by build pipelines whenever a new change is pushed, they are an excellent tool for determining the quality of code. Also, since they can be run and their results gathered before we deploy a change to production, the results can be used to cancel a change of insufficient quality or that might impact certain system functionality before deploying it to the next stage of a release pipeline. This way, only changes of sufficient quality propagate to the next stage.

- **The percentage of code covered by automated tests**: If a large part of the code is being tested by unit tests, this increases the quality of the software.

- **The change failure rate**: This is the percentage of deployments of new versions of the code that lead to issues. An example of this is a situation where the web server runs out of memory after the deployment of a new version of the application.

- **The amount of unplanned work**: The amount of unplanned work that has to be performed in any period of time can be a great metric of quality. If the team is creating a SaaS offering that is also operating, there will be time spent on operational duties. This is often referred to as unplanned work. The amount of unplanned work can be an indicator of the quality of the planned work. If the amount of unplanned work increases, then this may be because the quality has gone down. Examples of unplanned work can be live site incidents, following up on alerts, hotfixes, and patches.

- **The number of defects that are being reported by users**: If the number of bugs reported by users increases, this can be a sign that quality has been declining. Often, this is a lagging indicator, so once this number starts increasing, quality might have been going down for a while already. Of course, there can be many other reasons for this number increasing, such as new operating systems, an increase in the number of users, or changing expectations from users.

- **The number of known issues**: Even if there are very few new defects being found or reported, if defects are never fixed and the number of known issues keeps increasing slowly, then the quality of the software will slowly decline over time.

- **The amount of technical debt**: Technical debt is a term used to describe the consequences of sacrificing code quality for short-term gains, such as the quick delivery of code. Technical debt is discussed in detail in the next section.

Testing is an activity that is performed to find and report on the quality of software. Test results (insights into quality) can be used to allow or cancel a change progressing to the next release stage.

In the next section, another dimension of quality is explored: the amount of technical debt in a code base.

Technical debt

Technical debt is a term that describes the future costs of sacrificing code quality for something else. For example, to expedite the delivery of a new feature, a developer may choose to quickly expand an existing class with a few new methods. If the resulting class does not adhere to the principles of object-oriented design or grows to be too large, this can make for a class that is difficult to understand and maintain or change later. The term *debt* implies that something (time, quality, attention, or work) is owed to the solution. So long as this debt is not paid off, you have to pay interest in the form of all other work being slowed down a little bit.

Technical debt can take many forms, but some examples are as follows:

- Code that is not covered by any unit test where changes to the implementation of said code cannot be verified using the original tests that were used to create it
- Code that is not written in a self-explanatory fashion using meaningful variable and method names
- Code that does not adhere to coding principles, such as KISS, YAGNI, DRY, and/or SOLID
- Classes that are too complex because they have too many variables and methods
- Methods that are too complex because they have too many statements (flow control statements specifically)
- Classes or namespaces that have circular dependencies through different parts of the application
- Classes that do not adhere to the architectural design of the application

There are many forms of technical debt, and it can be daunting to oversee all of them. For this reason, there are many tools available that can measure the technical debt in a code base automatically and report on it. Tools for doing this will be discussed in the *Maintaining quality* section.

While technical debt is often considered a bad thing, there might be good reasons for creating technical debt on purpose. Just as with a regular debt, it is important to manage the height of the debt and ensure that interest can be paid and the debt itself can be paid off.

Companies often take on technical debt during the start-up phase, where it is often a conscious decision to quickly create a working solution. While this first version is used to validate the business proposition and attract funds, developers can pay off this debt by reimplementing or refactoring (parts of) the application.

Another reason might be a market opportunity or an important business event that has been planned months in advance. Taking on some technical debt to meet deadlines and deliver on time can be worth the cost.

However, never paying the debt and only taking on more debt over time will also increase the metaphorical interest to be paid every time a developer needs to make a change. The result will be that any change will take longer than the previous one. If this starts happening, it is unavoidable that at some point no change will be worthwhile anymore, since the cost always outweighs the benefits. At this point, a project or product has failed.

When talking about tests, it is important to understand which types of tests exist. The next section will go into this subject.

Understanding test types

In traditional software development, tests were often executed when *development was complete*, the *application was declared dev-done*, the *feature set was frozen*, or a similar situation. After declaring the development done, testing was performed, and often, a long period of going back and forth between testing and bug fixing started. The result was often that many bugs were still found after going live.

Shifting left is a testing principle that states that automated testing should be done earlier in the development process. If all activities involved with software development are drawn on a line from inception to release, then shifting left means moving automated testing activities closer to inception.

To do this, a wide selection of different types of tests is recognized—for example, unit tests, integration tests, and system tests. Different sources can suggest different types of tests, but these are some of the more well-known types. No matter the specific name of a type of test, when looking at tests with a high level of abstraction, they are often divided into the following two categories:

- **Functional tests**: Functional tests are used to test whether the desired functionality is actually realized by the application.

- **Non-functional tests**: Non-functional tests are used to verify whether the other desired properties of an application are realized and that undesirable properties are not present.

These types are further broken down into smaller subcategories, as shown in the following diagram:

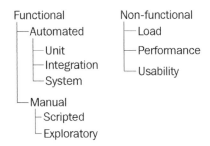

Figure 10.2 – Understanding test types

The following three sections contain brief recaps of the different types of functional and non-functional tests. This is to facilitate later discussions on which type of test to choose in which situation and how much of each type of test your project might need.

Types of automated functional tests

When talking about automated functional tests, the three most-used types are unit tests, integration tests, and system tests. These types of tests can be compared along several axes: the time it takes to create a test, the time it takes to execute a test, and the scope that they test:

- **Unit tests**: Unit tests are the quickest to write, and they execute very quickly, often in less than a millisecond. They test the smallest possible scope in an application, often a single class or method. This means that, once written, it should virtually never be necessary to change a unit test. For many systems, it is more likely that a test will be deleted rather than changed.

- **Integration tests**: Integration tests take more time to write since they are concerned with multiple units that have to be set up to work together. The execution of these tests should still be fast, averaging from below a second up to tens of seconds. Integration tests have a larger test scope, which means that, in return for this, they will cover a larger part of the code and are more likely to detect defects that are introduced with a change.

- **System tests**: System tests test a fully assembled and running application. Depending on the type of application, these are often API tests or automated UI tests. These tests take a lot of time to create since they rely on a deployed system to run and often require the setting up of an initial state in a database or another persistent store. The tests take a long time to execute, sometimes minutes per test. They are also less reliable and much more fragile than unit and integration tests. Even a minor change in an interface can cause a whole series of tests to fail. On the other hand, system tests can detect errors that both unit and integration tests cannot, since they actually test the running system.

> **Important Note**
>
> Please note that having a large test scope in a test has both an upside and a downside. The upside is that it can detect many errors. The downside is that a failing test with a very large test scope provides only a limited insight into what has gone wrong. Such a test failure will often require more investigation than a failing test with a smaller test scope.

The following sections explore each type of test in more detail.

Unit tests

Unit tests are used to test a single unit in isolation. When working in an object-oriented programming language, this will come down to having one test class for every class in an application. For full test coverage, the test class will then have one or more tests for every public method of the corresponding application class.

Unit tests should run extremely fast—on average, in a few milliseconds or less. To make this possible, each class is instantiated without its dependencies. This is enabled by the use of interfaces, where classes depend on interfaces instead of directly on other classes. For tests, the dependencies are then replaced with mock classes, as shown in the following diagram. On the left, the runtime configuration is shown; on the right, the configuration during tests is shown:

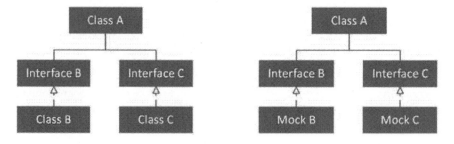

Figure 10.3 – Interface testing

A mock class implements the same interface but has no behavior associated by default. Specific behavior can be set up on a per-test basis. Mocks can also be used to verify that certain operations or functions on a dependency are called. As an example, take the following C# class:

```csharp
public class WorkDivider
{
    private readonly IMessageSender _messageSender;

    public WorkDivider(IMessageSender messageSender)
    {
```

```
        _messageSender = messageSender;
    }

    public void DivideWork(IEnumerable<WorkOrder> workOrders)
    {
        foreach(var workOrder in workOrders)
        {
            _messageSender.SendMessage(workOrder.GetMessage());
        }
    }
}
```

To instantiate this class in an automated test, an implementation of the IMessageSender interface is needed. To work around this dependency, a mocking framework such as Moq can be used to test WorkDivider, as follows. In these examples, **NUnit** is used as the testing framework:

```
[TestFixture]
public class WorkDividerTest
{
    private Mock<IMessageSender> _messageSender;
    private WorkDivider _subject;

    [SetUp]
    public void SetUp()
    {
        _messageSender = new Mock<IMessageSender>();
        _subject = new WorkDivider(_messageSender.Object);
    }

    [Test]
    public void
WhenSendingAnEnumerableOfWorkingOrders_
EverOrderIsSendToTheMessageSender()
    {
        var workOrder = new WorkOrder();

        _subject.DivideWork(new[] { workOrder });
```

```
        _messageSender.Verify(x => x.SendMessage(workOrder),
    Times.Once);
        }
    }
```

This means that it is not possible to write unit tests for classes that interact with other systems, such as databases, caches, or message queues. To ensure that this does not make it impossible to cover large parts of the application with tests, it is common practice to isolate the integration with other systems in separate classes. These classes contain the interaction with a remote system, but no business logic and as little code as possible. It is then accepted that these classes are not covered by unit tests. The typical design patterns that are used to do this are the Facade, Adapter, and Repository patterns.

> **Tip**
> Links to a more detailed guide on writing unit tests and how to mock classes are included at the end of this chapter.

Unit tests should be ready to run on the computer of every developer that clones the code base of an application. They should not require any special configuration or setup on the local computer and should be ready to go. This way, everyone who works with the code base can run the unit tests on their local computer. It is, therefore, a good practice for developers to run all unit tests on their own computers before pushing changes to the central repository.

Next to this local verification step, unit tests should also be a part of the continuous integration build. You will learn how to do this in the *Executing tests in a pipeline* section later on. As long as there are failing unit tests in a pull request, it is better not to merge the changes to the master branch. This can even be made impossible using Git repo branch policies, which were discussed in *Chapter 4, Everything Starts with Source Control*.

In the next section, the discussion of automated functional tests continues with integration tests.

Integration tests

Integration tests are used to test whether a group of components works together correctly. These tests are used for two purposes:

- Increasing the test coverage for those parts of an application that are not covered by unit tests—for example, classes that interact with other systems

- Addressing risks that are not addressed in unit tests and mitigating risks where individual components are interacting with other systems to verify correct desired outcomes

It can be hard to comprehend what integration risks may exist. Usually it is assumed that if the individual parts or components are working as per their specifications, the whole solution must also function properly. However, that invariably isn't the case, and many problems surface after the units are integrated. To understand this risk better, imagine that two components working together are responsible for climate control. One is written by measuring the temperature in degrees Celsius and the other is acting on that temperature, expecting its input in degrees Fahrenheit. It will quickly become clear that, while both components are working as intended, exchanging numbers and taking action based on those numbers, the combination will not produce the desired outcomes.

Integration tests, especially those that interact with other systems, will not only take longer to run than unit tests but often require more setup or configuration to run as well. This may even include secrets such as usernames, passwords, or certificates. To handle configuration such as this, a settings file can be created next to the tests from which settings are loaded before the tests are executed. Every developer can then create their own copy of that file and run the tests using their own configuration.

Continuing with the example from the previous section, let's assume that the `MessageSender` class that implements the `IMessageSender` interface needs a connection string to do its work. A test class for `MessageSender` might then look as follows:

```
[TestFixture]
public class MessageSenderTest
{

    private MessageSender _messageSender;


    [SetUp]
    public void SetUp()
    {
        var connectionString = TestContext.
Parameters["MessageSenderConnectionString"];
        _messageSender = new MessageSender(connectionString);

    }
}
```

`connectionString`, needed for constructing the `MessageSender` class, is received from the `Parameters` object on `TestContext`. This is the **NUnit** approach for making settings from a `.runsettings` file available. The exact approach can vary per test framework. An example `.runsettings` file would look as follows:

```xml
<?xml version="1.0" encoding="utf-8"?>
<RunSettings>
  <TestRunParameters>
   <Parameter name="MessageSenderConnectionString" value="secret-value" />
```

```
  </TestRunParameters>
  </RunSettings>
```

Moving the settings out to a separate file ensures that secrets are not checked into source control. In the *Executing tests in a pipeline* section, you will learn how to build a .runsettings file for running tests in a pipeline.

This is because integration tests should also be part of the continuous integration build if possible. However, there is a risk that this will make a continuous integration build too slow. To counter this, one of the following solutions can be implemented:

- Integration tests are executed in a separate build that is triggered in parallel to the continuous integration build. This way, the duration of the continuous integration build stays low while the integration tests are still continuously executed, and developers get fast feedback on their work.

- Integration tests are executed later in the pipeline, closer to the release of the software—for example, before or after the deployment to a test environment.

The downside of the first approach is that executing integration tests this way will mean that the tests will no longer work as a quality gate before code is merged to the master. They will, of course, continue working as a quality-reporting mechanism. This means that while errors might be merged, they will be detected and reported by the build.

The second approach does not have this risk since executing the tests is still part of the pipeline from source control to production; however, in this approach, the execution of the tests might be deferred to a later moment in time if not every build enters at least part of the release pipeline. This means that defects might become visible later on, extending the time between detecting and fixing an issue.

In either approach, failing integration tests will no longer block merging changes and you hence have to find another way to ensure that developers will take responsibility for fixing the defect that caused the tests to fail.

These trade-offs become even more evident with system tests, which often take so long that it is not possible to make them part of the continuous integration build.

System tests

The third and final type of automated functional test is the system test. These tests are meant to run against a fully assembled and running application. System tests come in two flavors, depending on the type of application: an API test or a UI test. System tests can take a long time to execute, and it is not uncommon for long tests with an elaborate setup of test data to take well over a minute.

> **Tip**
>
> You might come across something called coded UI tests. This is a now-deprecated Microsoft solution for writing UI tests. These tests could be executed from Azure Pipelines. Luckily, there are many alternatives, as referenced in Microsoft's deprecation message at `https://devblogs.microsoft.com/devops/changes-to-coded-ui-test-in-visual-studio-2019`.

System tests execute against a running application, which means that they will need configuration and setup before they can be run. The application needs to be running in a controlled environment and all of the integrations with data stores need to be fully operational. Integrations with other systems need to be either up and running or swapped out with a replacement mock to ensure that all operations that integrate with those systems will function properly.

These conditions make it less likely that developers will execute these tests on their local machines as they are making changes to the application. It is only when they are creating a new test or changing a test that they might do so. However, even then they may be executing these tests not against a locally run version of the application, but against a version that is already deployed to a test environment. This is not necessarily a good thing, but often just the reality in most teams.

> **Important Note**
>
> An introduction to creating API or UI tests is unfortunately beyond the scope of this book. There are many products available on the market and which one is the best to use will differ from project to project.

When executing system tests as part of the pipeline, they are often run after the code has been deployed to at least one environment. This will often be the test environment. This implies that the system tests are on the critical path from a source code change to the deployment to production. If this path becomes too long, they can also be taken out of the pipeline. They are then run on a schedule—for example, every night. Just as with integration tests, this speeds up the pipeline, but it removes the opportunity to use system tests as a quality gate.

System tests, and UI tests in particular, are often fragile and can stop working unexpectedly after minor changes. For this reason, it is advised that you keep their number as low as possible; however, keep in mind that these are the tests that can catch particular errors, such as misconfiguration or other runtime errors, database-application mismatches, or series of operations that create error states.

Besides automated function tests, there are also manual functional tests, which have value in many DevOps projects. These are discussed in the next section, but first, a note on flaky tests.

Flaky tests

Flaky tests are tests that fail with no evident change in code or configuration, or the code works on a local machine but fails with continuous integration. Upon retrying the test execution multiple times, the test eventually passes.

Flaky tests are unreliable and negatively impact the build quality confidence. One solution to eradicate the flaky test problem is to mute these tests so that continuous integration and release do not fail, and the unreliable test results are excluded from your automated test reports.

Types of manual functional tests

While automated tests are a great tool for receiving feedback on development work quickly and often, there are still things that will be tested manually. While automating repetitive tests is the best way to continuously monitor quality, some things will require the human eye.

Manual testing is the tipping point for shifting left. Whenever any type of test or validation is shifted left, this means that it is executed before manual tests are performed. The benefit of this is that all of these automated activities add to the amount of confidence that we might have in the version of the application that is being tested, increasing the chances that the version will also pass manual testing. In other words, when manual testing starts, it should be very unlikely that any new issues will be uncovered.

There are two types of manual tests:

- Scripted tests
- Exploratory tests

Both types of tests will be discussed in the following sections.

Scripted testing

Scripted testing is a technique that is used to minimize the amount of time spent on the test execution while still ensuring full coverage of all relevant test cases. This is done by splitting the testing into two distinct phases: test preparation and test execution. Test preparation is done in parallel to the development of the feature that is to be tested or even before development starts. During test preparation, the feature is analyzed and formal test cases are identified.

Once the test cases that must be executed are identified, manual test scripts are written that describe every step that is to be taken during the test execution phase later. These scripts are engineered in such a way that they are easy to follow and leave no room for questions or doubts. They are also written in such a way that the number of steps to execute is as low as possible. While this may take more time to prepare, all of it is done to ensure that as little time as possible is spent on the test execution.

A deeper discussion of test analysis and how to identify test cases is beyond the scope of this book. While you are responsible for test case creation, Azure DevOps supports you in this. Using the Test Plans service, you can create test plans and record the test cases within them for quick execution later on.

To create a new test plan, perform the following steps:

1. Open the Azure **Test Plans** menu.

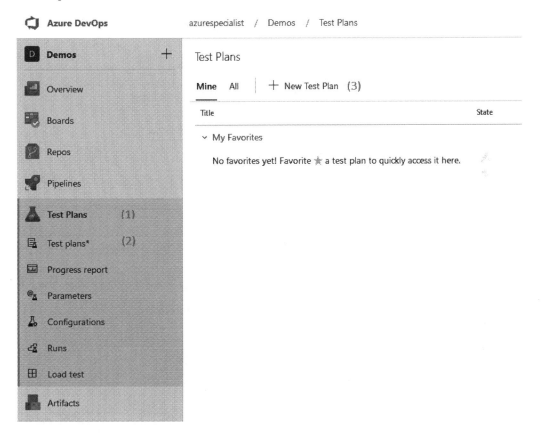

Figure 10.4 – Azure DevOps Test Plans menu

2. In this menu, click on **Test plans**. Here, you will be presented with an overview of all of the test plans you currently have.

3. Click the **New Test Plan** button to start creating a new test plan. This will open a new dialog, as shown in the following screenshot:

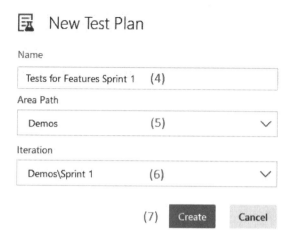

Figure 10.5 – Azure DevOps New Test Plan

4.   Give a meaningful name to the test plan, for example, a name that illustrates what the test plan is for.

5.   Link the test plan to the correct product area path.

6.   Select the correct iteration, or sprint, that this test relates to.

7.   Click **Create** to finalize creating the test plan. This will automatically open this test plan, as shown here:

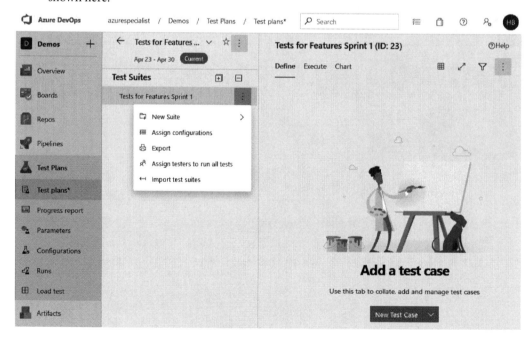

Figure 10.6 – Azure DevOps Test Suites

A test plan can be split into multiple test suites, which in turn can be split into test suites again. In essence, test suites are for tests what folders are for files. Suites can be managed by clicking the ellipsis button that appears when hovering over the test suite. This is shown in the preceding screenshot.

After creating a test plan, it is time to add one or more test cases to the plan. To do this, ensure that the **Define** tab is open for a test suite and click the **New Test Case** button. A new popup will open.

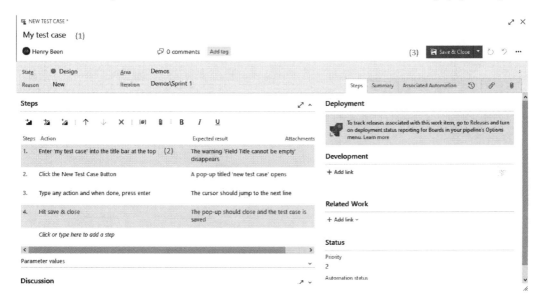

Figure 10.7 – Azure DevOps New Test Case

Here, the test steps and expected outcomes can be defined. To define a new test case, perform the following steps:

1. Enter a title for the test case.

2. In the dialog, enter one or more actions and expected results that describe the test case in detail.

3. Once the test case is completely described, click the **Save & Close** button to save the test case and return to the previous screen where you can manage the test suites.

Once the preparation is done and a feature is ready to be tested, all tests are executed. Since all tests are scripted in detail, this can be done quickly and effectively. There might even be developers, business analysts, or people from other parts of the company helping with the test execution. This means that the test execution itself will be really quick.

To start the execution of a test suite or plan, perform the following steps:

1. Navigate to the **Execute** tab.

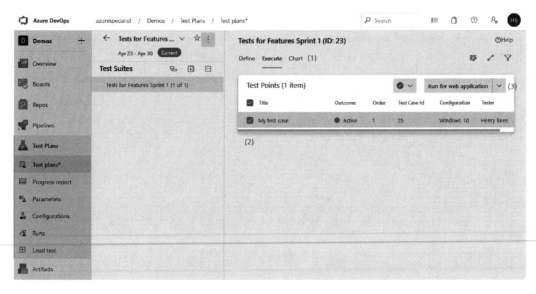

Figure 10.8 – Azure DevOps executing test cases

2. Select one or more test cases.

3. Select one of the run options at the top right.

When choosing to run the tests against a web application, a new browser window with a *test runner* will open. This test runner can be used to go through all of the test cases, and for every test case, through all of the steps, keep track of all successes and errors, as shown here:

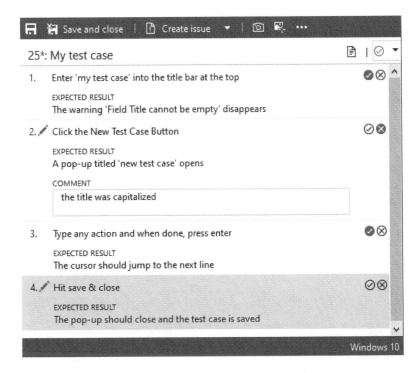

Figure 10.9 – Azure DevOps test case steps

The check mark or cross after every test step can be used to keep track of the outcomes for individual steps. If a step is marked as incorrect, a comment with the defect can be added. To mark a test case as passed or marked, the blue drop-down menu at the top right can be used. Once a test outcome is selected, the runner automatically progresses to the next test. Once all tests are performed, the results can be saved using the **Save and close** button at the top left.

To view the outcome of a test run, navigate to **Test Plans** and then **Runs** to get the following dashboard:

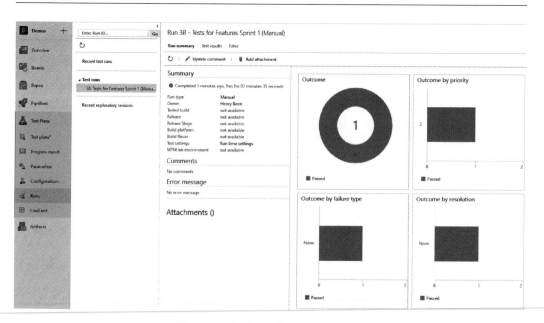

Figure 10.10 – Azure DevOps test runs

Here, you can select the run for which you want to see the outcomes to get a quick overview of the test outcomes. On the second tab, **Test results**, it is possible to view a list of all test cases and whether they passed or not.

A major benefit of having detailed scripts is that the same tests can be performed more than once, reducing the cost per execution. If a test plan is executed multiple times, all run history is maintained and can be accessed using the view shown in the preceding screenshot. This is useful if manual tests are used as part of a regression test; however, once this becomes the case, it is often even more beneficial to automate the tests using system tests, if possible.

> **Tip**
>
> It is possible to execute the same test multiple times, but for different configurations. When developing web applications, this is often done to test using different browsers. For desktop applications, this might be used to test for different operating systems. Working with configurations is detailed in the Microsoft documentation at `https://docs.microsoft.com/en-us/azure/devops/test/mtm/test-configurations-specifying-test-platforms?view=azure-devops`.

The next section will discuss a final form of functional testing, namely, exploratory testing.

Exploratory testing

Writing and executing detailed test scripts can take a lot of time from both the test engineer and test executioner, so often these tests are automated. Once they are automated, they will fall into the category of system tests, and automated UI tests in particular.

This does not necessarily mean that manual tests provide no value or no good return on investment at all. There are some things that the human eye will catch that a computer will not, such as interfaces that are not user friendly, misaligned interface elements, and text lines or images that are not fully displayed but get hidden behind other elements.

To catch these errors while not spending large amounts of time on detailed test scripting, exploratory testing might be a solution. In this approach, a tester opens the application and starts investigating those parts of the application that they feel contain the most risks with regard to the upcoming release. While exploring the application, the tester keeps track of which parts of the application they have visited and which test cases they have performed. Meanwhile, the tester also keeps track of new risks they identify or test cases they have not performed yet. In doing so, they are creating a list of covered and uncovered test cases while they are working. It also allows the tester to keep focusing on the most important risk and test cases all of the time. Once the exploratory test run is over, the tester can report on which application areas and test cases have been covered, which have not, and which risks are still not explored at all. This report can be valuable input for a product manager who must decide whether to move forward with a release or not.

A common misconception is that exploratory testing means that a tester is just clicking around to see whether the application is working okay. This is not the case, and the previous paragraphs have shown that exploratory testing is a highly structured activity that requires practice. If performed well, test preparation and test execution are interwoven during an exploratory testing session.

Exploratory testing is a great tool when there is limited time or the amount of time available for testing is not known upfront. Exploratory testing may yield findings that need to be recorded as defects. How to do this is discussed next.

Reporting manual test results

One of the activities that is also part of testing is the reporting of any defects or other issues found. This is often tedious and time-consuming work. You must try and reproduce the issue one more time, trying to remember how the issue manifested itself, and write down all of these steps. Then, both the desired and undesired outcomes must be described, screenshots must be taken, and everything has to be inserted into a bug tracker or work management tool, such as Azure DevOps.

To make this easier, there is a **Test & Feedback** extension for Azure DevOps available. This extension simply provides buttons for recording screenshots or videos and annotating them with text or drawings. Once an issue is found and documented by a recording or screenshot, it can be automatically submitted to Azure Boards.

This extension is freely available from the Azure DevOps Marketplace and runs in Firefox, Chrome, and Edge Chromium. A link to the extension is included at the end of this chapter.

> **Important Note**
> The Test & Feedback extension can be used when both executing scripted tests and performing exploratory tests.

This concludes the discussion of different types of functional tests. The next section will help you to decide which type of test to use in your projects.

Strategies for deciding which types of functional tests you need

With so many different types of tests, which type of test is the best for your project? Given the wide range of types of tests and their different properties, the answer is as you might expect: a mix of all of them, as they all have different properties.

The following diagram shows the relation between the time the different types of tests take to execute and the confidence in the quality of the software they provide. It shows that while manual tests that complete successfully have the highest likelihood of identifying any defects, they also take the longest to execute. For automated tests, the time taken for tens of thousands of unit tests to be carried out can often be kept to a few minutes, while 10 to 100 system tests can take over 30 minutes:

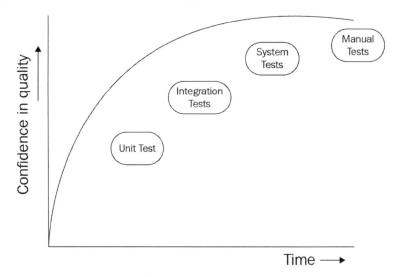

Figure 10.11 – Quality confidence versus test execution time

Looking at this trade-off, it often makes sense why unit tests are preferred over integration tests, integration tests over system tests, and any type of manual test over automated unit tests.

> **Tip**
>
> If the quality of unit and integration tests increases, then this line will climb even more to the top left. High-quality software architecture will also help reduce the need for system and integration tests and increase the chances of catching defects early, something that unit tests bring. Automated unit and integration tests run faster with consistent results that postively impact the overall build quality.

The understanding of this trade-off also helps with understanding two models that can be used in deciding on your testing strategy, that is, the testing pyramid and the testing trophy, which are discussed in the following two sections.

The testing pyramid

In many older projects, there are not too many automated functional tests. Often, many of these tests are slow to run, have a large test scope, are hard to maintain, and fail regularly without a clear cause. The value that these tests provide is often very limited. To counter the lack of good, automated tests, there are then many manual tests that are used to do a full regression test of the application before a new version is deployed. These automated tests are very time consuming and rarely executed. There is no fast feedback to developers and defects are often detected late. It is hard to practice DevOps in such a situation since the focus in DevOps is on creating new versions often and at a high rate.

Such a group of tests for an application is often called an ice-cream cone of tests, including many manual tests and a few automated tests, of which only a few are unit tests. The ice-cream cone of tests is an anti-pattern, yet often found in older and/or long-running projects.

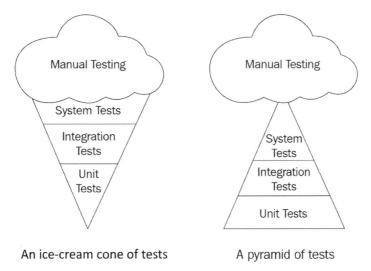

An ice-cream cone of tests   A pyramid of tests

Figure 10.12 – Testing pyramid for manual versus automated testing

To battle this, another, opposing, model was introduced: the test pyramid. This model advocates for having many unit tests that give feedback on the quality of the application within minutes, quickly pointing out most of the errors. On top of this, other types of slower tests are layered to catch only those errors that previous layers cannot catch. Using this approach, there is a good trade-off between test coverage and test duration.

> **Important Note**
>
> Please note that the test pyramid does *not* advocate a layered approach. Do not first build a layer of unit tests and only proceed to integration tests when all unit tests are done. Instead, it advocates proportions. You should have a healthy ratio between unit tests, integration tests, and system tests.

General advice on the best ratio between different types of tests is very hard to give. But in most projects, a ratio of 1:5-15 for each step in the pyramid can be reasonable.

The testing trophy

While the testing pyramid is a well-known and often-used approach for classifying tests and deciding on which types of tests to create, this approach has been criticized as well. While moving away from manual and system tests is widely accepted to be needed in DevOps teams, the focus on unit tests is not universally accepted. Some object to the fact that the testing pyramid hints at creating many more unit tests than integration tests.

The reasons for this objection are as follows:

- **Unit tests tend to be closely tied to the implementation that they test**. Looking back at the test of `WorkDivider` in the *Unit tests* section, we can see that it relies on knowing how the `DivideWork` method is implemented. The test verifies the actual implementation: the call to `SendMessage()`. Many unit tests have this characteristic and, as a result, adding many unit tests increases the effort needed to change the implementation of the class-level design of a solution.

- **Unit tests tend to have a higher rate of change than integration tests**. Unit test classes are closely tied to the class they test. That means that if the class they test is replaced, the unit tests for this class also lose all value. For this reason, it is argued that integration tests might have a higher return on investment.

- **Real value comes from integrating components, not from individual components**. Even when all units are working in isolation, there might not be any value delivered by a system. The real value of software only comes once it is integrated and ready to run. Since testing should confirm value delivery, it is argued that the focus should be on writing integration tests over unit tests.

To deal with these objections, the testing trophy was introduced by *Kent C. Dodds*. This model adopts the testing pyramid in the sense that it advocates as few manual and system tests as possible but differs in the fact that it does not emphasize unit tests over integration tests, but the other way around. The name testing trophy comes from the fact that if this were drawn, it would result in a figure that resembles a trophy.

Unfortunately, there is no silver bullet, and the best advice is to know about all three models and the reasoning behind them and apply the appropriate lines of reasoning to your current situation. When it comes to testing, there is no single best solution for all.

Types of non-functional tests

Functional tests are mostly concerned with verifying whether the behavior displayed by an application is the behavior that is expected; however, there are more risks when it comes to application development: whether an application performs actions quickly enough, whether this performance degrades if more users use the system concurrently, and whether the system is easy for end users to use. Tests that verify these properties of a system under test are called non-functional tests.

There are many types of non-functional tests, but three of them that are important in DevOps scenarios are as follows:

- Performance testing
- Load testing
- Usability testing

Let's go over them one by one.

Performance testing

Performance tests are executed to establish how quickly an application can perform an action, given a set of resources. Performance tests are often executed using specialized tools and run against a fully assembled system. If the tools used for automated API or UI tests record the duration of a test, the duration of these tests can be used as performance results as well.

To compare results over multiple test runs, it is important to ensure that all factors influencing performance are kept the same between tests. The setup of virtual machines for both test subjects and test runners should stay the same. The application configuration should remain constant and integration points should be in the same state as much as possible—for example, instead of reusing the same database, the same database should be restored from a backup before every performance test. This ensures that the results are comparable.

While performance and load tests are often mixed up, they are two different types of tests.

Load testing

Load tests are performed to measure how much load the system can take before it breaks. These types of tests are sometimes also called stress tests. Unlike in a performance test, there are many requests executed in parallel. What is measured is the average performance of all requests, while slowly increasing the number of requests to the system. In most cases, this will identify a breaking point, a specific number of requests per second at which the performance will suddenly decrease. This is the number of requests per second that the system can maximally serve. When executing a load test, gathering the average performance while increasing the maximum number of requests will often result in a graph like the following:

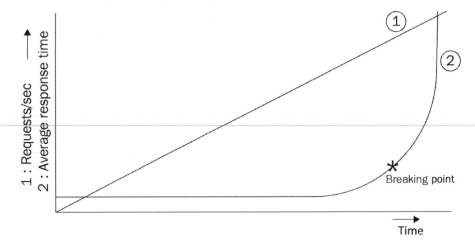

Figure 10.13 – Example of a load testing graph

This graph shows why it is important to know the breaking point of an application: too much load might crumble a system unexpectedly because of the sudden nature of the change in response times. Knowing where this point is allows operators to act before this point is reached in a production environment.

At the end of this chapter is a link to an online Microsoft lab for developers to practice load testing.

Azure now offers a fully managed load testing service. The Azure Load Testing service is under public preview and enables you to conduct load testing of your application by simulating traffic for a high-scale load. It can be used by developers, testers, and **quality assurance (QA)** engineers to identify and fix any application performance, scalability, or capacity issues. Azure Load Testing abstracts the complexity and infrastructure required to execute large-scale load tests. You can find out more about the Azure Load Testing service here: `https://azure.microsoft.com/en-us/services/load-testing/`.

Usability testing

Another important type of testing is usability testing. While other types of tests focus on verifying whether the implementation has the behavior desired by the product team, usability tests focus on verifying whether the expectations of the user are actually met. This means that the test scope is even larger, and these tests can identify UIs that are clumsy and help to find unclear text or user requests that were misinterpreted.

Usability tests are run by letting the user work with the final application on one or more tasks and observing or asking about how they interacted with the application. Results are often much more verbose than *passed* or *not passed*, and results are often given back to a product owner to write new user stories or change requirements.

A great technique for enabling usability testing is the use of feature flags. Feature flags enable us to gradually expose a new feature to more users. This capability can also be used to at first only expose a new feature to a select, limited set of users that are part of a usability study. This allows researchers or product owners to closely observe these users using the new feature, while other users cannot access it yet.

> **Important Note**
> Feature flags were discussed in *Chapter 6, Implementing Continuous Deployment and Release Management*, as a strategy for progressive exposure. The progressive exposure of new features is in itself a form of usability or user acceptance testing.

This approach can be extended to execute A/B tests. In these types of tests, half of the users are exposed to a new feature while the other half are not. Metrics are then gathered about all of the users to see whether the new feature brings users the benefits that were predicted for it—for example, if users use the application for more hours per day or not. This topic will be expanded upon in *Chapter 13, Gathering User Feedback*, which looks at how to gather user feedback.

Doing this shifts usability testing closer to the right in the release process. It can also be shifted to the left by performing usability tests not with the final application, but with mockups.

This concludes the discussion of the different types of tests. In the next section, metrics and tests will be used to automatically measure quality and implement quality gates.

Executing tests in a pipeline

Developers should execute tests on their local machine before opening a merge request for their code. That way, they can be confident that any of the changes they made did not break any of the previous behaviors of their code. In theory, this provides the guarantee that all code merged to the master branch compiles and has all tests passing. In practice, there are many reasons why this is not the case. Some can be as follows:

- Some tests might not be able to be run locally. They depend on confidential configuration values or are configured to run against a fully configured system. One or both of these are often the case for system tests. There are many situations where it is impossible to run system tests from the local system. Not all of these situations are necessarily desirable or insurmountable—but still, this is often the case.

- Developers are only human. They might forget to run the tests on their local machines after that one final tweak or are convinced that their changes did not break any existing behavior. Especially when delivering a bug fix under pressure, it can be tempting to skip running tests for the sake of speed.

To prevent these situations from allowing code that is not fully tested to propagate through the pipeline, it is recommended to have all tests also executed from within the pipeline. The following sections will show how to do this for unit and integration tests and for tests that are being run using other systems. First up are unit tests.

Running unit tests

For many languages, support for running unit tests from the pipeline is built into Azure DevOps. Unit tests can be executed for C#, TypeScript, Python, Maven, C++, Go, and many more.

For some of these languages, a single ready-made task is available. One example of this is tests written in C#. During the execution of .NET tests—for example, in C#—test results are automatically stored in an XML format that is understood by the build agent.

This allows the pipeline agent to interpret the test results and visualize them in the build results, as shown here:

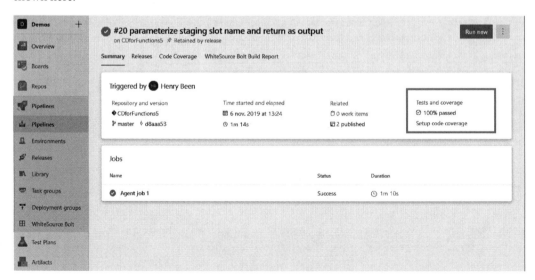

Figure 10.14 – Example for build results page showing automated test execution results

For some languages, more than one task has to be executed. For example, tests written in TypeScript are often executed via an NPM command. The following YAML snippet can be used to do this:

```
- task: Npm@0
  displayName: 'Run unit tests - npm run tests'
  inputs:
    cwd: src
    command: run
    arguments: test
```

This will execute a custom NPM command as specified in `package.json`. Unfortunately, this will not store the test results in a format that the pipeline agent understands. To translate the outcomes into the correct format, another task is needed. The following YAML snippet can be used to do this:

```
- task: PublishTestResults@2
  displayName: 'Publish Test Results'
  inputs:
    testResultsFiles: '**\reportTests\TEST-*.xml'
mergeTestResults: true
    condition: succeededOrFailed()
```

Whether test results are available directly or have to be translated varies from programming language to programming language. Besides publishing test results, it is also recommended to gather test coverage results.

Recording unit test code coverage

It is a best practice to not only run all unit tests during the build but also determine the percentage of the code base that was executed during any of these tests. This is called **unit test code coverage** and is an indication of how thorough the tests are. The build can also be configured to publish the code coverage achieved by unit tests.

To configure the build to publish test coverage for .NET Core unit tests, the following steps must be performed:

1. Install the `coverlet.msbuild` NuGet package in the unit test project.
2. Use the .NET Core task to execute the test and add two parameters to also generate coverage reports, `/p:CollectCoverage=true` and `/p:CoverletOutputFormat=cobertura`.

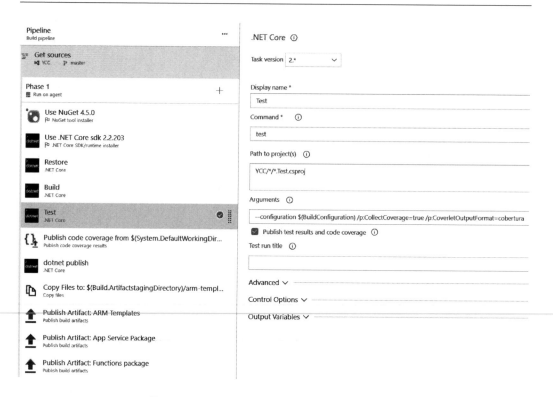

Figure 10.15 – Configuring unit test code coverage

3.   Add the **Publish code coverage** task:

I.   Set the code coverage tool to Cobertura.

II. Configure $(System.DefaultWorkingDirectory)/**/coverage.cobertura.xml as the summary file.

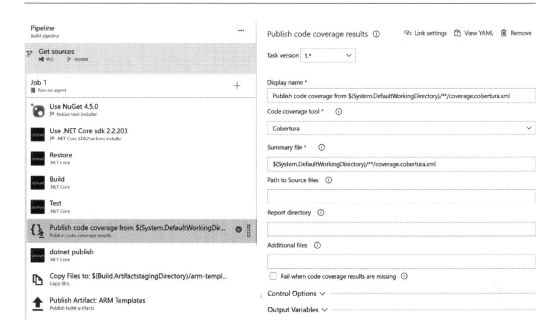

Figure 10.16 – Publishing unit test code coverage

4. The build's run details will now contain code coverage reports.

This is all of the configuration needed to generate detailed code coverage reports. The generated reports contain the number of covered and uncovered code blocks and the calculated coverage percentage. These reports are part of the build results page.

Next to unit tests, integration tests can also be run as part of the pipeline and they often come with the challenge of dealing with managing configuration settings.

Running integration tests

Integration tests are often written in the same framework as unit tests. Still, they come with a unique challenge of their own. Often, they require one or more settings that specify how to integrate with one or more other components that are part of the test. Looking back at the integration test of the MessageSender class discussed before, this is an example of this problem.

Remember how this test had a .runsettings file where you should specify connectionString to the queue that the MessageSender class will use. This connectionString setting cannot be checked into source control. Instead, a placeholder can be checked into source control, which is then replaced with the actual secret during pipeline execution.

In this case, this would mean that the following `pipeline.runsettings` file would be checked into source control:

```xml
<?xml version="1.0" encoding="utf-8"?>
<RunSettings>
  <TestRunParameters>
    <Parameter name="MessageSenderConnectionString"
value="#{MessageSenderConnectionString}#" />
  </TestRunParameters>
</RunSettings>
```

Before starting the actual test execution, another task is run to replace the placeholders with the actual values. These values can be securely retrieved from a variable group, key vault, or pipeline variable, as discussed in *Chapter 5, Moving to Continuous Integration*. There are multiple extensions for Azure DevOps available that can be used for replacing placeholders with actual values. The following YAML snippet is an example of how to do this:

```yaml
- task: qetza.replacetokens.replacetokens-task.replacetokens@3
  displayName: 'Replace tokens in pipeline.runsettings'
  inputs:
    targetFiles: $(System.DefaultWorkingDirectory)/
integrationtests- location/pipeline.runsettings
```

After the execution of the replace tokens task, the test runner can be invoked just as with unit tests. This **Replace Tokens** extension is available on the Azure DevOps Marketplace: `https://marketplace.visualstudio.com/items?itemName=qetza.replacetokens`.

Running external tests

Besides unit and integration tests, you will probably want to execute tests using other systems. For example, Azure DevOps has no built-in support for executing load tests or automated UI tests. For these types of tests, it is necessary to invoke other systems from the pipeline. Many systems can be integrated in this way.

How to do this differs from system to system, but most of the time, the following steps will apply:

1. Configure the tests in the external system.
2. Install an extension for Azure DevOps that makes new tasks available for calling into that external system from the pipeline.
3. Create a service connection to the external system.
4. Add the task to the pipeline.

For details on configuring integrations, a good starting point is often the website of the vendor of the third-party product.

Maintaining quality

The previous sections detailed various types of tests and metrics that can be used for describing the quality of an application. With these in mind, it is time to start thinking about the tools that can be used for maintaining high quality or even increasing quality.

Code reviews

One of the most powerful tools for guarding code quality is a code review. When working with Git, a pull request needs to be performed to merge the changes of a developer back into the mainline. A pull request allows one or more other developers to review all changes and comment on them. The developer that opened the pull request can review the comments and make changes accordingly, increasing the quality of the changes while they keep working.

For code reviews to work at their best, it is important not to see them as a gate that you must get your changes through with as little effort as possible. It is much more fruitful to have an open attitude based on the assumption that everyone is trying to create high-quality code and see the code review as the start of a discussion on code quality. It is important to change perspectives, from seeing the code review as an annoying ritual in software development where others will complain about your code to an opportunity for welcoming others to give their input about your code and help you write code of higher quality.

Once such an attitude is in place, code reviews will become a source of learning. They will result in discussions between peers about the best way forward for tackling an issue: the best way not just for now, but for the future as well, taking no technical debt and having enough unit and integration tests along with the code that is to be merged. Code reviews are also a great tool for mentoring junior developers, allowing them to receive feedback on their work. It can even be more valuable to have junior developers review the code of senior developers. This way, they can ask questions about things they do not yet know, and it will often lead to them pointing out overly complex solutions that might become technical debt over time.

Automatically gathering quality metrics

Next to manual reviews, there are also many tools available for automatically determining the quality of a code base. Some are built into Azure Pipelines, but more elaborate functionality comes from separate code-scanning tools. There are different mathematical approaches to measuring technical debt and using a tool to do so provides great insights into not only the quality of an application but also the changes over time.

One possible tool for measuring the quality of an application is SonarCloud. SonarCloud is the SaaS offering based on SonarCube. This tool can automatically scan a code base for possible bugs, security risks, technical debt, and other metrics for quality. This is a paid, separate offering that integrates with Azure DevOps pipelines. To work with SonarCloud, you have to create an account and retrieve a project key to invoke a SonarCloud scan from Azure DevOps.

For invoking SonarCloud, a set of three tasks is used that are part of an extension for Azure DevOps. After installing the extension and configuring a SonarCloud service connection, three tasks are added to the pipeline to set up the analysis, execute it, and (optionally) fail the build if the quality degrades. The first task is the only one that takes configuration, which is shown in the following screenshot:

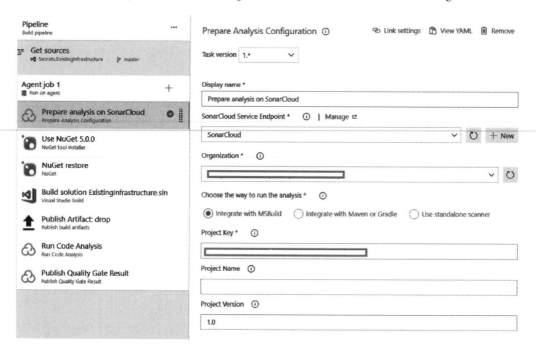

Figure 10.17 – Configuring SonarCloud – static code analyzer

Every build that is now executed will automatically have its code scanned by SonarCloud, where extensive reports about the quality will be available. On top of these reports, a dashboard is generated that provides a quick overview of some key quality metrics.

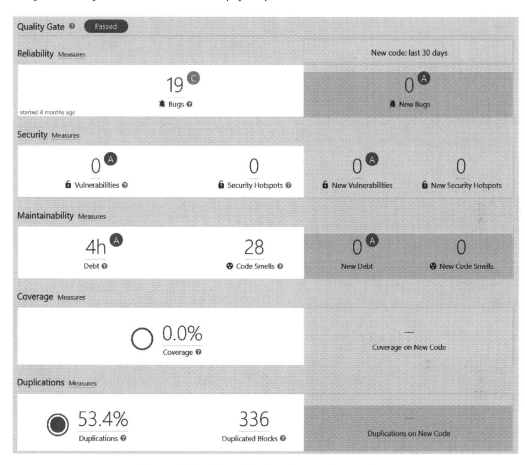

Figure 10.18 – SonarCloud quality metrics overview

Here is another look at the dashboard showing quality metrics:

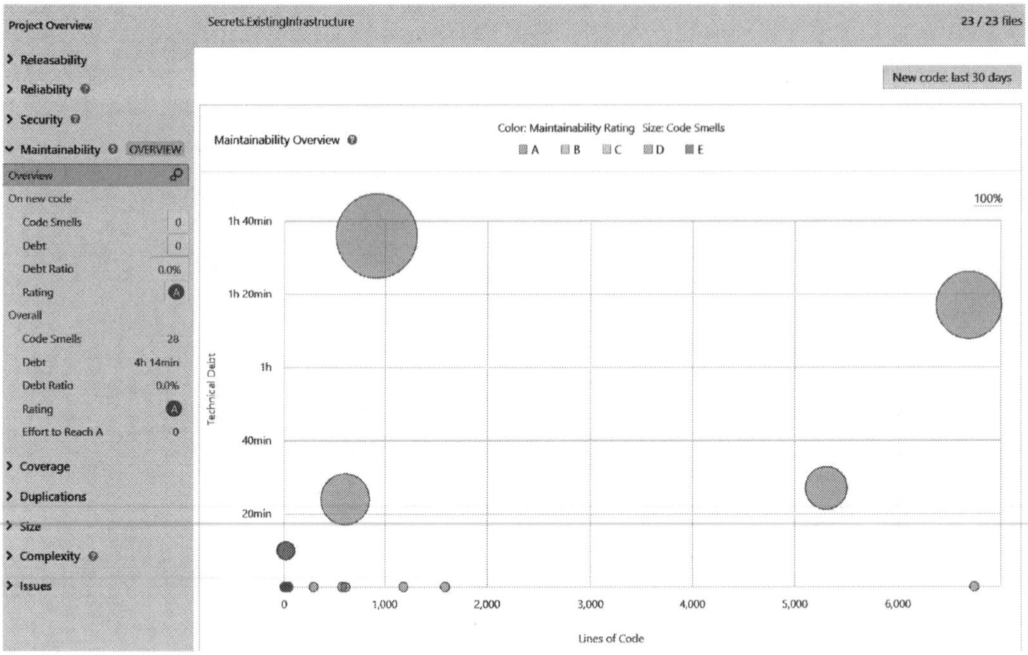

Figure 10.19 – SonarCloud quality gate dashboard

Code-scanning tools can be used for reporting the quality of the code but can also act as a quality gate that will stop the merge of changes or deployment to a specific environment if insufficient quality is detected.

Visualizing quality

Measuring the quality of an application continuously has no value unless it is acted upon. Dashboards can be a powerful tool for gaining continuous insights into the current level of quality and how the quality has changed over time.

Most code quality tools have built-in reporting options, and they can be valuable for QA engineers. They provide detailed insight into which parts of the application are of higher quality and which types of issues recently occurred more frequently.

The downside of this type of dashboard is that they can often be hard to read and correlate as they may exist in another tool that is different from Azure DevOps where developers perform most of their work. For this reason, it can be beneficial to also create dashboards in Azure DevOps to report on quality. An example of such a dashboard is shown in the following screenshot:

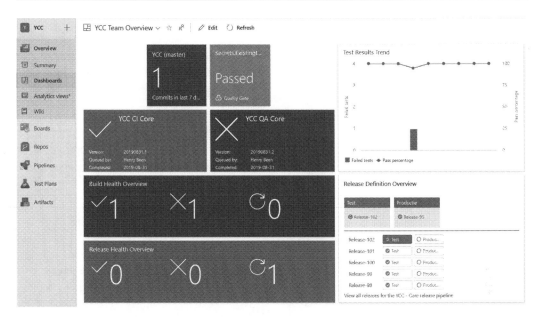

Figure 10.20 – Azure DevOps dashboard quality overview

This dashboard shows an overview of the current quality and application code, as well as some recent history. Here, you can find the following information:

- The number of recent changes is shown at the top, along with the result of the most recent SonarCloud **Quality Gate** outcome, which currently reads **Passed**. The results of the two different builds in this project are shown in the second row.

- The third and fourth rows show aggregations of all of the builds and releases within the project. Symbols are used to denote the status of the builds and releases: successful, failed, or still running.

- On the right, two widgets are used to show the percentage of failed tests and the corresponding number of failed tests over the last 10 builds.

- The results of the latest release runs per environment are shown below this.

Dashboards such as these can be created per team or per project using built-in widgets or extensions. There are many extensions available in the Azure DevOps Marketplace. For example, in the preceding dashboard, the **Team Project Health** extension is used. This extension is available on Azure DevOps here: `https://marketplace.visualstudio.com/items?itemName=ms-devlabs. TeamProjectHealth`.

Azure DevOps dashboards can be configured to automatically refresh every 5 minutes, making them usable as wallboards as well.

Quality gates

Measuring, reporting, and even visualizing quality is important and valuable; however, if no one is acting upon all of these metrics, it has no value to the development team. To prevent this, automatic quality gates or checks can be introduced.

One way to implement quality gates is by failing the continuous integration build whenever a test fails, the test coverage falls too low, or the thresholds that were set for the code-scanning tool are no longer being met. These are all things that have been discussed before. Another option to enforce standards is by adding gates or checks to pipelines. This way, certain conditions have to be met before the pipeline can continue.

How to do this differs between classic releases and YAML multi-stage pipelines.

Classic releases

One other option is the use of *gates* on Azure release pipelines. Here, it is possible to specify one or more conditions that have to be met before a release is allowed to be deployed to a specific environment. Gates can also be part of an extension, such as the SonarCloud extension, which was discussed before.

Gates can be added by selecting any stage in a release pipeline and editing the predeployment conditions. After enabling gates, one or more gates can be added. The following screenshot of a release pipeline shows how to disallow the deployment of any build of insufficient quality to an environment:

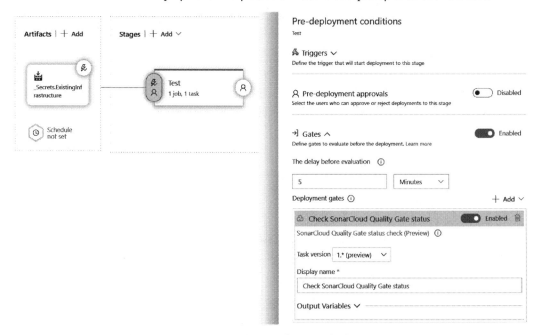

Figure 10.21 – Azure DevOps configuring deployment gates

The use of deployment approvals and gates is not mutually exclusive, so a mix of both can be used.

Multi-stage pipelines

Gates, as they are available for classic releases, are present in multi-stage YAML pipelines. In YAML pipelines, another mechanism is available: checks. Checks are configured to automatically validate whether one or more conditions are met before allowing a pipeline to continue. Checks can be added to resources that are used in a stage. If one or more checks are found on one or more resources in a stage, all of the checks have to be passed before the pipeline continues to that stage. Checks can be added to environments and service connections.

To add a check to an environment, navigate to that environment.

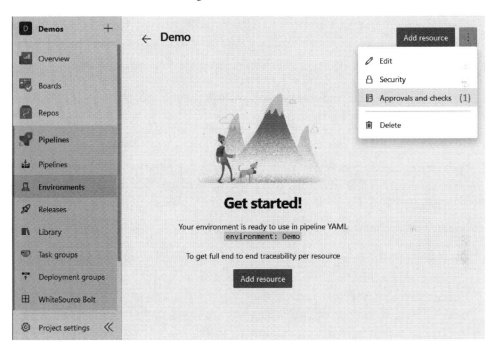

Figure 10.22 – Azure DevOps configuring environments

Now, perform the following steps:

1. At the top right, expand the menu and choose **Approvals and checks**.

2. In the new view that opens, click on **See all** to see all of the different types of checks that are available.

3. Choose **Invoke Azure Function**:

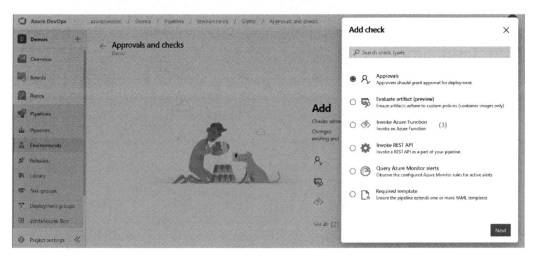

Figure 10.23 – Azure DevOps configuring environment approval and checks

4. In the popup that opens, configure the Azure function to be called. At a minimum, the function URL and key have to be provided.

5. Click **Create**.

Once the check is created, every deployment job (see *Chapter 6, Implementing Continuous Deployment and Release Management*) that targets the environment has to pass this check. The check is passed when the function that is called returns a successful response code.

The following types of checks are supported:

*   **Evaluate artifact**: Validate that an artifact of the container image type passes a custom policy. These policies are defined in a language called *Rego*.

*   **Invoke REST API**: Post details about the pipeline to an Azure function or REST API to execute custom logic. If the API returns a successful HTTP status code, the pipeline is allowed to continue.

*   **Invoke Azure Function**: The same as the **Invoke REST API** check, but with some defaults for Azure Functions.

*   **Query Azure Monitor alerts**: Only continue if the specified alerts are not in an active state.

*   **Required template**: Only allow the pipeline to continue if the current YAML pipeline extends one or more configured base YAML templates.

Checks can be a powerful mechanism for guaranteeing that one or more conditions are met before allowing a pipeline to continue.

Summary

In this chapter, you learned how to measure and assert the quality of software development processes. Releasing quickly and often requires the software that is written to be of high quality. Testing is needed to ensure that you write software of high quality with little technical debt. You learned about the different types of tests and the pros and cons of the different types of automated and manual tests. Finally, you learned how code reviews and tools can help to maintain high quality in your project, by reporting on quality and serving as a quality gate.

With this knowledge, you now understand the tests and test types to help you to decide which tests are needed for your applications, which risks you can address using which types of tests, and which ones you need and can omit. You are now also capable of setting up and configuring code-scanning tools to ensure that changes of insufficient quality are not merged to the mainline.

In the next chapter, you will learn about security and compliance, two topics that remain equally important when practicing DevOps.

Questions

As we conclude, here is a list of questions for you to test your knowledge regarding this chapter's material. You will find the answers in the *Assessments* section of the *Appendix*:

1. True or false: A unit test verifies the working of a single unit in isolation.

2. True or false: An integration test verifies the working of a fully assembled system.

3. Which of the following statements is correct regarding the principles of the testing pyramid?

    A. Have many integration tests, fewer unit tests, and even fewer system tests

    B. Have many unit tests, fewer integration tests, and even fewer system tests

    C. Have many system tests, fewer integration tests, and many unit tests

4. Which of the following is not a non-functional type of test?

    A. Load testing

    B. Usability testing

    C. Applicability testing

    D. Performance testing

5. Testing is about gaining insights into the quality of work. Which techniques can be employed to prevent work of insufficient quality from propagating through to production?

Self exercise

- Open the `packtbookslibrary-api` solution that we created earlier in *Chapter 6, Implementing Continuous Deployment and Release Management, Exercises section* and add a new project (select **NUnit Test Project**).

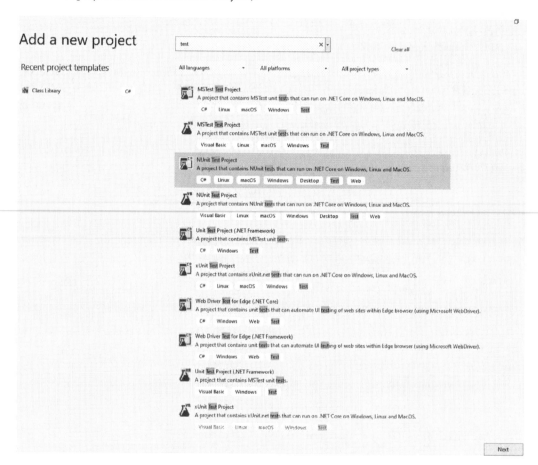

Figure 10.24 – Self exercise – adding a new test project

- Create a new test project.

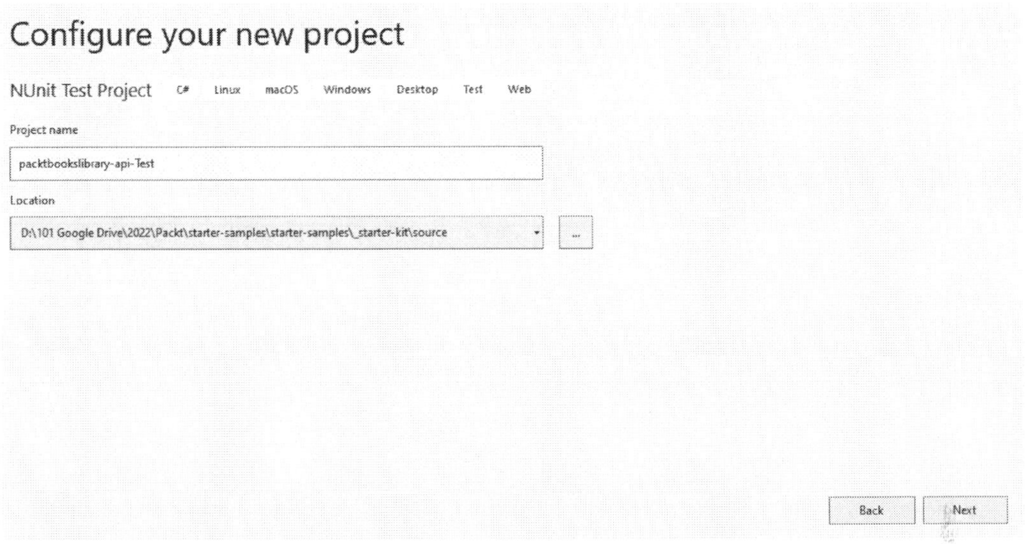

Configure your new project

NUnit Test Project   C#   Linux   macOS   Windows   Desktop   Test   Web

Project name

packtbookslibrary-api-Test

Location

D:\101 Google Drive\2022\Packt\starter-samples\starter-samples_starter-kit\source

Back   Next

Figure 10.25 – Self exercise – creating a new test project

- Once the test project is created, add a reference to `packtbookslibrary-api` in **Dependencies**.

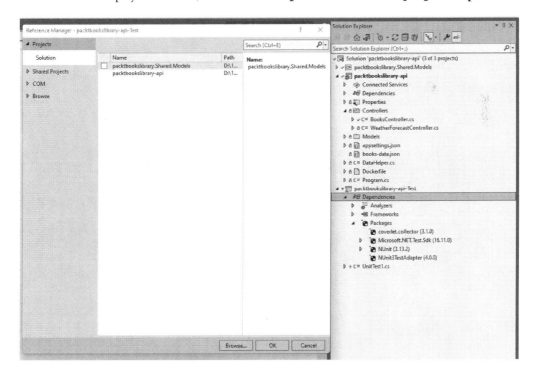

Figure 10.26 – Self exercise – configuring Dependencies

- Add a **Services** folder and then add the `IBookService.cs` interface and the `BookService.cs` class, which implements the `IBookService` interface.

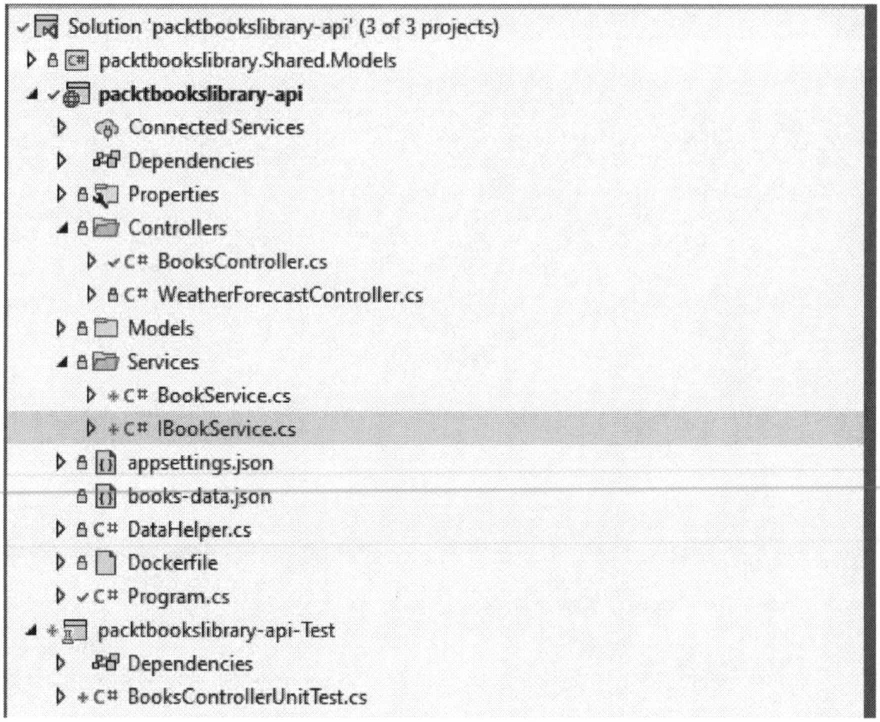

Figure 10.27 – Self exercise – adding the IBookService.cs interface

- `IBookService.cs` will have the following code:

```
using packtbookslibrary.Shared.Models;
using System.Text.Json;

namespace packtbookslibrary_api.Services
{
    public interface IBookService
    {
        List<Book> GetBooksList();
    }

}
```

- `BookService.cs` will have the following implementation:

```
using packtbookslibrary.Shared.Models;
using System.Text.Json;

namespace packtbookslibrary_api.Services
{
    public class BookService : IBookService
    {
        List<Book> IBookService.GetBooksList()
        {
            List<Book> books = new List<Book>();
            string jsonString = System.IO.File.
ReadAllText("books-data.json");
            books = JsonSerializer.
Deserialize<List<Book>>(jsonString);
            return books;
        }
    }
}
```

- Add the following code to `BooksController.cs`:

```
        private readonly IBookService bookService;

        List<Book> books = new List<Book>();

        public BooksController(IBookService bookService)
        {
            this.bookService = bookService;
            books = bookService.GetBooksList();
            //string jsonString = System.IO.File.
ReadAllText("books-data.json");
            //books = JsonSerializer.
Deserialize<List<Book>>(jsonString);
        }

        // GET: api/<BooksController>
        [HttpGet]
```

```
        public IEnumerable<Book> Get()
        {
            return books;
        }
    }
```

- Add a package reference to Moq:

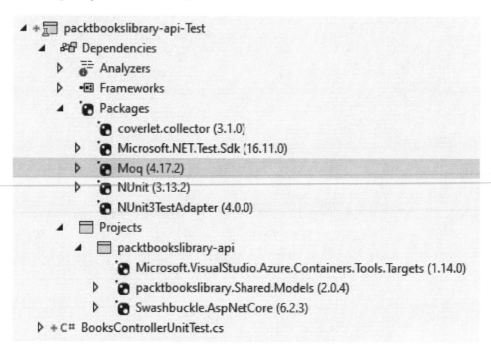

Figure 10.28 – Self exercise – adding a package reference

- Add code from BooksControllerUnitTest and execute a unit test in the pipeline. You can find the file here: https://github.com/PacktPublishing/Designing-and-Implementing-Microsoft-DevOps-Solutions-AZ-400-Exam-Guide

  You will notice that all test cases have successfully passed.

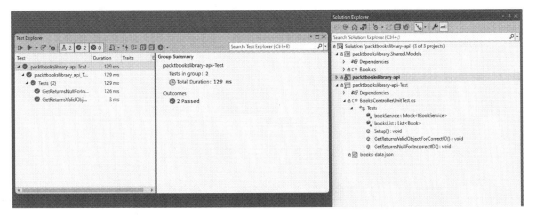

Figure 10.29 – Self exercise – executing BookControllerUnitTest

- Update nugget.config to add the Sources package:

```xml
<?xml version="1.0" encoding="utf-8"?>
<configuration>
    <packageSources>
        <add key="nuget.org" value="https://api.nuget.
org/v3/index.json" />
        <!-- add an Azure Artifacts feed -->
        <add key="PacktBooksLibraryFeed"
value="https://pkgs.dev.azure.com/aurigadev/
PacktBookLibrary/_packaging/PacktBooksLibraryFeed/nuget/
v3/index.json" />
    </packageSources>
</configuration>
```

- Add a test case step to the YAML pipeline to execute test cases as part of the build process:

```yaml
# Run your tests
    task: DotNetCoreCLI@2
    displayName: 'Run Tests'
    inputs:
    command: test
    projects: '**/*Tests/*.csproj'
    arguments: '--configuration ${{ parameters.
buildConfiguration }}'
```

- Execute **main-ci-pipeline** to run the pipeline and to check the **Test** tab for the results of the test execution.

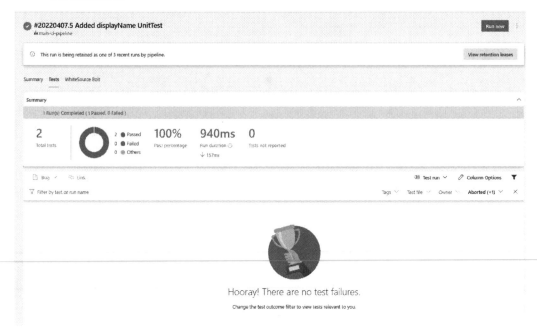

Figure 10.30 – Self exercise – executing a continuous integration pipeline to see the test results

Further reading

- More information about the testing trophy model can be found at https://testingjavascript.com/ and https://kentcdodds.com/blog/write-tests/.

- More information about writing tests using C# can be found at https://docs.microsoft.com/en-us/visualstudio/test/walkthrough-creating-and-running-unit-tests-for-managed-code?view=vs-2022 and https://docs.microsoft.com/en-us/dotnet/core/testing/unit-testing-best-practices.

- More information about the Test & Feedback extension can be found at https://marketplace.visualstudio.com/items?itemName=ms.vss-exploratorytesting-web.

- Practical labs to practice load testing can be found at https://docs.microsoft.com/en-us/learn/modules/load-test-web-app-azure-devops/ and https://docs.microsoft.com/en-us/learn/modules/run-non-functional-tests-azure-pipelines/index.

- Practical labs to practice automating UI tests can be found at `https://docs.microsoft.com/en-us/learn/modules/run-functional-tests-azure-pipelines/index`.

- More information about SonarCloud can be found at `https://sonarcloud.io`.

- The Team Project Health extension can be found at `https://marketplace.visualstudio.com/items?itemName=ms-devlabs.TeamProjectHealth`.

- More information about Rego can be found at `https://www.openpolicyagent.org/docs/latest/policy-language/`.

11

Managing Security and Compliance

As important as it is to ensure that your application performs the functions it needs to, you also need to ensure it doesn't do things that it shouldn't. In the previous chapter, you learned about quality and testing in order to continuously measure whether your application is doing what it is supposed to do. In this chapter, you will learn how to prevent any unwanted behavior. This is the subject of security and compliance. While increasing the flow of value to your end users – by deploying faster and shortened delivery cycles – you will still want to make sure that you are delivering secure and compliant software. In this chapter, you will learn how to address these concerns in your DevOps processes.

To do this, this chapter will start by discussing the perceived trade-off between speed and security, and it will explain how security is not decreased but might even be increased when embracing DevOps. Next, a specific dimension of security is addressed: how to handle secrets such as keys and passwords that your pipeline and application need securely. Following this, code-scanning tools for automatically identifying possible security risks in your application code and your dependencies are discussed. The chapter concludes by discussing how to keep your infrastructure and configuration deployments compliant, and how to detect runtime security risks and threats using Azure Security Center, now called Microsoft Defender for Cloud.

The following topics will be covered in this chapter:

- Applying DevOps principles to security and compliance
- Working with secrets
- Detecting application code vulnerabilities
- Working with dependencies
- Ensuring infrastructure compliance
- Monitoring and detecting runtime security risks and threats
- Other tools you can use

Technical requirements

To experiment with the techniques described in this chapter, you will need one or more of the following:

- An Azure DevOps project with access to build and release pipelines and the right to install extensions

- An Azure subscription (to sign up for Azure, you can go to `https://portal.azure.com` and follow the guide there if you do not have an account yet)

- PowerShell with the Azure Az PowerShell module installed (instructions on how to install the PowerShell Azure module can be found at `https://docs.microsoft.com/en-us/powershell/azure/install-az-ps?view=azps-7.3.0`)

- Optionally, subscriptions for WhiteSource Bolt, SonarCloud, or similar products

The preceding are all available for free or as a trial, for learning or evaluation purposes.

Applying DevOps principles to security and compliance

Concerns about security and compliance can be a reason for companies to be reluctant to accept a full DevOps mindset as it would hinder their ability to make releases very often. In the past, they used to have fewer releases that were all handed off for security or penetration testing before being deployed to production. This gave them the confidence that they were not shipping software that contained security vulnerabilities.

This practice of fewer releases and having a big final security test before the final release conflicts with a DevOps mindset, and this is where some companies struggle. They are looking for ways to ensure that they are delivering business value to their users with every release, but are not willing to compromise on security to do so. The question is whether this is a fair trade-off. Wouldn't it be possible to have both speed and security? Might it not actually be the case that releasing faster and more often, in combination with rigorous automation, can help to increase the level of security in software development? To answer this question, it is good to first explore how security is often practiced in non-DevOps environments and how this needs to be changed when adopting DevOps.

Bringing developers and security engineers together

In many companies, security engineers are part of a different department compared to developers. The thought behind this separation is that it is beneficial to have some distance between those who are writing code (that is, the developers) and those who are checking it.

In the past, the same separation often existed between software developers and software testers. However, recent insights have shown that putting developers and testers closer together does not result in unwanted behaviors such as groupthink, only testing what is already known to be working, or trying to cheat the tests by developing only for known test cases. Both experience and research show that the opposite is true. Putting developers and testers together results in products of higher quality. It is for this reason that movements such as Agile recommend that development teams incorporate, among other things, the discipline of testing.

It is by this same reasoning that the call for integrating security engineering into DevOps development teams is becoming louder. This movement is often called *DevSecOps* or *rugged DevOps*. Both movements advocate that using DevOps principles such as shifting left and automating as much as possible can help to increase security. They advocate that pen tests or vulnerability reviews of applications are no longer done manually, but that they are fully automated as part of the delivery pipeline. This enables automation, faster feedback loops, and continuous delivery and deployment practices.

It is also advocated that shipping software more often can also help to increase security further, for the following reasons:

- When a reliable mechanism for shipping software automatically is available, any change that addresses a security risk can be deployed swiftly. Being able to react quickly to a new finding is a great security improvement.

- Speed itself can be a security measure. If the working of a system changes multiple times a day, it is significantly harder to figure out what its inner workings are at any given time and to misuse them. Applying the principle of immutable deployments and using infrastructure as code ensures that the infrastructure that is running an application is refreshed quite often. This is good mitigation of advanced persistent threats.

One of the things this chapter will explore is how to configure delivery pipelines to add security scanning. Please note that running these tools from a pipeline is a different discipline, which ensures that these tools are properly configured and apply the correct policies and requirements. For these activities, a security background and a close collaboration with security engineers are still essential. This is just another area where close collaboration can make a difference. Particularly on the subject of security, collaboration with other disciplines will be necessary – to automate all security checks and avoid (or minimize) any manual verification processes.

Security concerns

The rest of this chapter will introduce a number of security concerns, but it is helpful to realize that some of the previous chapters have introduced security concerns already. As you already know from software development, security is not just something that you add in one place. Security should be applied everywhere. The following diagram shows different activities surrounding the creation and delivery of software. Next to each activity, the applicable security concerns are shown:

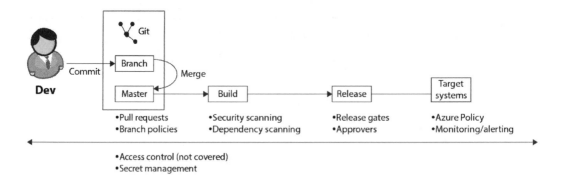

Figure 11.1 – Software development activities and security concerns

Let's walk through a quick recap of the security concerns at each of these stages:

- **Branch-master merge**: At this stage, the four-eyes principle is applied using pull requests. Pull requests allow another engineer to review the changes before they are merged into the main branch. Branch policies are used to make the use of pull requests mandatory, to ensure that code compiles and that the unit tests run. This was discussed in *Chapter 4, Everything Starts with Source Control*, and *Chapter 5, Moving to Continuous Integration*.

- **Build**: During this stage, a security scan of all source code and third-party dependencies is executed by adding additional tasks to the build pipeline. This prevents security risks from propagating unchecked. We will discuss how to do this in this chapter, in the *Working with secrets* section.

- **Release**: During the release, approvers can be configured. An approver is a user who has to give their approval before the deployment to a specific stage can continue. Additionally, automated release gates are used to ensure (and further enforce) that certain criteria are met before a release can continue. We discussed how to do this in *Chapter 6, Implementing Continuous Deployment and Release Management*.

- **Deployment environment (target systems)**: All applications will run in a target environment. This can be on-premises; however, in this book, the focus is on Azure. For runtime security and compliance concerns, this chapter will introduce Azure Policy and Microsoft Defender for Cloud, which was formerly known as Azure Security Center.

- **Cross-cutting**: All of the preceding points are only useful if there is sufficient access control within the Azure DevOps environment. While this is not in the scope of this book, it is an important angle to cover. Users should have enough rights to do their work, but they should not be able to make unauthorized changes to policies, builds, and deployment processes. Additionally, proper secret management is needed to keep secrets such as certificates, keys, and passwords secure during all phases of the delivery process. How we can do this is also covered in this chapter.

Now, with an understanding of how software and security engineers can come together to work on an application, it is time to address the different aspects of this work in the following sections. The next section will discuss how to handle secrets.

Working with secrets

An important security element is the handling of secrets. When deploying an application, there are always secrets involved. Especially when deploying to the cloud – that is, over the internet – handling these access keys in a secure way is very important. Besides the secrets that are necessary for deployment, there are also secrets that need to be inserted into the runtime configuration of an application. A common example is for accessing the database.

In *Chapter 8, Implement Infrastructure and Configuration as Code*, multiple mechanisms for delivering application configurations were discussed, including **Azure Resource Manager** (**ARM**) templates. However, templates require the input of external secrets, since they cannot be stored in parameter files in source control.

> **Important Note**
> Secrets should not be stored in source control.

If secrets cannot be stored in source control, then where should they be stored instead? Common options include storing secrets in service connections or variable groups.

Storing secrets in service connections

The first group of secrets that are needed for the deployment of any application is those secrets that are required for connecting to the target system. No individual person should have access to these secrets, as they are only used during deployments. This is why Azure Pipelines allows you to store them securely in service connections.

A service connection is the abstraction of another system that can be connected to, for executing tasks in Azure Pipelines. Service connections have a specific type – that is, to specify the family of systems they can be used to connect to. There are out-of-the-box service connection types for connecting to Azure, GitHub, Jira, npm, NuGet, and over a dozen more systems. New service connection types can also be added through the Azure DevOps extension mechanism.

Service connections can contain a reference to the location of another system – often, a URL. Next to the location, they can contain an authorization token, a username, and/or a password, depending on the type of service connection. Secrets that are stored inside a service connection can never be retrieved again, not even by administrators. Also, whenever any details of the service connection are changed, the secret must be re-entered as well. This is to prevent a previously entered secret from being misused to access another location. These details indicate how service connections are designed to provide a secure location for storing connection credentials.

Service connections can be managed in a central location for each Azure DevOps project. You can create new connections, edit existing ones, alter user permissions, and much more. Practice this by following these steps:

1. To open this view, navigate to **Project Settings**. A vertical list of various setting options will open.

2. From the list, click on **Service connections**. You will be able to view the various connections, as shown in the following screenshot:

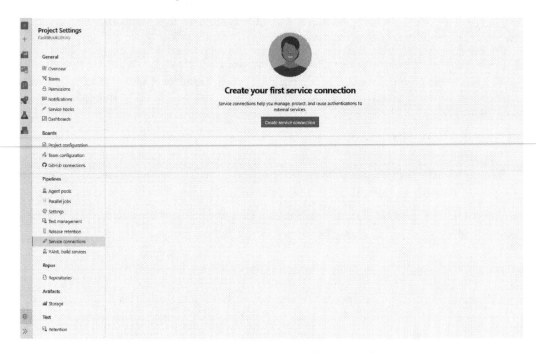

Figure 11.2 – Creating a new service connection

3. Now, click on the **New service connection** button at the top right of the screen if you wish to create new service connections.

4. To modify permissions, click on the **More Actions** submenu under **Security**. This will take you to a screen that is similar to the following screenshot:

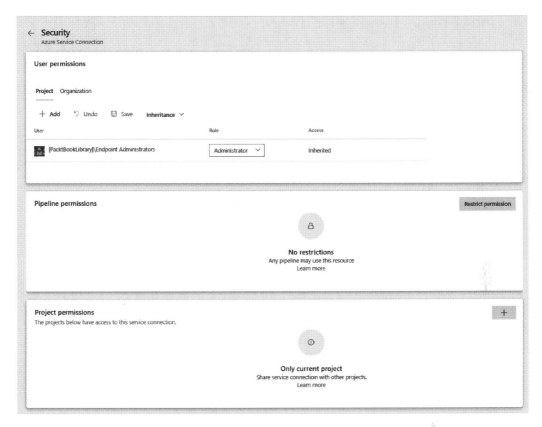

Figure 11.3 – Service connection security settings

From the **Edit and Security** view, you can now carry out these actions:

- Edit the service connection details.
- Alter user permissions.
- Restrict permissions.
- Add more users or groups and specify, for each, whether they can use or administer the endpoint.
- Specify which pipelines can use this service connection.

Every pipeline in the project should not have access to use the service connection by default. Instead, each pipeline that wants to use the service connection must be authorized by a service connection administrator first.

Storing secrets in variable groups

There are more secrets involved in application development than those that are required to connect to other systems. Examples include license keys, which are required during application compilation, or database usernames and passwords, which need to be passed on to the application after deployment or as part of an ARM template deployment.

These secrets can be stored in pipeline variables or variable groups, which we covered in *Chapter 3, Getting the Best Out of DevOps Tools*, in the *Creating a build definition in Azure DevOps* section. Microsoft will store all variables that are marked as secrets securely and make them non-retrievable through the user interface.

However, there might be reasons for not wanting to store secrets in Azure DevOps but in a specialized key store, such as Azure Key Vault, instead. Doing so will provide the extra guarantees that come with Key Vault and the ability to further control access policies using **Azure role-based access control** (**Azure RBAC**) and Key Vault access policies.

When storing secrets in an Azure key vault, they can still be used as a variable group as well, by connecting an empty variable group to the key vault through a service connection, as shown in the following screenshot:

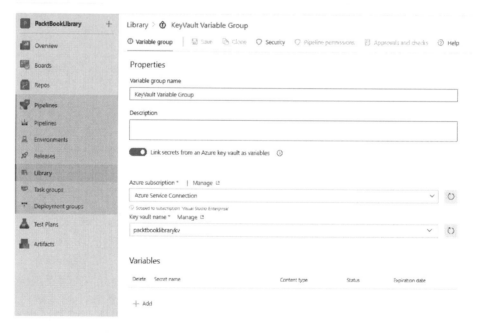

Figure 11.4 – Key Vault as the storage for a variable group

To use a key vault as the storage for a variable group, perform the following actions:

1. Enable the **Link secrets from an Azure key vault as variables** second slider to load the secrets from the key vault.

2. Select an already existing ARM service connection from the drop-down menu or create a service connection with a new managed identity for Azure on the fly by selecting an Azure subscription from the list.

3. Type in the name of the key vault that the secrets should be loaded into. You can also select one from the drop-down menu. In this instance, only key vaults that are accessible by the selected service connection are shown.

4. Access for specific users can be configured using the **Security** tab.

The proper authorizations for the service connection to Azure and the key vault can also be automatically created. Please note that both operations will make changes to the Azure security setup, so ensure that these are (still) correct.

Detecting application code vulnerabilities

The security assessments that were often conducted at regular intervals in the pre-DevOps era cannot be just left out when moving to a DevOps culture. This means that, instead of leaving them out, they must be conducted in some other way. There are two approaches to doing this.

The first approach is to keep doing pen tests, security reviews, and other security inspections at regular intervals just as before. However, instead of waiting for an okay from the tests before moving to production, code is deployed to production separate from the security assessment(s). This implies that there is an accepted risk that there might be vulnerabilities shipped to production that are found only during the next security scan, which will be addressed in the next release. Using this approach, it is possible to achieve speed, but then it also needs to be accepted that some vulnerabilities might exist for a while.

The second approach relies on making application security scanning part of the regular workflow for committing code to the source code repository. For example, security code reviews do not have to be done per increment or every two months. They can also be done per pull request – before the code gets merged. Now, all of a sudden, you are no longer detecting vulnerabilities but are instead preventing them. The same can be done with security vulnerability scans. They can become part of the delivery pipeline, or a full nightly **Quality Assurance** (**QA**) build that reports back on the quality of development every morning.

Of course, it is often not as black and white as that, and many companies use a combination of these approaches. They use automated feedback mechanisms to detect whatever they can, make security code reviews part of the pull request workflow, and then combine this with manual pen testing at regular intervals. This way, the speed of delivery is increased, while there is no increase or even a decrease in security risks, the latter being the consequence of the speed at which vulnerabilities can be mitigated.

OWASP Top 10

When it comes to the security of web applications, there are several types of security issues that are both common and responsible for the vast majority of all security issues. These types of issues comprise the OWASP Top 10. This is a list of the 10 most common types of security issues, published by the **Open Web Application Security Platform (OWASP)**. The list is reviewed every few years but has remained quite stable over the last couple of years.

Most of the errors in the OWASP Top 10 can be prevented by implementing automated security tests, either by using static code analysis for security vulnerabilities or with dynamic testing using the **OWASP Zed Attack Proxy (OWASP ZAP)**.

Implementing automated vulnerability scanning

In the previous chapter, in which continuous testing was discussed, SonarCloud was introduced as a code scanner for technical debt and code quality. Besides assessing the quality of application code, SonarCloud can also be used to scan for security vulnerabilities. In *Chapter 10, Integrating Continuous Testing*, you learned how to add a SonarCloud scan to your pipeline. There are other more specialized tools available as well, which we will discuss in the last section of this chapter.

These tools assess an application based on static tests. They scan the code to identify any risky code. This is called a white-box approach because they can see, inspect, and scan all of the code. In other words, everything is visible. This is the opposite of a black-box approach, where the running application is treated as a closed whole and is only tested by invoking it and observing the responses. One tool that can do this is the OWASP ZAP.

The OWASP ZAP

The OWASP ZAP is a tool that can perform the automated pen test of an application. This tool can run in two modes:

- **A baseline scan**: The baseline scan takes only a few minutes, and it is optimized to iterate over as many security risks as possible within those few minutes. This makes the baseline scan quick enough to be run early on in the deployment pipeline. It is even possible to run the security scan after every deployment to the first test environment, resulting in fast feedback to developers.

- **A full active scan**: The full active scan takes more time. In this type of scan, the proxy will examine every response from the application to identify other URLs that are part of the application, scanning them as well. In this way, the full application is discovered on the fly, using a spidering approach. This type of scan is more complete, but it also takes more time. For this reason, full scans are often run at intervals – for example, every night.

The OWASP ZAP tries to identify any possible security risks. Some of the most notable risks are SQL injections, JavaScript reflections, and path traversals.

The OWASP ZAP is an application that can be installed on any virtual machine. The disadvantage of this is that the virtual machine is always running, even when there is no scan running. This is more costly, and of course, the virtual machine itself needs to be patched and secured too. More recently, a containerized version of the proxy was also made available. This container can be run in Azure Container Instances, spinning up the proxy only when needed and tearing it down right after execution.

This completes our introduction to code-scanning tools and their implementation. With the help of these tools, you can detect vulnerabilities in your application and prevent any security issues. The next section will examine how you can scan application dependencies.

Working with dependencies

Next to the security risks that application code developed in-house poses, there is also a risk associated with components that are reused. Between 50% and 80% of modern application code is not developed in-house but is taken from other parties in the form of packages or dependencies. Some of these might be open source, but this is not necessarily the case. There can also be components that are bought from other development companies or binaries taken from galleries such as NuGet.

Dependencies not only pose security risks but also licensing risks. What happens if a team starts using a component that is published under the GPL license for a closed source component? If anyone ever finds out, they can be forced to open source their product, or at least suffer public shame for not using the work of others according to the license.

To mitigate these risks, a number of tools can be used to detect and scan all of the dependencies that are used when building an application. One of the tools available to do this is WhiteSource Bolt, which is available as an extension from the Azure DevOps marketplace.

Working with WhiteSource Bolt

To start executing scans with WhiteSource Bolt, perform the following actions:

1. Install the WhiteSource Bolt extension from the Azure DevOps marketplace.

2. Navigate to the **WhiteSource Bolt** menu under **Pipelines**.

3. Sign up and accept the license terms.

4. Add the **WhiteSource Bolt** scanning task to build or release definitions, as shown in the following screenshot:

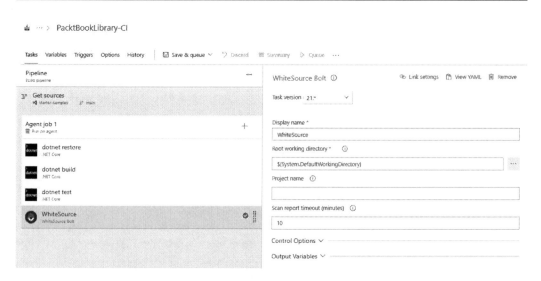

Figure 11.5 – A WhiteSource Bolt pipeline task

5.   Once a pipeline with the WhiteSource Bolt task installed has run, the page with the build results will contain an extra tab called **WhiteSource** that shows similar results, as shown in the following screenshot:

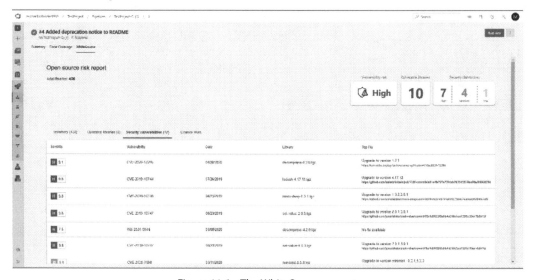

Figure 11.6 – The WhiteSource report

This completes our discussion on dependency scanning. As mentioned earlier, you can use these tools to your advantage to detect and scan all the dependencies that are used when building an application. In the next section, infrastructure compliance is introduced.

Ensuring infrastructure compliance

Another important topic is that of compliance. In many countries or markets, there are sets of rules and policies that must be implemented or adhered to when creating software. A fair share of these policies relates to the infrastructure that the applications are running on. If this infrastructure is deployed and managed on the Azure platform, Azure Policy can be a powerful tool for ensuring that the infrastructure complies with regulations.

In *Chapter 8, Implement Infrastructure and Configuration as Code*, the topic of ARM templates was discussed. ARM templates can be viewed as a technique for describing a complete Azure environment as a JSON array with many objects, each describing one resource in an application's infrastructure.

Azure Policy allows you to write policies that query this document and the changes that are being made through any of the APIs or ARM templates. Whenever a resource is found that matches the query, it can be prevented from being created or the match can be added to a list of audit results. Azure Policy can remediate or modify insecure configurations to prevent mistakes.

Next to writing custom policies, there are many policies readily available for all Azure users. These policies can be used to audit resources that do not comply with best practices or general advice. There are also groups of policies available, called initiatives, that describe the applicable parts of market standards.

Assigning an Azure policy or initiative

Policies can be assigned at different levels within Azure, either at the resource group level, subscription level, or management group level. This can be done through the portal, ARM templates or blueprints, or PowerShell.

To use PowerShell, the following series of commands can be used:

1. To retrieve a reference to the resource group and policy, use the following command:

```
$rg = Get-AzResourceGroup -Name myResourceGroupName
$definition = Get-AzPolicyDefinition | Where-Object {
$_.Properties.DisplayName -eq 'Audit VMs that do not use
managed disks' }
```

   The policy that is chosen here is a built-in policy that will audit all virtual machines that do not use managed disks but have custom disks in storage accounts. This policy definition will be used in the command in the following assignment.

2. To assign the policy to the resource group, use the following command:

```
New-AzPolicyAssignment -Name 'audit-vm-manageddisks' -
DisplayName 'Audit VMs without managed disks Assignment'
-Scope
$rg.ResourceId -PolicyDefinition $definition
```

Within 30 minutes of this assignment, the new policy will become active. At this point, a policy evaluation cycle is started, and all of the resources within the assignment scope will be evaluated against the policy. At the time of writing, there is no published SLA regarding how long such an evaluation cycle can take. Experience shows that this can be anything between 15 minutes and multiple hours, depending on the size of the assignment scope.

Writing an Azure Policy

While there are many built-in policies available, there are many use cases in which the creation of custom policies is needed. Just like any other Azure resource, a policy is written as a JSON document. The appropriate ARM resource type is called `policyDefinitions` and has the following structure:

```
{
  "name": "string",
  "type": "Microsoft.Authorization/policyDefinitions",
  "apiVersion": "2019-01-01",
  "properties": {
   "parameters": {
    "location": { ...}
   },
    "displayName": "...",
    "description": "...",
    "policyRule": {
    "if": {
     "field": "location",
     "equals": "[parameters('location')]",
     },
     "then": {
     "effect": "<audit|deny >"
     }
    }
   }
  }
}
```

The `parameters` object can be used to specify one or more parameters that need to be specified when assigning the policy later on. These parameters follow the same syntax and work the same as the parameters of an ARM template.

The `displayName` and `description` properties can be used to give the policy definition a meaningful name and description for later reference.

The body of the definition contains two elements, as follows:

- **The `if` statement** is used to specify a query that selects the Azure resources that this policy should apply to. There is a specific syntax for writing complex queries in JSON that is detailed in the ARM template reference, which is linked at the end of this chapter.

- **The `then` statement** is used to describe the action that needs to be taken for any resource that matches the condition. This can be *deny* – that is, to automatically deny the creation of any non-compliant resource. Another approach is not to deny non-compliant deployments but rather to audit them. While denying non-compliant deployments is very straightforward in theory, there is good cause for temporarily allowing non-compliant deployments. In such cases, an audit policy can help to keep tabs on these resources. All non-compliant deployments get audit records in their Azure activity log and can be viewed in the Azure portal, under **Azure Policy** in the **Compliance** tab. This is as follows:

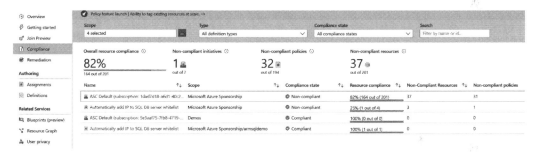

Figure 11.7 – Azure policy compliance details

After writing the policy definition, we need to create it within an Azure subscription for it to be usable. This can either be done through an ARM template or manually within the portal. From a DevOps perspective, writing policies in source control and delivering them through a pipeline as part of an ARM template is the recommended approach. This way, Azure policies are written in the same way as the application and can be reviewed and automatically deployed to Azure as part of a DevOps pipeline.

Initiatives

When working with Azure Policy, many companies find that they need to create many policies to define all the rules that they want their software developers to adhere to. For this reason, it might be beneficial to group policies. Such a grouping is called an *initiative*, and these are defined in JSON as well:

```
{
    "name": "string",
```

```
"type": "Microsoft.Authorization/policySetDefinitions",
"apiVersion": "2019-01-01",
"properties": {
 "displayName": "string",
 "description":  "string",
 "parameters": { ... },
 "policyDefinitions": [
 {
    "policyDefinitionId": "string",
    "parameters": {}
 }
 ]
 }
}
```

The body of an initiative is an array of objects. Each object must contain a `policyDefinitionId` property and, optionally, an object with `parameters` for the policy. The `policyDefinitionId` property must reference a valid `policyDefinitions` condition through its Azure resource ID. The `parameters` array should specify all of the parameters that the policy requires. Often, this is implemented by having the initiative specify the combined set of all parameters of all policies as an initiative parameter. The parameters for the individual policies are then specified with a reference to the initiative parameters.

Fetching audit results

After assigning a policy with the audit effect, the policy will automatically evaluate all of the resources within the scope of the assignment once it is active. There is no guarantee of how long this can take. For new resources, the results of policy evaluation are visible within 15 minutes, but often, this is faster.

Once the results are in, the compliance status for each policy or initiative can be viewed in the portal, resulting in an overview, as shown in the following screenshot:

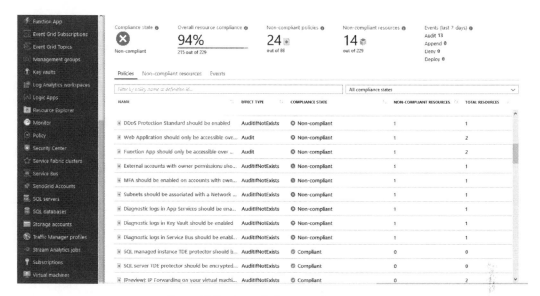

Figure 11.8 – Azure Policy compliance status

The difference between this report and other reports, which are the result of a manual audit, is that this overview is constantly updated to reflect the actual, current state of compliance – it is not a snapshot of compliance at a specific point in time.

An important benefit of this type of compliance is that the rules or policies are applied continuously to all the existing resources and any incoming change. This means that it is possible to ensure that the application environment is always compliant and always adheres to any rules and policies that apply.

Contrast this with the often-used approach of having security and compliance audits only every other month. Often, this results in environments that are only compliant just before the audit and with their compliance slowly decaying afterward – until it is time for another audit, of course, at which point it rises close to 100% again. At many companies, this results in a compliance graph as follows:

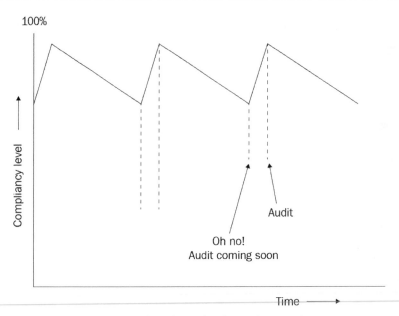

Figure 11.9 – Compliance level maturity over time

With this, we've discussed another example of how DevOps practices can help increase security and compliance – by ensuring infrastructure compliance. In the next section, several alternative tools previously mentioned in this chapter, such as Defender for Cloud, Sonar Cloud, and WhiteSource, will be discussed.

Monitoring and detecting runtime security risks and threats

All of the security tools that have been discussed up to this point have focused on preventing shipping vulnerable code to production environments. However, a complete, deployed software solution, including all its support infrastructure, is made out of so much more than just the code. On top of that, there are many interactions with a solution that may be unexpected or unplanned. Monitoring all of this continuously in production is necessary, not just to prevent security concerns but to also detect any security concerns that arise. In Azure, one of the tools available for doing just that is Azure Security Center. This and Azure Defender are now called Microsoft Defender for Cloud.

The Defender for Cloud tool provides security posture management and threat protection, and protects workloads running in Azure, hybrid, and other cloud platforms.

Defender for Cloud fills the following three needs as you manage the security of resources and workloads:

Figure 11.10 – Defender for Cloud

- **Continuous Assessment** – the solution will provide a brief overview of the current security posture.

- **Security recommendation** – the solution will harden resources and services with the Azure Security Benchmark, and recommend prioritized hardening tasks with detailed remediation steps to improve security posture.

- **Defend** – the solution will detect and resolve threats to resources, workloads, and services. These alerts appear in the Azure portal and can also be sent via email.

The following example shows recommendations to harden security for your resources and improve overall security posture:

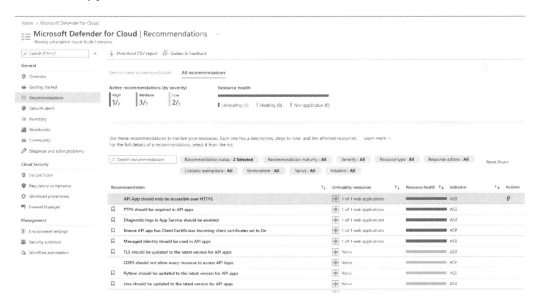

Figure 11.11 – Microsoft Defender recommendations

There are many more capabilities within Microsoft Defender for Cloud, and more are being added on an ongoing basis. When deploying in Azure, this is the place to identify and manage security risks.

This concludes our discussion of the various techniques for monitoring runtime environments for security risks. The next section looks at several alternative tools for performing some of the scanning tasks that were mentioned in earlier sections.

Other tools you can use

There are many tools available on the market for performing security scans of application code and dependencies. Some examples include WhiteSource, Black Duck, Veracode, and Checkmarx:

- **WhiteSource** is the paid version of WhiteSource Bolt. It offers the same services and more. For example, it doesn't only report risks at the time of the dependency scan; it also gives you alerts when new risks become available for dependencies that were present during the last scan of an application.

- **Black Duck** is a product that helps teams to manage the risks associated with using open source software. The services it offers are comparable to WhiteSource.

- **Veracode** and **Checkmarx** are code-scanning tools that are used to identify vulnerable code. Whereas **SonarQube** checks both code quality and security risks, these two products focus solely on security risks. In general, they are better at security scanning, with the downside being that they are more expensive.

- **Sonar Cloud** is a hosted environment for SonarQube and provides similar functionality as SonarQube.

- **CodeQL** is a security scanning tool to automate security checks. CodeQL treats code as data that can be queried and performs variant analysis. Variant analysis is a process that uses a known security vulnerability as a seed to find similar problems in your code. **Code scanning** is a feature that allows you to scan code in a GitHub repository to detect security vulnerabilities and coding errors. If code scanning detects a potential vulnerability or error in your code, GitHub notifies developers and prohibits them from contributing additional issues.

Summary

In this chapter, you have learned that DevOps and security are not two conflicting goals and that DevOps practices can help you to reinforce security. First, you learned how to handle passwords and other secrets when working with continuous deployment pipelines. Next, you learned how to enhance your pipelines with code and dependency scanning tools, applying the shift-left principle to security as well. Finally, you learned how to use Azure Policy to define constraints and rules for your infrastructure and how you can have these automatically applied, or have non-compliant deployments audited or automatically denied.

With the knowledge you have gained, you are now able to have a conversation within your company about how to address security concerns within your DevOps teams. You can cooperate with security engineers to configure the tools you work with and receive automated feedback on the security implications of your work.

In the next chapter, you will learn about application monitoring. Additionally, you will learn how to monitor whether your application is running smoothly and how to gather runtime metrics.

Questions

Here is a list of questions for you to test your knowledge regarding this chapter's material. You will find the answers in the *Assessments* section of the *Appendix*:

1. True or false – securing the delivery of software is just a single step in a deployment pipeline.

2. Which tool can be used for security testing, where a proxy is used to identify valid application URLs and then perform different attacks, such as injections on an application?

3. True or false – in most modern applications, over 50% of the code base comes from open source libraries.

4. What are the secure locations for storing the secrets needed during deployment or for running an application? (You can choose more than one answer.)

    A. Azure Pipelines variables that are marked as secret

    B. Azure Key Vault

    C. Azure DevOps Key Vault

    D. Azure variable groups

    E. Azure DevOps secure variables

    F. Azure DevOps service connection

5. Which two Azure offerings can be used to detect security risks at runtime?

Further reading

- Microsoft Security Code Analysis tool: `https://docs.microsoft.com/en-us/azure/security/develop/security-code-analysis-overview`.

- Code QL analysis engine: `https://codeql.github.com/docs/codeql-overview/about-codeql/`.

- The OWASP Top 10 and the details of every type of risk can be found at `https://owasp.org/www-project-top-ten/2017/`.

- A detailed walk-through on Azure Policy: `https://docs.microsoft.com/en-us/azure/governance/policy/`.

- WhiteSource Bolt can be found on the Azure DevOps Marketplace at `https://marketplace.visualstudio.com/items?itemName=whitesource.ws-bolt`.

- A detailed walk-through on using the OWASP ZAP can be found at `https://devblogs.microsoft.com/premier-developer/azure-devops-pipelines-leveraging-owasp-zap-in-the-release-pipeline/`.

- More information about the Azure Policy resource types and JSON specifications can be found as part of the ARM reference at `https://docs.microsoft.com/en-us/azure/templates/microsoft.authorization/allversions`.

- More information about the Microsoft Security Code Analysis Extension can be found at `https://secdevtools.azurewebsites.net/helpcredscan.html`.

- More information about WhiteSource Bolt and WhiteSource can be found at `https://bolt.whitesourcesoftware.com/` and `https://www.whitesourcesoftware.com`.

- More information about Black Duck can be found at `https://www.blackducksoftware.com/`.

- More information about Veracode can be found at `https://www.veracode.com/`.

- More information about Checkmarx can be found at `https://checkmarx.com/`.

Part 4 – Closing the Loop

DevOps is more than just accelerating the ability to ship quality products to production. Another very important aspect is to observe and measure the usage and other key performance indicators. The insights from the analytics offer critical feedback to shape the future of the product and even help prioritize other quality initiatives necessary to improve the overall reliability of the service.

This part will cover the process of effectively instrumenting applications in order to collect metrics that can be used to better understand application usage and user behavior. Another method for continual learning is to explicitly ask for feedback from within the product so that users get to share valuable suggestions as they use the software. Future improvements to the end user experience can be planned this way.

This part of the book comprises the following chapters:

- *Chapter 12, Application Monitoring*
- *Chapter 13, Gathering User Feedback*

12

Application Monitoring

In the previous chapters, you learned about applying DevOps principles to software delivery. You learned how to create a pipeline from source control all the way to production. You also learned how to ensure that your delivery is compliant and secure, without sacrificing speed or a focus on the delivery of business value. In this chapter, you will learn how to start transforming this pipeline into a DevOps loop, a continuous process of delivering new software, and then measure how your application performs. This is a continuous journey, as you evaluate how your application fares in production and learn how to proceed next.

To do this, this chapter starts by introducing a means for gathering application crashes. Almost every application will, at some point, throw an unhandled exception and crash. Ensuring that application crashes are gathered and reported will enable you to investigate the causes and address them. Then, attention will shift to instrumenting applications.

Instrumentation is the practice of gathering logs and metrics that help you understand how your application performs in production. You can use them to get alerts when things go wrong or, hopefully, before they go wrong. The chapter concludes by exploring several options for integrating with other tools.

The following topics are covered in this chapter:

- Investigating application crashes
- Instrumenting web applications
- Integrating with other tools

Technical requirements

To experiment with the techniques described in this chapter, you will need one or more of the following:

- An App Center account for gathering mobile application crashes
- A Raygun subscription for gathering desktop application crashes
- An Azure subscription for instrumenting web applications

Free-trial options are available for all of these.

Investigating application crashes

No matter how well an application is engineered, at some point, it will crash due to an unexpected condition. To learn from these crashes and to try and prevent them in the future, it helps to add code to applications to gather crash reports and send them to a central location. Here, they can be analyzed and grouped to identify application improvements. How to do this differs, depending on the type of application.

The following sections discuss how this process for mobile and desktop applications works. Regarding web applications, gathering crash reports can be done using the same tool as for instrumentation; we will discuss this in the *Instrumenting web applications* section later on.

Gathering crash reports for mobile applications

One of the many tools available for gathering crash reports and errors from mobile applications is Visual Studio App Center. Besides distributing mobile applications, **App Center** also allows applications to submit their crashes and errors for analysis.

To get started with crash reporting using App Center, the application first needs to be defined. This is called an app definition and how to work with it was discussed in *Chapter 6, Implementing Continuous Deployment and Release Management*. With this app definition, an app secret is created, which is needed to configure an application to send out crash reports. Along with crash reports, it is possible to track other errors, and exceptions that are of interest to developers. To start sending crash reports, the following steps need to be performed:

1. Install the `Microsoft.AppCenter.Crashes` NuGet package in the project.

2. Add the following code to the application initialization:

```
AppCenter.Start("ios={appSecret};android={appSecret
};uwp={appSecret}", typeof(Crashes));
```

Besides crashes, it is also possible to track other errors that are of interest to developers. This can be done using the following code:

```
Crashes.TrackError(ex);
```

All the unhandled exceptions are automatically caught and sent back to App Center. Here, they become available for analysis, as shown in the following screenshot:

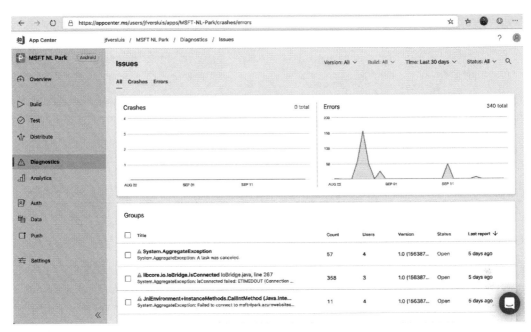

Figure 12.1 – An App Center diagnostics overview

Click on any of the reported errors or crashes to open a detailed view, as shown here:

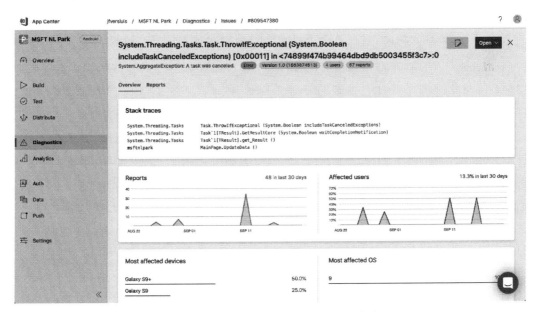

Figure 12.2 – An App Center diagnostics detailed view

A dashboard with the most important information is shown for each crash or error. This includes the number of reports and the number of affected users. Also, the impacted device types and operating systems are shown. At the top of the page, the stack traces are shown, which can be used by developers to investigate and, hopefully, fix the issue.

App Center has integration with Azure DevOps, Jira, and GitHub for bug tracking purposes. Refer to this link for more information: `https://docs.microsoft.com/en-us/appcenter/dashboard/bugtracker/`.

For any critical events, App Center can directly create a bug and send email notifications.

That covers gathering crash reports and errors from mobile applications. The next section introduces the same concepts for desktop applications.

Gathering crash reports for desktop applications

Crash reporting is also available for desktop applications. There are, again, many solutions available for desktop applications and most of them work in roughly the same way. One of these solutions is Raygun. Raygun is a commercial offering available for .NET applications but works for many other languages and platforms as well.

To gather crashes using Raygun, follow these three steps:

1. Sign up for a Raygun account.
2. Install the `Mindscape.Raygun4Net` NuGet package on the solution.
3. Catch unhandled exceptions and forward them to Raygun.

The following example shows you how to catch and forward unhandled exceptions to Raygun:

```
class Program
  {
    private static readonly RaygunClient _raygunClient = new
RaygunClient("myKey");

    static void Main(string[] args)
    {
      AppDomain.CurrentDomain.UnhandledException += HandleEx;
throw new Exception("Boom!");
    }

    private static void HandleEx(object sender,
UnhandledExceptionEventArgs e)
      {
```

```
        _raygunClient.Send(e.ExceptionObject as Exception);
    }
}
```

All the exceptions can be explored in the Raygun web interface. Here, exceptions are automatically grouped if stack traces are sufficiently similar. They can also be grouped and browsed individually, but in most cases, it makes sense to only focus on the larger groups of exceptions.

The following screenshot shows how these groups can be browsed in Raygun:

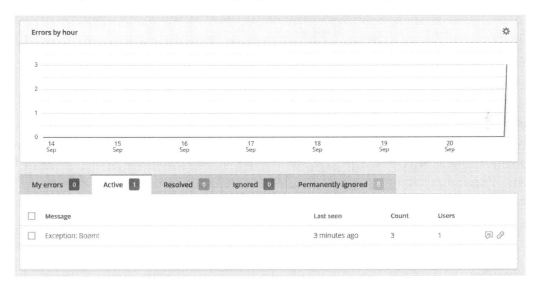

Figure 12.3 – The Raygun view for desktop application exceptions

Clicking on the exception message in this interface shows the complete stack trace and all the shared properties of any instance of the exception that has occurred.

This completes our look into gathering crash reports from mobile and desktop applications. Doing so allows you to find and investigate issues that customers face in production. In the following section, instrumentation for web applications will be introduced to further enhance our insight into how applications behave in production.

Instrumenting web applications

Web applications differ from mobile and desktop applications in many ways, including the fact that large portions of the application run on a server rather than a client. This enables developers to collect information on how web applications are run more easily than other types of applications. This is known as instrumenting an application.

Logs are text messages that are saved by a system to describe the execution path that the server follows. This helps developers go back in time and explore what has happened by examining the logging output. Structured logging is quickly becoming the standard for trace logging. **Structured logging** is a technique where logs are no longer only text messages. Instead, logs are parameterized text messages with a set of values for each parameter. This has two advantages – logs can be better compressed, and they can be searched more quickly.

Metrics are values that are recorded for an application. They take the form of a timestamp, metric name, and value. One example is recording the percentage of a CPU in use every second.

When instrumenting an application, it is easy to focus on many server-level types of logs and metrics. For example, many operators will, by default, start collecting metrics such as CPU usage, memory pressure, and I/O operations. While there is nothing wrong with these metrics, they are not always indicative of an application's performance from a user's point of view. Other metrics, such as response times or queue message processing delays, might yield better insights into the user experience. While there is nothing wrong with measuring system metrics (they are often great indicators of future issues), you should also try to gather user-centric metrics.

Azure offers the Application Insights service for instrumenting applications, with a focus on web applications. An Application Insights workspace can be created using the Azure portal, which opens up a workspace, as shown in the following screenshot. In Azure portal in overview section, **instrumentation key** field is plainly shown, it is recommended that you treat this as an application secret:

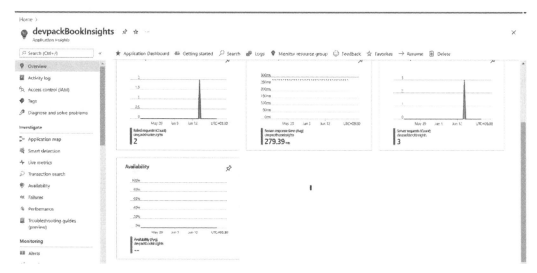

Figure 12.4 – Azure Application Insights Overview

The following subsections will go into detail about logging, metrics, and investigating individual requests.

Logging

One of the most basic types of instrumentation is adding logging statements to application code. In the past, these logs were saved to the disk of the server that ran the application. Retrieving and investigating these logs, therefore, took a lot of time and effort.

In modern hosting environments, logs are no longer saved on the local filesystem but instead stored remotely. With transient infrastructure and servers added or removed on the fly, it is no longer possible to store logs on a server and be sure that they can be retrieved later. For this reason, they are transmitted over HTTP to specialized log stores, such as Application Insights.

Emitting logs

To write log entries to a log store, such as Application Insights, from an ASP.NET application, two things must be done:

1. Log entries need to be emitted from the application code, where applicable, using the `ILogger` interface. This interface is available from the `Microsoft.Extensions.Logging.Abstractions` NuGet package.

2. The Application Insights NuGet package (`Microsoft.ApplicationInsights.AspNetCore`) needs to be installed and Application Insights needs to be registered as `LoggingProvider`. This way, all logs sent to the preceding interface are forwarded to the Application Insights code. In turn, this code forwards all the logs to the Application Insights service.

The following example code shows you how to use the `ILogger` interface from a class to emit a structured log entry:

```
public class Example
{
private readonly ILogger<Example> _logger;public
Example(ILogger<Example> logger)
   {
     _logger = logger;
   }


   public void DoSomething(User user)
   {
     _logger.LogWarning(
       "Doing something for user with id '{userId}' and username
'{username}'",
```

```
        user.Id, user.Username);
    }
}
```

> **Important Note**
>
> There should be no dollar sign (\$) at the start of the log entry. There is no string interpolation used here, but two placeholders are inserted into the text message. The structured logging entry will recognize these and, when showing the entry, insert the provided values.

With log entries emitted, a logging provider should be registered to capture these logs. This is done using the .NET Core built-in dependency injection.

After starting the application, all log entries at the level of warning and higher are automatically forwarded to Application Insights. To change which entries are forwarded and which aren't, filters can be configured. A link to more details on configuring Application Insights in detail is provided at the end of this chapter.

Searching logs

Within a few minutes of emitting a log entry to Application Insights, it becomes available on the interface for querying. To do this, open the Application Insights instance and navigate to **Logs** in the left-hand-side menu (**1**). This opens the view shown in the following screenshot:

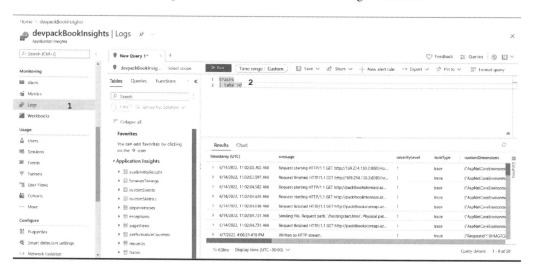

Figure 12.5 – The Application Insights Logs view

Here, it is possible to write queries (**2**) that search the recorded logs in **Kusto Query Language** (**KQL**). Application Insights is optimized for handling large amounts of data and most queries return results within a second or less, even when searching millions of log entries.

Alerting on logs

Gathering and searching logs is useful when troubleshooting specific situations or bugs in response to a user complaint. However, there are situations where it is better to be notified automatically when a certain condition arises. This is called alerting.

Within Azure, it is possible to create alert rules that notify developers whenever a certain condition is met. Alerting functionality is provided by the Azure Monitor offering that is integrated with many Azure services, including Application Insights.

To create a new alert rule, follow these steps:

1. Navigate to Azure Monitor using the portal.

2. Now, choose **Alerts**. This opens the view shown in the following screenshot:

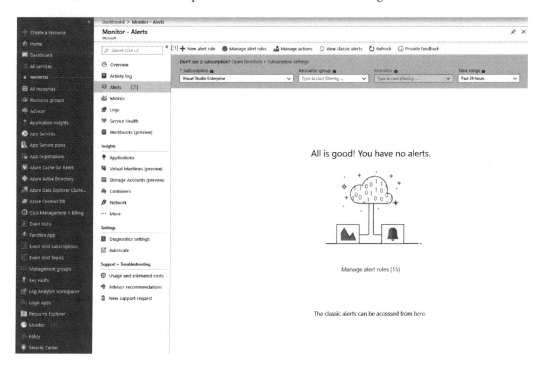

Figure 12.6 – The Azure Monitor Alerts view

If there are any alerts that need attention, they are shown here:

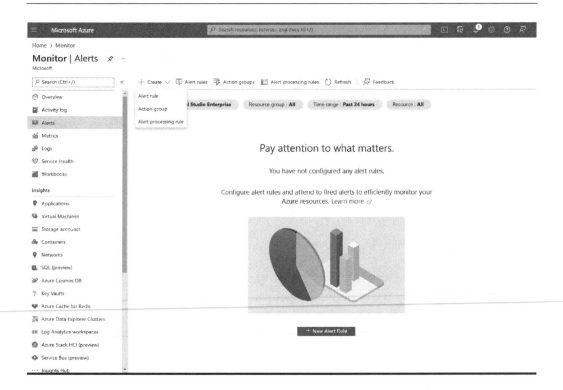

Figure 12.7 – The Azure Monitor alert creation view

Use the **Create** button at the top-left-hand side of the screen to add new alert rules. Doing so opens another view, as shown in the preceding screenshot. Here, the alerting conditions can be configured:

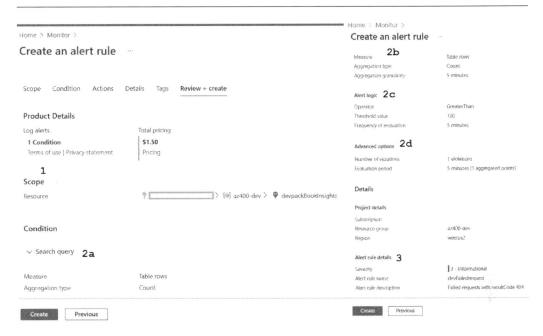

Figure 12.8 – The Azure Monitor alerts Review + create view

In the preceding screenshot, the view that opens to configure alerts – **Scope** – is shown. Here, it is necessary to make resource selections to create an alert.

3. This (**1**) is the resource that is the subject of the alert. This can be any type of resource, and in this instance, the alert will be on an Application Insights workspace.

4. These (**2**) are the conditions to alert under. To select these, the popup on the right opens. Here, a choice can be made between different types of alerts. Pick the **Log Search** alert type to open the detailed view shown here. Here, the following selections must be made:

- **A query mentioned below on the logs** (refer to **2a** in the previous screenshot): In this example, the requests log is queried for entries that failed with a 404 code result:

```
requests
| where success == False and resultCode == 404
```

- **A condition and operator for triggering the alert** (**2b**): In this case, the alert is triggered whenever requests are failed with a 400 code result.

- **The interval to evaluate the alert condition over** (**2c**): When specifying a query that matches a specific number, this determines the interval in which this amount must be met.

- **How often to evaluate the alert condition (2d)**: Evaluating an alert condition too frequently can result in too many alerts opening and closing in a fast series. Evaluating an alert condition too infrequently can result in alerts coming in too late. Experimentation will help you understand how to configure this.

5. This is the action to execute when the alert condition is met. Since there might be a lot of alerts that have to invoke the same group of actions, actions can be grouped, and these action groups can be referenced here. Some examples of actions are calling a Webhook or sending an SMS message or email.

6. The alert configuration is completed by putting in a name and description (**3**).

7. Finally, the alert can be saved.

After the alert is reviewed and created as per the preceding screenshot, activation is done automatically, and within a few minutes, the alert is ready to inspect application logs and signal whenever the alert condition is met.

Logging is a great method of gaining deep knowledge about what happened with a request and how an error came to be. Another technique for learning more about an application's behavior is by using metrics.

Metrics

Besides logs, an application can also emit one or more metrics. A metric is a series of values over time that describes one or more aspects of a system. Some examples of metrics are as follows:

- The number of users currently logged in

- The number of products viewed by users

- The number of database transactions

Gathering metrics such as these can provide insight into how a system is used and how it currently operates. Metrics are often used for creating dashboards and alerts.

Emitting metrics

To start working with metrics, they first have to be emitted by an application and stored in a centralized location. Besides logging, Application Insights can be used for metrics as well.

To use Application Insights for metrics, the following steps need to be taken:

1. Metrics need to be emitted from the application code where applicable, using the `TelemetryClient` class. This interface is available from the `Microsoft.Extensions.Logging.Abstractions` NuGet package.

2. Install the `Microsoft.ApplicationInsights.AspNetCore` Application Insights NuGet package.

3. Register `TelemetryClient` with the Dependency container. Do this by using the extension method on the container builder, as shown in the following code snippet:

```
builder.RegisterType<TelemetryClient>().SingleInstance();
```

4. Once this is done, the application is ready to start emitting metrics. This is done using the `TelemetryClient` class:

```
public class Example
{
private readonly TelemetryClient _telemetryClient;

public Example(TelemetryClient telemetryClient)
{
_telemetryClient = telemetryClient;
}

public void DoSomething()
{
_telemetryClient.GetMetric("doSomethingCalledCounter").
TrackValue(1.0);
 }
}
```

Emitting a metric involves two steps. First, a reference to the metric is retrieved using the `GetMetric()` method. Next, a value is submitted using the `TrackValue` method. Submitted values should be doubles or allow an implicit conversion to a double.

Once the metrics are emitted, they can be used to create graphs and metrics. However, before moving on to these topics, first, another type of metric needs to be discussed – namely, Azure platform metrics.

Besides the metrics that an application emits, there are also numerous metrics that can be recorded from the Azure platform that the system is running on. Some examples are as follows:

- The percentage of CPU used
- The number of messages on a service bus
- The number of database transactions per second
- The amount of free disk space

These metrics are often closely related to how an application performs and may even be leading indicators. For example, when the amount of free disk space reaches 0, most web servers stop working.

In Azure, each service emits a series of metrics by default. These are called platform metrics. Which metrics are emitted differs from service to service and cannot be influenced by the user. These metrics are also automatically gathered by Azure Monitor, and they can be used in the same ways for graphing and alerting as they are emitted by an application.

Platform metrics are integrated, cost-free, and for the majority of resources metrics are retained for 93 days.

Graphing metrics

All metrics that are gathered, either in Application Insights or in Azure Monitor, can be used to build graphs and dashboards that visualize the metric. Graphs can be created using the **Metrics** tab that is available on every Azure resource. Graphs can also be created using the Azure Monitor. This way, graphs for multiple resources can be combined on a single canvas. To do this, do the following:

1.   Open Azure Monitor, which is available from the menu on the left.

2.   Navigate to the **Metrics** menu. This opens the view shown in the following screenshot:

Figure 12.9 – Azure Monitor – Metrics

3.   Once the canvas opens, one or more graphs can be added to it. A graph is built using the graph builder at the top. Four selections have to be made here:

   •   The resource that a graph needs to be drawn for.

- **The metrics namespace belonging to the resource that a graph needs to be drawn for**: For every Azure resource type, there is only a single namespace. The only exception is Application Insights, for which there are two – one with default metrics and one with application metrics that are emitted using `TelemetryClient`.

- **The metric to draw**: For custom metrics, this refers back to the name chosen in the `GetMetric()` method from the previous section.

- **The mathematical operation to combine multiple measurements into a single point on the graph**: This can be the minimum, maximum, average, sum, or count.

- To add multiple graph lines to the same graph, choose **Add Metric** at the top. Repeat the preceding four selections to configure the new graph.

4. To make this graph part of a dashboard for easy reuse, click the **Pin to dashboard** button at the top.

5. Dashboards can then be accessed directly using the menu on the right:

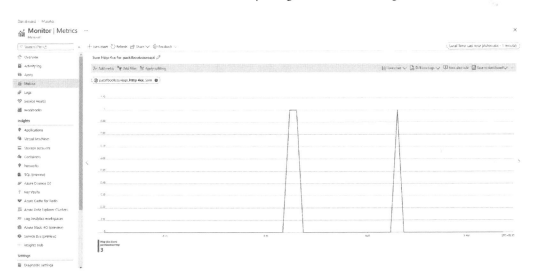

Figure 12.10 – The App Service Http400 metrics graph

Having a graph of a metric, or even multiple graphs in a dashboard, is great for investigating issues. However, no one likes to continuously watch dashboards to see how things are going. For that reason, it is also possible to configure alerts on metrics.

Alerting on metrics

Just as with log entries, it is possible to be alerted by Azure Monitor when a metric goes above or below a certain threshold. Log entries that require a follow-up could be related to only a single user or customer that is having trouble. Metrics, on the other hand, are useful for detecting situations where all users are impacted by an issue, or situations where an infrastructure no longer works or will stop working soon.

Creating alerts for metrics works in a way that is very similar to creating alerts from logs. To create a new alert rule, navigate to Azure Monitor using the portal and then choose **Alerts**.

Investigating requests

When using Application Insights for logging and metrics, there are many more built-in capabilities of Application Insights that you can use. One of these capabilities is the possibility to execute search queries against all types of data collected by Application Insights from one view, called **Search**.

Here, it is possible to search all the information collected by Application Insights, including the following:

- Logs emitted by the application code, which includes NuGet packages and the .NET Framework.

- **All dependency calls**: These are calls to databases and other systems that are automatically detected by Application Insights. Application Insights records the target system and duration.

- **All exceptions**: All exceptions that occur in an application are recorded by Application Insights, even if properly handled by the application code.

- **Requests**: Every user request that comes in over HTTP is logged. Important properties, such as the URL, duration, and HTTP verb, are also included.

To search for a specific transaction using the search view, open the correct Application Insights instance within the Azure portal and navigate to the **Transaction search** menu (**1**) to get the view shown in the following screenshot:

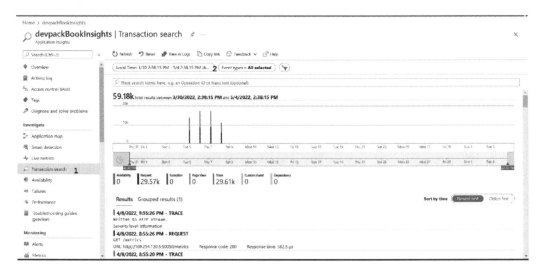

Figure 12.11 – Application Insights – Transaction search

In the **Transaction search** view, several search parameters can be configured (**2**):

- **An interval to search within**: This defaults to the last 24 hours.

- **The types of events to search in**: These can be requests, log entries, page views, exceptions, dependency calls, and so on.

- Any text to search for.

Within seconds, all matching results are shown in a bar chart. Each bar stands for a time period and shows how many matches there are within that time frame. Below this chart, all the individual matches are shown. These are a mix of all of the types of events available.

Clicking on any of the results opens a new view that shows the selected record in relation to all the other types, grouped per request. This allows you to quickly navigate to all the logs, dependency calls, and exceptions that are gathered by Application Insights during the execution of a single user request. The results can be displayed as a list and as a timeline.

This allows you to see very quickly what the server was doing when performing the user request:

Figure 12.12 – Application Insights – End-to-end transaction details

With all of these means to investigate applications and be notified regarding events, it is important to decide which alerts to create and which not to, not only in order to create a healthy working environment but also to balance monitoring with new work. This is the topic of the next section.

Optimizing alerting

Once teams start instrumenting their applications and adding alerts to metrics that they find important, it will not be long before the first alerts start coming in. At this point, it is important to not only respond to the alerts but also to investigate them and then close them. Alerts should also be evaluated and viewed as an opportunity for learning.

Optimizing alerts

An important thing to do after creating a series of alerts is to re-evaluate them on a regular basis. Two things that might come out of an evaluation such as this are as follows:

- **Changes in the alerting threshold**: Evaluating alerts regularly involves taking a look at the metric over time and seeing where the alerting threshold is at now. This might lead to the conclusion that the threshold is too low or too high.

- **Removing duplicates**: Looking at alerts that have been raised over the month(s), it is very likely you'll identify one or more groups of alerts that are always raised at the same time. For example, a set of alerts set on a specific web server can be so related that they are always raised at the same time. A common example is CPU usage and the average response time for an HTTP request; these two often rise at the same time. If this is the case, it is worth considering either removing one of them or downgrading one of them to be a warning only. Duplicate alerts increase the number of items that need an immediate reaction, leading to increased pressure on a team without a clear benefit.

Constantly optimizing the set of alerts not only helps to reduce waste but also prevents so-called alert fatigue.

Alert fatigue

If alert rules are not constantly reviewed and updated, they could negatively influence a team, especially when alert rules trigger too easily or too frequently, as people will no longer respond to them properly. If there are too many alerts, it will wear people out and they will become numb to the effect of an alert. It does not even matter whether they are false alerts or real alerts; just the number of alerts can be enough to get people into a state where they do not care anymore.

If a situation such as this is observed within a team, it is time to drastically change the way alerts are generated and responded to. If this does not happen, team members might fall ill or leave a company altogether.

One of the ways to prevent this situation is by implementing a healthy on-call schedule.

Which metrics to capture

One question that comes up frequently when talking about metrics is what metrics to emit and monitor. There are many possible metrics and even more opinions on this subject. As a good starting point, the following metrics are often gathered for web applications:

- **Requests per minute, transactions per minute, or something similar**: This is a metric that is intended to capture the current load or throughput on a web application.

- **The average response time**: This metric captures the response time for all requests within a time window.

- **The error rate**: This metric captures the percentage of all requests that result in an error. As a guideline for an error, all HTTP response codes of 400 and upward are often taken.

When these three metrics are captured and graphed together in a single graph, it provides the very first step in understanding an application's behavior. Let's explore a few examples:

- When the average response time goes up but the throughput (requests per minute) stays the same, this might be an indication that the infrastructure that hosts the application is having issues.

- When both the throughput and the average response times go up, this might be an indication that traffic is increasing and that the current infrastructure is not capable of sustaining that throughput at the same response times.

- When the error rate goes up but the other metrics stay the same, this might be an indication that a deployment has gone wrong or that a specific code path is starting to generate (more) errors.

Of course, these are just examples, and there are many more possible scenarios. Other metrics can help to rule out a specific scenario or try to avoid them. For example, also starting to monitor the database load as a percentage can help detect a specific instance of all three scenarios. If the database load gets close to 100%, it might be time to scale the database up to a higher performance tier to help to sustain the higher throughput at the same response times as before.

To conclude this section, there is one final recommendation – when starting with monitoring, there is often a tendency to focus on the systems that host the application. As an alternative, also consider monitoring metrics that have a direct business impact or metrics that are an indication of user satisfaction in terms of the usability of an application. This comes much closer to measuring business value than when only you watch systems.

Some examples of this are as follows:

- In an online shop, the number of books sold per minute can be a very valuable business metric. Just imagine the impact it can have on a business if this metric is available in near real time using Azure Monitor and custom metrics from the application code.

- For an online reading platform, the number of virtual page turns can be a valuable metric that signals whether users are happily working with the service. As soon as this number sees a sharp drop or rapidly increases, this might be an indication that something is going wrong.

To find out which metrics make sense in a given scenario, it might help to talk to business or subject matter experts.

Having an on-call schedule

Once alerts are configured and start to be raised, it does not make sense to configure them to not trigger before 8 AM and after 5 PM. In other words, it is necessary to make sure that alerts of a certain severity are followed up even outside of business hours.

In many companies where having alerts is new, there is some form of implicit expectation that some people will be available outside of office hours (alongside their regular duties) to handle these alerts. Sometimes, when an alert is raised only once or twice a year, and there are no agreements about response times, this might not even be a problem at all.

However, in many organizations – especially over time – there is an expectation that these alerts are responded to within a certain period of time. Besides that, the number of alerts may increase as systems become larger and more complex, or the number of systems grows.

The way to cope with this is by creating an on-call schedule and formal agreements on what is expected of engineers and how the organization will reward them for their efforts. This allows the organization to set clear expectations and allows engineers to manage their free time based on these agreements. Having enough system downtime helps the engineers relax between periods of higher stress. This allows them to stay alert when they are on call, ready to react when this is expected of them.

There is much material available on what constitutes a healthy on-call schedule and what doesn't, and the keyword here is *healthy*. Some general pointers are as follows:

- Those who are on call during non-business hours should not be on call during business hours as well.

- Provide engineers who are on call with reasonable compensation for being close to a phone, not under the influence, and so on. What is reasonable differs from situation to situation, but the more demanding being on call is, the higher the compensation should be.

- Provide the proper tools for being on call. For example, when a response time of 30 minutes or less is expected, provide those on call with a backpack with a laptop, phone, and means to connect to the internet.

- Ensure that every employee is not on call at least 75% of the time.

- Allow employees to take time off in lieu so that they can be late for work if they had to respond to an alert overnight.

After every disturbance of the normal operation of a system, whether this is during business hours or after, a live site incident review can be performed to learn what happened and how to reduce the chance of it happening again.

Live site reviews

After an alert is triggered and the team has responded and remediated the situation, it is time to evaluate what happened. This is called a live site incident review. Here, the whole team gathers to address the following:

- What happened – to start, a timeline should be constructed from the time the incident was discovered to the point that normal operations were restored. Next, the timeline is expanded with the events that led to the situation that triggered the incident.

- Next, the series of events is evaluated to learn what worked well in the response. If one member of the team used a new tool to quickly diagnose a problem, this can benefit other members of the team as well.

- Only then is it time to look at the possible points of improvement and translate these points into high-priority work for the team. Possible fail-safes are identified and scheduled for implementation or new alerts are identified that send an alert before a similar problem occurs again.

- The alert or group of alerts that triggered the initial response is evaluated to determine whether they are adequate or possibly contain duplicates.

The best time for a live site incident review is as soon after the incident itself as possible. In practice, this means giving everyone enough time to rest and recuperate and plan a meeting for the next business day.

This completes our overview of Application Insights and the Azure Monitor capabilities for instrumenting web applications. The following section describes several approaches for integrating Application Insights and Azure Monitor with other tools.

Integrating with other tools

Azure Monitor and Application Insights are excellent tools for gathering application logs and metrics, as well as storing them and making them searchable. However, there could be reasons why development teams or businesses prefer to work with other tools to visualize application performance or respond to alerts. One important driver for integration is often the primary tool used by a person or team. If a team operates mainly in ServiceNow or Grafana, it is often useful to integrate these with Azure Monitor instead of forcing these teams to work with multiple tools.

Many possible integrations exist; some examples are detailed in the following subsections.

IT service management applications

Action groups were introduced in the previous section where we looked at instrumenting web applications. Action groups are groups of actions to be performed in response to an alert.

Next to the rich built-in capabilities, it is also possible to automatically raise an alert in an existing **IT Service Management (ITSM)** solution. If there is already an ITSM solution in place within a company, it makes sense not to create a separate alerting channel using Azure Monitor. Instead, using an ITSM connector from Azure Monitor allows you to manage all the company-wide alerts from one solution.

Currently, there are integrations available with ServiceNow, Provance, System Center Service Manager, and more. These connections are created through the ITSM connector.

Azure Boards

In many development teams, Azure DevOps is the tool that developers spend most of their time with. This is also where they perform their backlog management using Azure Boards.

Meanwhile, operators (and hopefully, developers, too) perform investigative work in Application Insights to determine the cause of user errors and to drill down into the reasons for failure. This investigative work could result in new work that needs to be backlogged in Azure DevOps.

To facilitate this, integration between Application Insights and Azure DevOps can be configured from Application Insights by taking the following steps:

1. Navigate to the **Work Items** option on the left-hand side menu (**1**). This opens the view shown on the left in the following screenshot. Here, a connection to Azure Boards can be configured:

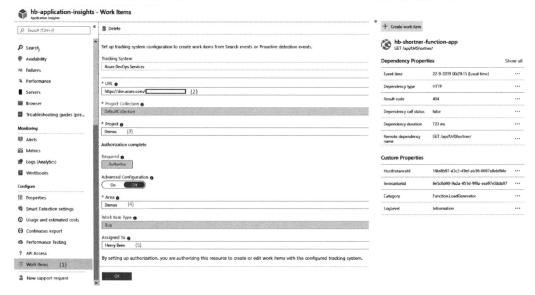

Figure 12.13 – Application Insights – Work Item integration

2. To configure the connection, the following details need to be filled out:

   - Enter the Azure DevOps link. Here, the name of the organization needs to be appended.

   - Select the Azure DevOps project to use. This can be selected from the dropdown.

- Select a product area where new items will be created. By default, this is the same as the name of the project, unless you change it.

- Provide the name of a user as the default owner of new work items.

After configuring this connection, a new + **Create work item** button is visible on the relevant pages in Application Insights. This button allows you to create a bug with all the relevant information directly on the backlog.

Grafana

Azure Monitor allows you to build simple, easy-to-use dashboards. The advantage of using Azure Monitor dashboards is that they integrate perfectly with all the other Azure practices, such as **Role-Based Access Control** (**RBAC**) and Azure Resource Manager templates.

However, teams may have already adopted other tools for visualization, such as Grafana. Grafana is a well-known platform that works well with operational dashboards. Grafana can be configured to connect using Azure Monitor and can query metrics for graphing. Grafana also has alerting capabilities.

To connect Grafana to Azure Monitor, the following steps need to be taken:

1. Create a new app registration in the Azure Active Directory account that is used by your Azure subscription. Take note of the **Tenant ID**, **Client ID**, **Subscription ID**, and **Client Secret** properties of this app registration.

2. Create a new RBAC role assignment for the app registration, with at least the **Reader** permissions set on the resources to monitor.

3. Configure a new data source in Grafana of the **Azure Monitor** type. Insert the properties collected in *step 1* for authenticating to Azure.

4. Add a new graph to the dashboard, selecting **Azure Monitor** as a data source.

By taking the preceding steps, a Grafana-to-Azure Monitor connection can be set up within a matter of minutes.

Summary

In this chapter, you learned how to start completing the DevOps loop. You also learned how to work with crash reports and gather them from all types of applications, as well as how to instrument web applications. You now know how to use Application Insights to centralize logs and metrics and to get insight into requests and dependency calls. You also learned how you can integrate Azure Monitor with other tools to further streamline your development processes.

With this knowledge, you can now start learning about how your applications operate in production. By doing so, you can not only deliver your software faster but also learn from its usage and start improving from there.

In the next chapter, you will learn about gathering user feedback to complement what you have learned from your system logs and metrics. You will also learn how to measure end user satisfaction with your application and new features.

Questions

As we conclude, here is a list of questions for you to test your knowledge regarding this chapter's material. You will find the answers in the *Assessments* section of the *Appendix*:

1. It is possible to capture custom metrics from the Azure platform offerings using Application Insights – true or false?

2. How long are platform metrics retained for in Azure Monitor?

3. It is possible to capture custom metrics from your own application code using Application Insights – true or false?

4. What do you call a situation where engineers start ignoring alerts as they are worn down by too many of them?

5. It is possible to call a Webhook when an alert fires in Azure – true or false?

Further reading

- More information about the App Center SDK can be found at https://docs.microsoft.com/en-us/appcenter/sdk/.

- Azure Monitor-supported metrics by resource type: https://docs.microsoft.com/en-us/azure/azure-monitor/essentials/metrics-supported.

- More information on Raygun can be found at https://raygun.com.

- More detailed information on configuring Application Insights is available at https://docs.microsoft.com/en-us/azure/azure-monitor/app/app-insights-overview.

- The KQL reference page can be found at https://docs.microsoft.com/en-us/sharepoint/dev/general-development/keyword-query-language-kql-syntax-reference.

13
Gathering User Feedback

In the previous chapter, you learned how to measure how your applications are performing in production. You learned how to gather crash reports and logs and how to instrument an application. However, the purpose of software is not just to deliver perfectly running applications, but to create business value. Gathering user feedback is necessary to determine whether your application is also achieving this higher goal. In this chapter, you will learn techniques to measure whether your users are satisfied, which features they are using and which they are not, and how you can use this information to steer future developments.

To do this, this chapter starts by introducing the concept of continuous feedback. Next, it moves on to introduce different approaches to asking users for feedback and recording their responses. This can be both in-application or via other channels. Besides gathering feedback directly, you can also tap into other, indirect channels. Examples are reactions to your software on Twitter and the usage of features in your application. Finally, this chapter will introduce hypothesis-driven development, an approach to software development practiced by Microsoft.

The following topics will be covered in this chapter:

- Understanding continuous feedback
- Asking for feedback
- Gathering indirect feedback
- Implementing hypothesis-driven development

Understanding continuous feedback

As explained in *Chapter 1, Introduction to DevOps*, DevOps is a cultural movement that tries to bring developers and operators closer together to help them to deliver business value faster and more reliably. Feedback loops are an important element in doing this. In the previous chapter, we saw numerous feedback loops:

- Developers can run unit tests on their local machine to verify that their changes did not break existing behaviors.

- After source code check-in, all unit tests are run again and a pipeline with more tests starts running.

- Besides functional tests, security tests and dependency scans can be run.

- After releasing, logs and metrics are gathered to determine whether the application is running smoothly.

All of this provides feedback on the technical quality of the work, and now it is time to add one more feedback loop—a loop intended to verify whether the application actually fulfills the needs of its users.

As obvious as this may sound, it is more often forgotten than most developers would care to admit. In many companies, there is faith in product owners or business analysts, and they are trusted to be able to predict which features users need and to sort them in order of priority.

This is while we know that developing software is a complex activity where the results of a change often cannot be predicted in advance. In such situations, it is important to continuously look for feedback from the user to identify whether features are delivering the value they should.

Continuously looking for feedback will help to make decisions such as the following:

- Removing features that are not being used by most of the users; this removes the need for maintenance on them, therefore reducing cost and freeing up development time.

- Expanding features that are most used by users, making them more prominent in the interface.

- Increasing or decreasing testing efforts based on the perceived quality of the application by users.

Going further along this line of reasoning, we might conclude that it is impossible to predict whether a feature will actually deliver enough business value to justify its existence or not. Companies that do this often adopt the practice of hypothesis-driven development, which will be discussed later.

The next section will introduce different approaches for asking application users for feedback.

Asking for direct feedback

One very straightforward way to collect user feedback is by just asking for it. Over the last few years, more and more applications have been enriched with feedback mechanisms built into the application.

Other approaches that are commonly used are publishing a public roadmap and engaging with customers directly.

Advantages of in-product feedback

Collecting in-product feedback is a good way to get started with direct user feedback. Examples of in-product feedback are grading a specific view or action, giving a thumbs up or down, or sending a happy or sad smiley face.

Collecting in-product feedback has the following advantages:

- It is one of the easiest ways for customers to give feedback, taking virtually none of their time.

- Due to the non-intrusiveness of this approach, a large number of end users of the application might choose to respond.

- Recorded feedback can be context aware.

- When recording a grade, smiley face, or thumbs up or down for feedback, an application can also record the current state and most recent user activities and send all of that along with the user feedback. This makes a single click by the user much more valuable than it seems at first sight. It allows quick insights into the most loved and most hated parts of an application.

- Finally, allowing in-product feedback makes the user feel heard and listened to.

> **Tip**
> Of course, recording data about users and how they use an application requires their consent. Your intentions need to be fully transparent regarding the information gathered about users. Also, an opt-in for explicit content is often required, as well as an option to revoke previously given consent. The precise requirements vary from country to country and are a legal consideration.

The disadvantage of this type of feedback is that it can be too much to analyze in detail. Also, since the results are often anonymized, it is not possible to follow up on feedback. This makes it hard to understand *why* a user was satisfied or dissatisfied with an application feature. Sometimes this is countered by adding a checkbox under the feedback box stating something such as *I give one-time permission to be contacted about this subject.*

If you want to understand the reasons for a user's feedback, other feedback mechanisms, such as interviews or focus groups, might be more appropriate.

Having a public roadmap

Another approach for gathering user feedback is by publicly sharing what is currently in the backlog and what isn't. One team that publicly shares which features they are working on is the Azure DevOps team. Naturally, this list does not contain all features the product group is planning. The reasons for this might be to keep a competitive edge or to keep some new feature secret until a big announcement. However, their backlog provides a good insight into what is currently brewing.

Adopting this practice allows the users of a product to reach out and comment on this public list. It allows them to request features to be moved up or down the list of priorities, and they can share which features they are missing.

This can bring the following advantage to a company: when users engage with feedback on the list of features, they are encouraged to specify why they make a certain request. This might provide new insights into customer demand and may lead to a shift in priorities.

There are also downsides to this approach:

- Not all users will engage in and provide feedback on a public backlog. This might result in a bias toward more vocal or more demanding customers in the group that provides feedback. While not necessarily an issue, it is good to keep this in mind.

- Engaging with users over feature requests or features that they want to be moved up or down the list can be very time-consuming. Especially when compared with in-product feedback, this approach takes more time.

As well as having a public feature roadmap, there are also other ways to give users an insight into what a company is currently working on and what they are planning. Some examples include the following:

- **UserVoice**: UserVoice is a platform that allows users to propose new features and vote on features proposed by others. It allows the gathering of user ideas without opening the actual backlog to users.

- **Bugtrackers**: If customers are very vocal about reporting bugs and errors in an application, it can help to open up a bugtracker. This allows users to see which issues are already known and if and when they might be fixed.

Public backlogs and UserVoice-like platforms are more common than open backlogs. Open lists of bugs or issues are more often seen in open source development.

Using interviews or focus groups

Other forms of requesting user feedback are one-on-one interviews and focus groups. While these are even more time-intensive than open backlogs and public discussions, they also have the benefit of allowing more balanced user selection.

For example, if an application is clearly targeting four different market segments, it can be beneficial to have five focus groups—one for each market segment and an additional one with a mix of them. The first four will allow us to focus on the specific needs of each group, while the fifth will incite a lot of discussions and provide insight into how different wishes from different groups compare.

Interviews and focus groups are also more suitable for not only getting feedback but also understanding the reasoning of users. Sitting face to face with users allows us to explore their way of reasoning and how they perceive an application.

This concludes the discussion of direct user feedback. In the next section, indirect user feedback is discussed.

Gathering indirect feedback

A well-known saying in software development is that users *do not know what they want*. While this may sound harsh, there are a few reasons why direct user feedback from discussions, interviews, and focus groups does not necessarily lead to good product feedback:

- One reason for this is that everyone wants to be liked. When conducting an interview, or talking to a group of users, there is a chance that they will only say what they believe the interviewer wants to hear.

- It has a high turnaround time. Scheduling interviews and focus groups takes time, and finding a time that everyone can attend can easily take days or even weeks.

- It is hard to keep asking the same group of users for feedback every few weeks. This is especially important when trying to determine whether the quality of a feature is improving with the newest updates or not.

For these reasons, it can be worthwhile to cut back on asking for feedback, but instead, measure how users are interacting with an application on a functional level and whether they are satisfied with the value they receive from an application.

One way to do this is by measuring user behavior in an application and emitting metrics based on that. In *Chapter 12, Application Monitoring*, **Application Insights** was introduced for gathering application-level metrics. While metrics are traditionally used for emitting metrics regarding application performance, metrics can also be used to emit metrics regarding application usage. Some examples are the following:

- How frequently is every page visited?

- How many times are specific operations performed?

- How long does it take to complete a certain view?

- How many users open a specific form, only to never complete it?

Gathering these metrics can deliver important insights into how users are interacting with an application and which parts they use or do not use.

Besides usage, another indicator of user satisfaction can be Twitter sentiment or the number of support requests.

Sentiment analysis

Besides gathering metrics in-product, there are also metrics that can be gathered outside of the product. One example source of information is Twitter. Using the Azure cloud and machine learning algorithms, it is now possible to continuously analyze all of the tweets that are directed to a Twitter handle or a hashtag and automatically detect sudden changes.

This even goes as far as an Azure Pipelines extension that allows continuously measuring Twitter sentiment and canceling the progress of a release to the next stage if sentiment turns too negative. This extension is implemented as a pipeline gate and is available in the **Azure DevOps Marketplace**.

Support requests

Just like the Twitter sentiment, there might be other indicators of user satisfaction that can be gathered automatically. Continuously collecting the number of support calls or emails per minute and detecting a certain spike can be a clear indicator of a user issue. Using machine learning and system integrations, this can be harnessed for automated responses or signposting a user to the results.

Adopting practices such as this can save minutes or hours when detecting production issues. Taking user feedback and making decisions based on that sentiment can go even further. This is called hypothesis-driven development, which is discussed next.

Implementing hypothesis-driven development

A risk in software development is that teams are so busy creating more and more features that they forget to reflect upon their business value, while everyone knows that not every feature is a success. Some features may not be used at all, or may even be disliked by users. As an industry, we have come to learn that product owners have a hard time predicting which features will be liked by users and which will not. Even when using all of the feedback mechanisms discussed previously, predicting what users want is difficult.

Another important thing to recognize is that every feature in the product also brings a future cost. Every feature requires documentation, support, and maintenance. This means that unnecessary features are driving costs up as well. From this perspective, it makes sense to not only leave non-value features but to even remove them from the product as soon as possible.

Hypothesis-driven development is a practice that starts with acknowledging that it is impossible to predict whether a feature will add value, add no value, or, even worse, decrease business value. Next, it recommends transforming features in the backlog into quick, lightweight experiments that are run in the product to determine whether a new feature adds value or not.

Such an experiment can be written in a similar shape as a user story, for example, like this: *We believe that users want a new one-field popup to quickly create an appointment, instead of the full dialog. We are convinced that this is the case when we see that over 25% of appointments are created using this new dialog and that the average approval rate of appointments goes up by 2 points or more.* The first part is called the hypothesis, and the second is the threshold for confirmation of that hypothesis.

Once this is written down, a minimal implementation of such a one-field popup is created, and its usage and the usage of the original form are monitored using metrics. Depending on the measurements, one of the following can occur:

- The belief stated in the hypothesis is confirmed to be true and the new feature adds value. More stories surrounding this feature can be added to the backlog to increase the business value the product provides.

- The belief stated in the hypothesis is not confirmed and further experimentation is not expected to yield different results. The feature is dropped from the backlog and the current, minimal implementation might even be removed from the product.

- The belief stated in the hypothesis is not confirmed, but experimentation continues. This can happen when there are numerous user complaints about a certain feature that the team is set on fixing. If one approach does not work, they might try another.

Using the approach outlined before, teams can increase the impact they make on business value by minimizing the time they spend on features that, after experimentation, do not add value and even remove them from the product again.

Often, hypothesis-driven development is combined with phased roll-out mechanisms such as **feature flags** or **deployment rings**. The experiment is then run on only a small percentage of the users, which makes it easier to pull the feature if it does not add enough value.

This completes the discussion about the means of gathering and using user feedback on applications and how user feedback ties into the DevOps goal of delivering business value to end users.

Summary

In this chapter, you learned how to measure the business outcomes of software development activities. First, you learned about the importance of feedback and how this helps to understand customer needs and whether those needs are actually being met. Then, numerous approaches to asking for feedback were introduced, both direct and indirect.

Finally, you learned about hypothesis-driven development and how a mindset of experimentation can help to cut down waste.

With this knowledge, you can now choose and implement feedback mechanisms that allow you to learn what the user sentiment regarding your application is. You are now able to implement an experiment-based approach to creating software, focusing on value-adding features and ignoring or even removing features that do not add value.

In the next chapters, you will learn all about containers. Containers are rapidly changing the way software is delivered and are often used for applying DevOps principles to both existing and new applications.

Questions

As we conclude, here is a list of questions for you to test your knowledge regarding this chapter's material. You will find the answers in the *Assessments* section of the *Appendix*:

1. True or false: There are no downsides to publicly sharing a roadmap.

2. What is an important concern to keep in mind when evaluating user feedback on a public roadmap?

3. What are two indirect indicators of user satisfaction that are relatively easy to capture?

4. Which of the following is not part of a hypothesis, as used in hypothesis-driven development?

   A. A hypothesis

   B. A confirmation threshold

   C. A conclusion

5. What are two benefits of interviews or focus groups over other means of gathering feedback?

Further reading

- The list of features planned for Azure DevOps can be found at `https://docs.microsoft.com/en-us/azure/devops/release-notes/features-timeline`.

- The Twitter Sentiment Analysis extension can be found on the Azure DevOps Marketplace at `https://marketplace.visualstudio.com/items?itemName=ms-devlabs.vss-services-twittersentimentanalysis`.

Part 5 – Advanced Topics

In this final part, you'll learn about the benefits of adopting a good DevOps culture in your organization . You will get to explore various scenarios that can serve as guidance while preparing an enterprise cloud adoption plan, which may have a direct impact on your business outcomes. At the end of the book, you can test your preparation for the certification by taking the mock exam.

This part of the book comprises the following chapters:

- *Chapter 14, Adopting the Culture of Continuous Improvement*
- *Chapter 15, Accelerate Cloud Adoption through DevOps*
- *Chapter 16, Containers*
- *Chapter 17, Planning Your Azure DevOps Organization*
- *Chapter 18, AZ-400 Mock Exam*

14

Adopting the Culture of Continuous Improvement

DevOps strategies deployed by teams mostly revolve around following a prescribed set of practices continuously and repeatedly as a part of every release iteration. However, high-performance teams approach everything with a learning mindset and identify improvements along the way to establish better discipline and becomes masters in doing things, such as effective **continuous integration (CI)/continuous deployment (CD)** practices for release agility, monitoring deployments to reduce failures, and addressing production issues in a timely manner.

No team can claim to be perfect in their implementation of DevOps practices. A culture of continuous learning must be inculcated as a must-have for the teams. Hence, listening to feedback coming from various stakeholders is the first step toward improving your DevOps hygiene.

Additionally, most DevOps tool vendors, including Microsoft, will periodically bring in newer enhancements and product innovations to the marketplace. Teams must constantly evaluate and plan to adopt these latest product features to maximize productivity. Adopting a culture of continuous improvement is critical to staying relevant in your DevOps journey.

This chapter focuses on the concept of **continuous improvement** and discusses a few of the approaches that organizations can make use of to learn constantly.

In this chapter, we are going to cover the following main topics:

- Measuring your DevOps success
- Value stream mapping
- A data-driven approach
- Operationalizing a feedback loop

Measuring your DevOps success

As discussed in *Chapter 1, Introduction to DevOps*, defining effective metrics and measuring your results against them is key to ensuring the success of your DevOps investments. This also serves as a compelling force to diligently follow the DevOps practices and improve them over time.

The insights derived from these metrics act as a motivator for engineering teams to pay greater attention to where they are lacking. Let's consider a few examples to illustrate this:

- Delivery cycle metrics such as story points delivered per sprint, overall productivity, and the number of defects delivered per line of code give insights to project administrators on progress made during a sprint and the quality of the output.

- Automated testing-related metrics such as test pass percentage, code coverage, and open defects offer insights into the readiness of the software before being released and deployed to production.

- After the software has been released, reports around usage and user activity, health monitoring metrics, and a count of errors indicate the adoption of your software.

From the examples shared, it is evident that dashboards and metrics have a strong bearing on the culture of a team and the habits it inculcates to achieve broader business objectives.

It is important to break down the **key performance indicators** (**KPIs**) into smaller and more meaningful metrics. A few examples have been listed as follows:

- KPI – lead time:

  - Metrics: Sprint velocity, defects status by severity, static code analysis results, and so on

- KPI – deployment frequency:

  - Metrics: Test case coverage, a unit test pass/fail rate, percentage build automation, the number of build pipelines, and the overall time for deployment

- KPI – mean time to restore a service

  - Metrics: The incident resolution time, a count of alerts per day, the service response time, and so on

- KPI – change failure percentage

  - Metrics: Server exceptions, a count of incidents by severity, and so on

Thus, we can conclude that the greater the number of DevOps metrics that you plan to measure, the more significant potential and benefit you will observe in the transformation of your DevOps practices.

In the next section, we will discuss the concept of value stream mapping as it applies to minimizing wastages in your DevOps life cycle.

Value stream mapping

Value stream mapping (**VSM**) is a concept that is quite popular in the manufacturing industry. It refers to the technique of creating a lean process, having very minimal steps to produce a product for the customer. This is an important approach to improve any business workflow or process, thereby eliminating waste and redundant steps that don't add any value, especially when viewed from a customer's perspective.

The main objective of VSM is to critically analyze any given process and reduce the number of handoffs required between different team members, thereby improving the overall efficiency and productivity. With greater emphasis on digital transformation journeys, organizations are reinventing their business strategy, with a rapid realignment of any existing business/IT processes. The overall goal is to realign, if necessary, the definition of *delivered value* for customers.

In the context of a DevOps life cycle, it may be considered as identifying a lean methodology, comprising only the steps that are necessary to produce value for the customer. The DevOps value stream serves as an optimization driver, thereby impacting people, processes, and products. The primary motivation is to minimize wastage while continuously delivering customer value.

The visualization of how work flows across the various stages of the development life cycle, from product ideation, feature prioritization, and developing a solution to the eventual release to the customer, is called the value stream map.

VSM-related activities comprise three major steps:

1. First, a baseline of the current as-is state is prepared.
2. Second, the target future state is defined, and the processes are redesigned by analyzing gaps or improvement areas.
3. Lastly, the gains from the VSM are analyzed to further iterate on this.

Two main KPIs that are impacted by VSM activities are as follows:

- **Lead time** (**LT**), also referred to as throughput time, response time, and turnaround time. Basically, this refers to elapsed time from the moment work is made available as an input to any particular stage of the value stream, until the time it is finished and delivered to the next stage or team in the value stream.

- **Process time** (**PT**), also referred to as processing time, touch time, work time, and task time. Basically, this is the time it takes a person to complete all the tasks as part of a process to transform an input into an output for one unit of work.

You can read more about how to apply VSM for your DevOps here: `https://www.lucidchart.com/blog/value-stream-mapping-for-devops`.

In the next section, we will look at how management teams can significantly benefit from data-driven DevOps by narrowing their focus on areas that require the most attention.

A data-driven approach

Deriving strategies for improvement through a data-driven approach has proven to be successful for most organizations. There is tremendous potential to improve your CI/CD processes and speed up the delivery and quality of software by adopting a data-driven culture. Most high-performance engineering teams gain insights from the numerous dashboards and KPIs being tracked. They make use of the insights to identify improvement areas and change themselves accordingly.

Let us look at some of the key aspects of data-driven DevOps:

- **Objectively measure what matters**: It all starts with identifying the important metrics and KPIs that must be tracked, and all measurements should be quantitative over qualitative. There is a saying that facts and figures don't lie. The measurement items must be expanded to derive concrete actionable items.

- **Report against benchmarks**: The reporting tools that you use must consistently produce reports for the consumption of the various stakeholders. There must be some initial benchmarks defined, and the reports should track variance against them. Any deviations must be highlighted for action.

    Reporting and subsequent analysis must be a periodic activity (every week at a minimum, if not daily) to make course corrections as early as possible.

- **Automate data delivery for immediate actions**: It is important to get data in a timely fashion to take corrective actions. Hence, we must rely on any existing automation available or explore additional opportunities to improve data capture and notification processes. Most of the DevOps tools today have rich automation capabilities, making it easier for decision making.

    For example, when a **pull request** (**PR**) is submitted, a build run checks the quality of the changes and can immediately send out an email to a developer if there were any automated test run failures. Thus, the developer can fix the issue and resubmit their changes, instead of waiting for hours for the full results to become available.

- **Develop insights for decision makers**: Measuring the success of your data-driven DevOps processes is important for any organization. There are typically two focus areas – first, the KPIs that give insights about the health of your engineering life cycle, and second, the main DevOps maturity index metrics that serve as feedback for the leadership team.

Teams must also conduct periodic reviews and analyses of data to identify opportunities for improvement. The use of techniques such as **Casual Analysis and Resolution** (**CAR**) and **fishbone analysis** can help teams identify the root source of issues and then act appropriately. You will find useful resources to discover more on these topics in the *Further reading* section at the end.

In the next section, we will explore how feedback loops can help in continuous improvement.

Operationalizing the feedback loop

The concept of feedback loops originated in **systems thinking**. Every organization can be modeled as a system, which refers to an interconnected ecosystem of people, processes, and tools that operates in an organized cohesive manner to achieve business objectives or outcomes. Feedback is an important concept in systems thinking, wherein the stimuli help to control the output of the system.

If you are new to the term *feedback loops*, imagine it as an interconnected relationship between entities or processes wherein a change in one leads to a change in the second, which eventually leads to change in the first. It is like a cause-effect sequence, where data produced as an outcome of an event or activity is used to regulate the outcome by controlling the original input action. A simplified view of feedback loops is depicted here:

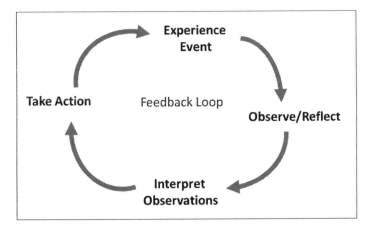

Figure 14.1 – A simple feedback loop

The DevOps processes within an organization can be subjected to systems thinking analysis by identifying the appropriate feedback loops aligned with the goal of continuous improvement. There are two types of feedback loops:

- **Reinforcing feedback loop**: A positive change or increase in the output of the first entity causes an increase in the second entity (positive feedback), which eventually leads to a greater increase in the first entity.

  For example, as the productivity of the team improves, the overall velocity increases. However, there is a stretch limit beyond which the quality may be impacted.

- **Stabilizing/balancing feedback loop**: A positive change or increase in the output of the first entity serves as a signal to decrease the second entity (negative feedback), which eventually leads to an adjustment in the output of the first entity, forcing it back into a balanced state again.

For example, as the team focuses on more quality-related checks as part of CI/CD processes, this adds up to the overall build time, thereby reducing the agility of the releases. Hence, teams are subsequently forced to optimize steps so that release agility can be brought back to an optimum state.

In the next section, we will look at the importance of designing effective feedback loops.

Implementing effective feedback loops

From the examples studied earlier, it is evident that not all feedback loops are important. Hence, it is crucial for organizations to design more effective feedback loops, and amplify the correct ones to achieve the right balance and trade-off between delivery agility, product quality, and the speed of releasing software to market. A few recommendations as initial guidance are shared here:

- Ensure that automated notifications are acted upon in a timely manner. Conduct periodic root cause analysis to reduce their occurrences.

- Make use of a VSM technique to uncover any redundant feedback loops that don't add any value.

- Achieve the right balance in your feedback systems between stability and positive change. Often, stability is more important than speed.

- Involve key stakeholders to participate as part of the feedback loops. Human interaction can offer more practical and contextual guidance that may be beneficial for your team.

- Make use of operational telemetry and metrics to serve as crucial feedback to improve your DevOps practices.

There is a popular saying that a one-size-fits-all approach will never work in any context. Hence, careful planning is required to identify the feedback loops that are important for your organization and team context.

Summary

In this chapter, we have reviewed a few of the important techniques to foster a journey of continuous improvement. To reap the true benefits of DevOps, organizations are expected to operate at the highest level of maturity. However, this is rarely the case, owing to numerous factors that are sometimes beyond anyone's control. Hence, by establishing a culture of continuous improvement, teams can ensure that processes, methods, and practices are as efficient and effective as possible.

Adhering to a systematic and structured approach to continuous improvement might turn out to be quite beneficial for the teams. This requires an organizational commitment to continuous learning and openness of the teams to scrutinize and suggest incremental improvements. There must be dedicated roles appointed to define, plan, and monitor the continuous improvement initiatives.

Also, periodic training must be planned for all personnel on DevOps-related topics, acting as a source of stimuli for the self-directed teams so that they stay committed to the organization's DevOps improvement. Team culture is fundamental to achieving engineering excellence through the demonstration of expertise in the various DevOps practices.

In the next chapter, we shall explore how organizations can expedite their cloud transformation journeys through DevOps.

Activity

- Organize your team and conduct a brainstorming session, preferably using a whiteboard tool.

- Create three vertical swim lanes – **Retain**, **Improve**, and **Discard**.

- Using sticky notes, advise your team to publish their thoughts on the whiteboard. Basically, identify an existing process and group them in the appropriate swim lane.

- Critically analyze the items grouped as Discard, and then verify whether they add any value while achieving the overall objectives of quality and efficiency, especially from a customer's point of view.

- Also, identify improvement areas for the existing processes by either simplifying them altogether or changing them.

- Publish a summary of your findings with the management team.

Further reading

- A fishbone analysis how-to: `https://citoolkit.com/articles/fishbone-diagram/`

- *Causal Analysis and Resolution*: `https://www.wibas.com/cmmi/causal-analysis-and-resolution-car-cmmi-dev`

- Optimize your CD pipeline: `https://www.atlassian.com/continuous-delivery/principles/value-stream-mapping`

- *How to Build a Data-Driven DevOps Decision Making Culture*: `https://www.launchableinc.com/how-to-build-a-data-driven-devops-decision-making-culture`

- *Understanding feedback loops in DevOps*: `https://otomato.io/udnerstanding-feedback-loops-in-devops`

- Systems thinking feedback loops: `https://medium.com/@myroslavazel/feedback-loops-in-system-thinking-7ef06e2ff310`

- VSM: `https://www.devopsinstitute.com/devops-value-stream-mapping-a-box-score-based-approach/`

15
Accelerate Cloud Adoption through DevOps

Digital transformation initiatives focus on making use of modern and emerging technologies to offer a competitive advantage in the marketplace. The adoption of cloud-based technologies has become an integral part of it. Likewise, DevOps also plays a crucial role in accelerating your cloud adoption journey.

However, organizations must first embrace a culture of experimentation, shrug off their old working styles, and shift toward a lean yet iterative software development methodology. DevOps provides just the right mix of tools, practices, and cultural philosophies that will enable organizations to adopt cloud platforms and deliver high-quality applications at high velocity.

In this chapter, we are going to cover the following main topics:

- The role of DevOps in digital transformation
- Modernization and cloud adoption
- Managing software delivery modernization
- Agile transformation and iterative planning
- Integrating DevOps in your cloud adoption plan

The role of DevOps in digital transformation

For any business, digital transformation is all about making use of modern and emerging technologies to deliver value to its customers and eventually create opportunities for greater revenue generation. There is no other alternative to survive in the competitive landscape.

DevOps, with its all-encompassing philosophy to bring the best out of people, processes, and tools, increases the chances of an organization being successful. With a heightened focus on automation, the evolution of modern cloud platforms has eliminated many of the bottlenecks that existed previously. The time to market of high-quality products has drastically reduced, reducing the amount of funding required as well. DevOps is all about optimization and the ability to achieve more with the same set of resources and people. It aims to improve any existing business processes through the use of technology. Also, the merging of the goals of the development and operations teams provides the right amount of cooperation for improved collaboration among teams.

The role of DevOps in digital transformation includes the following:

- To drive change in the cultural mindset of people and encourage the adoption of automation

- To promote collaboration between teams by breaking organization silos, thereby improving the overall productivity of the workforce

- To reduce wastage and costs associated with any manual or inefficient processes

- To expedite the product innovation cycle, resulting in a faster time to market

- To create opportunities to modernize existing IT assets with minimal disruption

In the next section, we will review the benefits of DevOps in the modernization and cloud adoption journeys of organizations.

Modernization and cloud adoption

Though cloud technologies have been around for a while now, the impact they can have on a business became obvious at the time of the Covid pandemic outbreak (in early 2020). Organizations that already had made investments in modernizing their businesses could survive the situation with minimal or no impact, whereas many traditional businesses had to incur huge losses. Here is an interesting article that explains the impact of the pandemic and how the future of work will pan out: `https://www.mckinsey.com/featured-insights/future-of-work/from-surviving-to-thriving-reimagining-the-post-covid-19-return`.

IT and business leaders understood that the adoption of cloud computing technologies was the way forward for the delivery of their services. IT was no longer seen just as an enabler; rather, it became an important tool for survival in the marketplace. Modern-day start-ups leverage technology to create a differentiating value proposition to attract customers. Enterprises have already begun to follow suit and one of the key strategic initiatives in every digital transformation journey is cloud adoption.

While cloud computing and DevOps are mutually independent concepts, the latter is important to achieve business objectives through cloud technology adoption. Thus, DevOps has become a core priority for enterprises to ensure business continuity. Be it optimization of IT spending, streamlining development processes, collaboration across teams, offering greater reliability of service, and so on, DevOps encompasses all aspects of your IT strategy.

DevOps is the foundation of modernization

There is a popular saying that any structure is bound to break in the absence of a solid foundation. Likewise, establishing rigor around your DevOps practices is critical in your modernization journey.

The key benefits of DevOps in modernization are as follows:

- Agility through automation
- Improved productivity through better internal collaboration
- Greater customer and employee satisfaction

DevOps drives cloud adoption

Cloud computing and associated technologies such as automation, **artificial intelligence (AI)**, devices, and so on open the door to a wide range of possibilities for your business. Increased productivity and agility lead to profitability, automation reduces IT costs, and real-time monitoring and feedback loops improve the experience for your customers.

The key benefits of DevOps in cloud adoption are the following:

- The automation of infrastructure modernization, on-demand provisioning, and scaling
- The reduction of IT management overheads, offloading many tasks to the cloud service provider
- Seamless integration with a variety of other platforms or products
- Increased deployment agility, improving time to market

In the next section, we will review how DevOps can impact the roadmaps for any software modernization initiatives within an enterprise.

Managing software delivery modernization

As organizations embark on their modernization journeys, they need to prepare a roadmap with clear goals and objectives, so that they can measure their success and outcomes against it. Typically, DevOps practices impact the four major pillars of software delivery modernization, namely **Software Life Cycle Management**, **Solution Architecture**, **Automation Practices**, and **Cloud Platform Adoption**:

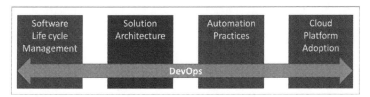

Figure 15.1 – DevOps impact on software delivery modernization

Let us review the role of DevOps across the four pillars in the next sections.

Software life cycle management

Organizations must adopt an iterative development methodology to achieve greater agility in releases. Agile and Kanban are better suited to offer flexibility and adaptability over the traditional Waterfall-based software development life cycle methodology.

Solution architecture

All modernization journeys typically involve two sets of initiatives:

- Migrating legacy applications to a cloud-based platform

- Developing new software products leveraging innovative technologies

Both require the convergence of the target solution architecture goals to a more microservice-based architecture over the traditional monolith-based approach. However, for legacy workloads, there will be challenges affecting their transformation.

Teams usually deploy three key strategies to modernize their IT assets in support of their cloud adoption journeys:

- **Rehosting** – Identifying assets that fall under the category of lift and shift and that can be moved to the new cloud platform infrastructure. Typically, these will be standalone-type applications with minimal dependencies. This offers businesses the instant ability to start operating from the cloud.

- **Refactoring** – This improves making small structural changes to your applications and repackaging them to take advantage of the cloud platform capabilities.

- **Rebuilding** – Certain applications (typically 10-15% of your existing assets) must be re-engineered to take advantage of cloud platform capabilities. These applications must be completely re-developed with a cloud-native architecture in mind.

DevOps practices such as *Infrastructure as Code, Configuration Management, Test Automation,* and *Application Performance Monitoring* can play a significant role in improving the overall efficiency of your migration process.

Automation practices

Automation is the key to faster delivery to the market. In DevOps, you merge both development and operations processes into a unified automated pipeline, such that all software components are continuously built, integrated, tested, and deployed. You discard any manual processes with the goal of achieving 100% automation in all aspects of software development. This ensures overall quality and improves the reliability of the software being released.

Cloud platform adoption

Implement all software products and solutions using a cloud-native design approach. This provides greater efficiency, thereby enabling organizations to stay focused on their core business priorities instead of managing infrastructure. The solutions built on top of a **platform as a service (PaaS)** model offer better scalability and manageability, and can quickly adapt to changing customer needs. The out-of-the-box monitoring capabilities provided by platform vendors make it relatively easy to detect faults and take corrective actions.

In the next section, we will discuss how iterative planning has to be adopted to deliver value during a cloud transformation journey.

Agile transformation and iterative planning

Agile transformation refers to the adoption of Agile-based project planning strategies within an organization to accomplish its vision. All teams function in accordance with the core values and principles of the Agile methodology. As an outcome, you can observe notable changes in the overall culture and behaviors of the teams.

Agile project management is all about incrementally delivering business value while having the flexibility to respond to change. Quite like other practices, even planning must be continuous. Align the portfolio of projects (or the product backlog) with the business objectives and initiatives, and the teams allocated to execute them, while continuously adjusting according to the needs of the customer or even changes in business priorities.

Roadmap for transformation

Creating an Agile transformation roadmap is never easy as each team and its requirements are unique. However, by adhering to the principles of Agile, you can derive an Agile transformation roadmap that can serve as some sort of blueprint for teams.

A sample representation of a very high-level Agile transformation roadmap will look something like this:

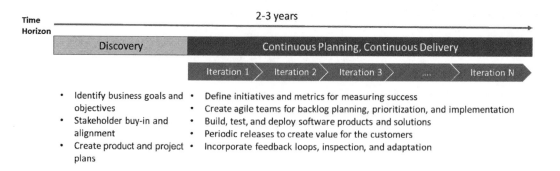

Figure 15.2 – Transformation roadmap

A more detailed Agile transformation roadmap should capture the key milestones, which can serve as a basis for creating more detailed plans. The detailed plans will capture more information about the roadmap items and action plans to achieve them. These plans help shift the mindset of the teams toward achieving an Agile transformation.

You can read more about iterative planning best practices here: https://www.scaledagileframework.com/iteration-planning/.

In the next section, we will review how to prepare your cloud adoption plan using a case study.

Integrating DevOps in your cloud adoption plan

DevOps and cloud adoption have fundamentally transformed the way teams build and deploy applications. In fact, in the past few years, organizations have realized the true power of cloud platforms through the adoption of DevOps practices.

Microsoft provides Cloud Adoption Framework, which lays down certain principles, and guidance that organizations can adopt to establish a cloud adoption plan. You can read more about Microsoft Cloud Adoption Framework for Azure here: https://docs.microsoft.com/en-in/azure/cloud-adoption-framework/overview.

Microsoft also provides great guidance on architecting applications for the cloud using the Microsoft Well-Architected Framework. You can read more about it here: https://docs.microsoft.com/en-us/azure/architecture/framework/.

In the next section, we will consider a case study and understand some of the key DevOps strategies that could be applied by an organization in its cloud adoption journey.

Case study

As part of this case study, we will consider a situation where a company named Packt Insurance Inc. would like to modernize its applications and deploy them on the Azure cloud.

> **Important Note**
> This case study is designed to simulate a real-world scenario. However, it is not meant to be comprehensive and exhaustive to cater to all business requirements or scenarios.

About Packt Insurance Inc.

Packt Insurance Inc., a company with a presence in over 10 countries (across America and Europe), offers a wide range of insurance products and services to its customers.

Over the last few years, the year-on-year growth of Packt Insurance has not been on par with the market opportunities. It is gradually losing to its competition due to a lack of market adaptability, high cycle time on innovation, and poor workforce productivity and collaboration owing to the use of legacy **line-of-business** (**LOB**) applications for running the business. Its cloud presence is limited and most of its applications are deployed as on-premises solutions.

In a recently concluded board meeting, the team took the decision to accelerate the digital transformation journey through its cloud adoption program. Packt Insurance wants to modernize even its LOB applications with a core priority of a cloud-first and mobile-first approach.

A summary of the key business drivers and stakeholder viewpoints is mentioned in the following sections. For this case study, it is meant to demonstrate how each stakeholder perceives the business problem and their requirements for the target solution.

Key business drivers

- To become a cloud-based digital business within the next 2-3 years
- To improve the speed to launch new services on the market on par with market trends
- To expand operations in newer locations and geographies

Stakeholder priorities

- **CEO**:
    - Achieve >10-15% growth, by expanding on the product offerings, broadening the distribution channels, and enhanced integration with channel partners.

- **CTO**:

  - I do not want to invest in IT infrastructure upfront but rather spend incrementally as we expand the business.

  - I want to know the profitability of our business units. I would like insights into our business that enable me to make decisions.

  - It would be great to know the sentiments of the customer about what they like and what they do not like about us.

  - I would like to be known as a technology innovator/pioneer in the domain and attract the new tech-savvy generation.

- **IT operations**:

  - The adoption of modern practices for cloud-based solution development and deployment across the enterprise.

  - To ensure compliance with security and data privacy standards.

  - The onboarding of new branch offices should be quick and seamless.

- **Product manager**:

  - To reduce the cycle time of new insurance products from the current 6-8 months to 2-3 months maximum

  - Would prefer it if actuarial rules could be directly updated without any IT intervention

Modernization roadmap

The executives at Packt Insurance have split the roadmap for the different IT initiatives to modernize their core LOB application into three phases:

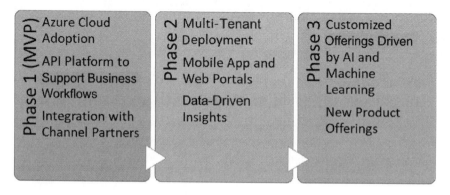

Figure 15.3 – Phases in the modernization roadmap

In the preceding figure, you can see the following:

- **Phase 1** – In this phase, the prioritized list of capabilities targeted for a **minimum viable product** (**MVP**) will be released. The objective of this phase is to quickly operationalize the first version of the platform.

- **Phase 2** – This is a continuation of *Phase 1*, and the team will start the next set of prioritized capabilities. Typically, in this phase, the first version of mobile apps and web portals will be released.

- **Phase 3** – This will be the continuous innovation phase where the use of AI and machine learning capabilities will drive newer product offerings and improvement of the overall digital services deployed.

Usual challenges and DevOps to the rescue

The team at Packt Insurance Inc. adopted DevOps practices and habits to activate the potential of the cloud transformation journey.

A high-level summary of the various actions taken by the team is given here:

- Cloud onboarding and governance – It established a **cloud center of excellence** (**CCoE**), merged operations and development teams, and established governance procedures for the cloud infrastructure.

- Organization change management – It organized training on Agile methodology and modern DevOps practices, with a greater focus on driving cultural change.

- Managing the portfolio of projects – It defined the key business objectives, identified the list of products and services, and created Agile teams for execution.

- Continuous planning – It created high-level release milestones and then prioritized the backlog as per those. The team planned to release an MVP within the first 6 months, followed by incremental major releases every 3-6 months as per the charter of the identified phases.

- Automating the life cycle – It invested in automation practices to drive predictability around the development, testing, and deployment of the products. The engineering teams achieved good velocity without compromising on quality.

- Legacy workload migrations – It initially deployed a hybrid cloud setup that retained some of the applications on-premises. However, at the proper time, these were retired and rebuilt for the cloud.

- Measuring success – It identified key DevOps metrics and tracked them effectively to measure their success.

- DevOps tools used – It used Azure DevOps, GitHub, and Azure Monitor as the primary tools for the implementation of the various DevOps practices.

Thus, we can observe that DevOps impacts all areas of the software development life cycle processes and change management within an organization.

Summary

In this chapter, we have reviewed how the adoption of a cloud platform reduces time to market and creates opportunities that fuel the transformation of a business. Be it managing your cloud infrastructure through automation, optimizing IT spending by leveraging monitoring capabilities, or planning and releasing great products, DevOps touches all aspects of your cloud-based digital transformation journey.

The cloud also enables teams to work from remote locations, in support of hybrid work situations. Cloud technologies make it easy for teams to collaborate using the required tools without losing any time or functionality. Research (the DORA report) shows that both DevOps and cloud adoption will significantly increase in the years to come until they become the norm across all organizations. In summary, we can conclude that, when done well, DevOps and cloud adoption strategies can significantly impact the bottom line of your organization.

In the next chapter, we shall explore the usage of containers when building scalable applications.

Additional reading

- Agile release trains: `https://www.scaledagileframework.com/agile-release-train/`

- Microsoft Cloud Adoption Framework: `https://docs.microsoft.com/en-in/azure/cloud-adoption-framework/overview`

- Modernization and cloud adoption through DevOps: `https://www.elyonstrategies.com/blog/modernization-and-cloud-adoption-devops`

- DevOps and cloud computing: `https://www.rishabhsoft.com/blog/devops-and-cloud-computing`

- Cloud migration decisions: `https://hentsu.com/cloud-adoption-decision-making-rehost-refactor-or-rebuild/`

- Agile transformation: `https://premieragile.com/steps-to-agile-transformation`

16
Containers

Over the last couple of years, containers have become a hot topic. They allow you to package any application or any tool, written in any language, and deploy it on a basic host or cluster. When implementing DevOps, containers can be of tremendous value. That is why DevOps and containers are often mentioned in the same breath. However, they are not the same thing. While DevOps is a cultural thing, containers are a type of technology, an alternative way of hosting your applications.

In this chapter, you will learn more about containers and how they work. This is achieved by exercises wherein custom container images are created and run on different hosting platforms, such as Azure Container Instances and Kubernetes.

The following topics will be covered in this chapter:

- An introduction to containers
- Building a container image
- Building images in Azure DevOps and running them in Azure
- An introduction to Kubernetes
- Kubernetes in action
- Upgrading containers
- Scaling containers and Kubernetes
- Deploying to Kubernetes with Azure DevOps

Technical requirements

To experiment with the techniques described in this chapter, you need one or more of the following:

- Docker Desktop
- Visual Studio 2019/Visual Studio Code
- An Azure subscription
- The Azure CLI

All these are available for free or can be obtained for a limited period for free for evaluation purposes.

An introduction to containers

Containers are the evolution of virtualization. With virtualization, the resources of physical machines are shared among several virtual machines. Sharing those resources also means that all virtual machines have their own operating system. This is different when using containers. With containers, not only are the resources shared but also the operating system kernel, making it very small in comparison with a virtual machine image.

Since the operating system kernel is shared, containers are also very portable. Images can be deployed on any type of host environment that supports running containers. This works because all the application's binaries and configurations are stored inside the container. As a result, environment variables outside the container do not impact the application.

Naturally, there are a number of caveats, however – a container shares the operating system kernel.

Containers provide the ability to virtualize an operating system in order to run multiple workloads on a single operating system. This is visualized in the following diagram, where you can see the difference between regular hosting, virtual machine hosting, and containers:

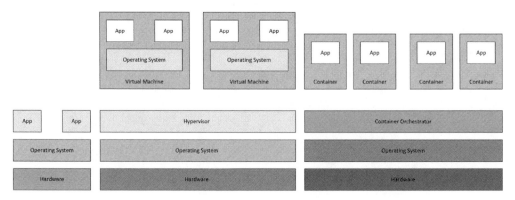

Figure 16.1 – Virtualization to containers

If you have ever heard of containers, you almost certainly have also heard of Docker. This is because Docker is one of the most well-known container engines that can be used for running containers.

The next section will delve into DevOps and containers, while the remainder of the chapter will go into more technical detail regarding containers.

DevOps and containers

As mentioned in the introduction, DevOps and containers are not the same thing. Containers are the technology that makes DevOps easier. This is because containers have benefits that make them *the* perfect tool for DevOps:

- **Consistent**: Because you build the container images, the hurdle of "*it works on my machine*" is eliminated.
- **Separation of concerns**: When using containers, your application will be distributed between separate containers, which makes it easier to maintain and separate the processes.
- **Platform**: The solution can be run on different platforms. It does not matter whether this is in Microsoft Azure, on Amazon Web Services, on Google Cloud, or in an on-premises environment, including even on your development machine.

That aside, DevOps is more cultural than technical and, as mentioned in *Chapter 1*, *Introduction to DevOps*, technical components are used to support DevOps. In the remainder of this chapter, we will focus on the technical side of things.

Hosting options

As mentioned previously, one of the benefits of containers is that they are extremely portable. This also means that containers can be hosted on numerous platforms and technologies.

To run the containers, there are a lot of options that will vary according to your use case. Some of these options are as follows:

- Azure App Service
- Azure Service Fabric
- Docker Swarm
- Docker Desktop
- Kubernetes

Depending on the demands of the application/container, it could run on all the options mentioned in the preceding list.

The images used to run containers (container images) also need to be hosted. These images are hosted in a so-called container registry. In a container registry, they are published privately or publicly. The two most well-known registries are Docker Registry and Azure Container Registry within the Azure platform.

Now that we have gone through some of the background information regarding containers, we are ready to go more deeply into the techniques behind containers and find out what is needed to create a custom container image.

Building a container image

This section will take you through the process of building a container image and executing it on your local system. To do this, we will first have to create an application and then add Docker support to it before we create an image and finally test it. So, let's begin!

Creating an application

To be able to test and check what is running on the container, an application is required. For this, a new application can be created, or you can use an existing application.

When creating a new application, the easiest option is to use the default ASP.NET Core website template within Visual Studio 2019. Container support can be added in a few clicks. This is simply done by checking the **Enable Docker** box when creating the project:

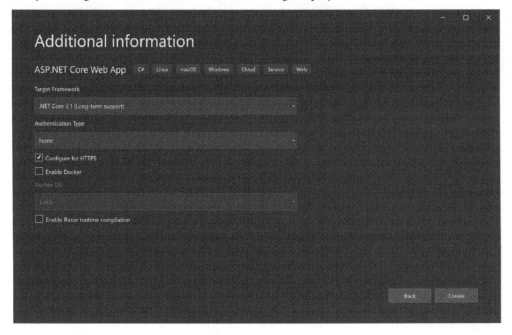

Figure 16.2 – An ASP.Net Core new application with Docker support

Keep the new application open or open your existing application. In the next section, we will investigate how Docker support can be added to an existing application.

Adding Docker support to an existing application

Adding Docker support to an existing application requires a couple of simple steps:

1. Open the project/solution in Visual Studio 2019 and right-click on the project.

2. Choose **Add** and select **Docker Support**:

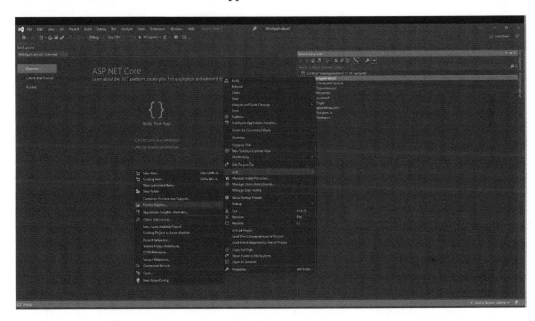

Figure 16.3 – An ASP.Net Core existing application with Docker support

Depending on your client tools and Visual Studio configuration, there may also be a **Container Orchestrator Support** option. With this option, the cloud orchestrator of your choice can be chosen. In this sample, we used Docker Compose because this format is supported by the major container orchestrators. Other cloud orchestrator options do exist, however:

- Docker Swarm

- Kubernetes

- Mesos Marathon

Depending on the cloud orchestrator used, a file is added to the project in the specific format for that orchestrator.

By adding Docker support, a new file is added to the project named `Dockerfile`. The Dockerfile is the specification of a container image. This file can be read by Docker, which sees it as instructions. The file is a text document that contains separate commands that can also be called within a command-line tool to assemble an image:

```
FROM mcr.microsoft.com/dotnet/aspnet:3.1 AS base


WORKDIR /app
EXPOSE 80
EXPOSE 443
EXPOSE 555
FROM mcr.microsoft.com/dotnet/sdk:3.1 AS build
WORKDIR /src
COPY ["WebApplication2.csproj", "."]
RUN dotnet restore "WebApplication2.csproj"
COPY . .
WORKDIR "/src/"
RUN dotnet build "WebApplication2.csproj" -c Release -o /app/
build

FROM build AS publish
RUN dotnet publish "WebApplication2.csproj" -c Release -o /app/
publish

FROM base AS final
WORKDIR /app
COPY --from=publish /app/publish .
ENTRYPOINT ["dotnet", "WebApplication2.dll"]
```

The example uses a technique called a multi-stage build file. This is because the file uses multiple FROM statements where there is a reference to a specific image.

Prior to the multi-stage build, it wasn't possible to use multiple FROM statements. During this time, it was hard to build efficient container images. Each statement in the file represented an additional layer on the image that resulted in it becoming larger and larger.

During this build process, it was also necessary to remove any components that were required during this process. For this reason, it was very common to have separate Dockerfiles for development and production.

As mentioned, the Dockerfile comprises instructions and the most commonly used instructions are as follows:

- **FROM**: The FROM command is used to specify on which operating system or base image the image will be based. In the preceding example, the `mcr.microsoft.com/dotnet/aspnet:3.1 AS` base image is used to build the production version of the application.

- **RUN**: The RUN command is used to install components or perform operations during the build process of the container image.

- **ENTRYPOINT**: The ENTRYPOINT command specifies what the entry point for a container image needs to be. In the preceding example, the entry point is specified as a .NET application that references the library that was built during the compilation process.

So far, we've created our application and added Docker support. Next, we'll see how to create an image with the application.

Creating an image with the application

To be able to create a Docker image, Docker Desktop needs to be installed, as Visual Studio uses this to construct the image. With a complete Dockerfile, the image can be built using the following steps:

Right-click the Dockerfile in Visual Studio and select **Build Docker Image**:

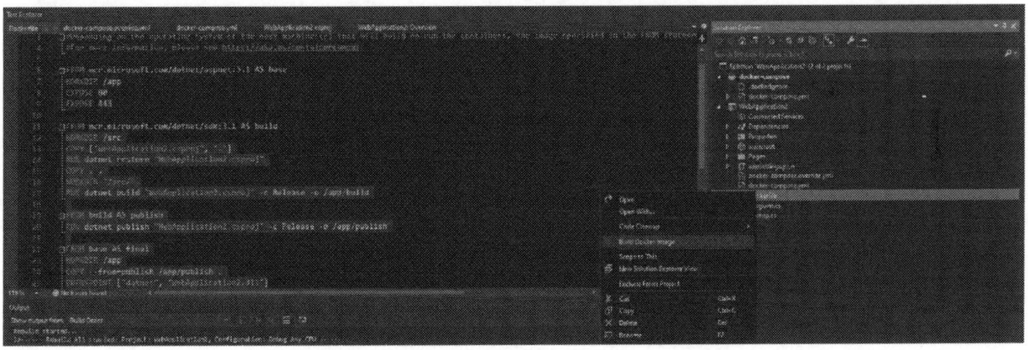

Figure 16.4 – An Asp.Net Core application build Docker Image

During the compilation and building of the image, take a look at the output window. Looking at it will provide more insights into the layered approach of container images.

Docker Desktop also makes it possible to run and store images locally. After building the image, open a terminal and run the following command:

```
docker images
```

The command displays all images currently on the machine. In this list, the base images that are downloaded during the creation of images are also listed:

```
C:\             >docker images
REPOSITORY                              TAG      IMAGE ID        CREATED        SIZE
mcr.microsoft.com/dotnet/aspnet         6.0      a7b911013ddb    10 days ago    208MB
packtbookslibraryapi                    dev      07ed90376bcf    12 days ago    208MB
webapplication2                         dev      29b2f45800dd    3 months ago   208MB
mcr.microsoft.com/dotnet/aspnet         3.1      f0220ee3f874    3 months ago   208MB
docker/getting-started                  latest   bd9a9f733898    4 months ago   28.8MB
```

Figure 16.5 – A Docker image list

We looked at how to add Docker support and make Docker images for current and new ASP.NET Core apps. The next part will explore how to run container images.

Running the container image

The container image can be started locally by running it within Docker. As we now have a container image, a container can be created:

1. Run the following `docker container run` command:

    ```
    docker container run --publish 8123:80 --detach --name
    [container name] [image name]
    ```

    The preceding command will start the container image specified at the end of the command. In addition, different arguments are specified:

    *   **Publish**: The `publish` argument opens a port from the host to the container. As mentioned in the example in the preceding section, this will open port `8123` and route traffic to port `80` within the container.

    *   **Detach**: The `detach` argument will run the container in the background and print out its specific ID.

    *   **Name**: The name for the container within Docker.

2. To list all running containers, use the **docker ps** command within the terminal.

3. With the container running, open a browser and navigate to `http://localhost:8123`. If everything works fine, this should show a default ASP.NET Core web page:

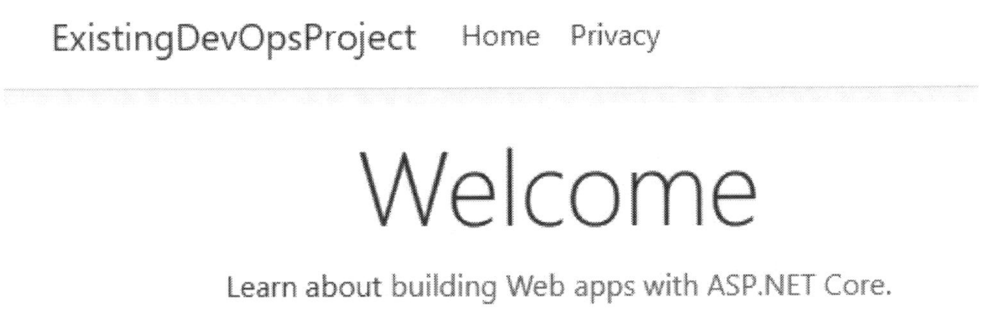

ExistingDevOpsProject   Home   Privacy

Welcome

Learn about building Web apps with ASP.NET Core.

Figure 16.6 – The ASP.Net Core default welcome page

Since building stuff locally and running it on your machine is not really the DevOps way of doing things, we will move to a different hosting platform in the upcoming sections.

Building images in Azure DevOps and running them in Azure

To support continuous integration and continuous delivery, the source files need to be shared in a repository. So, let's share the resources in Azure Repos and try to build our container by using Azure Pipelines. After building the container image, a place to store the images and run the container is also required. Within the Azure platform, there are two perfect services for this scenario:

- **Azure Container Registry (ACR)**: This service is a managed private Docker registry based on the open source Docker Registry. Here, you can maintain and register container images.

- **Azure Container Instance**: **Azure Container Instances**, also referred to as **ACI**, is a solution for running isolated containers without a lot of management.

> **Important Note**
> For the simplicity of this guide, the files are already added to the repository and the Azure resource is already created.

In the next section, we will explore how to create images in ACR and run them in ACI through Azure DevOps.

Creating a service endpoint

As already discussed within the book, connections within Azure DevOps with external services such as Azure and container registries are configured within a service endpoint. Because an image needs to be available in order for ACI to retrieve it, it needs to be published to a container registry. The connection from Azure DevOps to the registry is configured within a service connection.

Perform the following steps to configure the service connection:

1. In the Azure DevOps project, open the project settings.

2. Within the project settings, click on **Service connections**.

3. In the service connection overview, click on **Create service connection** and choose **Docker Registry**.

4. In the fly-out that appears, fill in the correct information and save the connection:

Figure 16.7 – A new Azure Container Registry service connection

Saving the connection will add a service connection to the project that can be used by the pipelines we will create, or that you will create in the future.

Creating a new pipeline

To be able to start building the container image and publish it to the registry, we will create a new pipeline. For this example, we will make use of the YAML pipeline experience.

Perform the following steps to get started with the pipeline:

1. Open your Azure DevOps project and click on **Pipelines**.

2. In the pipelines overview, click on **New Pipeline**.

3. Select **Azure Repos Git**, choose the correct repository, and then choose **Starter pipeline**:

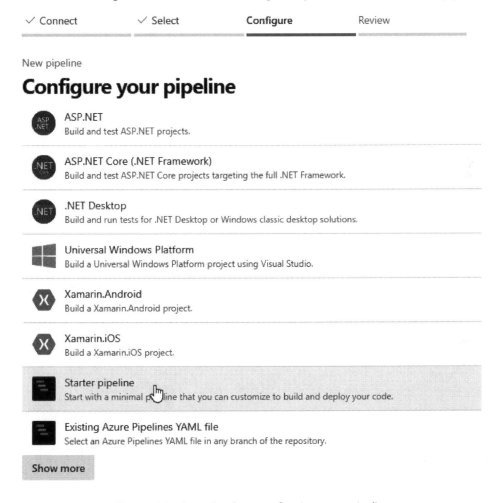

Figure 16.8 – Azure DevOps – configuring a new pipeline

4. From the starter pipeline, remove the two dummy script tasks and open the assistant.

5. In the assistant, search for the Docker tasks and add the tasks to the pipeline.

6. Choose the service connection created for the container registry and keep the other information as the default.

> **Important Note**
> Make sure to change the `buildContext` property of the tasks to point to the correct directory. This is required for Docker to be able to reference the correct paths when building your image.

When added, the YAML should look like this:

```
- task: Docker@2
  inputs:
    containerRegistry: 'MSFT Container Registry'
    repository: 'azuredevops'
    command: 'buildAndPush'
    Dockerfile:'**/Dockerfile'
    buildContext:
'$(System.DefaultWorkingDirectory)/ExistingDevOpsProject'
```

7. Save and run the pipeline. After the first run, the container image is created and published to the container registry.

   The images in the container registry can be retrieved by using a predefined URL. This URL comprises a few specific components:

   ```
   [container registry]/[repository]:[tag]:
   ```

   • **Container registry**: The base URL of the container registry.

   • **Repository**: The repository as specified during the process of publishing the image.

   • **Tag**: The tag for the specific version of the image. By default, the Docker tag used is `BuildId`.

8. Now that we have a reference to the container image, ACI should be able to retrieve the container and run it. The only thing needed for this is an Azure CLI command:

   ```
   az container create --resource-group [resource group]
   --name [ACI name] --location westeurope --image [Image
   reference] --dns- name-label [dns reference] --ports
   80 --registry-username [username of the registry]
   --registry-password [password of the registry]
   ```

Since the reference to the image is different for each build (`BuildId` for the tag value), `BuildId` is retrieved in the Azure CLI command via the `$(Build.BuildId)` variable:

```
az container create --resource-group aci-rg-devops
--name aci- demo-app --location westeurope --image
msftazuredevops.azurecr.io/azuredevops:$(Build.BuildId)
--dns- name-label aci-msft-demo --ports 80 --registry-
username
$(username) --registry-password $(password)
```

To execute the preceding script, the Azure CLI task is added to the pipeline. In this task, we configure the correct subscription via the service endpoint and set the inline script.

The script will create a container instance in the `aci-rg-devops` resource group with the name `aci-demo-app` and retrieve the `azuredevops` container image from the `msftazuredevops.azurecr.io` repository.

The complete YAML for this task looks like this:

```
- task: AzureCLI@2
  inputs:
    azureSubscription: 'Subscription MPN'
    scriptType: 'bash'
    scriptLocation: 'inlineScript'
    inlineScript: 'az container create --resource-group
aci-rg- devops -
name aci-demo-app --location westeurope --image
msftazuredevops.azurecr.io/azuredevops:$(Build.BuildId)
--dns- name-label aci-msft-demo --ports 80 --registry-
username
$(username) --registry-password $(password)'
```

Running this pipeline will result in an Azure container instance in Azure. That container will be running the exact same application that was running locally:

Figure 16.9 – An aci-demo-app instance running in ACI

When opening the Azure container instance in the Azure portal, you will see that it is a running instance and that there is a **Fully Qualified Domain Name (FQDN)** attached to the Azure container instance based on the value supplied, `dns-name-label`, within the Azure CLI command, `aci-msft- demo.westeurope.azurecontainer.io`. Open the URL in your browser and see the application we have pushed to the container:

Figure 16.10 – The aci-demo-app welcome page

It shows the same content as the container that was started locally. This is because, in both places, the same container image was started.

In this section, we started the container on ACI, but how will we manage running containers and restart them when there are problems? This is where Kubernetes comes in.

An introduction to Kubernetes

Kubernetes is another service for running your containers. Kubernetes is a cluster orchestration technology first developed by Google. It is now an open source platform for automating deployment, scaling, and operations of application containers across clusters of hosts, thereby providing a container-centric infrastructure. The term Kubernetes is often abbreviated as *K8s*. This is generated by substituting the eight letters of *ubernete* in the word with the numeral 8.

The functionalities of Kubernetes

As mentioned earlier, containers offer you a great way to package your applications. When running the applications, you need to make sure that applications keep running and this is where Kubernetes comes in, as it has the following core functionalities:

- **Service discovery and load balancing**: How a container is exposed is controlled within Kubernetes and, in addition, it is also capable of balancing the traffic within the orchestration.

- **Storage orchestration**: The ability to mount different kinds of storage providers to the platform.

- **Rollouts and rollbacks**: Kubernetes can automatically create and restart containers for the specified deployment.

- **Self-healing**: Kubernetes can heal containers when they are failing.

- **Secret and configuration management**: Kubernetes has a built-in functionality to manage secrets such as tokens, passwords, and keys.

In order to provide these functionalities, Kubernetes consists of a number of components.

Kubernetes core components and services

Kubernetes consists of a few core components that make it run. These components together make a great and stable product for running and managing containers. The next few subsections will go over each of these components individually.

Master node

One of the important components within Kubernetes is the master node. The node manages the cluster. It contains all the Kubernetes core components in order to manage the cluster:

- **kube-apiserver**: A component for exposing the Kubernetes API. This API is used by the management tools of Kubernetes, such as `kubectl`, and the Kubernetes dashboard.

- **etcd**: Used to maintain the state of the Kubernetes cluster.

- **kube-scheduler**: A component that selects nodes for the Pods to run on.

- **kube-controller-manager**: The controller manager oversees a number of smaller controllers that perform actions such as replicating Pods and managing node operations.

By using these components, the master node can maintain the desired state for the cluster. It is good to know that when you are interacting with Kubernetes, you are communicating with the master node. The master node will then communicate with the other components within the cluster.

Regular nodes

These are the nodes that will run the containers. Sometimes, they are referred to as worker nodes. They can be virtual machines or even physical machines. On these machines, the so-called `kubelet` is installed. `kubelet` is the agent that's used to run Pods/containers within the nodes.

As you may have noticed in the preceding sections, there are also other core services within Kubernetes, and we will discuss them next.

Pod

Within Kubernetes, Pods are used to run the applications. Within the Pods, it is specified which resources are required to run the application. The scheduler (`kube-schedular`) within Kubernetes checks where to run the application, depending on the demands and the nodes coupled to the cluster.

Pods have a limited lifespan and are removed when new versions are deployed. Also, when a node fails, Pods can be replaced by other Pods on the same or another node.

Service

The service is sometimes referred to as the load balancer and is used to provide a logical grouping of Pods and furnish them with connectivity (a way to connect).

The three major services are as follows:

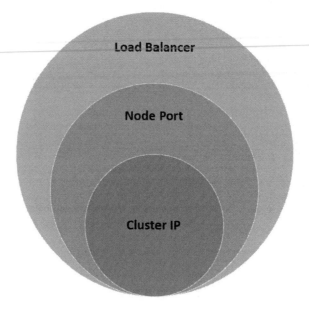

Figure 16.11 – The K8s services relationship

The three major services are as follows:

- **Cluster IP**: Adding an internal IP to a service. By selecting this option, the service is only accessible from within the cluster. This is the standard service type.

- **Node port**: The node port service establishes a port on each cluster node, hence the name, and routes traffic arriving on that port to the underlying service. It exposes services to external clients.

- **Load balancer**: This service adds a load balancer resource and configures an external IP address on the load balancer. On the external side, the load balancer will route traffic to the specific nodes based on the rules configured in the load balancer and internally to the correct Pod.

With these services, the internal and external connections for Pods are arranged. The services and Pods are all specified within a deployment.

Deployment

A Kubernetes deployment is a resource object that outlines an application's expected state. It specifies the number of replicas as well as the update strategy for that application. Kubernetes will monitor the health of the Pods and will remove or add Pods as needed to reach the desired state specified in the deployment.

These deployments are specified in a YAML file. For example, when running a container in Kubernetes, you must specify a replica set. A replica set ensures that a specified number of Pod replicas are running at any given time.

Operation of Kubernetes

When you are new to containers, and especially to Kubernetes, it is hard to figure things out immediately. However, to aid your understanding of the concept, take a look at the following diagram:

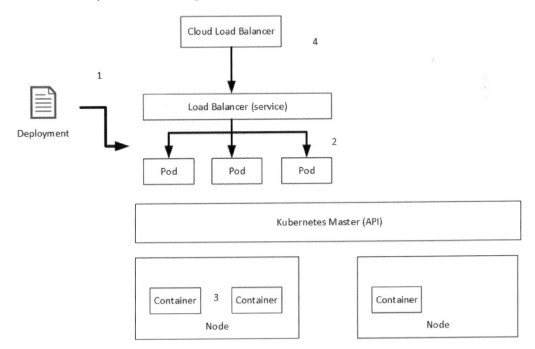

Figure 16.12 – An overview of Kubernetes operations

Deployments of containers to a Kubernetes cluster are defined in the so-called deployment file (**1**). In these deployment files, the desired state of the application is described. This desired state is described as a YAML file.

In this example, the desired state is a load balancer service and three Pods (**2**). These Pods are divided by the Kubernetes API on the nodes that run the containers (**3**). The service defined in the deployment file ensures that the traffic is routed to the specific Pods. The deployment can be changed by updating it.

The scheduler can also change deployments when, for example, automatic scaling is configured for the application. In that kind of scenario, a fourth Pod could be added to the cluster. In the service, there can also be an external load balancer to route traffic to the internal load balancer of Kubernetes (**4**).

Azure Kubernetes Service

Azure Kubernetes Service, or **AKS**, is the Microsoft implementation of Kubernetes. Setting up a regular Kubernetes cluster is a lot of work, but with AKS, it has been made easier. This is because AKS is a managed platform and the reason why almost all operational tasks are handled by the platform itself.

Some key functionalities of AKS are as follows:

- Azure manages critical tasks, such as health monitoring, scaling, and maintenance, including Kubernetes version upgrades and patching according to configuration and management requirements.

- The master node of Kubernetes is fully managed.

- Master nodes are free, and you only pay for running agent nodes. You only have to pay for the worker nodes; the master node is free because the Kubernetes cluster master is managed by Azure. You administer the cluster's agent nodes and only pay for the **virtual machines** (**VM s**) on which your nodes run.

By using AKS, a Kubernetes cluster can be operational within minutes and the master node is managed by Azure, so the focus will be on application development and deployment. Now, let's try to run a Kubernetes cluster with custom images.

Kubernetes in action

In the first few sections of this chapter, we created a container and deployed it to an Azure container instance. Let's now deploy this container to a Kubernetes cluster.

Creating a cluster can be done via the Azure CLI or an **Azure Resource Manager** (**ARM**) template. For ease of demonstration, the Azure CLI will be used.

First, a new resource group needs to be created to host the Azure Kubernetes cluster:

```
az group create --name mpn-rg-kubernetes --location westeurope
```

Now, we can create our Kubernetes cluster.

Creating a Kubernetes cluster

When the resource group is created, a new Kubernetes cluster can be added to the group:

```
az aks create --resource-group mpn-rg-kubernetes --name
mykubernetescluster
--node-count 1 --enable-addons monitoring --generate-ssh-keys
```

This command creates a new Kubernetes cluster with the name mykubernetescluster and with a single node. This means that there will be one VM created in the Azure portal that is configured as a node for the Kubernetes cluster. In addition, the monitoring add-ons will be enabled on the cluster.

The creation of this cluster will take a couple of minutes. In Azure, the mykubernetescluster service will be created in the specified resource group. Alongside this resource group, another group will be created by the Azure platform itself.

Kubernetes infrastructure

In this resource group, all virtualized infrastructure that is needed to run the cluster is created. This also means that in the future, new components can be added to this resource group depending on the demands of the application:

Figure 16.13 – The mpn-rg-kubernetes resource group

In the resource group created, you will find all the aforementioned resources to run the cluster:

Figure 16.14 – A list of a few resources required to run a cluster

With the Kubernetes infrastructure now up and running, the management and deployment of resources can begin.

Managing Kubernetes

To manage Kubernetes, the kubectl command line is used and installed locally (or used in Azure Cloud Shell). This is command-line interface tooling that will communicate with the Kubernetes API. Let's see how to work with Kubernetes with this command line:

1. First, download and install kubectl, and if you do not already have the Azure CLI installed, run the following command to install the Azure CLI on your machine:

    ```
    az aks install-cli
    ```

2. To connect to the cluster, the credentials need to be retrieved and saved to the local system. This can be done by using the az aks get-credentials command and specifying the resource group and cluster name:

    ```
    az aks get-credentials --resource-group mpn-rg-kubernetes
    -- name mykubernetescluster
    ```

3. With all the prerequisites configured, a lot of the base functionality can be run against the Kubernetes cluster. Take a look at these two commands for example:

- Retrieve the nodes of the cluster:

```
kubectl get nodes
```

- Get the Pods in the cluster:

```
kubectl get Pods
```

4. As well as to the preceding commands, you can also try the following Azure CLI command to open up the Kubernetes dashboard. This dashboard is a management interface built on top of the Kubernetes API that can be used next to the `kubectl` command line:

```
az aks browse --resource-group mpn-rg-kubernetes --name
mykubernetescluster
```

The dashboard is shown in the following screenshot:

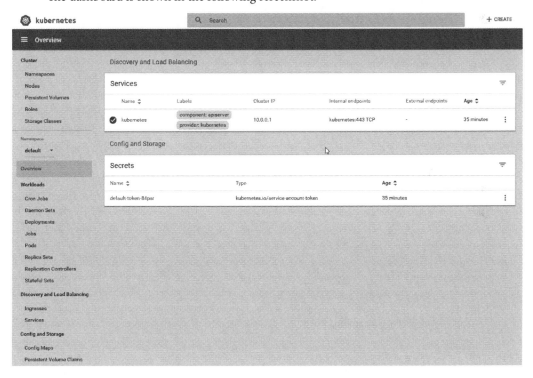

Figure 16.15 – Viewing the Kubernetes dashboard

A deployment file needs to be created to be able to run containers within the cluster. So, let's see how to do this.

Deploying a container image

We will create a deployment file and deploy it to Kubernetes. To do this, perform the following steps:

1. Make a new file in your favorite text editor and call it `deploy.yaml`. Add the following information to the `deploy.yaml` file:

```yaml
apiVersion: apps/v1
kind: Deployment
metadata:
  name: kubernetes-deployment
  labels:
    app: customapplication
spec:
replicas: 3
selector:
  matchLabels:
    app: customapplication
template:
  metadata:
    labels:
      app: customapplication
  spec:
    containers:
    - name: azuredevops
      image: msftazuredevops.azurecr.io/azuredevops:586
      ports:
      - containerPort: 80
```

In this example, the following is specified:

- A deployment is created with the name `kubernetes-deployment` (`metadata.name`).
- The deployment will create three replicas of the specified container (`spec.replicas`).
- The selector, in combination with the `labels` tag, is used to specify which components this deployment file will manage within Kubernetes.
- The deployment file will create a container for the `msftazuredevops.azurecr.io/azuredevops:586` image file.

2. To deploy this file to Kubernetes, we will again use the `kubectl` command line and make use of the `apply` command:

```
kubectl apply -f deploy.yaml
```

The `-f` argument is used to specify that a local path is used as a reference to a deployment file. After executing the command, you can open the Kubernetes dashboard to see the status and maybe even observe errors.

Important Note

It is possible that you encounter an error stating that pulling the image from your location failed. This could be a security issue. Under the hood, AKS is using a service principal. You should also see this when creating a new Kubernetes cluster. Make sure to give this service principal access rights on the Azure Container Registry.

3. Following a successful execution, try the `get Pods` command to see whether there are three Pods within the system. If everything proceeded correctly, there should be three Pods running within Kubernetes, but the application is still not available to the outside world.

    To make it available, we need to add a service to the deployment file.

Important Note

If you want to add a service to the same file, add a line with the `- - -` characters between the deployments. This is not required when you also define separate files for deployment.

In the `deploy.yaml` file, add the following section:

```
---

apiVersion: v1
kind: Service
metadata:
  name: customapplication-service
spec:
  type: LoadBalancer
  ports:
  - port: 80
  selector:
    app: customapplication
```

This YAML section creates a load balancer and attaches it to the specified selector (`spec.selector.app`), meaning it will be used for the Pods, as we previously specified.

In the background, Kubernetes will create an Azure load balancer and a public IP address for connection to the Pods.

4. To retrieve the external IP address of the service, use the following command until it displays the external IP address:

```
kubectl get service
```

This will return all services and their external IP addresses if they are present. Also, take a quick look at the additional resource group of Kubernetes to see which Azure resources are created.

Well done! In this section, you learned how to create a Kubernetes cluster and deploy a container image on it via `kubectl` and deployment files. In the next section, we will take this forward and learn how to upgrade these containers.

Upgrading containers

In Kubernetes, applications are very easily updated. For this, Kubernetes uses rolling updates, which means that traffic to a container is first drained before the container is replaced. During an upgrade of the application, Kubernetes will deploy an additional Pod and run it through some specified probes.

A probe is a diagnostic that is periodically performed on a Pod to check its status. During the upgrading or creation of a Pod, Kubernetes brings up the additional Pod and makes sure that it passes the liveness and readiness probes.

If the newly created Pod succeeds with both probes, the traffic to a single, old Pod is terminated and traffic to the new Pod is opened. For this termination, Kubernetes uses a termination grace period. During this period, the connection to the load balancer is stopped and active connections are processed successfully, and new traffic is routed to a running Pod. During the 30-second default grace period, the Pod is in a termination state and all previous traffic to it is diverted to the other Pods.

This process continues until all Pods are replaced with the new version. All of this is default behavior within Azure Kubernetes. Deployment is simply triggered by adjusting the deployment file and applying it with the same command as used previously:

```
Kubectl apply -f [file]
```

By default, `httpGet` probes are added to Pods that are being exposed, but they can also be customized by adding the readiness probe or liveness probe to the deployment:

```
readinessProbe:
    httpGet:
        scheme: HTTPS
        path: /index.html
        port: 8483
        initialDelaySeconds: 5
        periodSeconds: 5
        successThreshold: 1
```

This readiness probe performs an `httpGet` request on the Pod and has the following options:

- `path`: The path it should call for the `httpGet` request.
- `port`: The port number it should use for the call. This is also configured in our deployment file.
- `initialDelaySeconds`: The seconds it waits before running the probe once the container is started.
- `periodSeconds`: The number of seconds the probe waits before it times out.
- `successThreshold`: The minimum amount of success necessary for the probe is 1.

As mentioned, a deployment has a default rolling upgrade scenario configured. The configuration of the rolling deployment can be retrieved by using the following command:

```
kubectl describe deployment kubernetes-deployment
```

> **Important Note**
> If you are interested in doing so, build a new version of your container and upgrade it within Kubernetes. Before running the upgrade, make sure you have the dashboard open, refresh the page during the update, and you will see extra Pods coming up and old Pods being terminated.

In this section, we learned how to upgrade containers, which will help you stay up to date with the latest version. Moving forward, in the next section, we will look further into the scaling of containers and Kubernetes.

Scaling containers and Kubernetes

As the demand for your application grows, you will need to scale the application. Scaling the application can be done in multiple ways and different components can be scaled:

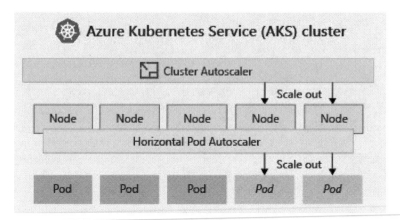

Figure 16.16 – The autoscaler in AKS

The preceding diagram shows you the different ways to scale your application or cluster, which we will discuss over the upcoming subsections.

Scaling Pods manually

Pods can easily be scaled by updating the number of replicas. Try getting your Pods by using the kubectl get Pods command, and increase the number of replicas by using the following command:

```
kubectl scale --replicas=[number of Pods] deployment/
[deploymentname]
```

This command scales the Pods up or down, based on the number of replicas. The scale is adjusted, as shown in the deployment configuration.

Autoscaling Pods

AKS also supports autoscaling. The scheduler will then update the number of Pods, depending on CPU utilization or other metrics that are available.

Kubernetes uses the metrics server for this. The metrics server collects metrics from the summary API of the kubelet agents that run on the nodes within the cluster.

The autoscale functionality also requires some configuration on the deployment side of Kubernetes. For deployment, you need to specify the requests and limits for the running container. These values are specified for a specific metric – for example, the CPU.

In the following example, there are requests and limits specified for the CPU metric. The CPU metric is measured in CPU units. In Azure, one unit stands for one core. On different platforms, a unit can have a different meanings:

```
resources:
  requests:
    cpu: 0.25
limits:
    cpu: 0.5
```

This part can be added to the container in the deployment file, and this will make sure that the Pods can be autoscaled when large numbers of requests need to be served.

With the updated deployment file, deploy it and make an autoscale rule within the Kubernetes cluster:

```
kubectl autoscale deployment [deployment name] --cpu-percent=60
--min=1 --max=10
```

This rule will update the deployment with autoscale functionality. If average CPU utilization across all Pods exceeds 60% of their requested usage, the autoscaler increases the Pods up to a maximum of 10 instances. A minimum of one instance is then defined for the deployment:

After creating the autoscaler, you can check it by running the following command:

```
kubectl get hpa
```

> **Tip**
> **HPA** stands for **Horizontal Pod Autoscaler**.

Try creating a CPU-intensive operation within an application and checking automatic Pod creation during execution. The Kubernetes cluster will notice the significant amount of CPU usage and will scale out the cluster automatically by creating multiple Pods.

Once the intensive operation is finished, Kubernetes will scale the number of Pods down to the minimum.

Scaling nodes

Alongside scaling Pods, Kubernetes can also scale the number of nodes that run within the Kubernetes cluster. The number of nodes can be scaled using the following commands:

1. First, get the information pertaining to the current environment by requesting the number of nodes:

    ```
    az aks show --resource-group mpn-rg-kubernetes --name
    mykubernetescluster --query agentPoolProfiles
    ```

2. Then, use this command to update `nodepool`. Extract the name of `nodepool` from the result of the last command:

    ```
    az aks scale --resource-group mpn-rg-kubernetes --name
    mykubernetescluster --node-count 2 --nodepool-name
    nodepool1
    ```

Scaling the number of nodes up can increase the performance drastically. This will also make the cluster more expensive. By scaling the number of cluster nodes down, costs can decrease, and you are only using the resources that are actually required by your application. To keep track of this, the nodes can also be autoscaled.

Autoscaling nodes

Alongside the manual scaling of nodes, nodes can also scale automatically by updating the Kubernetes cluster. This can be done by using the `az aks update` command. With this command, you can set the minimum and maximum node counts. The autoscaler will then make sure that nodes are created when needed:

```
az aks update --resource-group mmpn-rg-kubernetes --name
mykubernetescluster  --update-cluster-autoscaler --min-count 1
--max-count 5
```

AKS also has the option to scale out with ACI. To use this option, a specific configuration needs to be applied when creating the AKS cluster. This is mainly required because ACI needs a specific subnet within the virtual network.

In this section, we learned to scale containers and the cluster to drastically increase performance. Next up is deployment from Azure DevOps to facilitate continuous deployment.

Deploying to Kubernetes with Azure DevOps

We have seen a lot of options for deploying and configuring the Kubernetes cluster via the command line. When working with DevOps, however, changes need to be applied in a continuous way.

For this, there is the Kubernetes manifest task within Azure DevOps, which contains a lot of functionalities to manage a Kubernetes cluster:

```
task: KubernetesManifest@0
  inputs:
  action: 'deploy'
  kubernetesServiceConnection: '[service connection name]'
  manifests: '[path to your deployment file]'
  containers: 'msftazuredevops.azurecr.io/azuredevops:$(Build.
BuildID)'
```

In the preceding example, the following is configured:

- `action`: The kind of action we want to perform. In this example, the `deploy` action is used because we want to deploy/apply a deployment file.

- `kubernetesServiceConnection`: The service connection to the Kubernetes cluster.

- `manifests`: The path to the manifest file. As we are using the deploy action, this should be a reference to the deployment file.

- `containers`: A special field where you can override the version of the container being deployed. By specifying the preceding, every image is specified in the deployment manifest with the `msftazuredevops.azurecr.io` reference, and the `azuredevops` repository is replaced by the new value as configured in this field.

Using a Kubernetes destination environment within Azure DevOps pipelines also has the advantage of seeing the environment running within Azure DevOps. This will show the number of running Pods within the cluster.

Try it out with the following stage configuration for a build that will publish the deployment files to the artifact location of Azure DevOps:

```
stages:
  - stage : Build
    displayName : Build
    jobs:
    - job:
      pool:
        vmImage: 'ubuntu-latest'
      continueOnError: false
      steps:
      - task: Docker@2
```

```
        inputs:
            containerRegistry: '[Container Registry service
connection]'
            repository: 'azuredevops'
            command: 'buildAndPush'
            Dockerfile: '**/Dockerfile'
            buildContext: '$(System.DefaultWorkingDirectory)/
[folder path for docker]'
        - task: CopyFiles@2
          inputs:
            SourceFolder: '$(system.defaultworkingdirectory)/[path
to the deployment manifest files]'
            Contents: '*'
            TargetFolder: '$(build.artifactstagingdirectory)'
flattenFolders: true
        - task: PublishBuildArtifacts@1
          inputs:
            PathtoPublish: '$(Build.ArtifactStagingDirectory)'
            ArtifactName: 'drop'
            publishLocation: 'Container'
```

Next to the build stage, add the following release stage. Following the initial execution of the pipeline, a new environment will be available within Azure DevOps. In the environment created by the release, attach the Kubernetes cluster to see information on the running Pods:

```
- stage : Release
  displayName : Release
  jobs:
  - deployment: KubernetesDeploy
    displayName: Deploy Kubernetes
    pool:
      vmImage: 'ubuntu-latest'
    environment: 'Kubernetes'
    strategy:
      runOnce:
        deploy:
          steps:
            - task: DownloadPipelineArtifact@2
```

```
            displayName: 'Download pipeline artifacts'
            inputs:
              buildType: 'current'
              targetPath: '$(Pipeline.Workspace)'
          - task: KubernetesManifest@0
            inputs:
              action: 'deploy'
              kubernetesServiceConnection: '[Kubernetes service
 connection]'
              manifests: '$(Pipeline.Workspace)[deployment
 manifest]'
              containers: '[container registry]:$(Build.
 BuildID)
```

In the example, two stages are specified for a multi-stage pipeline. The first stage will build the container image via the Docker task and publish it to a container registry. After publishing the image, it also publishes a number of build artifacts – in this case, the Kubernetes manifests.

The second stage deploys to a specific environment called Kubernetes. This environment will also be created in Azure DevOps if it has not already been added. During the remainder of the process, it retrieves the published artifacts of the build stage and uses the Kubernetes manifest task to deploy the Kubernetes resources.

Summary

In this chapter, you have learned what containers are and how they relate to DevOps. Where DevOps is more of a cultural thing, containers are a way to support it technically. You have also learned how to create container images via a Dockerfile, specifically by using a multi-stage build file. Finally, we dived into Kubernetes, where we learned a way to host containers and also manage the running containers by using the `kubectl` command.

Using the knowledge acquired in this chapter, you are now able to deploy applications to Kubernetes and make sure that it scales with the number of requests it receives.

In the next chapter, you will learn more about facilitating the DevOps process by using Azure DevOps. You will learn what works for your organization and team and what doesn't, and how to implement that structure and your approach using Azure DevOps.

Questions

As we conclude, here is a list of questions for you to test your knowledge regarding the material covered in this chapter. You will find the answers in the *Assessments* section of the *Appendix* chapter:

1. What are the benefits of containers for DevOps?

2. A specific container can be hosted on different platforms (Azure/**Amazon web Services** (**AWS**)/ **Google Cloud platform** (**GCP**)) – true or false?

3. Is it possible to add container support to an existing application?

4. What is the RUN command used for within a Dockerfile?

5. Kubernetes can be scaled on different components. What are they?

Exercises

- Let's create and publish an image of our application into Azure Container Registry and deploy it on an Azure Kubernetes cluster.

- The following Azure resources need to be configured for this lab:

  - ACR

  - AKS

- Set up the environment – create AKS and ACR:

  ```
  az aks create  --resource-group az400-dev
  --name  packtsbookaci --generate-ssh-keys --location
  eastus
  az acr create --resource-group  az400-dev  --name
  packtbookacr --sku Standard --location eastus
  ```

- Configure ACR integration with an existing AKS cluster:

  ```
  az aks update -n 'packtsbookaci' -g 'az400-dev'
  --attach-acr 'packtbookacr'
  ```

- Refer to `azurecontainercluster-pipelines.yml` in the repository or create a new YAML file with the following contents:

  ```
  trigger:
  - main

  pool:
  ```

```
    vmImage: ubuntu-latest

variables:
  buildConfiguration: 'Release'

steps:
- script: echo Hello, world!
  displayName: 'Run a one-line script'

# Authenticate nuget.exe, dotnet, and MSBuild with Azure
Artifacts and optionally other repositories
- task: NuGetAuthenticate@1
  #inputs:
    #nuGetServiceConnections: MyOtherOrganizationFeed,
MyExternalPackageRepository # Optional
    #forceReinstallCredentialProvider: false # Optional

- task: DotNetCoreCLI@2
  displayName: Restore
  inputs:
    command: restore
    projects: '**/*.csproj'
    feedsToUse: config
    nugetConfigPath: $(Build.SourcesDirectory)/nugget.
config

- task: DotNetCoreCLI@2
  displayName: Build
  inputs:
    command: build
    projects: '**/*.csproj'
    arguments: '--configuration $(buildConfiguration)' #
Update this to match your need

- task: Docker@2
  displayName: Build an image to container registry
  inputs:
```

```
        command: build
        repository: 'SampleStarter'
        dockerfile: '**/Dockerfile'
        containerRegistry: 'packtbookacr'
        tags: $(Build.BuildId)
        arguments: '--build-arg FEED_ACCESSTOKEN=$(VSS_NUGET_
ACCESSTOKEN)'

- task: Docker@2
  displayName: Build and push an image to container
registry
  inputs:
    command: push
    repository: 'SampleStarter'
    dockerfile: '**/Dockerfile'
    containerRegistry: 'packtbookacr'
    tags: $(Build.BuildId)
```

- Note that the containerRegistry name is packtbookacr, which is the same as when you created AKS and ACR. The containerRegistry name packtbookacr must be globally unique, so you won't be able to use the same name.

- Update dockerfile with the following contents:

> **Important Note**
>
> The endpoint is masked with *** in the following example. Please use an appropriate and valid endpoint for your NuGet feed.

```
#See https://aka.ms/
containerfastmode to understand how Visual Studio
uses this Dockerfile to build your images for faster
debugging.

FROM mcr.microsoft.com/dotnet/aspnet:6.0 AS base
WORKDIR /app
EXPOSE 80
EXPOSE 443


FROM mcr.microsoft.com/dotnet/sdk:6.0 AS build
```

```
WORKDIR /src

RUN curl -L https://raw.githubusercontent.com/
Microsoft/artifacts-credprovider/master/helpers/
installcredprovider.sh | sh


COPY ["packtbookslibrary-api.csproj", "."]
COPY ./nuget.config .
ARG FEED_ACCESSTOKEN
ENV VSS_NUGET_EXTERNAL_FEED_
ENDPOINTS="{\"endpointCredentials\":
[{\"endpoint\":\"https://pkgs.dev.azure.com/*****/
PacktBookLibrary/_packaging/PacktBooksLibraryFeed/nuget/
v3/index.json\", \"password\":\"${FEED_ACCESSTOKEN}\"}]}"
RUN dotnet restore "./packtbookslibrary-api.csproj"
--interactive
COPY . .
WORKDIR "/src/."
RUN dotnet build "packtbookslibrary-api.csproj" -c
Release -o /app/build


FROM build AS publish
RUN dotnet publish "packtbookslibrary-api.csproj" -c
Release -o /app/publish


FROM base AS final
WORKDIR /app
COPY --from=publish /app/publish .
ENTRYPOINT ["dotnet", "packtbookslibrary-api.dll"]
```

- We use **Azure Artifact Credential Provider** here to automate the acquisition of the credentials required to restore NuGet packages.

- After successfully executing the azurecontainercluster-pipelines.yml file through the Azure DevOps build pipeline, you will notice that an image with tags is created in ACR:

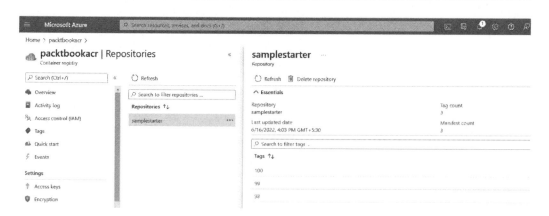

Figure 16.17 – An ACR list

- You may need to establish and authorize an Azure DevOps Service connection with ACR, as created in the preceding paragraph, to successfully execute a build pipeline:

Figure 16.18 – Establishing an ACR service connection

Further reading

- Information on installing the Azure CLI: `https://docs.microsoft.com/en-us/cli/azure/install-azure-cli`.

- Information on installing Docker Desktop: `https://docs.docker.com/desktop/windows/install/`.

- More information on Kubernetes: `https://kubernetes.io/docs/home/`

- You can find more information regarding Azure Kubernetes at the following link: `https://azure.microsoft.com/en-us/topic/what-is-kubernetes/`.

- Information on ACR: `https://docs.microsoft.com/en-in/azure/container-registry/container-registry-get-started-portal`.

- More information regarding multi-stage builds: `https://docs.docker.com/develop/develop-images/multistage-build/`.

17

Planning Your Azure DevOps Organization

In previous chapters, you learned about many techniques and practices concerning DevOps. In this chapter, we will take a step back and look at how you can build a strong DevOps organization and what you need to think about when doing so. After that, you will learn what this can bring to you with regard to security and traceability. From there on, you will learn how you can consolidate your toolchain portfolio, thereby standardizing your development life cycle mostly on using Azure DevOps.

We will begin by creating an Azure DevOps organization where you will learn which constructs are available to lay out your products and teams in the tool. You will also learn about licensing and the security implications of the different approaches. After that, you will learn about traceability and how that can be used to create a verifiable software development process. Next up is the consolidation of the tools used. As you progress on your DevOps journey, you may find that each team uses different tools that it is familiar with and enjoys working with. While DevOps is all about empowering people, some level of standardization might be desirable, and you will learn how to go about this. Finally, you will learn that you might have to accept that you will never be completely done adopting DevOps.

The following topics will be covered in this chapter:

- Setting up an Azure DevOps organization
- Ensuring traceability
- Consolidating tools
- Accepting there is no end state

Technical requirements

To follow along with the practical parts of this chapter, one of the following is needed:

- A Microsoft Live account, also called a personal account

- A work or school account

Setting up an Azure DevOps organization

To practice with one or more of the technologies and techniques described in the previous chapters, an Azure DevOps organization might have been created specifically for this use, or maybe one was available already that could be used for this purpose. However, creating an organization for a company from scratch takes a little more consideration. Taking the time to properly plan the layout of the organization can save a lot of time later on.

This section describes the components out of which Azure DevOps is built, how you can use this to organize a fitting security model, and licensing options and costs.

How Azure DevOps is organized

The top-level construct in Azure DevOps is called an organization. For most companies, a total of one organization will suffice, but it is possible to create more than one.

Each Azure DevOps organization is hosted in a specific region. Most of the data (source code and work items) for the organization is guaranteed to be located in the region for the organization, but some information is always stored in other data centers due to the global reach of the service. Having a distributed organization with teams and products in different geographies can be one reason for using more than one organization. For example, if some teams are located in Australia and some in West Europe, it makes sense to create two separate organizations and host all teams in the geography closest to them. This will ensure that the bulk of the Azure DevOps services are hosted within a data center in a region that is physically closer to the teams, greatly reducing latencies when working with Azure DevOps.

An organization can be linked to **Azure Active Directory** (**AAD**). If this link is enabled, only users (both members and guest accounts) that are inside that particular AAD are allowed access to the organization. Using a company AAD is not mandatory; an organization can also be created using a Microsoft account. Administrators can also allow users with a GitHub account access to the organization. However, it must be noted that when creating an organization with a work account, it will automatically be linked to the home (default) tenant linked to the AAD account. Tenant administrators can prevent their work accounts from being linked to new organizations.

In each organization, one or more projects can be created. A project is an isolated container of work items, source control repositories, pipeline definitions, and all other Azure DevOps artifacts. There are only limited sharing and linking possibilities between projects. At the time of writing, only work items, pipelines, and agent pools can be related across projects. This way, projects can serve as a strong isolation boundary for enforcing rigid security between products or teams if needed. In general, it is recommended to have as few projects as possible, with the goal of having only one if possible when the count of teams is very few (<10).

The following diagram shows a possible organization of Azure DevOps organizations and projects. It shows that there are two organizations connected to AAD. One is located in West Europe and the other one in Australia. In West Europe, there are two projects in the organization, while in Australia there is just one:

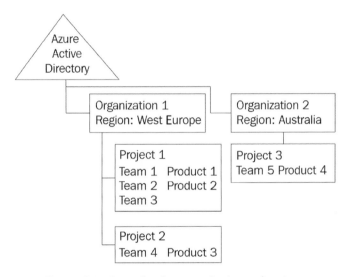

Figure 17.1 – Azure DevOps organization and projects

As stated before, the recommendation is to go with as few organizations and projects as possible. But in this example, the latency from Australia to West Europe is a good argument to split into two organizations to have Azure DevOps hosted close to the teams. The split into two projects in West Europe might be due to the need for a high level of isolation for team 4, which is working on product 3.

Combining teams 1 to 3 and products 1 and 2 into one project has been done on purpose. The reason for this is that within a single project, multiple product areas and multiple teams can be defined. Having all of these in a single project enables the easy linking of work items for portfolio management. This way, working items from one team can also be related to the commits or pull requests of another team on another product. This is helpful if features are spread over multiple products or applications (components).

Azure DevOps provides area paths, teams, and iterations that help you organize and execute the life cycle processes on your product backlog. Hence, you must choose the level of granularity carefully to achieve a greater degree of parallelism in your development life cycle. A few simple rules to follow would be the following:

- Avoid linking users to multiple teams. Rather, create teams as a logical, self-contained unit.

- Create an area path for each major product (or team) in the organization. Create subarea paths as applicable.

- Create separate team projects only if you want fine-grained control over all aspects of the DevOps life cycle.

To make defining all products and all teams in a single project possible, it is important to know about the Azure DevOps security model and how to use this for implementing access control.

Creating an Azure DevOps organization and project

Creating a new Azure DevOps organization and one or more projects is a task often completed by administrators who will also be responsible for managing these environments later. These organizations are most likely connected to an **Azure Active Directory (AAD)**. To create an organization for private use or training and learning practices, it might be better to use a personal account.

To create a new organization using a personal account, do the following:

1. Navigate to `https://dev.azure.com`.
2. Choose **Start free** to start the creation of a new Azure DevOps organization.
3. When prompted with a login dialog, log in using a personal account.
4. After logging in, select the correct country of residence and opt in/out of tips and other service updates using the following dialog:

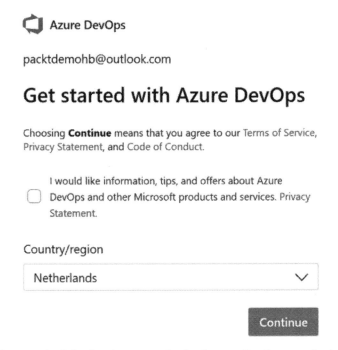

Figure 17.2 – Selecting the country/region for your DevOps organization

5.   Press **Continue** to create a new organization.

Once the organization is created, a new wizard will automatically start to create the first project. To create a project, do the following:

1.   Provide a project name.

2.   Choose between making the project public or private. Private projects are the default setting and are intended to create software within an organization and not allow anonymous access. Public projects are intended for open source development.

Once a new organization and a new project are created, it is possible to make changes to these choices using the management interface.

> **Important Note**
> Please keep in mind that renaming the organization or a project will change the URL, so all existing integrations and links may break.

It is even possible to change the location of an organization later. This must be requested and is not as easy as changing other settings.

Once an organization and project are available, it is time to set up security.

Azure DevOps security model

Within Azure DevOps, authorization can be assigned to individual users or security groups. A security group is either a logical wrapper around an existing AAD group or can be defined within Azure DevOps itself. In general, it is recommended to assign authorization as much as possible to groups, and limit individual user assignments.

To configure authorization for a user or security group, two complementary approaches are available:

- Organization- and project-level authorizations
- Object-level authorizations

When working with the on-premises product, Azure DevOps Server, there are also server-level security groups and settings available:

> **Important Note**
>
> In Azure DevOps Services, an organization is called a project collection and a project is called a team project. Sometimes, these names are also used in Azure DevOps.

- **Organization- and project-level authorizations**: To allow a user to perform a specific action on every object of a certain type, an organization- or project-level authorization can be set. As an example, look at the built-in groups, `Project Collection Build Administrators`, or `[ProjectName]\Build Administrators`, which, by default, have permission to view, manage, and edit build definitions and build resources.

  The permissions that can be set at the organization and project level are automatically applied to all individual resources in the organization or the project.

- **Object-level authorizations**: On most of the objects in Azure DevOps, individual permissions can be assigned to users or groups. These permissions are set using an **access control list** (**ACL**) on the object itself. The following example shows a classic build definition:

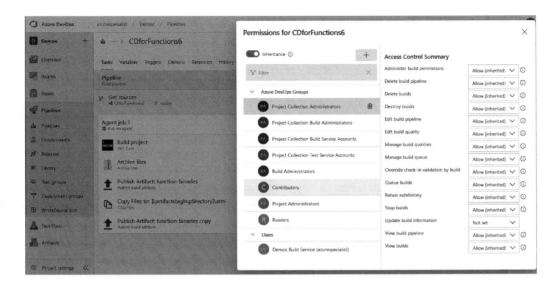

Figure 17.3 – Setting up permissions for your project

For each group, for each action, it is possible to configure the **Allow**, **Deny**, **Not set**, or **Allow(inherited)** permission. When an action is configured with **Deny**, access is never allowed, not even if a user is part of a group that has the authorization specified as **Allow**. In other words, when there are two conflicting assignments (**Allow** and **Deny**), **Deny** will take precedence over **Allow**. **Not set** is to be interpreted as an implicit deny that does not take precedence. In other words, when there are two conflicting assignments (**Not set** and **Allow**), the user will be allowed access.

Some artifacts in Azure DevOps are part of a hierarchy. For example, pipelines can be in a folder. Whenever inheritance is enabled, permissions from a higher (parent) level in the hierarchy will propagate to the artifact. This means that when a user has access to a pipeline folder, all of their rights will propagate to all underlying folders and pipelines if, and only if, there are no more specific authorizations set.

While the security model determines which authorization a user has, user actions are also limited by their assigned access level, which follows from their license.

Azure DevOps licensing

Another aspect of creating an Azure DevOps organization is managing licenses. Within Azure DevOps, every user needs to have an access level assigned before they can log in to the product. There are three access levels defined:

- **Stakeholder**: Stakeholders are free users who can log in to the product but have limited access to its features. Stakeholders can manage work items, manage pipelines, and view dashboards. They do not have access to any of the other product areas, making this license level usable for non-development roles only.

- **Basic**: Basic users have a paid license that gives them access to all parts of the product, except for test management and advanced test execution functionality.

- **Basic and Test Plans**: Users of the Basic and Test Plans license option have access to all parts of Azure DevOps. They have the same access as basic users but are also provided with access to test management and tools for user acceptance testing, test execution, and test result reporting.

The first five basic licenses for every organization are free. This means that experimenting with the product and learning how to use it can be done without incurring any costs. Additionally, Visual Studio subscribers can also get free licenses. Professional subscribers get a free Basic license and Enterprise subscribers get a free Basic and Test Plans license.

Licenses can be assigned and re-assigned at any point, so for a company or team with many joiners and leavers, it is not necessary to buy more licenses than they have people active at any given point.

Licensing costs are not the only costs that come from using Azure DevOps; it is important to also know about the pay-per-use costs.

You can refer to this link for more information: `https://docs.microsoft.com/en-us/azure/devops/organizations/security/access-levels`.

Consumption-based costs

Licenses give users access to the product and, from there on, they can use all of the services in the product at a fixed cost, except for the following two:

- Azure Pipelines parallel executions

  By default, every Azure DevOps organization is provided with one Microsoft-hosted parallel execution job with limited monthly execution time. This means that while there can be as many pipelines defined as needed, there can be only one pipeline executing at a time. Of course, this number can be increased, but this comes at the cost of buying more Microsoft-hosted parallel execution jobs.

As an alternative, it is also possible to buy self-hosted jobs. For these jobs, the execution agents are not provided by Microsoft but have to be provided by the organization itself at an additional cost. This provides the opportunity (and responsibility) to fully control the hardware.

- Azure Artifacts storage

  When working with Azure Artifacts feeds, the first 2 GB of storage used is free. Any extra storage used will be charged extra as per the rate card.

  Once more and more of the users of a team have a license for Azure DevOps and perform their work there, this can be used to increase traceability for software development.

Refer to this link to understand more about Azure DevOps billing: `https://docs.microsoft.com/en-us/azure/devops/organizations/billing/overview`.

Ensuring traceability

One of the advantages of Azure DevOps over some of the other tools covered in this book is that it is a fully integrated suite of tools, each supporting specific DevOps processes. This end-to-end integration allows for detailed and lengthy traceability, from work described on the board to the related binaries being deployed to an environment.

When working with a set of other tools that support only a part of the DevOps process, integrating them is often possible and, of course, this will result in some traceability. For example, when working with Jira and GitHub, it is possible to relate commits, pull requests, and other changes in GitHub back to work described in Jira. When picking merged changes up in Jenkins to build and deploy the product, there will also be traceability from Jenkins back to GitHub. However, there will be no direct visibility on which work item was completed with which Jenkins deployment.

The disadvantage of this is that a product owner who works in the Jira tool cannot see whether a completed user story is associated with a release already. They would have to visit multiple tools to find the answer to that question; in GitHub, they would have to find all commits relating to the story and then see whether those commits have been released already using Jenkins.

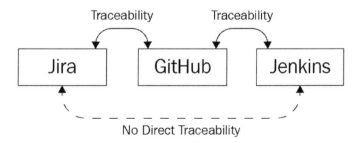

Figure 17.4 – Traceability options between tools

When working with Azure Boards, Repos, and Pipelines, this is different. When using all of the Azure DevOps services, traceability is possible from story to deployment and the other way around. The following is an example that highlights how to see which commits were deployed for the first time to an environment with a specific deploy:

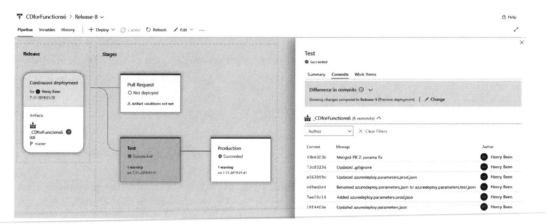

Figure 17.5 – Viewing commits that are part of the pipeline run

Having this type of end-to-end traceability enables a number of questions to be answered quickly, including the following:

- Has work on this work item already started? (Branches and pull requests can be related to work items.)

- Is this work already part of our nightly build? (Commits and build pipelines can be related to work items.)

- Is this bug already fixed and is the solution available to our customers on ring two already? (Releases and environments show which new commits and work items were part of the latest deployment.)

> **Important Note**
>
> One thought that is particularly important to reinforce when talking about traceability is that it is not about blame. Traceability is not about finding out who made which mistake, but about finding out what the state of things is and how objects relate. As soon as traceability becomes the basis for blame, engineers will soon find ways to hide their work. This will result in more errors and less visibility, only making problems worse.

With the benefits of traceability clear, let's explore how consolidating tools can help us to reap these benefits.

Consolidating tools

One trend that can be observed in the market is that of traceability and DevOps products that extend their offerings to include more than just source control, pipelines, or deployments. Examples are GitHub and GitLab, which are adding new services. More integrated **Application Lifecycle Management** (**ALM**) or DevOps suites are emerging, but Azure DevOps has been offering this for years now.

However, there are many companies where these integrated suites are not in place. Teams operate in different ecosystems, leading to different tool choices. Or maybe teams just have different preferences or started adopting DevOps practices at different points in time, with other tools to choose from. No matter the reason, there are many companies that have several tools running for the same job.

Unfortunately, several drawbacks are associated with having disconnected tools or multiple tools for the same thing:

- Collaboration between teams is hindered if they are using different tools. No matter the personal preference of developers, it can prove to be a hindrance to productivity when one half of the organization is using Jenkins and the other half is using Azure Pipelines. By extension, switching teams or helping others out is severely impeded when they are using another tool.

- When there are more tools, there are also more costs. Even when all of the tools are open source and free, there are still costs involved. These costs can consist of, for instance, support contracts or requests, training, or the time needed to investigate and overcome specific issues. The same holds for upgrades and maintenance. When there are more tools, the total costs increase.

- Multiple distributed tools suggest multiple efforts for security and monitoring, which can lead to many issues and breaches.

To overcome these challenges, many large companies decide to standardize which tools are used, either completely or at least to some extent. As an alternative or intermediate solution, it is also possible to use integration between tools as a way of starting a consolidation.

Standardizing tools

To combat these drawbacks, most companies accept one of two strategies:

- Centralized decision making to select one tool (for each DevOps area) for the whole company
- Centralized adoption of a limited set of tools, out of which teams can choose which to adopt

In **complete centralization**, one central team or department decides, on behalf of everyone, which DevOps tools will be used within the organization. Once such a decision has been made and implemented, this reduces costs and makes it easier for engineers to assist other teams.

The downside is, of course, that one single tool is not necessarily the best choice for everyone, while for the organization as a whole, the selected tool might be the best—such standardization can do damage in a number of edge cases.

Limited centralization is used by some companies to prevent this. Instead of just one tool, a group of tools is chosen as the company's standard. Teams are now able to make their own choice out of two or three tools, depending on their specific needs. This limits many of the drawbacks of full decentralization, while not sacrificing the productivity of teams with very specific needs.

Adopting one of these two strategies might mean that some existing tools will be deprecated or decommissioned altogether. This can be a slow and painful process, especially in large organizations where there are often conflicting interests. There are many ways to go about this, but there are strategies to make such a migration less painful.

Migration strategies

Reducing the number of DevOps tools in use often means one or more tools must be decommissioned. This can be difficult since, often, these tools are used to implement governance and compliance, as required by laws and regulations. In practice, this means that one of two things can be done:

- Old tools are not completely decommissioned but just no longer used, to maintain the change history.

- History must be migrated to the new tools as well before the old tools can be decommissioned.

When choosing to do a migration, there are four ways to go about this:

- Azure DevOps Server to Azure DevOps Services migration

- Big-bang migration

- Synchronization

- Rebuilding

> **Tip**
> Azure DevOps Server used to be called **Team Foundation Server** (**TFS**). Older versions of TFS need to be upgraded to one of the latest versions of Azure DevOps Server before they can be imported into Azure DevOps Services. The import service always supports the latest two versions of Azure DevOps Server.

All four of these are detailed in the following sections.

Azure DevOps Server to Azure DevOps Services migration

For organizations wanting to move from working with Azure DevOps Server to Azure DevOps Services, there is a high-fidelity migration service available. Every project collection that currently exists in the on-premises Azure DevOps Server environment can be migrated to an Azure DevOps organization using the Azure DevOps Server import service. All of the assets currently existing in the on-premises project collection will be migrated to Azure DevOps: work items, source control repositories, and build and release definitions.

The migration of a project collection consists of the following high-level steps:

1. Validating whether a project collection is ready for migration: This step does not make any changes but only checks whether all preconditions for a migration have been met.

2. Preparing the migration: In this step, a JSON file is generated that describes how the migration should be performed. A second file can also be supplied for linking on-premises identities to AAD identities to ensure that all of the history is still correctly linked to who made the change after the migration.

3. A dry run of the migration is done to verify that the import process will result in the expected outcomes.

4. The actual migration: In this step, the collection is taken offline, a **Data-Tier Application Package (DACPAC)** is generated from the project collection database, the DACPAC and files from step 2 are uploaded, and the migration is initiated.

5. After the import, all assets need to be verified and, in specific scenarios, some post-import actions have to be taken.

For using the migration service, a comprehensive guide with checklists and step-by-step instructions is available and linked to at the end of this chapter.

Big-bang migration

The second possible strategy is a big-bang migration. At some point, the old tool is switched off, all data is migrated to the new tool, and the new tool is made available. It has a high potential for issues, and often, there is no turning back. This is usually not a good migration strategy.

However, one situation where such an approach might make sense is the migration of source control. There are tools available for migrating from different sources to any type of hosted Git solution, including Azure DevOps. Source control also has the benefit that change history is built so deep into the system that migrating with history is often easier than for other types of data.

Synchronization

Another strategy for migration is allowing for a period of time where both tools can be used at the same time.

One way to do this is by using a tool that can be used to sync between the old and the new tool. This can be either in one direction, from old to new, or in both directions. This way, an in-between situation is created where both tools can be in use at the same time. Every team can choose its own time for migration within a certain window. This avoids a forced migration window. Teams can also opt to use both tools next to each other for a while. This allows them to learn the new tool, while still being able to switch to the tool that they know if they are under pressure. After a period of transition, the old tool can be made read-only or decommissioned completely. This approach often works well for work-tracking systems. Between these systems, the concepts are often very similar (epics, features, stories, and sprints), which makes synchronization a feasible approach.

Rebuilding

A slightly different approach is that of asking teams to rebuild in the new tool. This approach also creates an in-parallel situation, but there is no automated migration or synchronization. Teams will have to redo their process or way of working in the new tool. Since this can take a while, the old tool will remain while teams are working on this. One situation where this is often a good approach is that of build and/or release pipelines.

No matter the strategy that has been chosen, in all cases, it helps to make sure that the new tool or tools are an improvement for the teams over the existing tools. This should improve performance, traceability, ease of use, or integration with other company tools. A positive vibe around any migration can improve the outcomes dramatically.

As an alternative to migrating to a single tool, integrations between tools can be used to bring existing tools together.

Integrating tools

As an alternative to replacing no-longer-preferred tools, it is also possible to integrate them with the preferred tool. Especially when it has been decided to move to Azure DevOps, this can be a powerful strategy. In many of the previous chapters, for each topic, different tools were listed that integrate with Azure DevOps.

When pursuing end-to-end traceability, these integrations can be used as a means to bring tools closer together. Consider the following example.

An organization is using Azure DevOps for managing work items, hosting Git repositories, and executing build pipelines. Deployments are done using Octopus Deploy for historic reasons. Since a full migration is too costly, as an alternative, an integration strategy is chosen. Triggering Octopus Deploy not manually but automatically from Azure DevOps meets several goals:

- End-to-end automation is achieved.

- Release management can now also be done in Azure DevOps, even though each deployment in Azure DevOps does nothing more than trigger Octopus Deploy.

- Having release management in Azure DevOps now allows for end-to-end traceability.

When consolidating tools, and really all things regarding DevOps, one thing that you must be ready to accept is that you are never done.

Accepting there is no end state

It is fair to expect that, at any point in time, there will be one or more improvements that teams want to make to their applications, toolchains, or way of working. To cope with this, it is recommended to not keep changing everything all of the time.

Instead, try to implement changes in batches or a series of well-defined steps. Also, note there is a natural order to things. It is impossible to practice **continuous deployment** (**CD**) without having a proper **continuous integration** (**CI**) process first. Also, adopting **infrastructure as code** (**IaC**) will deliver the most value when a CD process for application code is already in place. Next, automating governance and security measures works best when having infrastructure and configuration code is common practice. Once all of these practices have been implemented, new things will come up on the radar—future improvements that may be necessary.

Besides this series of improvements, it is also important to realize that not every team is at the same place in this journey, not every team can move at the same pace, and that development is not always this linear.

But this does not mean that it is impossible to track and plan future changes and have learnings from one team applied to other teams as well. One oversimplified approach to tracking this can be a table, as shown here.

Here, we see the adoption of different DevOps practices or ideas among five teams. All teams are practicing CI. Some of them are practicing CD, while team 3 is still working on that **work in progress** (**WIP**) and the fifth team has not started yet. Finally, team 2 is already experimenting with IaC. Finally, as there is no end state, it is only a matter of time before the next practice or idea will pop up and a team will start experimenting:

	CI	CD	IaC	next ?
Team 1	✓	✓		
Team 2	✓	✓	experimenting	
Team 3	✓	WIP		
Team 4	✓	✓		
Team 5	✓			

If a table similar to the preceding one is updated, evaluated, and expanded upon frequently, it helps to foster continuous learning and improve the way software is created and delivered. Learning and improving will become the standard and this will help to improve the delivery of value to end users. It also shows that adopting DevOps is never done.

It also provides the means to see which teams are at the forefront and which teams are following along. By giving teams who are in the lead more room for experimentation and knowledge sharing with other teams, organizations can encourage their leading teams to improve even more, while at the same time accelerating other teams as well.

And with this remark about the need to keep learning, experimenting, and pushing yourself, it is a great time to wrap this book up. Let's recap this chapter in the next section.

Summary

In this chapter, you learned how to configure your Azure DevOps organization and how to create a layout for your products and teams. You learned what the implications are regarding the different configuration options and how to apply those. After that, you learned how you can use Azure DevOps to add traceability to your development process. You learned how to capture ideas and tasks in stories and tasks and how these can be traced all the way to deployment, and the other way around. The next thing you learned about is how to approach the consolidation of tools used within your organization and when to stop trying to consolidate tools. Finally, you learned that it is important to continuously keep improving.

With the things you learned in this chapter, you are now capable of setting up and configuring Azure DevOps for your team, teams, or organization. You can create a structure that fits your organization and start using it with just one or multiple teams. You are also able to slowly standardize your way of working and consolidate the teams on the same set of tools.

This completes the final chapter of this book. You can refer back to this book to help you prepare to take the AZ-400 exam, as most of the topics are along similar lines. However, in order to be well prepared for the exam, I recommend reading more about it from other sources as well and trying to get as much hands-on experience as you can. As a practice tool, the concluding chapter contains a mock exam to help you prepare for the final exam.

Good luck!

Questions

As we conclude, here is a list of questions for you to test your knowledge regarding this chapter's material. You will find the answers in the *Assessments* section of the *Appendix*:

1. True or false: All data stored in Azure DevOps by users is guaranteed to be contained within one region.

2. Reorder the following Azure DevOps concepts in such a way that each element acts as a container for the next concept in the list:

    *   Work item

    *   Organization

    *   Region

    *   Project

3. True or false: The general recommendation is to create a new project for every application that is developed by your organization.

4. Which two elements limit the actions any user can perform within Azure DevOps?

5. What is the main benefit of using a single tool for ALM/DevOps as opposed to a suite of tools?

Activity

Consider a scenario where your organization is planning to develop the next-generation customer relationship management online service. The engineering team is organized using departments, wherein each department is entrusted with the ownership of building products or services for an identified focus area. The following diagram depicts a summary of this:

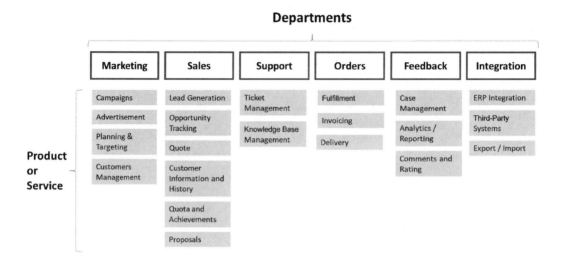

Figure 17.6 – Organization structure

Within each department, there would be multiple feature teams (for example, infra, web, mobile, core API, and so on) working on these products or services.

For the scenario under evaluation, identify an approach for setting up your DevOps organization using projects, area paths, and teams. One of the considerations is that each department would prefer to have complete ownership of their DevOps components and the project life cycle.

Further reading

- More information on Azure DevOps projects and when to create more than one project can be found at https://docs.microsoft.com/en-us/azure/devops/organizations/projects/about-projects?view=azure-devops#when-to-add-another-project.

- More information about the Azure DevOps security model can be found at https://docs.microsoft.com/en-us/azure/devops/organizations/security.

- Up-to-date information on Azure DevOps pricing can be found at https://azure.microsoft.com/en-us/pricing/details/devops/azure-devops-services/.

- More information about the Azure DevOps Server import service can be found at https://docs.microsoft.com/en-us/azure/devops/migrate/migration-overview?view=azure-devopsviewFallbackFrom=vsts.

18
AZ-400 Mock Exam

Designing a DevOps Strategy

1. You are tasked with introducing Azure DevOps into your organization. Right now, there are many other tools being used for deployments. You are asked which of the following tools can integrate with Azure DevOps. [There can be any number of answers.]

    A. Octopus Deploy

    B. Jira

    C. Jenkins

    D. App Center

2. You are asked to create a dashboard for your team that displays information about how your team is working. You should focus on displaying metrics and charts that encourage Agile and DevOps ways of working. Which metrics do you choose? [Choose three.]

    A. A widget that shows the average cycle time for work items

    B. A widget that shows the outcome (success or failure) for the most recent deployments

    C. A widget that shows the number of lines of code added per day

    D. A widget that shows the number of pull requests currently open within the team

3. You are asked to implement static code analysis within your project. What is the best time to do this?

    A. During the build stage, just before artifacts are published

    B. During the deployment stage, just before the actual deployment to the target environment

4. You are running **Team Foundation Server (TFS)** 2015 on-premises. You are asked to migrate all assets on this server to Azure DevOps using high-fidelity migration. Put the following tasks in the correct order.

    A. Run the Migration Validation tool.

    B. Perform a complete end-to-end dry run of the import process.

    C. Create a portable backup of the TFS Project Collection(s).

    D. Upgrade your TFS to one of the two most recent versions of the Azure DevOps server.

    E. Run the `import` service for each Project Collection.

5. One of the core principles of DevOps is *to continuously deliver value to our end users.* Which of the following is not used to do so?

    A. People

    B. Practices

    C. Process

    D. Products

6. You are working for a large enterprise and have to automate the assignment of licenses to new hires. To do this, you have created a small application that is connected to the HR application. Which type of authorization do you use between your application and Azure DevOps?

    A. User accounts

    B. Personal access token

    C. OAuth tokens

    D. One-time secrets

7. You need to migrate an existing Git repository to Azure DevOps. Which of the following do you need to do? [Choose two.]

    A. Create an initialized Git repository.

    B. Create an uninitialized Git repository.

    C. Execute `git remote rm origin; git remote add origin <new-repository-url>; git push`.

    D. Execute `git remote redirect origin <new-repository-url>; git push`.

8. You are working in a heterogeneous environment with teams using different DevOps tools throughout the company. One of your builds is running within Azure DevOps, but another team wants to consume your pipeline artifacts from another tool. Which of the following can you use for staging build artifacts to connect from other tools?

   A. Pipeline artifacts

   B. Artifactory

   C. Octopus Deploy Binary Server

   D. Artifact feeds/universal packages

9. You are tasked with configuring source control for your team in Azure DevOps. Which of the following requirements can only be fulfilled by using **Team Foundation Version Control (TFVC)**?

   A. You need to enforce the four-eyes principle.

   B. You need to configure access to specific folders for one user only.

   C. You need to configure access to specific files for one user only.

   D. You need to connect to classic build pipelines.

10. You need to execute and record exploratory testing sessions. In addition to executing tests, you should also be able to automatically report bugs on your Azure Boards backlog. You plan to use the Test & Feedback extension for this and assign all testers a testing license. Does this complete the goal?

   A. Yes

   B. No

11. You need to execute and record exploratory testing sessions. In addition to executing tests, you should also be able to automatically report bugs on your Azure Boards backlog. You plan to use the Test & Feedback extension for this and assign all testers a Basic and Test license. Does this achieve the goal?

   A. Yes

   B. No

12. You need to execute and record exploratory testing sessions. In addition to executing tests, you should also be able to automatically report bugs on your Azure Boards backlog. You plan to use the Test & Feedback extension for this and assign all testers a Basic license. Does this achieve the goal?

   A. Yes

   B. No

13. You are tasked with identifying metrics that can be used to measure the impact of adopting DevOps. Which of the following do you advise to be used? [Choose two.]

    A. Amount of work in progress at the same time

    B. Velocity

    C. Cycle time

    D. Sprint duration

14. Which of the following is not a DevOps habit?

    A. Team autonomy and enterprise alignment

    B. Maximizing the amount of work not done

    C. Hypothesis-driven development

    D. Live-site culture

15. You are tasked with creating a test strategy for the new application that you are creating with your team. Which of the following recommendations should you make?

    A. For verifying that the most critical user scenarios are still working correctly, one or more system tests should be written.

    B. For verifying that the most critical user scenarios are still working correctly, a stress test should be performed before every deployment.

    C. For every ten unit tests, there should be at least one integration test.

    D. Before enabling a new feature in production, a final smoke test should be performed on the production environment.

16. Source code is one of the most valuable assets for your company. You want to implement multi-factor authentication for access to Azure DevOps when users are not connecting through the corporate network. Which of the following can you use to do this?

    A. Azure Active Directory Conditional Access

    B. Azure Active Directory Network Allowance

    C. Azure DevOps Network Controls

    D. Azure Active Directory Account Groups

17. You are working in a team that provides Azure subscriptions and resource groups to other teams. As part of your work, you want to monitor whether all teams implement recommended Azure best practices for security. Which of the following do you use?

    A. Azure Policy

    B. Azure Security Center (now Microsoft Defender for Cloud)

    C. Azure Key Vault

    D. Azure Security Monitor

18. You are tasked with providing the means for starting SonarCloud scans from within Azure DevOps. Which of the following steps create a complete solution? [Choose two.]

    A. Update the SonarCloud configuration in your Azure DevOps project.

    B. Create a new SonarCloud service connection.

    C. Activate the SonarCloud integration pack.

    D. Install the SonarCloud extension.

19. You need to apply an update to a deployment within Kubernetes—which command should you use?

    A. `kubectl apply`

    B. `kubectl deployments`

    C. `kubectl get services`

    D. `kubectl deploy`

20. What are the basic tools you need to use when managing an Azure Kubernetes cluster? [Choose all that apply.]

    A. Azure CLI/PowerShell

    B. kubectl

    C. Azure DevOps

Implementing DevOps Development Processes

21. You are developing a Microsoft .NET Core application and want to analyze the application to check whether there are any open source libraries with known security vulnerabilities being used. Which of the following products can you use for such an analysis? [Choose two.]

    A. Jenkins

    B. WhiteSource Bolt

C. Snyk

D. App Center

22. You are currently using (i) JIRA, (ii) GitLab, and (iii) Octopus Deploy for some of your DevOps processes. You want to consolidate your DevOps tools and have chosen to go with Azure DevOps. Which Azure DevOps services should you use to replace these? Choose the correct service to replace these three services. [Match three pairs.]

A. Azure Pipelines

B. Azure Repos

C. Azure Boards

D. Azure Artifacts

23. You are evaluating different options for build agents. What are valid arguments for opting for private agents over Microsoft-hosted agents? [Choose two.]

A. You need custom software to be available on the agent before any job is executed.

B. You need to ensure that the same environment is used for executing only one pipeline job before being destructed.

C. You need direct network connectivity from the build agent to your on-premises network.

D. You need to ensure that you are always running on up-to-date images.

24. You are responsible for managing the settings of the applications your team deploys to Azure App Service. Which of the following offerings cannot be used to achieve this?

A. Azure App Configuration

B. ARM templates

C. Azure Policy

D. Azure Key Vault

25. You are tasked with creating a large number of build pipelines for your team. Almost all pipelines need to have the same structure. Which Azure DevOps Pipelines construct can help you?

A. Branch Policies

B. Task Groups or Templates

C. Azure Artifacts

D. Deployment Groups

26. You are using Entity Framework as the database access layer from your application. You are responsible for managing database upgrades and want to use Entity Framework for this as well, to manage the database schema from code. Which type of schema migration should you use?

    A. Migrations-based

    B. End-state based

27. You need to save your local changes to a Git repository. Which commands do you need to use? [Choose two]

    A. `git clone and git push`

    B. `git commit and git push`

    C. `git add, git commit, and git push`

    D. `git add and git commit`

28. You need to prevent anyone from merging changes to the master branch if the changes do not compile or any of the unit tests fail. Which of the following can you use to accomplish this?

    A. Branch protection center

    B. Azure Repos branch policies

    C. Azure Repos branch security

    D. This is not possible in Azure DevOps; you need to use another product, for example, GitHub

29. Your company uses GitHub Enterprise on-premises for hosting source control. For implementing continuous integration and deployment, you are looking to use Azure DevOps. Which of the following components form a complete solution to make this possible? [Choose two.]

    A. An external Git service connection

    B. Opening the firewall for HTTPS connections from Azure Pipelines to GitHub Enterprise

    C. A Git sources proxy for HTTP

    D. On-premises agents

30. A new team joins the company, and they have to start work on a new application. They ask you to recommend a branching strategy that allows them to work on multiple features in parallel and deploy a new version at any time and minimizes the need for merging changes late. Which of the following do you recommend?

    A. Create an eternal branch per team member and cherry-pick commits to merge.

    B. Create a branch per feature and merge this branch upon completion.

C. Create a branch per task and merge this branch upon completion.

D. Create and merge a branch as often as possible when a shippable piece of work has been completed.

31. You are tasked with configuring source control for your team in Azure DevOps. Which of the following source control systems do you choose, preferably?

A. TFVC

B. Git

32. Which of the following is true?

A. You can have as many Git and TFVC repositories in an Azure DevOps project as you want.

B. You can have at most one Git repository and at most one TFVC repository in an Azure DevOps project.

C. You can have at most one TFVC repository and as many Git repositories as you want in your Azure DevOps project.

D. You can have either Git repositories or TFVC repositories in an Azure DevOps project, but not both at the same time.

33. Your team is creating a mobile application and wants to use App Center for distributing the application to both the app stores and the testers within the team. Which of the following should you use? [Choose two.]

A. Invitation-only pre-release groups

B. Push-to-store integration

C. Store connection

D. Distribution groups

34. You are creating a series of microservices for a new project. You are looking for a way to manage configuration from a centralized point. There are many configuration settings shared between microservices. Which of the following solutions best fits this use case?

A. Azure Key Vault

B. Azure App Configuration

C. Azure Configuration Center

D. ARM templates

35. You have to ensure that code cannot be checked into the master branch of a repository when it has not been viewed by at least two people. Which of the following is a complete solution for this? [Choose three.]

    A. Enforce the use of a pull request for merging changes to the master.

    B. Reset approval votes on the pull request for a branch when a new commit is pushed to that branch.

    C. Have a minimum of at least two reviewers but allow everyone to merge their own changes.

    D. Have a minimum of at least one reviewer, not being the person who opened the pull request.

36. You have to sign the binaries (DLLs) that your team produces so that other teams that consume them can verify the binaries are not altered and really are the binaries originating from your team. You have to store the certificate used for signing securely. Where can you do this and still have the file available for use in your pipeline? If multiple answers fit, choose the simplest solution.

    A. Azure Pipelines Library

    B. Azure Key Vault

    C. Encrypted in source control

    D. Azure DevOps certificate store

37. You have to ensure that every build pipeline contains a task group that is pre-shared by your team. Which of the following Azure DevOps constructs can you use to do this?

    A. Pipeline decorators.

    B. Pipeline verifiers.

    C. Pipeline pre-execution tasks.

    D. This is not possible—you have to implement a manual auditing process.

38. Your sources are stored in a Subversion source control system. You want to move to Azure DevOps Pipelines for continuous integration. You do not want to move your sources and connect from Pipelines to Subversion. Is this possible?

    A. Yes

    B. No

39. The development team is creating a containerized application. The solution needs to be deployed to a Kubernetes cluster in Azure. You need to create the cluster and ensure that the application is running as it should. Select which commands you should perform and place them in the correct order of execution.

    A. `kubectl apply`

    B. `az group create`

    C. `az aks create`

    D. `az appservice plan create`

    E. `kubectl get deployments`

    F. `az aks get-credentials`

    G. `kubectl get hpa`

    H. `kubectl get services`

40. A great advantage of running containers instead of virtual machines is that containers share the operating system kernel. This also makes container images smaller than virtual machine images. Is this correct?

    A. Yes

    B. No

Implementing Continuous Integration

41. Order the following types of tests based on the size of their scope. Start with the test types with the smallest scope.

    A. Integration tests

    B. Unit tests

    C. System tests

42. Which of the following are true? [Choose more than one.]

    A. Stress tests are performed by applying an ever-growing load onto a system, to identify the breaking point of the system.

    B. Integration tests always include the database.

    C. Performance tests are performed to measure how quickly the system can perform a given task.

    D. Usability tests are performed to identify use cases where the system is too slow to respond.

43. You are creating an Azure DevOps dashboard to provide the team with insight into the quality of the code being written. Which of the following widgets does not belong on such a dashboard?

    A. A widget that shows recent deployments and whether they were successful or not

    B. A widget that shows the number of check-ins per day

    C. A widget that shows how the unit test code coverage changes over time

    D. A widget that shows whether the latest build has failed or not

44. Which of the following is not a valid merge strategy?

    A. Squash commit

    B. Rebase

    C. Interleave

    D. Merge commit

45. Which of the following is not part of the OWASP Top 10?

    A. Injections

    B. Sensitive data exposure

    C. Least privilege principle violations

    D. Using dependencies with known vulnerabilities

46. Your team is creating container images that should be deployed into Azure later on. Which of the following can you use to store your images? [Choose two.]

    A. Azure Container Instances

    B. Azure Container Registry

    C. Azure Kubernetes Service

    D. Docker Hub

47. You want to be notified whenever any integration build fails. You configure an email subscription on your Azure DevOps project. Will this achieve this goal?

    A. Yes

    B. No

48. You want to trigger a YAML pipeline whenever a new version of an artifact hosted in an Azure Artifacts feed becomes available. Is this possible?

    A. Yes

    B. No

49. You want to use a mix of hosted agents, private agents in the cloud, and an on-premises agent in the same stage of a multi-stage YAML pipeline. Is this possible?

    A. Yes

    B. No

50. You want to create a release pipeline that is triggered at the same time every day of the week. You also want to exclude Sunday. Is this possible?

    A. Yes

    B. No

51. The developer team is creating a container-hosted application and wants to share the image on the internet. The team builds the image via Docker and tries to host it via Kubernetes. Is this the correct way?

    A. Yes

    B. No

52. Which of the following are places where you can store container images? [Choose all that apply.]

    A. Azure Container Instance

    B. Docker Hub

    C. Azure Container Registry

    D. Azure Container Storage

Implementing Continuous Delivery

53. The company you are working for is using ServiceNow as the change management system. There is a rule that ServiceNow should be used to track every deployment to production environments. You are responsible for ensuring that your application is not deployed to the production environment if there is no valid change registered in the change management system. Which of the following will accomplish this? [Choose two.]

    A. You implement a deployment callback that checks for a valid change in ServiceNow.

    B. You add a deployment gate as a precondition to deployment to the production stage.

C. You add a deployment gate as a postcondition for completing deployment in the QA stage.

D. You create an environment and call it `Production-ServiceNow check`.

54. You need to deploy an application to twelve on-premises virtual machines, grouped into three subnets. Which of the following actions should you perform to have a complete, working solution to do this? [Choose three.]

A. Create a new deployment group and add the correct agents to that group.

B. Download and install Private Agent on all of the virtual machines that you need to deploy to.

C. Add a selection job to your release pipeline to select which deployment group to use.

D. Download and install Private Agent on precisely one virtual machine in every subnet.

E. Add a deployment group job to your release pipeline to execute the tasks necessary for deploying the application.

F. Configure a username and password on your deployment pipeline to configure how to connect to the agents.

55. You need to configure a release pipeline to meet several conditions before deployment to the production environment can be started. These conditions are (i) that at least two out of four members of an approval board should approve of the deployment and (ii) that Azure Monitor should be checked for any alerts in the first hour after the release. Can this be done using Azure DevOps Pipelines?

A. Yes

B. No

56. You are using **SQL Server Data Tools (SSDT)** for describing your database schema as code. You want to use SSDT for schema upgrades as well. Which type of schema migration should you use?

A. Migrations-based

B. End-state-based

57. You are working with a schema-less database. Does this remove the issue of schema management completely?

A. Yes

B. No

58. Your team must follow regulations that state that every new version has to be approved by the test manager manually before it can be deployed to production. Which of the following changes fulfills this requirement in the most meaningful way?

    A. You add a pre-deployment gate to the production stage that verifies the sign-off in a home-build system where all application versions that are signed off can be recorded.

    B. You add a post-deployment gate to the QA stage that sets the test manager's approval in the designated system if all automated tests have succeeded.

    C. You add a post-deployment approval to the QA stage that must be given by the test manager.

    D. You disable automated approval to the production stage and instruct everyone to only start deployment after consulting the system that contains all signoffs by the test manager.

59. You are creating several release pipelines for your team. Many of the pipelines will use the same configuration values for some tasks. Which of the following can help you to repeat their values as a complete solution?

    A. Variable groups

    B. Task groups

    C. Variable containers

    D. Azure Key Vault

60. You want to automatically generate release notes out of the stories completed in a deployment. You want to do this without using any extensions or add-ons—only the built-in capabilities of Azure DevOps should be used. Is this possible?

    A. Yes

    B. No

61. You want to deploy an application to Azure Service Fabric from Azure DevOps. Do you need to install an extension for tasks to do this?

    A. Yes

    B. No

62. You need to apply an update to a deployment within Kubernetes. Which command should you use?

    A. `kubectl apply`

    B. `kubectl deployments`

    C. `kubectl get services`

    D. `kubectl deploy`

63. What kind of task is used within Azure DevOps to deploy containers to Azure Kubernetes?

    A. Kubernetes manifest

    B. Kubernetes

    C. Kubernetes general task

    D. Kubectl

64. What kind of file is most appropriate to deploy resources to a Kubernetes cluster?

    A. ARM template

    B. Terraform document

    C. PowerShell script

    D. YAML deployment file

Implementing Dependency Management

65. You are using Azure Artifacts for hosting NuGet packages that your team creates. You have a new requirement for making one (and only one) of the packages that you create available to all other teams in your organization. Which of the following are valid solutions? [Choose more than one.]

    A. You create a new feed and allow any user in your Azure Active Directory to use packages from this feed. You move the package to be shared to this feed.

    B. You allow all users within your organization to use your existing feed.

    C. You create a new feed and allow any user in your organization to use packages from this feed. You move the package to be shared to this view.

    D. You create a new view in your existing feed and publish the package to be shared to this view. Next, you configure that all members of your organization can read packages from this view.

    E. You add your existing feed as an upstream source to the feed that is used by any other team so they can pull your packages as well.

66. Which of the following are valid arguments for splitting your solution into multiple smaller solutions and using shared packages or libraries for assembling the complete application from these smaller solutions? [Choose two.]

    A. You have over 25 C# projects in a single solution.

    B. Your code base is becoming so large that compilation and/or running unit tests is starting to take too long.

C. Your team is becoming too big and is split into two. Splitting the solution as well will establish clear ownership: one solution per team.

D. You are approaching the Git limit of 10,000 files in a single repository.

67. For which of the following does Azure Artifacts support upstream sources? [Choose two.]

A. Composer

B. Python

C. Gems

D. Maven

68. You are working with Azure Artifacts feeds for dependency management. You are taking a new dependency on a library that is publicly available through NuGet. Which of the following can you use to consume this package through an existing feed?

A. Upstream sources

B. External views

C. Upstream views

D. Dependency views

69. You have a library that is used in two applications but only within your own team. Which of the following strategies is the best way to share this library?

A. Link the shared library as a shared project in the two consuming solutions.

B. Have the library in a separate repository and use a build pipeline to build the library and upload it as a NuGet package to Azure Artifacts. Consume it from there in your two applications.

70. You want to use universal packages for distributing application components from Azure DevOps to different deployment orchestrators. Is this possible?

A. Yes

B. No

Implementing Application Infrastructure

71. You are working on an application that will be deployed in two different Azure Regions to allow for failover scenarios. Which of the following together make a valid solution? [Choose two.]

    A. You create one ARM template with two parameter files. The first parameter file corresponds to the first Azure region, and the second parameter file to the second Azure region. You use the ARM templates to update the infrastructure.

    B. You create an ARM template and parameter file to update the infrastructure in one region only. In the other region, you update the infrastructure manually to prevent configuration drift.

    C. You first update the infrastructure in both regions. Only when the infrastructure is updated successfully do you deploy the application to both regions.

    D. You first update the infrastructure in one region, followed by the deployment of the application. Only when this succeeds do you update the infrastructure in the other region and deploy the application to the other region.

72. You need to deploy an Azure Resource Manager template to an Azure resource group using an Azure DevOps pipeline. Some of the parameters that you need to use are stored in Azure Key Vault. Which of the following options combined is not a necessary part of a complete solution?

    A. Create a new variable group and link it to the correct key vault using a service connection.

    B. Give the Azure Active Directory service principal a Reader RBAC role on the correct Azure key vault.

    C. Configure a new Azure Resource Manager service connection in your Azure DevOps project and create a new Azure Active Directory service principal that way.

    D. Give the Azure Active Directory service principal the following access policies on the correct key vault: list and get.

73. You are tasked with creating and configuring several virtual machines in Azure. Which combination of tools should you use? [Choose two.]

    A. Azure Automation DSC

    B. Azure Runtime Runbooks

    C. ARM templates

74. You are configuring the Azure resource group where your application will be deployed later. You are provided with a pre-created service principal for doing the deployment from Azure DevOps Pipelines. Which RBAC role assignment should you give to this service principal to deploy resources?

   A. Reader

   B. Contributor

   C. Deployer

   D. Owner

75. You have to set up the RBAC role assignments for your teams. You want to follow the principle of least privilege. You also need to ensure that access to your team resources is available to whoever needs it. Which of the following solutions is best?

   A. You add the principal used for deployments and all team members to an Azure Active Directory group. You assign this Azure Active Directory group the contributor role on your Azure resource group.

   B. You give the principal that is used for deployment contributor rights on the resource group and all team members the reader role.

   C. You create two new Azure Active Directory groups: reader and writer. You add the service principal used for deployments to the writer group. You add all team members to the reader group. You assign the reader role to the reader group and the contributor role to the writer group.

   D. You create a new Azure Active Directory group. You add the service principal used for deployments to this group. You assign the group the contributor role. You create an escalation procedure for team members to be temporarily added to this Azure Active Directory group.

76. Which of the following tools cannot be used for managing Azure resources?

   A. Terraform

   B. Azure DevOps CLI

   C. Azure PowerShell

   D. CloudFormation

77. You are practicing infrastructure as code and want to deploy an ARM template from Azure DevOps as part of your deployment process. Which of the following solutions does this in the simplest way?

   A. You execute an Azure CLI script from a Cmd task in your deployment pipeline.

   B. You execute a PowerShell script from your deployment pipeline.

C. You use the built-in task for the deployment of the ARM template.

D. You upload the template to an Azure storage account and use an HTTP REST call to start the deployment of the ARM template.

78. You are transforming the way your team delivers its application by practicing *everything as code*. Which of the following cannot be created using Azure Blueprints or ARM templates?

A. Azure subscriptions

B. Azure Active Directory security groups

C. Azure RBAC custom roles

D. Azure RBAC role assignments

79. You are working in a team that provides Azure subscriptions and resource groups to other teams. As part of your work, you want to limit the types of Azure resources a team can create. Which of the following do you use?

A. Azure RBAC roles and role assignments

B. Azure Policy

C. OWASP Zed Attack Proxy

D. Azure Security Center (now Microsoft Defender for Cloud)

80. What is not a benefit of working with infrastructure and configuration as code?

A. Minimizing configuration drift

B. Peer-review support

C. Lower lead time on configuration changes

D. Source control history of configuration changes

Implementing Continuous Feedback

81. You have to gather crash reports from the applications that your team creates. Which tools can you use to do this? [Choose two.]

A. Snyk

B. Raygun

C. App Center

D. Azure Automation

82. You are configuring many alerts. Some alerts need to result in a warning per email, others are critical errors and need to result in an SMS text message that's sent out. Regardless of the alert being a warning or an alert, you also need to update a home-build system with the alert being fired.

   You create the following solution: one action group for warnings both sends the email and calls a WebHook on the home-build system. One action group for errors both sends the SMS text message and calls a WebHook on the home-build system. For alerts that are a warning, you configure action group one. For alerts that are an error, you configure action group two.

   Is this a complete and correct solution?

   A. Yes

   B. No

83. You are configuring many alerts. Some alerts need to result in a warning per email while others are critical errors and need to result in an SMS text message being sent out. Regardless of the alert being a warning or an alert, you also need to update a home-build system with the alert being fired.

   You create the following solution: One action group sends an email, sends an SMS text message, and calls a WebHook on the home-build system. You configure this alert group on all alerts and add an alert condition configuration to only send emails for warnings and to only send SMS text messages for errors.

   Is this a complete and correct solution?

   A. Yes

   B. No

84. You are configuring many alerts. Some alerts need to result in a warning per email while others are critical errors and need to result in an SMS text message that's sent out. Regardless of the alert being a warning or an alert, you also need to update a home-build system with the alert being fired.

   You create the following solution: One action group for warnings sends an email. A second action group for errors sends the SMS text message. A third action group calls a WebHook on the home-build system. For alerts that are a warning, you configure action groups one and two. For errors, you configure action groups two and three.

   Is this a complete and correct solution?

   A. Yes

   B. No

85. You want to invite your users to provide ideas and suggestions on your product. This should be in a public place so that other users can comment and vote on those suggestions. Which of the following tools can be used to do this in the simplest way? [Choose two.]

    A. Azure Blob storage static site

    B. GitHub issues

    C. UserVoice

    D. Azure Boards public views extension

Answers

1. A, B, C, D

2. A, B, D

3. A

4. D – A – C – B – E

5. B

6. B

7. B, C

8. D

9. C

10. D

11. A

12. A

13. A, C

14. B

15. A, D

16. A

17. B

18. B, D

19. A

20. A, B

21. B, C

22. A – (iii), B – (ii), C – (i)

23. A, C

24. C

25. B

26. A

27. B, C

28. B

29. A, B

30. D

31. B

32. C

33. C, D

34. B

35. A, B, C

36. A

37. A

38. A

39. B, C, F, A

40. A

41. B, A, C

42. A, C

43. B

44. C

45. C

46. B, D

47. A

48.	A		68.	A
49.	A		69.	B
50.	A		70.	A
51.	B		71.	A, D
52.	C		72.	B
53.	B, C		73.	A, C
54.	A, B, E		74.	B
55.	A		75.	D
56.	B		76.	D
57.	B		77.	C
58.	C		78.	B
59.	A		79.	B
60.	B		80.	C
61.	B		81.	B, C
62.	A		82.	A
63.	A		83.	B
64.	D		84.	A
65.	C, D		85.	B, C
66.	B, C			
67.	B, D			

Assessments

Chapter 1, **Introduction to DevOps**

1. True. In traditional organizations, development is often tasked with creating changes to software, while operations is responsible for maintaining the stability of the target systems for these changes. Since changes inherently carry risk and may disturb stability, operations is often resistant to change.

2. False. While, in theory, it is possible to apply the different DevOps practices in isolation from one another, the real value comes from combining them. For example, continuous deployment without continuous integration and test automation not only makes very little sense, it is actually dangerous to continuously deploy changes without the quality assurances that continuous integration and test automation offer.

3. The incorrect answer is D. DevOps is not a job title, but a cultural movement. Actually, creating a new DevOps team in between development and operations is often at loggerheads with the DevOps philosophy. Instead of two teams or departments with their separate goals, there are now three.

4. Fastlaning is an approach to expediting unplanned, high-priority work over planned work, all while maintaining a single sprint board for the whole team.

5. There are many definitions of DevOps. Some of the main elements that are frequently included are business value, end users, continuous deployment, automation, and collaboration.

Chapter 2, **Site Reliability Engineering Fundamentals**

1. True. SRE team's primary responsibility is to maintain reliability for applications. The reputation and success of a business or product are dependent on the reliability of cloud solutions in a production environment.

2. False. Generally, availability is expressed in nines. For instance Three nines (99.95% availability percentage) will have an average in a year 4 Hours 22 Minutes and 58 Seconds of allowed downtime .

3. True. SRE adopts automation to resolve common and recurring problems. Response time for common problems is reduced as a result of automation.

4. 95% availability implies allowed downtime:

   - Weekly: 8h 24m 0s

   - Monthly: 1d 12h 31m 27s

   - Yearly: 18d 6h 17m 27s

5. The correct answers are A, B, and C. DevOps Management and Bug Tracking do not impact or create challenges to maintaining reliability.

6. True. The level of service reliability needs to be defined by key stakeholders and the SRE team will help to maintain these service reliability levels using SLOs and SLIs.

7. Toil is the kind of work tied to running a production service that tends to be manual, repetitive, automatable, tactical, devoid of enduring value, and that scales linearly as a service grows.

Chapter 3, Getting the Best Out of DevOps Tools

1. False. You can sign up for Azure DevOps for free with either a Microsoft or GitHub account.

2. True. Azure Boards allows multiple teams to collaborate and work together on a single project.

3. True. Application Insights is a feature of Azure Monitor that provides extensible **application performance management** (**APM**) and monitoring for live web apps.

4. True. You can use Azure Pipelines to automatically build, test, package, release, and deploy your GitHub repository code.

5. False. GitHub is an enterprise scale offering from Microsoft that supports both Public and Private repositories.

Chapter 4, Everything Starts with Source Control

1. The main difference between centralized and decentralized source control is that in a decentralized source control system, every user of the system has the full history of the sources. In a centralized system, only the server has the full history. Decentralized systems work best when working disconnected from the server, whereas centralized systems often allow for more detailed access control.

2. True. Git is the best known decentralized source control system.

3. The correct answer is B. Rebasing is not a branching strategy, but a merging strategy.

4. When working with Git, a pull request is used to merge changes from one branch with another. Pull requests can be reviewed, approved, or denied. To enforce the use of pull requests, Git policies can be used.

5. The correct answer is B. Trunk-based development is not a merging strategy, but a branching strategy.

Chapter 5, **Moving to Continuous Integration**

1. False. Continuous integration is about integrating the work of every developer with that of their colleagues at least daily and building and testing the integrated sources. Just running a daily build does not constitute continuous integration.

2. True. A classic build pipeline is always connected to a source code repository. It might be that the sources are not used in the build pipeline, but the connection is always there.

3. False. It is possible to create a YAML pipeline that starts directly with a stage. A link to a source control repository is no longer mandatory.

4. The correct answer is C: a service connection. Service connections are configured in the organization or project that contains the pipeline that needs to call into the external tool. Once a service connection is configured, it can be used from one or more pipelines.

5. The correct answers are A and D: access to closed networks and the ability to install extra software. Self-hosted agents are deployed on infrastructure owned by you. This means that you can deploy them on networks that you control, giving them access to that network. Since the agents are deployed on your infrastructure, you can also decide which software is installed (and which is not). Tasks and extension tasks are automatically downloaded to the agent before it executes a job. You can have as many parallel pipelines as you want without using self-hosted agents. However, you will need to buy extra parallel executions from Microsoft for this purpose.

Chapter 6, **Implementing Continuous Deployment and Release Management**

1. False. It is also possible to trigger a new release on a schedule or manually.

2. All of the answers are correct.

3. A and C are correct. Both ring-based deployments and canary deployments expose only a limited group of users to the new version of your application. Feature toggles are also used for progressive exposure but are not used to limit the risks of a deployment but that of a new feature release.

4. True. Deployment groups are used to perform tasks from a release pipeline not on one agent in the group, but on all agents. Deployment groups are intended to be used to deploy software on the machine that is also running the agent.

5. One possible advantage is that end-to-end traceability of all steps is retained in Azure DevOps. If you also manage your work items and source code in Azure DevOps, you will keep end-to-end traceability from the work item to release within Azure DevOps, and all this while still using the App Center for actual deployments.

Chapter 7, **Dependency Management**

1. False. A version of a package can be visible in more than one view.

2. False. Pipeline artifacts can only be consumed from within other pipelines within Azure DevOps.

3. True. Azure Artifact feeds can be used to share universal packages to other products. This allows you to compile an application in Azure DevOps, upload the binaries as a universal package, and download it again in another product. This is useful when using another deployment tool, for example, Octopus Deploy.

4. True. The three main aspects of dependency management are standardization, package formats and sources, and versioning.

5. The correct answers are B and D. Answer A is incorrect since the package references (either in a `.csproj` file or in a `nuget.config` file) should only reference packages by name and version. Answer C is incorrect since `consumer` is not a valid access level in Azure Artifact feeds. The correct access level is reader (or higher), making answer B correct. Answer D is also correct. You need to add the package location to your NuGet configuration.

6. One motivator can be the size of the solution. If compiling and testing the solution is taking so long that developers have to wait for feedback in relation to their work, it can be better to split the solution into smaller parts. This will shorten the feedback loop for developers, thereby increasing speed. Another motivator can be that multiple teams are working on an application, and they want to increase the amount of isolation between teams.

Chapter 8, **Implement Infrastructure and Configuration as Code**

1. True. ARM templates allow you to specify the end state for all resources in an Azure resource group. Applying an ARM template will always result in the creation of missing resources and updates for existing resources. If the deployment mode `complete` is specified, even resources not in the template will be removed.

2. The correct answer is B. Modules, Run As accounts, and variables are all constructs that were discussed in *Chapter 8, Implement Infrastructure and Configuration as Code*.

3. False. ARM template parameters allow the referencing of values in an Azure Key Vault, so as to prevent users from having to enter secrets or other sensitive information in source control. At the time of deployment, the secrets are retrieved and used within Azure, provided the identity that starts the operation has access to that key vault.

4. True. You can define one or more schedules within an Azure Automation Account and then link these to a Runbook.

5.   Many benefits can be expected when practicing infrastructure as code. Two oft-cited examples are the prevention of configuration drift and the ability to create new environments on demand. Configuration drift is prevented by reapplying the same infrastructure specification to an environment on a schedule. Environments on demand can be used to quickly create a new test environment, performing tests and then removing the environment again. This allows for more repeatable test results and, possibly, savings in terms of testing infrastructure.

Chapter 9, Dealing with Databases in DevOps Scenarios

1.   True. Entity Framework and Entity Framework Core both have built-in support to generate a migration after changes to the schema definition have been made.

2.   False. Most migration-based approaches use an extra table to keep track of which migrations have already been applied to the database.

3.   True. End state-based approaches work by comparing the current schema to the target schema. This results in the generation of a one-time SQL script that is run against the database to update the schema. There is no state stored between runs.

4.   The correct answers are A and B. Running side by side, if done correctly, reduces change risks dramatically. If there are issues, you can always remove all new code, along with the database copy, and restart afresh from a working situation. Having both situations working correctly also allows for very precise performance measurements regarding the production workload. However, one of the disadvantages is that the cycle time is actually very likely to increase. You have to move multiple smaller changes to production one by one, which increases the total time taken.

5.   False. Your schema (either implicit or captured in data objects) still changes. However, this only becomes visible when reading an object back from the database that was persisted with a previous version of the object. In essence, you are only delaying coping with the issue of schema changes.

6.   You can choose to not use database-level coding techniques, such as stored procedures and triggers. The more of your logic you capture outside of the database, the smaller the total number of database changes you have to make.

Chapter 10, Integrating Continuous Testing

1.   True. In a unit test, an individual component is tested in isolation. In an object- oriented language, this is often a single class.

2.   False. In an integration test, the correct working of a group of components is verified, and not the entire assembled system. If the entire assembled and deployed system is tested, this is referred to as a system test.

3. Answer B is correct. The testing pyramid prescribes a large set of unit tests that verify as many requirements as possible. Integration tests are added only for those risks that cannot be covered using unit tests, resulting in a lower number of integration tests. Even fewer system tests are added, only to cover the risks not covered by either unit or integration tests.

4. Answer C is correct. All other types of testing are covered in this chapter.

5. Two techniques that can be mentioned here are code reviews and pipeline gates. Code reviews allow developers to review the work of their colleagues to help each other maintain high quality. Pipeline gates can be used to prevent a build or version of an application from propagating further down a pipeline if certain conditions are not met. Example conditions can include certain quality metrics, or minimum standards for test coverage or test results.

Chapter 11, Managing Security and Compliance

1. False. To securely create and deliver software, the whole process, and especially the pipeline, needs to be secured. Just adding security at the end will not work, as security has to be woven through all different steps of the delivery process.

2. The OWASP **Zed Attack Proxy** (**ZAP**) can be used for this type of testing.

3. True. In modern applications, up to 80% of the code can be from open source libraries or frameworks.

4. The correct answers are A,B, D, and F. There is no such thing as Azure DevOps Secure Variables or Azure DevOps Key Vault.

5. Azure Policy can be used to prohibit or list unwanted Azure configurations, often relating to infrastructure provisioning or configuration. Azure Security Center (now Microsoft Defender for Cloud) can be used to identify and remediate runtime security risks.

Chapter 12, Application Monitoring

1. False. The platform metrics that are emitted by Azure are defined by every individual service and cannot be changed.

2. 93 days. This number guarantees that there are always at least three months of history.

3. True. Custom metrics can be calculated in your own application code and emitted to Application Insights through the SDK or REST API.

4. Alert fatigue.

5. True. Azure allows for the creation of action groups that can contain webhooks to be called in response to an alert being raised.

Chapter 13, **Gathering User Feedback**

1. False. One possible downside is losing a competitive edge in the market. If competitors know what you are going to develop next, they may preempt you in that regard.

2. Possible concerns are that some users or groups of users are more vocal than others, which might result in a difference between the general opinion and the opinion that is heard. Also, feedback on a public roadmap is most likely coming from existing users only. While it is important to retain those, prospects might not comment on your roadmap with features they are missing.

3. Two examples that are discussed in this chapter are sentiment on social media channels and the number and severity of support requests.

4. Answer C is correct. A hypothesis states a belief that a certain feature is needed. In the hypothesis the second part is a measurable user response that is to be observed before the belief is confirmed. This is called the confirmation threshold. A hypothesis does not yet have a conclusion.

5. Possible benefits of user interviews or focus groups are that they are often conducted at a smaller scale, allowing not only for the measuring of feedback, but for also understanding the reasons behind it. Another benefit is that participants can be carefully selected to be representative of all users or a particular segment.

Chapter 16, **Containers**

1. The benefits of containers for DevOps are consistency, the separation of concerns, and platform portability.

2. True. Depending on the host operating system, it does not matter where the container is hosted.

3. Yes, this is possible. This can be done by adding Docker support and a project level.

4. The RUN command is used for the installation of components or for performing operations during the process of building the container image.

5. Nodes and pods can be scheduled within Azure Kubernetes Service. Both of these components can be scaled manually or automatically.

Chapter 17, **Planning Your Azure DevOps Organization**

1. False. Some information can travel to other regions or is available globally. For example, sometimes agents are running in other regions when capacity in the chosen region is low.

2. **Work item | Project | Organization | Region**. An Azure DevOps organization is the top-level construct that can be created by users. Every organization is in precisely one region, which is maintained by Microsoft. Within an organization, one or more projects can be created. In turn, a project can contain many work items, such as user stories, features, or epics.

3. False. The general recommendation is to have just enough projects: the fewer the better. Isolation and very strict authorization boundaries may be reasons for choosing to use multiple projects.

4. Authorizations and licensing. Authorizations can be set up to the limit that can be accessed by every individual user or a group of users. The license assigned to a user can also prohibit the use of certain features. For example, users with a stakeholder license cannot work with source control.

5. End-to-end traceability. When executing work management, source control, building, artifacts, and deployments from a single tool, it is possible to trace the deployment

Index

B

Packt.com

Subscribe to our online digital library for full access to over 7,000 books and videos, as well as industry leading tools to help you plan your personal development and advance your career. For more information, please visit our website.

Why subscribe?

- Spend less time learning and more time coding with practical eBooks and Videos from over 4,000 industry professionals

- Improve your learning with Skill Plans built especially for you

- Get a free eBook or video every month

- Fully searchable for easy access to vital information

- Copy and paste, print, and bookmark content

Did you know that Packt offers eBook versions of every book published, with PDF and ePub files available? You can upgrade to the eBook version at packt.com and as a print book customer, you are entitled to a discount on the eBook copy. Get in touch with us at customercare@packtpub.com for more details.

At www.packt.com, you can also read a collection of free technical articles, sign up for a range of free newsletters, and receive exclusive discounts and offers on Packt books and eBooks.

Other Books You May Enjoy

If you enjoyed this book, you may be interested in these other books by Packt:

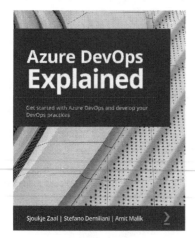

Azure DevOps Explained

Sjoukje Zaal, Stefano Demiliani, Amit Malik

ISBN: 9781800563513

- Get to grips with Azure DevOps
- Find out about project management with Azure Boards
- Understand source code management with Azure Repos
- Build and release pipelines
- Run quality tests in build pipelines
- Use artifacts and integrate Azure DevOps in the GitHub flow
- Discover real-world CI/CD scenarios with Azure DevOps

Learning DevOps - Second Edition

Mikael Krief

ISBN: 9781801818964

- Understand the basics of infrastructure as code patterns and practices

- Get an overview of Git command and Git flow

- Install and write Packer, Terraform, and Ansible code for provisioning and configuring cloud infrastructure based on Azure examples

- Use Vagrant to create a local development environment

- Containerize applications with Docker and Kubernetes

- Apply DevSecOps for testing compliance and securing DevOps infrastructure

- Build DevOps CI/CD pipelines with Jenkins, Azure Pipelines, and GitLab CI

- Explore blue-green deployment and DevOps practices for open sources projects

Packt is searching for authors like you

If you're interested in becoming an author for Packt, please visit `authors.packtpub.com` and apply today. We have worked with thousands of developers and tech professionals, just like you, to help them share their insight with the global tech community. You can make a general application, apply for a specific hot topic that we are recruiting an author for, or submit your own idea.

Share Your Thoughts

Now you've finished *Designing and Implementing Microsoft DevOps Solutions AZ-400 Exam Guide*, we'd love to hear your thoughts! Scan the QR code below to go straight to the Amazon review page for this book and share your feedback or leave a review on the site that you purchased it from.

`https://packt.link/r/1803240660`

Your review is important to us and the tech community and will help us make sure we're delivering excellent quality content.

Made in the USA
Columbia, SC
18 September 2023

23011891R10267